King Charles of New York City

AuthorHouse™
1663 Liberty Drive
Bloomington, IN 47403
www.authorhouse.com
Phone: 1 (800) 839-8640

Published by AuthorHouse 05/05/2015

ISBN: 978-1-5049-0867-2 (sc)
ISBN: 978-1-5049-0866-5 (e)

Library of Congress Control Number: 2015906429

Print information available on the last page.

King Charles of New York City

The Life of Charles Barnes Towns

How a Poor Georgia Farm Boy Became a World
Authority on Drug and Alcohol Treatment

Gary W. Neidhardt

authorHOUSE®

For my wife

Mary Jean Neidhardt

Contents

Preface... vii

Foreword... ix

1) Introduction... 1

2) Beginnings 1862-1904... 8

3) Connections 1904-1908.. 20

4) China 1908-1909.. 23

5) King Charles of New York City 1909-1919...................... 33

6) *The Century Magazine* Articles 1912............................ 43

    a. *The Injury of Tobacco,* March 1912

    b. *Help For the Hard Drinker*, June 1912

    c. *The Peril of the Drug Habit,* August 1912

    d. *The Drug-Taker And the Physician,* October 1912

7) The Harrison Act, December 1914................................ 78

8) *Habits That Handicap,* August 1915........................... 90

    a. Chapters I-III on Drug Addiction

    b. Chapter IV – Psychology and Drugs

    c. Chapter V-VII on Alcoholism

    d. Chapters VIII-IX on Tobacco

    e. Chapter X – The Sanatorium

    f. Chapter XI – Preventive Measures

    g. Chapter XII – Classification of Habit-Forming Drugs

    h. Chapter XIII – Psychology of Addiction

    i. Chapter XIV – Relation of Alcohol and Drugs to Insanity

9) *Medical Review of Reviews* December 1914–July 1917....144

10) *The Peak*, December 1916 – December 1917..................179

11) *Medical Review of Reviews* August 1917–April 1918....208

12) The Towns Treatment...229

13) The Fall from Grace...237

14) Four Brochures to Attract Physicians............................253

15) *Reclaiming The Drinker* – 1931.................................265

16) *Drug and Alcohol Sickness* – 1932...........................287

17) Dr. William D. Silkworth Hired by Towns 1929-1951....296

18) The Job Offer at Towns Hospital – 1937?.....................311

19) Towns' Contributions to Alcoholics Anonymous.............321

20) Epilogue...329

21) Appendix..340

Towns Bibliography..356

General References and Suggested Readings.....................357

Index..363

Notes...379

Figure Cross Reference...404

Image Sources...406

Listing of Figures

Figure 1 - Charles Barnes Towns as he appeared in the November 29, 1913 Collier's Magazine Article_____ 3

Figure 2 - One of the Paul Thompson pictures of Charles Towns in the October, 1912 The American Magazine article _____ 23

Figure 3 - Charles Barnes Towns in the October, 1912 The American Magazine _____ 33

Figure 4 - Ad in the June, 1914 The Medical Times, with the 81st Street address included _____ 39

Figure 5 - July, 1915 ad in The Medical Times with the 81st street address, plus reference to the Annex on 82nd St. _____ 40

Figure 6 - August, 1914 The Medical Times ad announcing the move to 293 Central Park West _____ 41

Figure 7 - Towns' ad in The Medical Times, October 1914, in which he claims the hospital to have been founded fourteen years ago _____ 41

Figure 8 - Full Page ad, December, 1914 in The Medical Times. This ad also appeared in the Maryland Medical Journal for the months of January, February, and March, 1915. _____ 42

Figure 9 - A rather typical syringe ad for the times _____ 60

Figure 10 - Towns Hospital in New York City _____ 90

Figure 11 - Representative sanitariums ads of the times that appeared in the December, 1916 The Modern Hospital. Please note the two spellings: sanitarium and sanatorium. _____ 115

Figure 12 - The Modern Hospital, December 1916 This sanitarium was a prominent advertiser for the times and was often encountered in the various magazines of the 1910's. In another ad in the New York State Journal of Medicine in 1915, they advertised for treating cases of drug addiction. _____ 116

Figure 13 - Ad included with May 1916 Article complete with misspelling of Shakespeare_____ 152

Figure 14 - Charles Barnes Towns in the October, 1912 The American Magazine article _____ 179

Figure 15 - Ad for Towns Hospital that appeared in the December, 1916 The Modern Hospital_____ 181

Figure 16 - Page 1 of a two-page ad appearing in the January, 1917 The Modern Hospital_____ 189

Figure 17 - Part two of a two page ad appearing in the January, 1917 The Modern Hospital _____ 190

Figure 18 - Towns Hospital ad that appeared in the February, 1917 The Modern Hospital_____ 195

Figure 19 - Part I, Page 1 of The Modern Hospital ad that began in March, 1917, which covered three months. _ 198

Figure 20 - Part I, page 2 of The Modern Hospital ad that began in March, 1917, which covered three months. _ 199

Figure 21 - Part II, Page 1 of The Modern Hospital ad, which appeared in April, 1917._____ 200

Figure 22 - Part II, Page 2 of The Modern Hospital ad, which appeared in April, 1917. _____ 201

Figure 23 - Part III, Page 1 of The Modern Hospital ad. This part appeared in May, 1917. _____ 202

Figure 24 Part III, Page 2 of The Modern Hospital ad. This part appeared in May, 1917 _____ 203

Figure 25 - The Towns Hospital The Modern Hospital ad for June, 1917. _____ 205

Figure 26 - The American Journal of The Medical Sciences Ad by Towns Hospital in the December 6, 1917 issue _ 206

Figure 27 - Ad that may have led to Towns dismissal from writing for the Medical Review of Reviews _____ 222

Figure 28 – An ad in the Boston Medical and Surgical Journal capturing the mood towards prohibition in the times of World War I. _____ 225

Figure 29 - A January, 1921 in The Medical Times on Insomnia. A curiosity: Towns Hospital is listed as 292 Central Park West A previous December, 1920 ad in the same magazine carried the 292 address. _____ 241

Figure 30 - February, 1921 Towns Hospital ad on Hypnotics in The Medical Times _____ 242

Figure 31 - March, 1921 Towns Hospital Ad in The Medical Times again on Insomnia _____ 244

Figure 32 - April, 1921 Towns Hospital Ad in The Medical Times on Prohibition _____ 245

Figure 33 - May, 1921 Towns Hospital ad in The Medical Times on treating tobacco as a poison _____ 248

Figure 34 - June, 1921 Towns Hospital Ad in The Medical Times on nervous disturbances _____ 249

Figure 35 - July, 1921 Towns Hospital Ad in The Medical Times on "The Pathological Aspect of Prohibition." The address of 292 Central Park West appears in all the Towns ads in this magazine. _____ 250

Figure 36 - Charles Towns as he had appeared in The American Magazine in October, 1912 _____ 329

Figure 37 - A June, 1911 Ad in the Boston Medical and Surgical Journal showing the health properties of a pure malt product, which of course contained alcohol _____ 340

Figure 38 - A June 29, 1911 ad in the Boston Medical and Surgical Journal, which recommended how doctors should prescribe "The Best Tonic" and not some cheap imitation. _____ 341

Figure 39 - Ad in the June 1911 Boston Medical and Surgical Journal for Glyco-Thymoline of a medication to be placed in an infant's food or used with an enema _____ 342

Figure 40 - A second ad for Glyco-Thymoline in the Boston Medical and Surgical Journal. Not only was the medication good for nursing babies, included here was a half dozen additional projected usages for the product. The ad also appeared many times in the1915 Maryland Medical Journal. _____ 343

Figure 41 - A March, 1917 Ad appearing in The Modern Hospital Magazine for Liquid Petrolatum used to treat intestinal problems. The product may not have contained alcohol, but at the same time, the remarks that claim it not to be habit forming. _____ 344

Figure 42 - An ad place in the April, 1917 issue of The Modern Hospital magazine by The J.L. Mott Iron Works featuring their work done at Towns Hospital with hydrotherapy _____ 345

Figure 43 - An ad for a hypnotic containing alcohol that appeared in the March, 1917 medical magazine The Modern Hospital _____ 346

Figure 44 - a May, 1917 ad in The Modern Hospital featuring an extra dry champagne as being a health tonic _ 347

Figure 45 - A 1916 ad in The Modern Hospital featuring three kinds of whisky, which includes a "safe, medicinal whisky" that a doctor should consider safe to give to his patients _____ 348

Figure 46 - Boston Medical and Surgical Journal, January, 1917. A March ad for this very same product promised relief from hemorrhoids _____ 349

Figure 47 - Boston Medical and Surgical Journal, February, 1917. A rather unusual 'outstanding food' that promised favorable results for "infants, invalids, and the aged." _____ 350

Figure 48 - Boston Medical and Surgical Journal, February, 1917. Top ad for The Fisk Hospital includes endorsement from a Towns' colleague Robert C. Cabot M.D.. Contains a physician advertising prices. Lower right shows an ad for the Towns Treatment _____ 351

Figure 49 - December, 1914 ad in The Medical Times. This same ad appeared in the Maryland Medical Journal for January and February, 1915 _____ 352

Figure 50 - The Medical Times ad of February, 1913 suggesting that if you had $5.00, Home Treatment for alcoholism could be yours. _____ 353

Figure 51 – The Pepto-Mangan ad found in the August, 1915 Maryland Medical Journal spoke volumes for the nature of patent medicines still available during these times. Patent medicines accounted for half of all drug sales as late as 1929 (See The Origin of Compulsory Drug Prescriptions by Peter Temin, 1978, p.2) _____ 354

Figure 52 - This ad in the April, 1915 New York State Journal of Medicine was a result of the Harrison Ac _____ 355

Preface

Charles B. Towns is one of the most compelling and enigmatic figures in the history of drug policy and the history of addiction treatment in the United States. He is perhaps best known for the institution bearing his name and the role he and it played in the early history of Alcoholics Anonymous (A.A.). In spite of the recent flurry of new biographies on key figures in the birth and early evolution of A.A., the story of Charles Towns, the Charles B. Towns Hospital for Drug and Alcohol Addiction, and the "Towns Cure" for alcoholism and other addictions have, until now, not been fully revealed. In the pages that follow, Gary Neidhardt unravels this story, using to the greatest extent possible Towns and his contemporaries' own words.

The history of addiction treatment and recovery in America is engaging reading in part because it is filled with such captivating characters, few of which rival the colorful tales and legends that surround Charles Towns. The task of separating fact from self-promotional myths and competitor attacks is not an easy one, but Gary Neidhardt has waded into this fray with considerable courage and competence. The result is a meticulously researched account of Towns: the man, his ideas, his institution, and the controversies he stirred. Students of addiction treatment and recovery and the larger arena of drug policy will be drawn for years to this account of an individual whose rarely acknowledged influence continues to echo within policy debates, professional discussions of medication-assisted addiction treatment, and within the meeting rooms of A.A. and other 12-Step fellowships.

The chapters that follow present key excerpts and analysis of Towns written work and the historical context in which this work unfolded, but they also contain photographs that capture the spirit of the man and cultural climate in which both his ideas and his unique approach to curing addiction flourished. This visual storytelling is itself a valuable contribution.

Many mysteries remain about the life of Charles Towns, but *King Charles of New York City* provides the most complete and engaging account to date of one of the most fascinating chapters in the history of addiction treatment. So, let the tale begin.

William L. White

Author, *Slaying the Dragon: The History of Addiction Treatment and Recovery in America*

Foreword

A king of New York City many years ago? Fiorello H. La Guardia? Maybe a Wall Street tycoon? A star of a George M. Cohan Broadway show? Lou Gehrig? Or an ally of Al Capone? Some gangster of the prohibition era? Or an Elliot Ness that arrested bad guys?

How about a champion of freedom from all mind altering substances?

Freedom from opium, heroin, cocaine and morphine! Any narcotic! Alcohol and tobacco as well! This king favored the elimination of any substance that interfered with clarity and serenity provided by the five human senses. And who was this king? Charles Barnes Towns.

His passion was fired not by the forces of any temperance movement or religious crusade! Education and logic would be enough to convince those with rational, open minds. Based on common sense, which nature had gifted mortal men, reason and enlightenment through government would be enough to save the world from the evils of substances that inevitably turned men into slaves before driving them insane. The human race would be better off if all of these substances could be cleansed from the memory of the human race. Mankind had the chance to make such a dream come true if they could break the shackles of the substances that imprisoned them, and, above all, chose to follow Charles Barnes Towns.

He set his goals no lower than that! Since Towns was an acknowledged atheist, his personal crusade was based upon man assuming the throne of reason and common sense. Towns soon gained the ear of three U.S. Presidents, the United States Congress and many of the finest medical minds in the country. For a brief shining moment in the second decade of the twentieth century, he was believed to possess the world's only proven cure for opium addiction. He enlarged the promises of his remedy when he claimed it would work for any stimulant or narcotic compulsion. His articles in prominent medical magazines provided a prestigious podium to address leading doctors throughout the country. His ads in prominent medical magazines were second to none in both square inches and promotional capability. (Many of his ads are included in this book. As there were as many as 339 different medical magazines published throughout the world, as listed in the 1915 *Medical Review of Reviews*, the Towns ads included within may be but a small sample). With his castle located on Central Park in downtown New York, he provided convincing rhetoric that he possessed the one and only medical solution to addiction. Furthermore, to convince the skeptical physician of the sincerity of his motives, he was willing to give away the knowledge of his solution for free to anyone qualified to employ it.

All this was from a son of a Confederate lieutenant born in La Grange, Georgia in 1862 who never finished middle school. He learned to break horses that other men could not ride, and through his acquired sense of determination, he became what was reputed to be the top insurance salesman south of the Mason-Dixon line. Upon heading north to New York to become part of a brokerage business, that enterprise soon failed. But soon he was intrigued by a mysterious gentleman that provided Towns with an alternative potential income source, which was a solution for opium addiction. Towns soon was experimenting with this treatment, which took every bit of the iron nerve that he had brought with him from Georgia. Through sheer determination and persistence, he gained the attention of an influential New York medical man. Through that contact, he was recommended to represent the United States as a goodwill ambassador to China to help provide a solution to their admitted opium problem. He insisted on traveling to China at his own expense to perfect the treatment. He successfully overcame the opposition from the Empress of China when she favored other opium treatment approaches. His reported courage helped build him a legendary reputation of a conquering hero upon his return to the United States in 1909. Soon some top medical men were referring to Towns as one of the most persuasive personalities in the world. His medical solution was written up in the *Journal of the American Medical Association* as a state of the art approach to solving narcotic addiction. Towns had arrived!

The timing of the book is also rather fortuitous. The centennial of Congress having passed The Harrison Narcotic Act was December, 2014. It became the law of the land in March, 1915. This law, modeled after New York State legislation that Towns himself claimed to have authored, seems known to relatively few today. Many works of history fail to even mention it. The interpretation of the Harrison Act by the courts, through prosecutions filed by the U.S. Treasury Department, led to outright narcotic prohibition by 1919—close to the start of alcohol prohibition, but without the necessity of a Constitutional Amendment.

There has been a recent thirty minute video of William L. White where Ernest Kurtz was interviewed about a variety of matters. Whereas I cannot quote Ernest Kurtz exactly, he mentioned how some significant new information has been discovered since 1979 when he wrote what has been the definitive work on the history of Alcoholics Anonymous: *Not God*. He called for amateurs to get involved in the study of the history of recovery. When I was searching around for an established author to examine this manuscript, Mike Fitzpatrick suggested I contact William White, who graciously did so. He has written the preface to this book and has been a very encouraging influence overall.

This book hopefully is a sample of what Kurtz desired: an amateur using his time and resources to shed light on an enigmatic personality that has remained rather obscure to all but a few recovery historians. Many have not learned that Towns made an invaluable contribution to the future recovery community despite the fact that the spirituality of Alcoholics Anonymous was foreign to most of what he had written himself over the years. Towns, an acknowledged atheist, controversial and opinionated, nevertheless made a couple of crucial decisions very late in his life. He helped create a spiritual fellowship of A.A., which undeniably has benefitted a few million people so far. Such a story has elements of a fictional novel. Yet, the story is true.

This work is but a step in the direction of a still larger story. My hopes are that this book will uncover some treasure chests of Towns documents and letters as of yet unexplored. Questions are many. When Bill Wilson admitted having been treated with belladonna, with what frequency did he receive the medicine and for how long during any of his four visits? When treating addicts had become criminal for the treatment professional, did Towns continue treating them "under-the-table" and risk being arrested himself? When Dr. Robert H. Smith used belladonna in Akron, Ohio, how did he use it? How did he learn of it? Where did Towns work when he made his reputation as a Georgian that he could convince a granite gatepost to buy life insurance? Why did he go to New York City in the first place in 1901? Who was the man that introduced the belladonna treatment to Towns and when did that happen? When did Towns make the job offer to Bill Wilson, which may have sabotaged the fellowship of Alcoholics Anonymous by tempting its co-founder into becoming a professional lay therapist?

I look forward to the day when progress is made on answering these questions. Until then, I hope this book to be a step in the ongoing search to find more of our cultural origins. From that process, mistakes made in the past may not be repeated as often in the future.

Acknowledgements

Thanks should be provided to John Bowles, who nine years ago had his picture taken in front of Towns Hospital and thereby piqued my interest in that address; to Mack Scaife, who suggested I attend a William L. White seminar on *Slaying The Dragon* long before I knew anything about this scholarly work; to John Holmes of Hilton Head, South Carolina, who introduced me to Mike Fitzpatrick in 2010 through which I was put back into contact with William L. White; to Mike Fitzpatrick, who has been a wonderful resource and sounding board,; to Dr. William Doverspike, who went through the manuscript making enhancements and corrections; to William L. White for his recommendations and support; to my sister Carol Neidhardt; who provided consistent encouragement throughout; and last, but by no means least, my wife Mary Jean Neidhardt, who consulted with me often, edited the manuscript, made recommendations, and provided consistent help whenever needed.

Note on 8 ¼ x 11" Format Chosen

Many of the ads included in this book among the 52 Figures tell a story of their own. Many of the magazines in which these ads appeared were printed on pages that were as least as large, if not larger, than the display size used here. Shrinking them into a smaller size made them unacceptably difficult to read and subtracted from their value. This double spacing format remained for purposes of readability, as a result.

1) Introduction

Who was Mr. Charles Barnes Towns? As a means of introduction, here are some descriptions of the man according to those who either knew him personally or who have studied him closely.

"Of all the cure proclaimers there was an undisputed king, or perhaps emperor, so magnificent were his accomplishments and so influential his lobbying: Mr. Charles B. Towns. He worked at such a high level of national and international efforts to control narcotism that he appeared to many to be above mercenary considerations."[1]

"And it would not surprise me, for one, if the world sooner or later should discover that it must listen to Towns. I believe the fact is now established that with reasonable intelligence and care the treatment can be applied anywhere, particularly with the advice and aid of Towns himself."[2]

"The story of the Charles B. Towns Hospital is the story of a most fascinating institution by a most fascinating man. He was so personally persuasive and dominating that some observers even questioned whether the results of his treatment for addiction might be more attributed to the power of his personality than to the medical protocol used at his hospital. As one physician noted, 'The Towns treatment would be all right if you could mix in about a grain of Towns with every capsule of the specific.'"[3]

"He will be, as he is, simply the experienced, enthusiastic leader of what is perhaps the first really intelligent crusade against these most insinuating and baffling enemies to the human character – alcohol and drugs. Excepting perhaps those few open-minded physicians who had worked close to him, it transpired that nobody in the world knew quite so much about these matters as Towns. Above all this, he had happened, through one of the chances that Nature seems sometimes to arrange, to be the right man in the right place. The problem had stirred the genius within him and found an answer there."[4]

"Here's an odd story of an odd man with odd adventures, whose virile personality backed a nationwide campaign in which not one individual in America was without a personal interest."[5]

"Any one who knows Mr. Towns knows one of the most persuasive and dominating personalities in the world . . . "[6]

"No one could possibly talk with Charles B. Towns for the briefest period without being impressed with the sincerity of purpose that has made him a benefactor to humanity, or without noticing the combativeness that has led him, singlehanded, to wage relentless warfare against alcohol, tobacco, and all habit-forming drugs."[7]

"Towns rose in the esteem of the medical profession's elite and in the opinion of the political powerwielders who were under pressure to do something about opium addiction in the Philippines, China, and the United States. Towns achieved a national and even international role. His techniques as a salesman and his imposing personality took him far, and he was eventually accepted as one of the most knowledgeable and altruistic addiction experts in the United States."[8]

The praise for Charles Barnes Towns, once literally King Charles of New York City

narcotic treatment, and pioneer of what was believed to be the only proven solution for addiction and alcoholism in the world, gathered national attention as if he were P.T Barnum. Towns was a Harold Hill, who many decades ahead of *The Music Man* sounded a warning about the game of pool not because of the game itself, but because cigarettes were often smoked there to corrupt young men! He was an

Figure 1 - Charles Barnes Towns as he appeared in the November 29, 1913 Collier's Magazine Article

Elmer Gantry, who preached with equivalent passion. One easily could become convinced Towns' only wish was for humanity to be clean of drugs, alcohol, tobacco, caffeine, and any other substance that might interfere with the joy of living clean and sober. The preceding praise was but a sample of the nature of his accolades at one time. But as of this writing, when we are experiencing the one-hundredth anniversary of the Federal Legislation advocated by Charles Towns, which led to nationwide narcotic prohibition, his name has been all but entirely forgotten. Of the relatively few that do recognize his name, he is remembered as the proprietor of the "drunk tank,"[9] named Towns Hospital, where Bill Wilson, co-founder of Alcoholics Anonymous, dried out after his fourth visit. Wilson had his "white light experience" there in late 1934 that led to thirty-six years of continuous sobriety until his death. Otherwise, Towns' name has been all but lost to history. If his name is mentioned at all, he is often dismissed as a quack that persecuted drunks with a remedy for addiction worse than the affliction it was meant to treat.

It may seem very strange to a reader of today that in the United States of America, in the latter half of the nineteenth century, people could go to their local druggist to purchase as much morphine or opium as they could afford for themselves or anybody else of any age. In the years that followed prior to the beginning of the twentieth century, cocaine and heroin were added to that list after they were discovered and publicized. In the book *Drug War Politics*, narcotic drugs and cocaine were described at the beginning of the twentieth century in this manner.

> In 1900 opium and its derivatives morphine and heroin, cocaine, and cannabis (marijuana) were all legal substances, readily available to anyone that wanted to acquire them. Not only were they prescribed by doctors to relieve pain and sleeplessness, but they could be purchased in grocery and general stores as well as by mail order. They were found in numerous unregulated patent medicines, claiming to cure everything from stomach aches to head colds to corns.[10]

If someone did not feel well and simply decided to go the druggist for any of the prolific numbers of patent medicines that were being sold, the medicine could have contained any combination of those four drugs and alcohol too! Up until 1906 when the Pure Food and Drug Act became national law,[11] there was no requirement for the label of any patent medicine to list any of its ingredients, so the purchaser may have "felt better" through the use of a "medicine" without having any idea why. Of course, the "medicine" had little to do with treating the actual symptoms of the malady, but if the patient "felt better," was not that a fair deal? Such reasoning seemed to dominate the times. As the authors of *Drug War Politics* observed, "Addicts were not stigmatized. They were not thought of as degenerates and certainly not as criminals. The idea that a national policy was needed to handle problems of addiction—let alone that such addicts should be punished under federal law—was nowhere in evidence."[12]

Today there can also be very much of a mistaken conception of what the title "doctor" meant back around the beginning of the twentieth century. Many could designate themselves as a "doctor?" How better to compete with druggists and their patent medicines for the medical dollar when the "medicines" could be concocted for almost nothing and sold with large profits? While the American Medical Association was founded in 1847, it was not incorporated until 1897, and it did not achieve publication of standards for national medical schools until 1910.[13] David F. Musto referred to the AMA by 1913 as a "relatively small group centered mostly in the eastern states" that had a membership of only 8,500 doctors in 1900.[14] Charles Towns was to accuse doctors of being the primary creators of drug addiction in the United States as well as asserting that some of them were addicts themselves, the latter assertion of which was proven to be undeniably true for a minority of them.[15] Clearly the people of United States of one hundred and ten years ago had a widely different conception of the "drug problem" if they had ever heard of it. A much larger concern around the beginning of the twentieth century than drugs was alcohol and the various temperance movements associated with that perceived curse. Charles Towns reigned supreme mainly during the second decade of the twentieth century, when the American way of dealing with drugs took form through legislation that he either supported or helped originate.

Nevertheless, as influential as Charles Barnes Towns once was, his name seems to have been forgotten almost entirely. History has not been very kind to the medical model of addiction and alcohol treatment that Towns believed to be his miraculous and invaluable contribution to mankind, and a methodology he thought should have been taught in medical schools as part of their standard curriculum. Towns Hospital simply became one more "drunk tank" for the affluent, and the medication popularized there was discredited and eventually discarded.

However, the story behind the story becomes how such an influential personality, "one of the most persuasive and dominating personalities in the world" of his times, could ever have been so entirely forgotten by so many that actually may be in his debt. After all, without Charles Towns, most likely the doctor that loved drunks, Dr. William D. Silkworth, may have never met the co-founder of Alcoholics Anonymous (A.A.) Bill Wilson and become the right doctor at the right time to assist Wilson to benefit from his "white light" experience. Without Charles Barnes Towns, most likely the book *Alcoholics Anonymous* would not have been published in April of 1939, because Towns provided as much as fifty percent of the funding that financed the book when loans were hard to come by. Without Towns, the book may have never attracted the publicity as early as it did that first led to the September 30, 1939 *Liberty Magazine* article, which was followed a year and a half later by the much more famous March, 1941 *Saturday Evening Post* feature by Jack Alexander that made A.A. nationally prominent.

The second decade of the twentieth century ended, however, as a very bad decade for kings and royalty. Kings of those times paid dearly for promises they could not deliver and practices contrary to their country's best interests. The decade of World War I brought these flaws to the attention of their populations. Revolution or abdication was a common result.

During that decade, Towns rose to heights of medical authority and prestige, a King Charles of

New York City, far beyond any qualifications of an eighth-grade education from Georgia. But

after 1920, he was no longer considered worthy of any throne. He was just one more fellow

that owned a hospital where the well-to-do could dry out. No longer was he to be

contemplated as "Charles Barnes Towns." No, towards the end of his life, he was called

"Charlie" if he was remembered at all.

2) Beginnings 1862-1904

Charles Barnes Towns was born during the American Civil War in LaGrange, Georgia on January 12, 1862, and only vague references are made to his education, which may not have been beyond the eighth grade.[1] Charles' father Jarrel Oliver Towns was a major in the Georgia Militia in 1852 and then a Second Lieutenant in the 2nd Georgia Cavalry during the Civil War. Charles' lack of formal education may have been directly related to shortages and turmoil related to the aftermath of the Civil War reconstruction in Georgia. Charles married Mary L. Barbour on October 10, 1887 when he was twenty-five years old.[2] Any biographies up to the age of 39 years old and his arrival in New York City in 1901, tend to be rather brief – a paragraph or two. The late Bill Pittman, in *AA The Way It Began*, wrote the following about "Charlie" in 1988.

Charles B. Towns was born in 1862 on a small farm in central Georgia.[A] During his youth he broke horses and mules and steers that no other person could conquer. But the farm became too easy for Charlie and he took to railroading. He used his spare time to study arithmetic and grammar. Railroading yielded somewhat to his aggressive disposition, but he soon tired of it and turned his attention to life insurance. Towns, with his threatening index finger, with his hypnotic eye and prehensile jaw, could convince a granite gatepost that it stood in immediate need of life insurance. He set a record for selling more life insurance than any other man had ever written south of the Mason-Dixon Line up to that time (1901). Soon after, he went to New York to seek a larger arena for his talents. There he found something that excited him even more – the stock market.[3]

[A] LaGrange, Georgia is located almost on the Alabama border in the west central part of the state

The biographers of Towns seem to be particularly fascinated with his ability to break the will of an animal, implying that this talent became quite useful in his legacy of defeating drug addiction: he could convince addicts that their habits could be broken no matter what!

He breaks the horse and the mules and the steers that no other will can conquer, and does it mostly without violence, by the coolest, strongest will and a courage that will take a dare from nobody.

But the farm gets too easy for Charlie, and he takes to railroading. Here he had to turn about and brush up his book knowledge; but he goes after the grammar and the arithmetic between hours, just as he used to go after a refractory bull, and he cons and curbs them both and kicks them with contempt for something mastered and unfeared. Thereafter railroading yielded somewhat to his aggressive disposition, but when transportation problems began to be halter broken his interest flagged and turned to life insurance.[4]

A very consistent theme throughout most any description of Charles Towns included the Dynamic and bull-breaking nature of his will and courage. Dr. Richard C. Cabot of Massachusetts General Hospital and Harvard was the doctor that proclaimed Towns to be "one of the most persuasive and dominating personalities in the world."[5] He was described similarly by Samuel Merwin in *The American Magazine* in 1912.

His sympathy for the unfortunate is as deep as his understanding of him. It is simply unlimited. But you can't beat Towns. You can't outwit him. You can't bully him. Now and then some misguided person tries it. It is quite impossible to convey, on the mere printed page, any adequate idea of what such a speech could mean, coming from Towns. The candid and dominant eye, the astonishing physical vitality, the utter sense of mastery, the admonishing finger waved before a retreating nose. No, you couldn't defeat Towns. You could kill him, perhaps, but you couldn't defeat him.[6]

So, according to Samuel Merwin, neither he nor any author could adequately portray Charles Towns through the use of the written word. He had to be encountered to be fully appreciated and recognized.

Towns was described in *Pass It On* as one who "radiated an animal vitality" who was "perfectly proportioned, a physical prodigy" and who was a "great believer in gymnastics."[7]

In *Bill W. My First 40 Years*, written in Bill Wilson's autobiography, Bill described Towns.

Charlie was one of those American success stories. He had been a poor Georgia farm boy and later, banging around the world, his travels had taken him to China . . . Charlie stood about six-one, perfectly proportioned and, even in advanced years, was a physical prodigy. He radiated an animal vitality that hit people like a ton of bricks. Charlie lectured me, as he apparently did all the others. He was a great believer in gymnastics, spending about two hours a day in the New York Athletic Club himself. He never missed if he could help it.[8]

No explanation has been found why Charles left his success story of selling insurance in Georgia and moved to New York City. All that has been learned is that he did arrive there in 1901 and "Towns became a partner in a brokerage business, and what that business did to him is far too sad a tale to tell. But Towns is game. He hung on three years. At the end of three years he was one of the wisest, humblest men from Georgia in all New York."[9]

This sentence may very well be the only time in this entire biography of Charles Towns that one should expect to encounter the word "humble" or "humblest" regarding him.

Some years passed by before the public learned of Charles Towns being in New York City, and just when he began to come into the publics' eye remains unclear. But fifteen years later in the March, 1916 issue of *Medical Review of Reviews*, a professional medical publication, Charles Towns wrote an article entitled "My Relation to the Medical Profession" in which he eloquently told of his introduction to his "life work" that took place while, according to the article, he was still a newcomer in the brokerage business.

In 1901, a man who was not a physician told me he believed he had a remedy that would free an addict from the drug habit. At that time I knew nothing about medicine, and less about drug habits. I had never been afflicted with any such habit, and had never paid any attention to anyone who had. I thought it was preposterous for this man to suggest that I take up this matter, and I told him so. I asked him why he did not appeal to a physician, and he answered that no physician believed it possible to treat cases of drug addiction in a definite way.

By a strange stroke of fate, it happened that on that very day I found it necessary to call in my family physician to see one of my children.[B] I told him of the conversation that I had had, and he made all manner of fun of me for even permitting the man to take up my time. He told me how nonsensical it would be to treat such a case in the way that this man suggested. He himself had had several cases, but he usually sent them to medical institutions, where they were kept over long and indefinite periods, and finally turned adrift—uncured and incurable, and this, he said, was the experience of the profession.

The dogmatic attitude of my physician incited me to investigate the matter further. I secured for treatment a real fiend—a man who was taking forty grains of morphine a day. I hired a small apartment in a New York hotel—and a physician to stand sponsor for the treatment. It was terrible therapy—the patient went wild, and tried to tear the house down; he swore he would have us all arrested, if we did not desist at once. He wanted to quit, the man with the formula wanted to quit, the doctor wanted to quit. But I saw that this was not the time to quit. For three days and nights I remained in that room—with my prisoner. On the fourth day the man claimed he no longer craved morphine, and on the sixth day he returned to his home. Two years ago I saw this man. He had never touched the drug since that day, and was in splendid physical condition.[10]

Three years earlier, in 1913, Peter Clark Macfarlane described Charles Towns' entry into

---

[B] "One of my children" is a bit of a puzzling quote. Charles Towns had but one child, Ed., born in 1895, that lived into adulthood·and eventually took over his father's hospital. There may be more to be discovered here.

treating addicts with a dynamic touch that fully illustrated the nature of Towns' forceful personality. In this version, however, the physician appeared only after there was an emergency.

Towns' first move was to get his family doctor to agree to stand by him, to be responsible for the medical supervision of just one treatment. His next was to get a patient. He did this by advertising in the 'Herald' for a morphine addict who wanted to be helped. There were two responses; one called to see him – a gent with his arms and chest literally covered with needle marks. He was the first morphine user Towns had ever seen. The man's condition was pitiable, his dependence upon the drug so absolute that he had to have a 'shot' while the call was in progress and Towns observed the operation curiously. The man was evidently of some refinement . . .

The addict consented readily enough to make a test of the treatment, but dared not tell his wife. By subterfuge they slipped him out of his home and to a suite which Towns had hired in the old Abington Square Hotel. They were three; Towns, the unnamed possessor of the formula, and the patient. The medicines were also three; little vials from which were to be administered, at given intervals, the powerful agents that were to undo in this man's tissues the accustomed habit of a dozen years and set him free in a few days an unmarked man among his fellows!

In five or six hours the patient became very restless; in two or three more he was threatening to go home, but Towns quieted him and went downstairs to supper. Soon his unnamed partner came hurrying down in great excitement.

"The patient is dressing to go home," he said.

"Well, he'll not go," gulped Towns, swallowing his coffee.

"But we can't keep him against his will," protested the formula possessor weakly.

"But we will keep him," declared Towns, rushing upstairs.

The man had fully dressed himself and was packing his bag. "You have no right to keep me here," he affirmed, vehemently.

"I know we have no right," said Towns cooly, "but we are going to keep you just the same." And then he walked over and laid his hand on the man's shoulder and said in such a tone of quiet but thrilling determination as is easy with Towns but is rare with most men:

"My friend, you entered into an agreement with me and I am going to cure you or hand you a harp!"

The patient wrung his hands a moment, then turned like lightning to the mantelpiece on which stood, among other things, a vial containing a powerful sedative, and before he could be restrained had seized the vial and drained the whole ounce.

"Quick! An emetic!" commanded Towns, and he seized the man. His partner rushed to obey.

"And a stomach pump!" added Towns. In the next fifteen minutes this ex-life-insurance agent gave a remarkable – and a successful, else this tale had not been telling—exhibition of life-saving. After which he judged the time had come to send for his doctor.

In the meantime his nerve-stricken partner—just at this stage accomplice might seem the better word—was pleading to have the treatment abandoned and the man sent home.

"Not on your life!" affirmed Towns. "I never quit but one thing in my life, before I whipped it; and that was too recent to pile up another instance right now."

"Is he in any danger?" Towns asked, a trifle anxiously, after his doctor had concluded a very thorough examination.

"No," was the reply; "his pulse is all right."

"Then we go to it," declared Towns decisively, and they did. The patient became more and more violent, the formula possessor more and more chicken-hearted; Towns more and more determined. As the crisis approached Towns had to have the assistance of a male hospital

attendant as strong as two policemen and the doctor too had to stay very close, watching every

symptom, every roll of the eye, or spurt or sag of the pulse.

At the end of fully eight hours, however, the divide was crossed and the man's condition

returned toward normal. He was offered a hypodermic of the drug without which he had been

unable to live, and he declined it. After the fourth day he went home a cured man. He has

never taken morphine since.[11]

Thus, we have the first "successful" application of what eventually became named "The

Towns Treatment."   Around thirty-five years later Bill Wilson would refer to it as "the so-called

belladonna treatment" in the basic text of *Alcoholics Anonymous* and claim to have been the

recipient of the medicine.[12] By then, it had been called by some other names, including "The

Towns-Lambert" treatment (Lambert being Dr. Alexander Lambert, who published the

methodology in the *Journal of the American Medical Association* in 1909.)[c] However, after the

rather bizarre events associated with the first application of this "cure," Towns realized that the

ingredients needed some definite modifications. He needed to experiment on more patients

and "fine tune" how the medicines were administered.

Towns wrote of that first episode:

[c] More than one historian has confused Dr. Alexander Lambert, of Cornell University and Bellevue Hospital, the first doctor that listened to and supported Towns, with Dr. Samuel W. Lambert, who later became a medical consultant at Towns Hospital, and at that time was dean of the College of Physicians and Surgeons at Columbia University. These two men, who were brothers, are both listed on page 319 of *The American Disease* by Dr. David F. Musto. *Pass It On*, p. 101, incorrectly lists Dr. Sam Lambert as a creator of the Belladonna treatment in the sentence "The belladonna treatment at Towns had been developed by Dr. Sam Lambert . . ." Towns got the formula first from his anonymous layman, refined it, and then provided it to Dr. Alexander Lambert.

In spite of the horrible impression which this whole thing gave me, I saw that something definite had been accomplished, and from time to time I picked up a case in the New York tenderloin.[D] They were treated under the most unfavorable conditions, sometimes in their own environment, sometimes in nursing homes. Beginning as I did, I came in contact with the most undesirable and worthless types of drug habitués. At the outset the patients without an exception were from the underworld, and among them were some of the best-known confidence men of their time, men whose names were known to the police all over the world as the leaders of their special line of work—race track touts, gamblers, women of the street. But without this assistance my work to-day would be incomplete. At every step I was discouraged by the medical profession; seeking for information, I found skepticism, ridicule and rebuffs instead. I learned nothing from them—except that a definite treatment for drug habits was something entirely unknown to medicine.

But I had entered upon my life-work. I began to solve one problem after another in carrying out this work. I modified the treatment, making it less drastic and more successful. At the end of the first year I had radically improved the original formula, and had reached a period where it was possible for me to establish an institution for the care and treatment of cases of addiction. When I began to make progress, every medical step that I took was on virgin soil. And I kept a clinical history of every case.[13]

Might a lesser man have abandoned the idea altogether? Towns, however, was intrigued, and evidently very determined! He was not a "lesser man!"

[D] Tenderloin definition from Merriam-Webster: [from its making possible a luxurious diet for a corrupt police officer] : a district of a city largely devoted to vice

There are also the characteristics of a pattern that, sad to say, seems to be repeated throughout much of recovery literature: when it comes to dates, they are quite often a best guess. The history makers, drunk or sober, clean or high, virtuous or otherwise, characteristically were not writing down events when they were taking place. Sometimes years later, they wrote down what dates they remembered. Sometimes the dates used were as they wished them to be remembered. They were often close to the truth. Sometimes, however, the dates might be considered chosen to enhance one's reputation, and Towns did not seem immune to this practice.

While Towns clearly stated that he was approached in 1901 with the formula, the preceding dialogue from Macfarlane's "The 'White Hope' of Drug Victims" article contained Towns saying that "I never quit but one thing in my life, before I whipped it; and that was too recent to pile up another instance right now."[14] This sentence probably indicates that the year of the first experiment was actually no earlier than 1904. A later date than 1901 accounts for the failure of his partnership in the brokerage business, which lasted three years after his arrival in New York. How had he been able to break away from that business to have been with his first addict for something like six days consecutively without any break whatsoever? Somehow there seems to be a lot of room to doubt that 1901 was the year for his first patient. Rather, 1904 seems at least as likely.

Towns would later claim repetitively that his hospital was founded in 1901 as well. But using Towns own words as quoted by Macfarlane, "They were treated under the most unfavorable conditions, sometimes in their own environment, sometimes in nursing homes."[15] There was no mention of any hospital of his being opened simultaneously with the early experiments with the secret formula. Whereas the date that Towns Hospital first opened remains disputed, the actual date may have been as late as 1909 at a West 81st Street address after his triumphant return from China. The son of Charles Towns, Colonel Ed Towns, who took over running Towns Hospital by 1944, claimed the hospital opened in 1909.[16]

We should also consider that some salesmen have been known to stretch reality at times if the practice resulted in making sales. Towns, as we shall repetitively see, fit the stereotype. He lacked of formal education. He was a newcomer to New York. He began to claim expertise in a subject for which he had no medical training whatsoever. Thus, there appears to be reason to suspect that he was often guilty of making claims that distanced himself further from modesty while increasng his chances for success. Later on, he was to claim that he never took medical responsibility for any of his patients—that he always had a doctor present. In the previous dialog already provided, supposedly he saved the life of his first patient through the use of a stomach pump without any doctor being present.

One may suppose it would be Towns' desire for such trivialities to be overlooked. He would wish that any critics were as determined as he was to find a solution to morphine addiction, which would lead to the betterment of all of mankind. Towns, being who he was, set his sights no lower than that.

Towns quickly was to sever his connections with the unnamed fellow that presented him with the rudiments of the morphine remedy. Towns learned that this partner was offering the formula for sale through a doctor without Towns' consent and that Towns' very own doctor had been offered the secret formula for $50. Towns went to that very same doctor.

"Here," exclaimed Towns, "for nothing!" And he wrote out the formula. "But," he added, "It isn't safe yet. You don't dare to use it. Nobody does!"

That is, of course, nobody except Towns, who would dare anything. All the time, however, he was working to relieve the treatment of its drastic features, and he made progress too.[17]

The challenge was to find a way that would allow an addict to be removed from his affliction with as little trauma as possible. As Towns was to write in detail in years to come, he considered most addicts of that era to be innocent victims. They were begging to be relieved of the curse of addiction that was given to them legally, but, unfortunately, by their doctor or druggist. Towns considered himself to be just the man to be up to the challenge of relieving humanity from the awful agony of addiction.

But to do so, he would need connections.

But one connection he severed right then and there was his relationship with the mysterious fellow that gave him the formula that soon was to be called the Towns Treatment. That person has remained unknown to this day, which was what Towns intended as an appropriate punishment for that fellow going behind his back.

3) Connections 1904-1908

As Towns reported previously, he was discouraged by the medical profession whenever he approached a physician with his discovery. Somehow, and no one knows exactly when or how, Towns attracted the support of a very influential physician by the name of Dr. Alexander Lambert, "professor of clinical medicine at Cornell University, for years a visiting physician at Bellevue" Hospital in New York City. Dr. Lambert was also "considered to be the best advised man in New York on drug habits and alcoholism."[1] This physician was to have a most persuasive and significant role in giving medical validation for Towns' innovation to the point that eventually some named the medical approach as the Towns-Lambert Treatment.[2]

The two men reportedly became good friends. Dr. Lambert was to offer Towns the ability to treat patients under the doctor's supervision, and the results of these first experiments were recorded. No precise information has yet been located to determine exactly where all these early treatments took place, how much time Dr. Lambert spent overseeing the work, or how many patients Towns treated. However, the results seemed to impress Dr. Lambert quite favorably. Dr. Lambert's enthusiasm had to be somewhat limited, however, by the fact that Towns, at this time, "would not reveal the secret formula."[3] Still, when some world events brought the dilemma of drug addiction to the United States government in 1906, Towns' relationship with Lambert was to soon lead Towns to be considered qualified to become an international narcotic problem-solver for the United States. Lambert introduced Towns as "a straightforward, honest man—no 'faker,' who had a most useful solution for drug addiction."[4]

Dr. Alexander Lambert had been a personal physician to the President of the United States Theodore Roosevelt. The physician had become a confidant of the Secretary of War William Howard Taft as well, who had previously been Governor-General of the Philippine territory before being appointed by the President to be Secretary of War in 1904. By 1906, the problem of opium addiction in the Philippines had been reported back to the Roosevelt Administration by a letter written by the American missionary Bishop Charles Henry Brent. The missionary had reported that there was no known solution of how to treat millions of opium addicts. The problem had reached crisis levels in the opinion of the Chinese government, he reported. He proposed an international meeting of great nations to help China with their opium dilemma.[5]

Peter Clark Macfarlane wrote of what followed the Brent letter, which resulted in Towns eventually traveling to China by 1908.

> One day, down in Oyster Bay [Roosevelt's home], Dr. Lambert told Secretary Taft about Towns and his treatment. The Secretary immediately invited Towns to Washington, and through the Surgeon General turned over to him three pronounced drug cases, one a Chinaman, and two Americans. Towns treated all successfully.[E] The Secretary was for sending Towns at once to the Philippines at the Government expense; but Towns wanted to go at his own charges, and upon conditions which the Philippine Commission did not accept.[6]

[E] The *New York Times* obituary for Charles B. Towns reported this story differently following Towns' death February 20, 1947: "Working always with physicians, he treated successfully many cases of drug addiction. In 1907, the late President, then Secretary of War, sent twelve soldiers to Mr. Towns' hospital, where under clinical observation of Army physicians, they were successfully treated." This is one more date that very much leads to confusion of when Towns Hospital originally opened, which is believed to be not until Towns returned from China with all the favorable publicity in 1909 – see *New York Times*, June 6, 1965, on the closing of Towns Hospital. There Col. Ed Towns, the son of Charles Towns, stated the hospital was opened in 1909.

Though Towns never went to the Philippines, soon afterward he met Samuel Merwin, the American playwright, and author, in New York City, who had just returned from China. Towns informed Merwin about the Philippine proposal, and Merwin suggested that Towns go to China where Merwin said an imperial edict had just been made against their opium problem. An estimate had been made, however fantastic, that there were 160,000,000 opium addicts in China at the time.[7] A few years later, after Towns' triumphant return from China, Merwin was to praise and publicize Towns in a manner that money cannot buy.

Macfarlane continued the story.

The job was just about big enough to appeal to Towns, and he had just exactly faith enough in himself and his remedy to make him willing to go over there and undertake it. In Washington Towns met our then Minister to China, Rockhill, who voiced the same idea as Merwin, a very billiken[F] of good humor, who was the last to press his hand as he departed . . . With him Towns had taken, besides his "almighty nerve," a stock of drugs sufficient to treat 10,000 patients.[8]

Thus began a story that became almost worthy of an Indiana Jones movie.

[F] Billiken – from Wikipedia, "The Billiken was a charm doll created by an American art teacher and illustrator, Florence Pretz of Kansas City, Missouri, who is said to have seen the mysterious figure in a dream."

4) China 1908-1909

Figure 2 - One of the Paul Thompson pictures of Charles Towns in the October, 1912 *The American Magazine* article

Samuel Merwin, in *Fighting The Deadly Habits, The Story of Charles B. Towns*, written after Towns' triumphant return from China, relayed the story of Towns in such a manner that the saga simply is included as it was written.

[In 1908] Towns went to China with an idea worthy of Mark Twain's Connecticut Yankee in King Arthur's Court. The Chinese government had undertaken the colossal task of putting down opium. Towns knew from long experience with drug addicts that the habit can seldom be broken without medical aid, and further than no really effective treatment for this curse has ever been known in all of medical history—unless it were, as he believed, the method that he had perfected. Therefore, it seemed, the Chinese Government needed him. He carried with him to China the outline of a plan by which the Government could administer his treatment to a hundred million unfortunates without preliminary expense and at a very low cost to the individual. Provision was made, within the scope of the plan, for the treatment of millions of free cases.

He spent five months at Peking, making representations to the Government and privately treating several thousand cases with success,[G] only to learn that the Government did not want him. He could not even get a permit enabling him to open a single public hospital. Something was wrong; he was baffled. It occurred to him to have a chemical analyses made of the "cures" that had been officially adopted [by the Chinese Government instead of the Towns' Treatment, resulting in Towns not receiving a permit]. He found that each contained morphin[sic] or some other derivative of opium. Each was worse than opium smoking. The Government of China had fallen among grafters in high places.

That settled it for Towns. He promptly rented a house, and put up signs announcing a treatment for opium smokers. Before noon of the first day he was informed that unless the signs were down by three in the afternoon the Minister of Police would take them down by force. Towns replied that he would be on hand to shoot the man that touched them. Nobody came. The signs stayed up. Later the reluctant Government gave him the right to open hospitals anywhere in China and accorded him the privileges and protection of a missionary.[1]

Towns later was to claim that he had 4,000 successful results in China and to have

---

[G] This assertion of Samuel Merwin is highly questionable, especially when compared to how MacFarlane tells the story. In any case, the prose is written in a colorful and vibrant style, which is almost assuredly exaggerated.

opened three hospitals in Peking, Tien-Tsin and Shanghai, but his story version seemed dwarfed when compared to the excitement and adventure of accounts written first by Merwin, and then by Macfarlane.

Peter Clark Macfarlane's version of the story differed significantly but was by no means any less dramatic, and concluded identically. According to Macfarlane, Towns was immediately met in China with bureaucratic delay. He was not allowed any "private treatments" as Merwin reported. The U.S. Ambassador counseled Towns to be patient with the Chinese government, but only after a significant amount of time passed did Towns discover that the delay was because local competition had formed a monopoly already. Just as Merwin reported, the competition's "cure" was simply opium repackaged as a phony medicine. The U.S. ambassador abandoned helping Towns after the repeated delays, saying there was no more that could be done, which only made Towns "Georgia mad" and readied him to take matters into his own hands.

The words of Macfarlane now follow.

And Mr. Towns, formerly of Georgia, late of Manhattan, now of the Flowery Kingdom, once a farmer and horse wrangler, then a railroad man, insurance agent and broker, now the only man in the world, as he believed, with a practical and efficacious cure for the drug habit, and not dodging round the edges of the problem, either, while making money out of the misfortunes of the sufferers, but right here in China at his own expense, challenging the whole nation with his little green mixtures—this Mr. Towns, I regret to say, got mad—not angry, you understand; nothing so diplomatic as that—just plain, American, Georgia mad! and said to the United States Minister what I should think was a very dangerous thing to say when in the midst of heathendom, where a certain flag with certain stars and divers stripes upon it might at some moment become very useful as a shield for bullets or long, sharp, weary-edged knives—but that did not bother Mr. Towns a bit, while his temper lasted, or after, for that matter.[2]

Towns promptly dismissed the U.S. minister, and the minister left angrily saying that Towns should not expect any additional help from him. Towns could not have cared less.

Macfarlane continued:

Thereafter, immediately, Towns rented this house opposite the French Embassy outside the city walls, and moved into it without bothering to get the permit required of any foreigner before he could take up his residence there. Immediately upon his occupancy he raised the two signs which proclaimed in Chinese characters that the said house was now the "Charles B. Towns Anti-Opium Institute." After twenty-four hours came the order to take down the signs and Mr. Towns' refusal, which scared pale and spotted his interpreter, an Englishman but Chinese bureau bred. The same day came a second order, more peremptory; and Mr. Towns returned another refusal, still less diplomatic, which still more frightened his interpreter, so that his teeth were fairly chattering when he translated the last ultimate ultimatum to the effect that if the signs were not down by three o'clock the soldiers of the Empire would take them down.[3]

Macfarlane described how Towns reacted to this threat.

[Towns was] keeping guard over the signs . . . he has returned the impertinent intimation that the Government send out for the pulling-down job men whose lives can best be spared from the service. And this man on the soap box, with only a revolver in his lap and another on his hip, is just as alone as he appears. The United States Minister has washed his hands of him as a trouble maker. There is absolutely nothing between him and death for his American impudence, save his Georgia-born nerve. Yet there he sits, one lone white man, in the midst of four hundred million Chinamen, waiting for the soldiers . . . to come and try to take down the signs.[4]

Towns was not a gunman; he had never carried a gun; had never met an enemy he could not quell with his eye or outpalaver with his tongue; but now he was at a disadvantage. He could not manipulate this chow talk. He was just one high-tempered American in the midst of millions upon millions of Orientals who needed him greatly, but to whose good he was not permitted to minister. . .

[But after three o'clock came and went] no legions appeared—not a pigtail—not a stinkpot—nothing! Towns waited and waited, a grin gradually overspreading his features. Along about sunset, with a crick in his neck from so much craning, he got tired and went inside, which was just as well, for nothing happened until the next day.

What came then was no army with guns, but a messenger of state carrying a formidable-looking document, which proved to be a permit from the Government to open a hospital in Peking or any other part of the Empire that he chose, and therein to practice his healing arts to what extent he might. . . .

Towns stayed in China seven or eight months and treated 4,000 Chinamen, concluding his Oriental career by standing up in Shanghai before the first International Anti-Opium Conference, recounting his experience . . .[5]

However, there was far more to Towns' experiences in China than the United

States desiring to send him as a drug ambassador to help save Chinese lives from the perceived

"evils" of opium addiction. There were very clear politics involved, a hidden agenda, which

David Musto described in his classic book *The American Disease* which explained why the

Chinese may have been so reluctant to enforce their demand for Towns to take down his signs,

or for that matter, why Towns was sent to China in the first place.

Chinese in the United States received some of their worst treatment during America's period of

expansion of 1904 in the Far East. Tension between China and the United States reached a

climax over the determination of Congress to exclude Chinese laborers. Brutality in the United

States against Chinese travelers and immigrants of all kinds furnished ammunition to the anti-

imperialists in China. With an inadequate army, and knowing that burning the American

Embassy would only bring back the marines, Chinese merchants protested by organizing a

voluntary embargo against American goods in 1905. Although formally disavowed by the

Chinese government, the embargo was popular and in certain trading areas effective. The

growth of the embargo, and a fear of what total cessation of trade would mean to those who

thirsted after the endless Chinese market,[6] agitated American traders. President Roosevelt

privately admitted the justice of the Chinese protest but felt it unmanly to allow America to be

pushed around: he asked Congress for $100,000 to send troops to the Far East.[7]

It was in the summer of 1906 that the missionary to China, Bishop Brent, wrote to

President Roosevelt to urge an international meeting of the United States and other great powers, including Japan, to help China deal with its opium problem. Such a humanitarian movement seemed to meet with Roosevelt's objectives to ease Chinese anger against the United States and to decrease the desire of the Chinese to continue their embargo. Three commissioners were selected to represent the United States at the American-initiated conference, and one of those chosen commissioners introduced a third key player, along with Towns and Dr. Alexander Lambert, of advocates to what eventually led to American narcotic prohibition: "the dashing, ebullient Dr. Hamilton Wright."[8] Some were to declare later that Dr. Wright by himself was to become "the father of American narcotic laws"[9] even though he began his crusade from a staff position in the U.S. State Department. Another author, John Helmer, asserted doctors "Wright and Lambert deserve to be regarded as the founding fathers of American drug policy."[10] Those two doctors are the ones that gave Towns the boost, which led him to gain a reputation as an American crusader for healing drug addicts and alcoholics during the second decade of the twentieth century.

Missionary Bishop Brent became chairman of the three-man commission in July 1908. The three delegates, the second being Wright and the third being Charles C. Tenney, began coordinating efforts to begin an international conference in Shanghai at the beginning of 1909.[11] Meanwhile, Dr. Wright, who "had always enjoyed the political side of medical work," had a rather high regard for his own opinions. He became quite enthusiastic regarding the opportunity that the China opium problem represented for advancing his career. Wright researched the opium problem to the best of his ability and sent the President his own memorandum without consulting with his two other committee members.

This direct communication to the President reflected Wright's view of his role in government: a subordinate in the State Department because of technicalities, he was in reality independent of formalities—a distinguished scientist trying to accomplish quickly and efficiently an important political assignment.

Secretary of State Root, to whom Roosevelt turned over Wright's memorandum for comment, did not share Wright's perception. To Root, this attempt to attract the attention of the President would only confuse consideration of the subject and was a nuisance. "Dr. Wright should report to the State Department under which he is serving," admonished Root. "If Wright would go on and attend to his business the information he acquires will be used in the proper place. . . .

[A] responsibility of the convening nation, [the United States], was to have exemplary opium laws. Here there was a more serious difficulty, for while calling on other nations to aid in the eliminating of the opium problem, the United States had no national laws limiting or prohibiting importation, use, sale, or manufacture of opium or coca leaves and their derivatives. This situation simply reflected the traditional constitutional reservation of police powers to the states. Nevertheless, the lack of a federal law embarrassed the commission officials, who believed that other nations would not understand the intricacies of the American Federal system. Wright and Root wanted federal anti-narcotic legislation before the Shanghai meeting, only a few months away.

Wright may have believed it necessary to stress the evil of opium in America in order to secure passage of domestic legislation. His statistics were usually interpreted to maximize the danger of addiction, dramatize a supposed crisis in opiate consumption, mobilize fear of minorities, and yet never waver from the exuberant patriotism which colored the crusade for the Shanghai conference.[12]

The challenge of enacting such a law to control opium, however, was a huge step in an era in which the Federal government had very limited police powers, nor an effective manner of enforcing any legislation passed by Congress regarding opium. Some reduced objective was, therefore, necessary in order to get any legislation passed by Congress that was thought to be constitutional, while showing the world that the United States was committed to solving the opium curse. So Wright and Root reduced their objectives to just the importation of opium used for the purposes of smoking.

> Root made no claim he was proposing a definitive law to deal with the opium problem in the United States. No new methods of enforcement were proposed, and only the importation of opium for smoking was actually outlawed . . . When the Act was approved (9 February 1909), the American delegation proudly and with dramatic flourish announced the victory to the [Shanghai] commission, then in session.[13]

Thus, the first antinarcotic federal law was passed not because of the desire to control the opium problem domestically, but to accomplish a "face-saving" political objective. The Secretary of State wished to reduce the economic impact of a Chinese embargo on American business interests. Little did anyone know that this first Opium Law of 1909 would be the first step in the outright prohibition of all narcotics not related to direct medical treatment in just ten short years. The actual results of the conference itself, in retrospect, retain only the slightest historical significance.[14]

It was after the Shanghai convention that Towns emerged as an American hero. Not only had the United States passed narcotics legislation to prove the nation's commitment regarding the world-wide curse of opium, the United States also had the individual that had invented the world's only known solution: Charles B. Towns. Towns had announced that 76 reputed so-called opium cures contained opium themselves, and, therefore, were not cures at all.[15] Towns not only announced how he had effectively treated 4,000 opium addicts, but he also announced the contents of his gift to the world. For the first time, he announced the contents of what had previously been his secret opium remedy, and it contained no opium! He then returned to the United States as a hero. Dr. Alexander Lambert published in the *New York Times* that the "obliteration of the craving for narcotics is not a matter of months or weeks but is accomplished in less than five days. The result is often so dramatic that one hesitates to believe it possible."[16] Plus, many perceived Towns had put his selfish economic interests second to the priority of healing the world of the opium curse! As a salesman, nobody could have asked for a better angle to become famous and enjoy all the benefits derived from being a magnanimous, patriotic, and dedicated American. He had gained a noble reputation for facing down China's Empress with his truth. In the midst of all this praise for his narcotic solution, he returned back to his adopted new home to begin his reign as "King Charles of New York City."

5) King Charles of New York City 1909-1919

Figure 3 - Charles Barnes Towns in the October, 1912 *The American Magazine*

Some months after Towns' triumphant return the states, Dr. Alexander Lambert provided Towns invaluable publicity and medical validity by publishing the Towns Treatment in the September, 1909 issue of the *Journal of the American Medical Association*.[1] Before China, Towns had kept the Towns Treatment secret, but not anymore! Four thousand patients in China evidently had been quite a confidence builder that the flaws had been removed. *Colliers Magazine's* Peter Clark Macfarlane wrote about Towns in a manner that cannot be superseded. Macfarlane's praise in the November 29, 1913 article captured the essence of Towns' crusade to help the world become addiction free.

[Dr. Lambert] published the Towns formula for the world, backing it with his own indisputable clinical records and giving it the indorsement[sic] of his own great name. The day that this was done, though many called him a fool for foregoing monetary profit, Towns was a very happy man. In less than ten years he had taken the drastic formula which the Unnamed is supposed to have got from some country doctor who had hit upon it in his practice, had stripped it of its severities, had its effects scientifically observed in unnumbered cases, brought it to the point where for several years no improvement in it had been found possible, and now, with the indorsement[sic] of eminent practitioners, he had given it out freely for the benefit of suffering men and women the world over. He, a layman, had done this!

Because he was a layman, Mr. Towns had encountered much prejudice and much suspicion, but now he had been able to make a final demonstration, both of the value of his remedy and the unselfishness of his own aims.

For years Mr. Towns has had a private hospital in New York where patients are treated under his formula, and out of this hospital he makes a generous living; but the treatment is, nevertheless, free to every physician and to every hospital, with the best advice that Towns can print or give.[2]

By now Towns Hospital was doing a lucrative business with an address of 119 West 81st Street since being opened in 1909.[3] He soon was receiving praise from some of the most prestigious doctors in the country, such as Dr. Richard C. Cabot, who taught at Harvard and was on the staff of the Massachusetts General Hospital from 1898-1921. Truly, Towns had the best references from some very high places that were earned by example. Dr. Cabot wrote the highly favorable article "The Towns-Lambert Treatment for Morphinism and Alcoholism" in the esteemed *Boston Medical and Surgical Journal* published on May 11, 1911.

> I then went to New York and spent several days in Mr. Towns' private hospital, watching the progress of alcoholic and morphine cases at different times of the day and in different stages of their treatment. I was struck at once by the small amount of suffering undergone by these patients as compared with the much severer suffering with which I had been previously familiar in watching the results of withdrawing morphine either suddenly or gradually.[4]

This paragraph represents a key to understanding the nature of the praise that Towns was earning from some top medical men. The Towns Treatment had the appearance of allowing the addict to be parted from his addiction with a "small amount of suffering." Dr. Lambert and Dr. Cabot were no strangers to morphine, heroin, and opium addicts. These brilliant men, at the top of their profession, were unquestionably impressed with Charles Barnes Towns and had no better methodology for detoxing an addict without severe, even unbearable, agony. Towns was thought to be providing them a modern solution that was thought to be relatively painless as well as effective.

Dr. Cabot was the one that said, "Any one who knows Mr. Towns knows one of the most persuasive and dominating personalities in the world."[5] Dr. Cabot was quoted in October of 1912 that he "was anxious to find out whether the treatment could be carried out with equal success by anyone else"[6] and for a time was involved in a clinic in Boston that had used the medicine and reported effective results.

Here is what Dr. Cabot was attributed to have said in the January, 1916 issue of *Medical Review of Reviews*.

Richard C. Cabot, of Harvard, whose training and traditions are such as to make him withhold his endorsement until absolutely convinced. "I do not hesitate to say that Mr. Towns knows more about the alleviation and cure of drug addictions than any doctor I have ever seen."[7]

Macfarlane reported how Towns was endeavoring to get the Towns Treatment, or "the Towns-Lambert Treatment, as it is exactly called in the medical profession, or the Lambert Treatment, as it is denominated by those medicos unwilling to admit that a layman can teach them anything," accepted as a standard solution for addiction throughout the nation. As he had the appearance of advocating such a course without any pecuniary interests in the outcome beyond running just a single hospital in New York City, his advocacy seemed to almost take on the nature of a philanthropist. A book review in the *New York Times* in 1915 was to associate Towns with impeccable motives worthy of a great benefactor.

The treatment he gives for the cure of the drug habit and the methods he employs In the hospital he has established for that purpose have aroused the interest and won the commendation of physicians and philanthropists.[8]

Samuel Merwin described Towns' noble motivations in this manner in October of 1912.

That a layman should give the medical world not only a new and accurate lot of information regarding the effects on the human system of alcohol and habit-forming drugs, but also a new and effective method of obliterating the craving for those narcotics, is remarkable enough. That a business man, developing this treatment and building up a private hospital in as efficient and unsentimental a manner as he would have built up a manufacturing or trading business, should steadfastly put behind him repeated offers to capitalize and commercialize his discoveries, should win his way into the confidence of that closest of close corporations, the medical world, should publish his most valuable secrets and devote his life to giving away broadcast the benefit of his discoveries and his experience—this is extraordinary.

All this is what Charles B. Towns has done. He will never, now, be the millionaire head of a country-wide chain of money-making private hospitals. He will be, as he is, simply the experienced, enthusiastic leader of what is perhaps the first really intelligent crusade against these most insinuating and baffling enemies to the human character alcohol and drugs. . . .
It is enough here to say that the treatment has been so perfected that by its use the narcotic craving is often eliminated within a few days, and that the old laborious and painful efforts at cure by slow reduction of the dose . . . is no longer necessary.[9]

David F. Musto noted in the 1973 book *The American Disease*:

Towns was so prominent in authority on addiction that some newspapers and nonmedical periodicals occasionally referred to him as "Dr." Towns, an understandable error . . .[10]

Such high praise, and inevitably the lucrative business of running a well-publicized narcotic and alcoholism hospital led to it moving to a new, prestigious location, 293 Central Park West, in the summer of 1914. That address carried a great deal of status then, and that address is no less impressive one hundred years later: the hospital fronted the body of water that in 2014 is called the "Jacqueline Kennedy Onassis Reservoir" of the famous New York Central Park.

Towns had "looked about him and saw a world sodden with alcohol, dazed with drugs, and befuddled with tobacco. He saw the terrific pressure of commercial need and greed driving these habits in upon us from every quarter. He saw that many druggists were feeling the resulting abnormal desires almost with impunity. He saw physicians casually employing alcohol where it was neither indicated nor needed, and leaving in their wake a gloomy trail of morphinists—many of these latter actually victims of the hypodermic syringes left in their hands by physicians . . . He saw, all about him, men and women going down under this scourge . . . And he coined the phrase—driving a hard fist into the palm of the other muscular hand by way of emphasis—"I tell you, anything that acts like an opiate, *is* an opiate!"[11]

Now the king of narcotics had his "castle," Towns Hospital, located in the heart of one of the wealthiest, most prestigious addresses in New York City. He praised the location in an advertisement in the April, 1917 *The Modern Hospital* magazine.

First of all, to give you some idea of the unusual situation of this Hospital and of the advantages it has for carrying on a helpful personal work for its patients, let me point out that the Hospital building itself faces Central Park, overlooking it at its highest point, with the fashionable

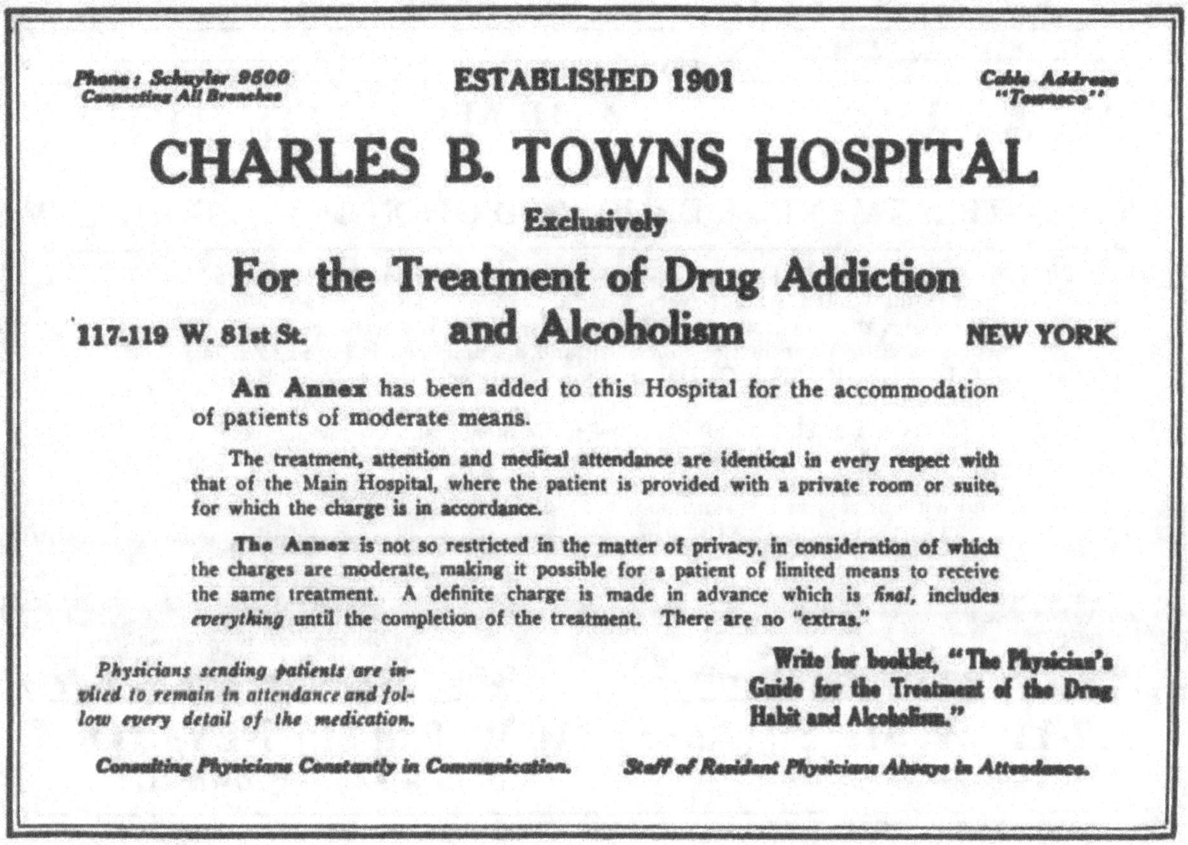

Figure 4 - Ad in the June, 1914 *The Medical Times*, with the 81st Street address included

residences section of Fifth Avenue in the distance. There is no more beautiful view of the Park to be had anywhere. There is a park entrance immediately at our door, and we are within two minutes' walk of the great Croton Reservoir, which has a one and three-fourths miles' walk around it, while the Drive and Bridle Path are right in front of us.

The Metropolitan Museum of Art is within sight, and can be reached by a ten minutes' walk across the Park. The American Museum of Natural History stands on the same street with ourselves (Central Park West) and is only a few blocks away. Within a ten minutes' walk is Riverside and street car lines are at hand to carry one quickly to the centers of amusement and business, uptown and downtown, respectively. I would not exchange the situation of this

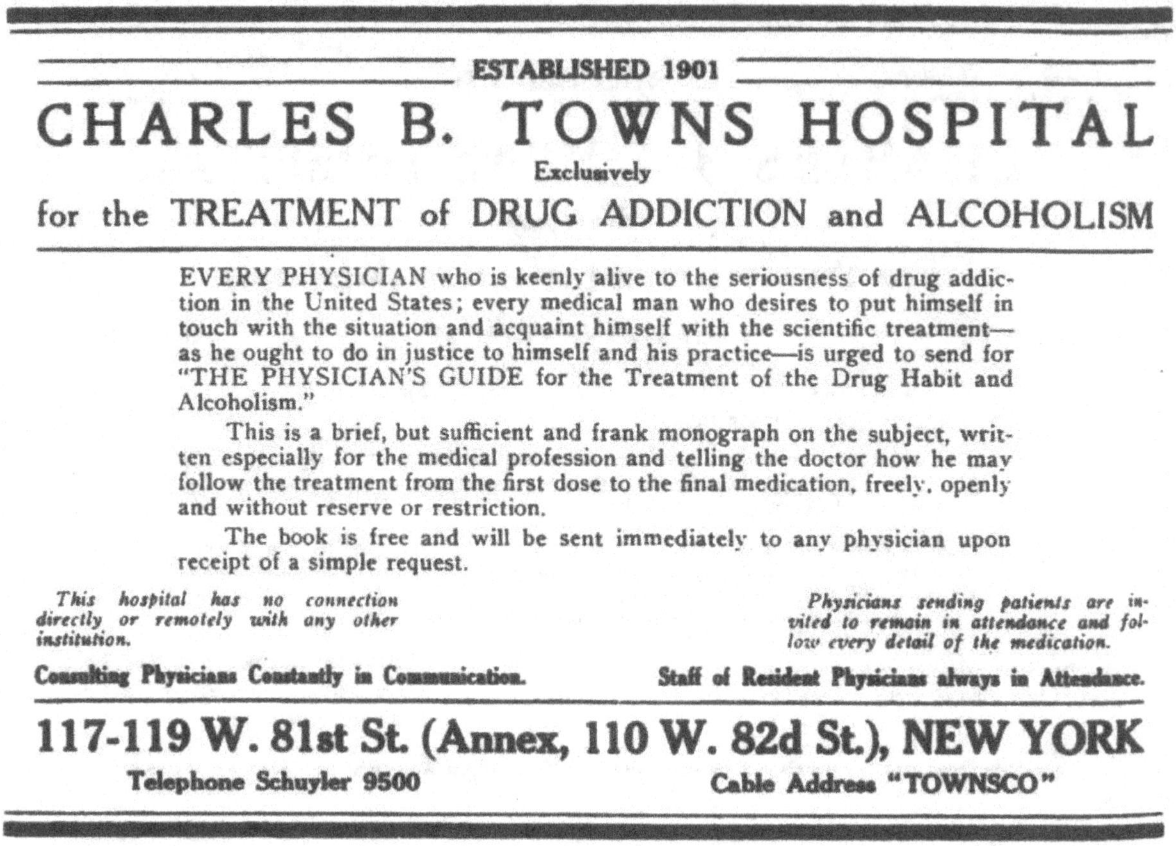

Figure 5 - July, 1915 ad in *The Medical Times* with the 81st street address, plus reference to the Annex on 82nd St.

hospital or its equipment and facilities for those of any other institution that I know anything about, city or country.[12]

King Charles had strengthened his rule through such advertising and publicity. Beginning a few years before in 1912, at the age of 50, he had been given the opportunity to write articles for a very popular monthly magazine for the times, which had begun his literary career, and revealed many of his deep-seated opinions, which would remain predominant for the rest of his life regardless of the upheavals and changes that were to come in dealing with alcoholism and drug addiction.

Announcement!

THE CHARLES B. TOWNS HOSPITAL
for the Treatment of Drug Addiction and Alcoholism

Formerly on West 81st Street
is now permanently located at

293 Central Park West at 89th Street, New York City

which property has been acquired by purchase. This modern building is designed for a select private hospital, is perfectly located,
splendidly planned, fully equipped and is provided with single rooms
for patients of moderate means and with rooms *en suite* for those
desiring such accommodations.

*Physicians are invited to inspect the
new Hospital where every courtesy
and attention will be shown them.*

Telephone 6710 Riverside

Figure 6 - August, 1914 *The Medical Times* ad announcing the move to 293 Central Park West

An Invitation To Physicians

The Charles B. Towns Hospital, for the Treatment of Drug Addiction, Alcoholism
and Nervous Diseases, 293 Central Park West, at 89th Street, New York City,
extends an invitation to all physicians to visit its new quarters, recently purchased, and
familiarize themselves with the method and treatment. The Towns Hospital has been
established 14 years. It is operated under conditions which render the alienation of the
patient from his physician impossible. There is nothing secret; physicians are kept informed from the first to the final dose of medication and a complete bedside history of the
case is fully charted. Physicians are not only welcome during the treatment but are invited to follow every detail of its administration. The Towns Hospital is everything its
name implies—a hospital in the strictest sense, under the direction of physicians and trained
nurses experienced in the work. The active treatment requires only a few days and its
brevity is a distinct advantage to out-of-town physicians who may desire to accompany
their patients to the city. Rooms may be had en suite for those wishing such accommodation and special provision is made for patients of moderate means.

*The treatment in detail has been fully explained in articles
appearing in the Journal of the American Medical Association,
and reprints, together with a booklet and articles which have
appeared in other publications, containing full information relative to the treatment, terms, etc., will be mailed on request.*

Consulting physicians constantly in
communication. Staff of four resident
physicians always in attendance.

Telephone, Riverside 6710

Figure 7 - Towns' ad in *The Medical Times*, October 1914, in which he claims the hospital to have been founded fourteen years ago

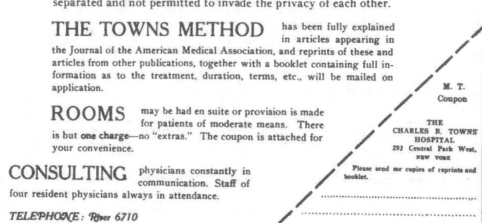

Figure 8 - Full Page ad, December, 1914 in *The Medical Times*. This ad also appeared in the *Maryland Medical Journal* for the months of January, February, and March, 1915.

6) The 1912 *The Century Magazine* Articles 1912

Towns wrote the following four articles for *The Century Magazine* during 1912. Surprisingly, his first article was not about opium, nor any other drug with which he had condemned previously. Nor was the article about alcohol, for which the Towns Treatment had been adapted. The subject of the article was the only addictive substance that Towns ever admitted having used himself: tobacco.

***The Injury of Tobacco And Its Relation
to Other Drug Habits,*** March, 1912

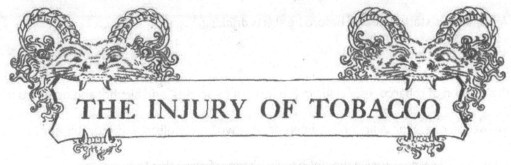

THE INJURY OF TOBACCO

AND ITS RELATION TO OTHER DRUG HABITS

BY CHARLES B. TOWNS

He claimed to have given up smoking sixteen years prior to writing this article. His personal memories may have led him to write in such an unsympathetic manner when it came to tobacco, and particularly cigarettes.

The odor of a cigarette is probably as offensive to most of those who do not smoke as any other smell under heaven.[1]

I consider that cigarette-smoking is the greatest vice devastating humanity to-day, because it is doing more than any other vice to deteriorate the race.[2]

What extraordinary statements about this conveniently available nicotine delivery system![3] He went all the way to China to fight the opium curse, yet cigarettes had been a greater vice since they were the starter substance that led to the hell of addiction. "The narcotic tobacco" in the form of cigarettes he considered to be a gateway to abuse of other substances, along with being a filthy, smelly habit on its own. As a corrupting influence on boys, Towns considered that the influence of cigarettes was virtually unsurpassed.

A boy always starts smoking before he starts drinking.[4]

The relation of tobacco, especially in the form of cigarettes, and alcohol and opium, is a very close one. For years I have been dealing with alcoholism and morphinism . . . and I have never seen a case . . . which did not have a history of excessive tobacco.[5]

The action of any narcotic is to break down the sense of moral responsibility. If a father finds that his boy is fibbing to him, is difficult to manage, or does not wish to work, he will generally find the boy is smoking cigarettes.[6]

Furthermore, all business men will tell you that tobacco damages a boy's usefulness in his work. This is necessarily so, since anything which lowers vitality creates some kind of incompetence. For the same reason the boy who smokes excessively not only is unable to work vigorously, but he does not wish to work at all.[7]

The narcotic tobacco? In the early decades of the twentieth century, the term narcotic was not comparable to the manner in which it is used today. A "narcotic (from the ancient Greek to make numb) [was] originally referred medically to any psychoactive compound with any sleep-inducing properties."[H] Following that line of reasoning for the times, alcohol was considered a narcotic as well. Drunkenness often led to drowsiness or the drunk passing or blacking out, thus, "the narcotic alcohol" was not an unusual concept at the time. Towns considered "the narcotic tobacco" to be no less detrimental than smoking opium.

The more you compare smoking and drinking and drugging, the more resemblances you see. Opium like tobacco and alcohol, ceases to stimulate the moment the effect of it is felt: it then becomes a narcotic. The history of the three as a resort in an emergency is precisely the same. . . The inhaler of tobacco gets his effect in precisely the same way that the opium-smoker gets his . . . It may be news to the average man to hear that the man who smokes opium moderately suffers no more physical deterioration than the man who inhales tobacco moderately.[8]

The preceding is an extremely important quote of Towns to remember, and one that he may have wished he never wrote. The ominous clouds of war soon began to appear. Narcotics, almost overnight, became thought by an increasingly outspoken minority to be a threat to the very soul and future security of the United States.[9] Towns and many others were to assert that there were no such men who smoked opium moderately. The term "drug fiend" quickly emerged as a common part of the American vocabulary. And while alcohol and drugs were

---

[H] The Wikipedia definition continues: "In the United States it has since become associated with opiates and heroin and their derivatives, such as hydrocodone. The term is, today, imprecisely defined and typically has negative connotations. When used in a legal context in the U.S., a narcotic drug is simply one that is totally prohibited, or one that is used in violation of strict governmental regulation, such as codeine or morphine."

soon to be banned, tobacco was to remain entrenched in the American pastime despite Towns

insistence that cigarettes were an equivalent to opium smoking and the number one vice of

humanity.[10]

Towns' passionate views rarely referenced any data or evidence to support his

assertions. His writing was most often without footnotes and did not include any validation or

sources of his opinions. He reported what he considered obvious truths, and as a persuasive

salesman, he was more than ready to make quite a few bold assertions. In such practices, one

risks being proved flat wrong. Here's an example:

> It is very significant that in dealing with alcoholism no real reform can be expected if the patient
>
> does not give up tobacco. Again, most men who have ever used alcohol to excess, if restricted
>
> voluntarily or involuntarily, will use tobacco to excess. This excess in tobacco produces a
>
> narcotic effect which temporarily blunts the craving for alcohol. Another way of saying the
>
> same thing is that when smokers are drunk they no longer care to smoke.[11]

Beginning in 1935 and for quite a few decades afterward, the rooms of Alcoholics

Anonymous were known for their cigarette smoking. Bill Wilson and a host of other recovered

alcoholics remained heavy smokers for their entire sober adult lives, including during crucial

periods of early sobriety.[i] Many recovered alcoholics still smoke to this day, suggesting that

---

[i] On page 135 of *Alcoholics Anonymous*, Bill Wilson, who died on January 24, 1971 of emphysema after a lifetime of smoking, was to write a story that declared smoking was by far the lesser of evils when compared to drinking alcohol. In retrospect, these words may have been directed at Charles Towns for his opinions that one had to quit smoking in order to quit drinking alcohol. Of course, Bill Wilson did quit drinking alcohol without ever quitting smoking. So have a host of A.A. members over the years.

while Charles Towns had many opinions on many topics, those opinions were typically very strong, right or wrong. He did not mind sharing them, in print or otherwise, nor would he shy away from his critics. One of his opinions, which seemed to be among his strongest, was that most any unfavorable criticism of him resulted because of the failure of his observer to change and have an open mind. The following paragraph regarded how he would expect the effects of morphine to be understood by one with an open mind (italics added for emphasis).

Morphine, as it is well known, will distort the moral sense of the best person on earth; it is part of the action of the drug. Since the way morphine gets its narcotic effect is very similar to the way tobacco gets its effect, one would naturally suppose that tobacco would produce in a milder degree something of the same moral distortion. This may seem a startling conclusion, but *change your mental attitude and observe*. Have not smokers undergone a noticeable moral deterioration in at least one particular? They have a callous indifference to the rights of others . . . But a smoker may with impunity pollute the air, offend the nostrils, and generally make himself a nuisance to everybody in his vicinity who does not practice his particular vice.[12]

According to Towns, the distorted morals of a cigarette smoker were similar to that of a morphine user because the effects of both drugs led to a callous indifference of the addict to

---

"One of our friends is a heavy smoker and coffee drinker. There was no doubt he over-indulged. Seeing this, and meaning to be helpful, his wife commenced to admonish him about it. He admitted he was overdoing these things, but frankly said that he was not ready to stop. His wife is one of those persons who really feels there is something rather sinful about these commodities, so she nagged, and her intolerance finally threw him into a fit of anger. He got drunk.

Of course our friend was wrong—dead wrong. He had to painfully admit that and mend his spiritual fences. Though he is now a most effective member of Alcoholics Anonymous, he still smokes and drinks coffee, but neither his wife nor anyone else stands in judgment. She sees she was wrong to make a burning issue out of such a matter when his more serious aliments were being rapidly cured." *Alcoholics Anonymous*, p. 135

the needs of others. Get it? If you did not, according to Towns, that was because one failed to "change your mental attitude and observe." Might such an approach seem rather argumentative, even domineering? To further understand Towns during much of his life, one should not be surprised by a great deal more of the same insistence that he knew the truth. As a matter of fact, he approached the truth seemingly as he approached bronco busting earlier in his life: if he rode the truth long and hard enough, eventually the truth would surrender to him and be conquered. Someone with an open mind inevitably would recognize the motives behind his noble mission, and become willing to become not only one of his supporters, but also one of his knights at his roundtable.

Help For the Hard Drinker – What Can Be Done to Save The Man Worthwhile, June 1912

HELP FOR THE HARD DRINKER

WHAT CAN BE DONE TO SAVE THE MAN WORTH WHILE

BY CHARLES B. TOWNS

Author of "The Injury of Tobacco" [1]

Previously cigarettes had been described by Towns as "the greatest vice devastating humanity to-day." In this June, 1912 article, alcohol was condemned with such an equivalent intensity that one may conclude Towns thought alcohol was even worse.

With increasing unanimity the thinkers of the world are saying that in alcohol is found the greatest of humanity's curses. It does no good whatever; it does incalculable harm . . . and [alcohol has] worked greater havoc in the aggregate than all the plagues. If not another drop of it should ever be distilled, the world would be the gainer, not the loser, through the circumstance. Yet the use of alcohol is continually increasing. The number of its victims sums up a growing total. Sentimentalists have failed to cope with it, and the law has failed to cope with it. In combating it, the world must now find some method more effective than any it has yet employed.[13]

So what was worse: tobacco, which he described as "the greatest vice devastating humanity to-day;" or alcohol, which Towns considered "the greatest of humanity's curses?" Towns seemed to follow a technique of dramatic presentation that was not to be diminished by what he may have written previously. To ask him to clarify such statements might have reduced the full impact of his truths, he might have responded. Then, Towns probably would have accused the questioner of not being willing "to change his mental attitude and observe."

Towns seemed to begin to show sympathy for the alcoholic in a manner not shown to cigarette smokers.

As a rule [alcoholics] are naturally highly nervous, or, through some systemic defect, crave abnormally the excitation which alcohol confers. For these reasons, granting favorable opportunity and no great counterbalancing check, they are foredoomed to drink to excess. Some are predisposed to alcoholism by an unstable nervous organism bequeathed to them by intemperate parents or other ancestors; others are drinkers because they do not get enough to eat, or fail, for other reasons than poverty, to be sufficiently nourished; and others, possessing just the favorable type of physique, become alcoholics through worry or grief. All these kinds of people are victims of a habit which, properly speaking, they did not initiate, and of which, therefore, censure must be very largely tempered.[14]

A much friendlier, sympathetic Charles Towns became revealed. Alcohol was legal and could be found on almost any city street corner. People were only human. If society was so careless to provide temptation everywhere to everyone, then society, as a whole, should be prepared, without complaint, to pay for the consequences. No one need have been surprised by wayward souls overwhelmed by falling to the temptations of drinking alcohol. Behind the rhetoric was a significant implication: some wonderful, admirable people were alcoholics.

By general admission the alcoholic often possesses many qualities of mind and temperament which the world admires and pronounces of the utmost value when rightly developed. Even the careless weakling who drinks to excess is proverbially likely to be generous, magnanimous, warmly impulsive, even quixotic. The finest sensibilities, the most delicate perceptions—from all of which qualities great constructive results may be expected—are notably the most exposed to alcoholism.[15]

Almost makes a nonalcoholic wonder if he would be more appreciated as an alcoholic! Clearly, this tone was far friendlier than his approach with cigarette smokers. Towns asserted so many alcoholics were ending up in mental institutions, jails, and prisons because society did not know what else to do with them. They had succumbed to temptations they should never have been offered in the first place. Rapid deprivation of alcohol drove many into wet-brains and permanent insanity. He thought there was a significant percentage of institutionalized mental defectives that could have become healed of their alcoholism had his remedy been provided to them at the right time. Towns was going to attempt to right this preventable wrong: his approach should become part of a standard curriculum in medical schools for combatting alcoholism in this country and throughout the world.

Not bad assertions for Towns, with no more than an eighth-grade education!

Towns described his understanding of the current shortcomings of treating alcoholics in New York hospitals without his humanitarian discovery (italics added for emphasis).

The man whose drinking has so disarranged him physically or mentally that he is obviously ill is, it is true, taken to the alcoholic ward of some hospital, but even there no effort is made to treat the *definite disease of alcoholism*. For example, Bellevue and Kings County Hospitals, where New York's two "alcoholic wards" exist, are institutions devoted especially to the treatment of emergency cases. As a matter of course, the alcoholics taken to them are merely "sobered up." As soon as they are sobered and have achieved sufficient steadiness of nerve to make their discharge possible, they are turned out again into the liquor-ridden city, with their craving for the alcohol which has just mastered them no weaker, with their resolution to resist its urging no whit stronger, than they were before the crisis in their alcoholic history engulfed them. There is as of yet no public institution in New York City where a man, either as a paying or a charity patient, may go for medical treatment designed to alleviate the craving for liquor . . . This, then, is at present the treatment accorded by the public to the *victims of this serious disease*. There are no clinics devoted to the study of alcoholism, although it is the ailment of probably one third of the sick people in the world today.[16]

Clinics of his design should be created that would treat "victims of this serious disease" that were suffering from "the definite disease of alcoholism." Towns eventually may have regretted having written words contained in his *The Century Magazine* articles, because, in just three short years, he would insist that alcoholism was not a disease! Instead, he would insist that alcohol, as well as other addictive substances, caused the retention of poisons in the body. Until these poisons within the patient were purged, the physical cause for the craving of alcohol would remain. The alcoholic would be doomed to return to drinking alcohol. His solution had all the appearances of a revolutionary humanitarian approach to the baffling problem of alcoholism. He expressed himself with such conviction, and provided such examples of what appeared to be effective remedies, that Charles Barnes Towns was appearing to become a national authority on this dilemma.[17] He was to be provided the opportunity to write his opinions in sophisticated medical journals because no one seemed to have any better approaches in an era when such solutions seemed almost as part of the American Manifest Destiny.

The preceding Towns' quotation has a rather extraordinary assertion as well: that alcoholism "is the ailment of probably one-third of the sick people in the world today." No study is referenced to support the assertion; no outside data whatsoever, just his personal opinions. Towns had benefitted already from the assertion that there were 160,000,000 opium addicts in China. Who knows what Towns thought the percentage of sick people there were in the world from all addictive substances combined? Rarely was such supporting data required or supplied by him. He seemed to consider such references might clutter the minds of his readers, which might detract from the power of his truths.

After all, he wished to appear as the best friend an alcoholic could have! He desired a long-time misbehaving drunk to keep his job despite the trail of damage left behind because of his alcoholism. He wished to build sympathy for those with the disease and help the alcohol afflicted stay out of jail where they should never have been sent in the first place.

The world's loss through alcohol has been incalculable. No community ever existed which could afford to relinquish the services of all its citizens who drink to excess or even of those who frequently got drunk. Yet society has continually maintained that when encountering the alcoholic it has crime, not disease [there's that word again!], to deal with. Hence the crudely ineffective idea of penalization as a preventative.[18]

The Towns Treatment would remove the craving of the alcoholic in just five to seven days, so that he may never drink again. He thought that alcoholics should not be treated as criminals, but it was criminal to withhold alcohol suddenly from the alcoholic. Instead, they "should be treated as invalids"[19] and, therefore, be treated with sympathy and understanding; they should be removed from alcohol through his humane remedy that involved a relatively gentle withdrawal. Society was all wrong in the manner of how alcoholics had been treated. Most alcoholics were misunderstood! Towns went so far as to assert that the alcoholic should be expected to lie, and he should be forgiven for lying because that is what untreated alcoholics do.

Not only must the physical yearning be eliminated, but the mental willingness to drink must be destroyed before reform can be accomplished. It is at this point that the sentimentalists fail. A promise made by one in whom the craving for the stimulant [in this case, alcohol] exists cannot be properly be considered binding, for such a one is not responsible for what he promises. If a body proves stronger than the mind in such a battle, he is merely an unfortunate, not really a liar or a weakling.[20]

Punishment has never yet cured a disease.[21]

The alcoholic should be treated not as a criminal, but as a patient with a disease that can be treated intelligently. The alcoholic's employer should recognize that his employee most often is a good man that will return to his job sober and healthy if just given the medication with the understanding and compassion that went with it.

The employer who discharges a good man from his position because of drunkenness not only fails to deal intelligently with the man or with the subject, but may very likely be committing a crime against society by robbing it of a useful citizen and at the same time forcing a useless one upon it . . . If one of these [drunks] is found to have employment at the time of his arrest, great care should be exercised not to let the fact that he has been arrested prejudice his employer against him, and as far as possible, he should be spared humiliation.[22]

Towns asserted it was a crime against society to discharge an employee inflicted with alcoholism, which, after all, he would not have had society not made alcohol so omnipresent that it could not be avoided. The employer should be careful, as well, not to humiliate his employee for being arrested for being drunk. A reader who had a drinking problem could have understood Towns as someone that wanted to be his very best friend and public defender.

Towns insisted that the alcoholic was the victim! His body tissues had deteriorated from the over-consumption of alcohol. No wonder he behaved so badly! He had been poisoned!

Excessive use of alcohol really deteriorates tissue, and tissue degeneration transforms for the worse the entire physical and mental make-up of a man. The confirmed alcoholic is in a state which, save in rare instances, nothing short of specialized medical treatment can correct. Mere general building up of the bodily tone is as ineffective with alcoholics as is enforced deprivation or punishment.[23]

Thus, as a direct result of the Towns' discovery, the entire criminal system could be relieved of large numbers of prisoners. His proven remedy would make them, once and for all, free men no longer enslaved by substances that caused their cravings. This rapid, innovative solution, which took just a few days, also implied that recovery hospitals would not have to be very large since the beds would turnover so quickly. Charles Towns' medications were "completely effective" and the ingredients were "a very simple prescription" that were "purchasable at any drug store." Towns did not bother to describe the methods employed because "every physician already knows it or can easily obtain it without cost . . ." The mixture could be administered "without publicity and in a few days" so that the patient "need not even be missed from his neighborhood, and an ordinary cold might keep him longer from his business." Towns related how many alcoholics were "afraid to take any treatment for alcoholism" because of potential embarrassment, but the brevity of the Towns' solution directly addressed that the "self-respect [of the alcoholic] must be protected at every stage."

My purpose in writing this article is to show that the only chance of reforming most alcoholics lies in giving them opportunity through this physiological change to reestablish confidence in themselves. [24]

After the patient had left the hospital a free man, Towns insisted that he would be required to abstain from all alcohol in the future, regardless of circumstances. In addition, extreme care was necessary to shield the recovered alcoholic from anyone that had relapsed.

Finally, Towns concluded his article with the admission that not every alcoholic could be helped. Some alcoholics never had been useful citizens and would not be useful in the future. How did he decide who was likely to be treatable? The man who had a job was worthy, the man who was not employed tended to be hopeless.

It is possible to discriminate between the worthy and the unworthy by the simplest of expedients. Usually the question, What is this man willing to do in return for help?[J] will, with its answer, also supply the answer to the inquiry as to his worthiness. No man of sufficient mental fiber to make helping him of any actual value is willing to accept charity . . . My eleven years of experience[K] have proved to me that the sense of personal obligation is of great moment in this matter. Even when it becomes necessary for a relative, employer, or friend to assist a patient by the payment of his bills, it should be regarded as a part of the treatment to consider this a loan, which must be repaid, and not a gift. It follows, sadly enough, that the most hopeless alcoholic is the rich young man to whom financial obligations incurred for treatment means nothing

---

[J] One would think there should be a quotation before "What" and after "help?" but it was not written that way.
[K] "Eleven Years" should be considered highly questionable regarding the exact date, which may not ever been conclusively proven, of when he first started treating patients with his formula.

whatsoever, and to whom responsible employment is unknown . . . I cannot say with too great emphasis that self-respecting pride is the main hope of the alcoholic.[25]

Towns was not a religious man and probably wrote the preceding without any cognizance of The Seven Deadly Sins, which are also known as the capital vices or cardinal sins, which in Christian ethics "has been used since early Christian times to educate and instruct Christians concerning fallen humanity's tendency to sin."[26] The very first and greatest, of these sins, is pride. Nevertheless, Towns wished to appeal to a man's self-respect, his pride, and without the ability to do that, the patient was considered hopeless. Thus, along with the very rich, the very poor were hopeless too. Towns insisted that payment for treatment in his hospital was done upfront, and he wished for that payment to come directly from the pocket of the patient. That would make him responsible; he would not be likely to waste his own money. Estimates of the fee vary from $50 to $350 depending upon the year and location of the hospital.[27] The patient, by being self-supporting through his own contributions, would take his recovery seriously and, therefore, be more willing to persevere through any obstacles that otherwise may tempt him to return to his old self-destructive habits.[28]

Towns wanted the fee to be fixed and for the stay at the hospital to be as brief as possible while remaining effective. The quicker the patient could be treated and released, the more money the hospital would make. He was to confront the sanitarium industry directly with their common practices of charging by the week. He called that a corrupting influence, which most often would lead to the exploitation of the patient. Later, he was to recommend that new special public hospitals be created dedicated to administering the Towns Treatment despite the reality that they directly would compete with private physicians for the medical dollar. Towns would complain about how his ideas were not properly accepted because of prejudice. He remained unaware, so it seemed, that far more significant than prejudices were his procedures and politics, which advocated a much more active participation in the medical industry by government than many doctors and druggists thought warranted.

The Peril of the Drug Habit And The Need of Restrictive Legislation, August 1912

THE PERIL OF THE DRUG HABIT
AND THE NEED OF RESTRICTIVE LEGISLATION
BY CHARLES B. TOWNS
Author of "The Injury of Tobacco" (The Century for March), "Help for the Hard Drinker" (The Century for June), etc.

With this article, Towns directly confronted physicians, the sanitarium industry, druggists, nurses, and the entire medical industry. His self-confidence was never more pronounced. Any concession to other ideas would only diminish the truth that he boldly announced to the country. The drug problem was solvable! What was necessary was to implement the genius of Towns' policies, and the drug problem eventually would become nothing more than a distant, unpleasant footnote of history.

Towns was even more sympathetic with drug addicts than he was with alcoholics. It was his opinion that most drug addicts were innocent victims of either their physician or their druggist. The problem was not illegal drugs, at least not yet since almost every drug was legal in most places. Doctors and druggists, being only human, could not resist the temptations of making repetitively paying customers out of previously unsuspecting patients, and pocketing the endless profits that resulted.

Towns thought the first step to stopping the drug insanity should be a relatively small one. He wished to control the syringes that he thought were being provided haphazardly by physicians to their patients to inject themselves with morphine.

[Those patients] were not properly safeguarded from forming the habit or properly helped to overcome it. It has been criminally easy for any one to acquire the drug habit. Few physicians have recognized that it is not safe for most persons to know what will ease pain. When an opiate is necessary, it should be given only on prescription, and its presence should then be thoroughly disguised . . . it is clear that the physician who uses his syringe without extreme urgency is greatly to be censured, for the patient who has once seen his pain blunted by the use of a hypodermic eagerly resorts to this means when the pain returns. Conservative practitioners are keenly aware of this responsibility, and some go so far as never to carry a hypodermic on their visits . . . One of the busiest and most successful doctors of my acquaintance has used as little as half a grain[L] a year, and another told me he had never gone beyond two grains.[29]

[L] A grain is a unit of measurement of mass equal to 64.79891 milligrams. ½ a grain would be, therefore, 3/100ths of a gram, an incredibly small amount by volume, but not necessarily a small psychoactive effect.

The course of recommended pain relief, as advocated by Towns, seemed rather heartless. He thought most dosages of morphine were unnecessary, that most episodes of pain could be quickly resolved, and that patients never needed to learn about syringes to minimize episodes of their pain. Towns asserted "it is perhaps a conservative estimate that only ten percent of the entire drug consumption in this country is applied to the purpose of blunting pain. Thus ninety percent of the opiates used are, strictly speaking, unnecessary."[30] He believed that if patients were not taught how to use syringes, morphine addiction could be reduced significantly. Thus, the doctor should keep as much secret about the method of pain relief as possible whenever it had to be administered. Apparently Towns expected the physician to approach the patient with a syringe while the patient could not view what the physician was doing. Did Towns not want the physician to inform the patient of why he might feel discomfort during the injection? Exactly how the doctor was to accomplish this was not described.

Thus, according to Towns, a large part of the problem of morphine addiction would be solved simply by the doctor exercising discretion. The physician should not tell the patient

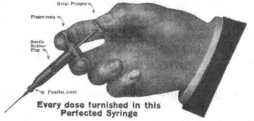

Figure 9 - A rather typical syringe ad for the times

anything about morphine, not show him what a syringe looked like, and keep the patient ignorant about such things for his own good. Such views of Towns reflect a marked paternalism.

> With few exceptions, I have found that the first knowledge of [morphine] came through the administration of a hypodermic by a physician. It is the instrument used which has shown the sufferer what was easing his pain. I consider that it has been the chief creator of the drug habit in this country.[31]

He claimed to have made that exact assertion in front of the House Ways and Means Committee in 1911.[32] Most addicts, according to Towns, were victims. The time soon arrived when "the pleasurable part of the effect—if it was ever present—cease to be obtained; and in order to get the soothing or stimulating effect, the dose must be constantly increased as assimilation increases." While some pain sufferers were medicating themselves out of necessity, Towns thought that the percentage of users was very small. "The rest [were] impelled simply by craving—that intolerable craving which arises from deprivation of the drug."[33] Every drug user would become hooked, and then a threat to himself and everybody with which he came in contact. This peril of the drug habit could not be underestimated.

> [Whether] a man has acquired the habit knowingly or unknowingly, its action is always the same. No matter how conscientiously he wishes to discharge his affairs, the drug at once begins to loosen his sense of moral obligation, until in the end it brings about absolute irresponsibility. Avoidance and neglect of customary duties, evasion of new ones, extraordinary resourcefulness in the discovery of the line of least resistance, and finally amazing cunning and treachery—this is

the inevitable history. [He knew of] mothers and wives who became indifferent to their families; clergymen of known sincerity and fervor who became shoplifters and forgers; shrewd, successful business men who had become paupers; . . . Under the sway of opium a man does venturesome or immoderate things that he would never think of doing otherwise, simply because he has lost the sense of responsibility.[34]

The implication of this line of thinking should not be underappreciated. The individual had no control after his introduction to drugs. The result of drug usage was always irrational and self-destructive behavior. Towns believed society, in order to protect the general welfare, must take action, for the general good, to remove the potential for such tragedies to take place. If the individual always became a victim, overwhelmed by forces he did not understand and introduced to him most often by his well-meaning physician, the individual could not be held responsible. Towns considered himself a pioneer in the field of addiction, and he firmly believed that the answer to the problem rested with appropriate government legislation that needed to be enacted as soon as possible. Towns made this following claim.

[As early as 1911] he had "personally secured the act which was passed by the New York legislature in February, 1911, to restrict the sale of [syringes] to buyers on a physician's prescription." Before that time all drug stores and most department stores sold hypodermic instruments to any one who had the money. A boy of fifteen could buy a syringe as easily as he could buy a jack-knife.[35]

He believed the issue to be so important that he took the issue personally. He announced the expansion of his mission in this article. He would become a vocal public advocate for restrictive drug legislation and for laws to be passed not only in State of New York, not only in the nation's capital, but internationally as well because of his perceived necessity to combat a "habit which now alarms the world."[36] He did not find it necessary in the article, however, to list the names of any of the countries that allegedly were alarmed.

Towns asserted that too many druggists and patent-medicine manufacturers were making large profits by hooking people into becoming repeat customers. "It is of course to the interest of every druggist to create a lasting demand for his article,"[37] Towns asserted. Patent medicines routinely contained cocaine, opium, heroin or morphine, and up until the Pure Food & Drug Act of 1906, the ingredients of patent medicines did not need to be disclosed. As of 1912 when Towns was writing this article, the ingredients were being declared, but he asserted the addiction had not been significantly reduced. The way to reduce addiction was clear to him. Narcotic drugs should be administered only through prescription and should not be available to the public without a doctor's continued supervision. A single prescription should allow for not more than three weeks of medicine until the prescription had to be renewed to obtain more of the drug by another visit to the doctor.

Towns was downright suspicious, if not insulting, regarding druggists and their professional associations that were resistant to his views.

There is obviously not so much profit in a medicine that cures as in one that becomes indispensable. Hence arises the great inducement, from the druggist's point of view, in soothing-syrups and the like. In this country all druggists, wholesale and retail, are organized, and the moment a bill is brought up anywhere to correct the evil in question, there is enormous pressure of business interests to secure its dismissal or satisfactory amendment. {Towns emphasized] the essential selfishness of their position . . . [38]

He considered "easy accessibility to drugs in medicinal form [was] more dangerous than the moralists cared to admit."[39] He then referenced his observations of opium smoking in China. Opium smoking was popular there because it was commonly available. He reasoned that injecting opium in this country was becoming common also because of the availability of the syringe. If one removed the syringe, "lack of opportunity is everywhere recognized as a great preservative of virtue."[40] He continued (italics in original).

[The] alkaloids of opium administered hypodermically or as ingredients in many patent medicines *are* thus convenient, and as a result this phase of evil *has* reached overwhelming proportions. Nor have we any cause for congratulation upon our particular form of the vice, for opium smoking is vastly less vicious than morphine-taking.[41]

Overwhelming proportions? No statistical evidence was volunteered. But because of this emerging threat, he advocated strict controls on opium from the moment the substance entered the country since druggists and physicians had proven they could not be trusted to administer narcotics responsibly.

[There never would be proper] accounting until there is government monopoly in the drug. Indeed, there can be none until there is cooperation of all the governments of the world. If Congress were to pass a stringent law for the United States tomorrow, unless there were some international arrangement, it would not prevent any person from importing the drug, or, if the law did not allow him to import it, from smuggling it.[42]

Some years before the President of the United States, Woodrow Wilson, would advocate the creation of a League of Nations, Charles Barnes Towns advocated the founding of an unnamed international league to be created to combat what he perceived to be the evils of drug addiction. Government should monopolize the production and sale of narcotics not only in the United States, but individually in countries throughout the world. An international association of some kind needed to be formed to ensure that narcotics were being handled responsibly among nations. Towns thought international government legislation to be the only possible solution.

Stopping importation, then, is a farce, unless at the same time there is rigid governmental control in those countries that produce or import the drug. And, therefore, unless there should be a cooperation of all governments, it is futile to try to regulate the traffic. As long as people can get opium, they will smuggle it.[43]

Not only was government regulation the only solution, but also government was an extremely practical solution.

It has been demonstrated to be quite practicable for all the opium-producing countries to make the drug a government monopoly; it would be equally practicable for them to sell directly to those governments that use it for governmental distribution. The only obstacle to an international understanding is that the producing countries knew very well that government regulation would materially lessen the sale of the drug.[44]

The profit motive needed to be removed from the distribution of narcotics. According to Towns, this goal could be achieved by making drug production, distribution and sale a world-wide government monopoly. The problem of narcotic addiction could be solved once and for all! Narcotics of all kinds would be sold that were collected and distributed by governments only, including whatever patent-medicines proved useful, if any. Written prescriptions would track the distributed medicine.

Government would be more than sufficient to handle and distribute all of the drug that is needed for legitimate purposes . . . The drug would serve only its legitimate purpose, because the druggist could sell it only on prescription . . . The physician would thus have to shoulder the entire responsibility for the use of any habit-forming drug. With Government as the first distributor and the physician as the last, the whole condition of affairs would assume a brighter aspect, for it would be a simple matter to get from the physician a proper accounting for what he had dispensed. If he knew he must answer for every case of drug-taking which he was a factor in creating, he would be very careful in his administration of the drug. Thus the new crop of users would be small, and less than ten per cent of opium at present brought into this country would be sufficient to meet every legitimate need.[45]

Resistance to this approach of a government solution to addiction was compared by Towns to be comparable to resistance against the slave trade.[46] He claimed that school-children were buying cocaine in Jersey City.[47] Dealers in drugs were going to continue to sell their addictive substances as long as there were no consequences for them doing so. Towns considered the status quo intolerable. Immediate regulation was the only answer.

The prevalence of the drug habit, the magnitude of which is now startling the whole civilized and uncivilized world, can be checked in only one way—by controlling the distribution of habit-forming drugs. With Government as the first distributor and a physician as the last, drug taking merely as a habit would cease to exist . . . By such restriction the intense misery due to the drug habit would be decreased by nine tenths, indeed, by much more than this; for when a physician dares no longer be content with the mere alleviation of pain, which is only nature's way of announcing the presence of some diseased condition, he will seek the more zealously to discover and remove its cause.[48]

Here was the conclusion and triumphant assertion of Charles Towns in his third article written for *The Century Magazine*. His first article concerned cigarettes, which by and large he considered a disgusting, selfish habit that fouled the air. His second article was about alcohol, which he considered a curse. As he was not a temperance advocate, he had implied only that society would be better off if alcohol was not manufactured for drinking anymore. His third article, however, that concerned drugs, was international in scope, and revealed a faith in the purity and efficacy of government that is truly startling. His policies advocated unprecedented enlargement of government in the United States that some would have considered socialist in nature. However, he would have replied that such criticism as quite unfair. He was an addiction specialist, not a politician. He considered his motives were entirely sensible and humanitarian. His nature was that of a philanthropist interested only in the betterment of mankind. Had not he proven himself to be above simple pecuniary motives already, by his free donation of his addiction solution to the world? How much proof did anyone need of the pure motives of his proposals?

The Drug-Taker And The Physician And The Need of Adequate Specific Treatment, October 1912

THE DRUG-TAKER AND THE PHYSICIAN

AND THE NEED OF ADEQUATE SPECIFIC TREATMENT

BY CHARLES B. TOWNS

Author of "The Injury of Tobacco" (THE CENTURY for March), "Help for the Hard Drinker" (THE CENTURY for June), "The Peril of the Drug Habit" (THE CENTURY for August), etc.

Towns made his position clear in the previous article of how regulation by government of narcotics was considered essential, and that he thought the physician was the main creator of the drug habit in the United States. Towns asserted that the physician could be the solution to the drug problem as well.

Since the physician, by the administration of these drugs in his practice, has so large a share in the creation of the habit, he is the person who may be expected to lessen it; and justice demands that he be made responsible for the entire distribution of such drugs to the public.[49]

Before, however, full government regulation was to be implemented for limiting the problem of drug addiction in the future; Towns was very sympathetic to the poor souls that had been afflicted with the habit already. What would become of them?

He then entered into opinions, which seemingly cannot be adequately paraphrased or summarized. To fully appreciate Charles Barnes Towns, his words resemble what today might be called a stereotypical thinking on steroids.

Until some provision has been made [for current addicts], it might be an unwise and perhaps hazardous thing to put all such drugs entirely out of their reach. To do this would tend to let loose upon society a multitude of scheming and really desperate sufferers. No one will go to greater lengths than the drug-taker bent upon obtaining his dose at the usual time. Only death or rigid incarceration will keep him from it, and records show that penitentiary-bars have not been able to do so . . . When opium is simply withdrawn and he survives the ordeal, he usually takes to alcohol. Between the opium-user and the excessive alcoholic—for after the forcible withdrawal of opium he becomes excessive—there can be no doubt which is the more hostile to society. The man with an inflamed brain is more dangerous than the man who wishes to be let alone. The alcoholic is usually uproarious, and wants to keep in the foreground; the morphinist is passive, and wants seclusion. While the one turns night into day, the other turns day into night. An alcoholic wishes to take care of everybody's business; a morphinist is satisfied not to take care of his own. Thus, that the drug-taker may not become even more mischievous to society than he already is, the question of enabling him to recover from his habit becomes of paramount importance. It must be considered and if possible settled before restriction of the sale of the drugs can become absolutely effective.[50]

Towns insisted that if opium addicts were not removed from their slavery first before drug legislation cut off their supply, there would be hell to pay. Most opium users would turn to alcohol. Since their brains were inflamed by the drug already, they would be far more hostile to society as craving, drunk, lunatics suffering from withdrawal than just average alcoholics. He wanted the Towns Treatment to be made available to these victims, and then drugs to be restricted by law. Through such compassion and procedures, the risks of future harm from addicts being withdrawn from opium would be minimized.

He then briefly introduced a description of the drug habit in the United States but provided no statistics or studies beyond a passing reference to the Internal Revenue Service. He said the IRS reported an increase in the importation of narcotics that was increasing much faster than the population was through births and immigration. He asserted that immigrants were not the source of increased drug use, since "I have never seen an Italian, a Hungarian, a Russian, or a Pole" that was a drug user.[51] His opinion on Jewish immigrants, which Towns probably intended as being complimentary, resonated as an ethnic stereotype.

I have met with only four cases of drug-taking Hebrews. Few Jews—except in the under-world—acquire the habit knowingly. It may become fastened upon them through the use of medicine the danger of which they do not realize, but once freed, they will not again come under its power. The practical sagacity of their race is their surest safeguard.[52]

Towns then made some observations that some may find surprising and suggest that he was ahead of his time: the reason Americans were prone to drug usage was because of the pace of the American lifestyle.

> What is commonly spoken of as the "American type," highly nervous, living under pressure, always going to the full limit, or beyond, is peculiarly liable to disorders that lead to the habitual use of drugs. We are all hypochondriacal by nature, prone to "take something" whenever we feel badly. Lack of opportunity alone, of knowledge of what to take and how to procure it, has saved many a person under severe physical or mental strain from recklessly resorting to drugs.[53]

The restriction of drugs simply would make drugs harder to obtain. Fewer people would know what the drug experience offered if fewer people were exposed to it. Society would be vastly better off and healthier through restrictive legislation.

While to some this line of reasoning seemed plausible, if not paternal, Towns then identified who many drug addicts were. While physicians, according to Towns, had created the drug habit in this country and were also to be the solution to drug addiction, physicians also comprised fully one half of the drug patients treated at Towns Hospital. These were potentially dangerous people.

> Reputable medical men, writing on this subject, have alleged that fifteen percent of their own profession are addicted to drugs. As compared with my own experience, this seems a gross exaggeration, for though it is true that one half of all my drug patients have been physicians, I am inclined to believe that the percentage of drug-takers among the profession is much below

five rather than fifteen. This percentage is quite high enough, however, to be a standing menace to society. To realize this, one has merely to recall that the drug-taker is a confirmed evader of responsibility; and the physician of all men, is in a responsible position . . . It is a characteristic of the drug-taker, no matter who he is or how he acquired the habit, on the smallest excuse to advise others to take the drug whenever pain or fatigue gives the slightest occasion for it. While he grows callous to everything else, he has an abnormal sympathy with suffering. Thus it will readily be seen that there are few more dangerous members of a society than the physician who is addicted to a drug.[54]

A full fifty percent of the patients at Towns Hospital were physicians! But Towns apparently did not want to insult them any more than he had already. So, he was "inclined to believe" that the percentage of addicted physicians did not begin to approach the high percentage of patients at Towns Hospital. Due to the expensive upfront fee at Towns Hospital, ranging up to $350, most often only the affluent could afford Towns' services. In addition, most of his publicity to date had been to physicians. The highly favorable Samuel Merwin article in *The American Magazine* had only been published this very same month, and the *Colliers Magazine* article by Macfarlane would not be written for another thirteen months. Consequently, the patients at Towns Hospital would not reflect the percentages of the general population that were addicted. Bellevue Hospital or Kings County Hospital in New York City would have been a much more accurate patient sample than Towns Hospital.

The article continued with the assertion that nurses that had become addicted to drugs were potentially more hazardous to patients than physicians because nurses spent more time with patients. Towns also discussed the dilemma of addicted pharmacists, and how irresponsible they were if they were inflicted by the substances they distributed. Just how restrictive drug legislation was going to improve the future, for those who already handled narcotics as part of their professional responsibilities, Towns never clarified beyond an implied significance of a paper trail through collected written prescriptions. Towns apparently never considered an effective forgery of a paper trail to be a major consideration. Nor was there any consideration of the costs to effectively monitor large amounts of rather sterile paperwork, not to mention the additional burdens on professionals to fill out the paperwork in the first place.

Towns then portrayed competitive alternatives to his medical model in a very negative manner. Treating an individual as an out-patient was considered ridiculous, and the related patent medicines advertised to treat such addictions were addictive themselves.

> In many of the periodicals and daily papers are carefully worded advertisements setting forth that a man may be cured of a drug habit quickly, secretly, painlessly, and inexpensively . . . In almost all cases he wishes to be freed from the habit, but at the same time to avoid the disgrace of being classed with "drug fiends"; he is unwilling that even his family or his intimates should know of his condition. He has an exaggerated sensitiveness to pain upon which also the advertisement relies. Furthermore, attention is directed to the fact that the patient may take the alleged remedy without spending much more money than he is now spending for the drug itself, naturally a powerful appeal to a man of limited means . . . I have encountered few patients who have not at some time or other taken a "home cure."[55]

He then noted the implausibility of attempting to treat opium addiction with opium, which was precisely the approach of seventy-six so-called opium cures that were condemned by him back in 1909 at the Shanghai conference. Towns continued to insist that any self-induced reduction method as advertised in home cures was futile: "a treatment of this sort must, except in case of a miracle, be administered by another and under continuous medical surveillance" because the addict already has become "utterly unable to deal justly with himself, for it is the nature of the drug to destroy his sense of responsibility."[56]

Next Towns asserted the risks and economic exploitation he had observed in the sanatorium industry in treating addicts. Most physicians were sending their patients to such places since they did not know what else to do with them. They already knew the futility of trusting an addict's word of what he administered to himself at home. Constant surveillance was required for effective results. The embarrassment of friends and relatives of being around an addict was most often intolerable, which led to indefinite stays by the addict in sanatoriums. The patient would not be released until the victims of his addiction thought him cured. The sanatoriums that were charging week by week had every economic incentive to keep the addict as a patient as long as possible, rather than rapidly treating him and returning him to be a productive member of society.

> The sanatorium becomes merely a convenient and pleasant boarding-establishment where everything is done to secure the homelike atmosphere usually advertised. The man who charges by the week is tempted never to end the treatment; on the other hand, a patient will pay by weekly driblets much more money than he would think he could afford in a fixed sum.[57]

Worse still was that an addict in a sanatorium would be forced to congregate with other addicts, and Towns considered exposure of the addicted to others of their kind to be counterproductive. Here, again, Towns provided strong opinions that could only be described today as stereotypical to a fault.

> The gravest aspect of these long stays at a sanatorium is the unavoidable colonization. Picture to yourself a group of from a half a dozen to fifty morphine patients, eating together, walking together, sitting on the veranda together . . . All the more on this account is there a general and eager discussion of previous history and present situation. For where the alcoholic is quite indifferent, the morphine victim has an insatiable interest in symptoms. He has also an excessive sympathy with all who have been through the same mill with himself. Thus, in a matter where individual and isolated treatment is imperative, most sanatoriums deal with patients collectively. Furthermore, these are peculiarly a class of unfortunates who ought never become acquainted. Whatever moral restraint the habit has left in a man is completely relaxed when he hears constant bragging of trickery and evasion and has learned to envy the cleverness and resources so exhibited. The self-respect and pride which must be the main factors in his restoration are sometimes fatally weakened. Colonization should be restricted to the hopeless mental cases, and to them only because it is unhappily necessary.[58]

Towns Hospital offered individual hospital rooms and offered complete confidentiality. There were to be no benefits in patients learning anything about each other. Reliance on pride and self-respect were considered essential to recovery, and putting addicts together were thought to only lead them to glorify their past and share counterproductive stories elevating past misdeeds. Towns then continued to claim the virtues of a treatment hospital with the sole purpose of fighting addiction and how any other approach was inferior.

He concluded this article with words that, again, cannot be adequately summarized. His views represented a most unfortunate dismissal of what would become a biproduct of the American drug culture of today: the big business and big money that drive some addicts to live on the street just as long as they can get their next hit.

It may be noted that I have not dwelt upon the expense of the habit. The consideration may be omitted from the case. To the average addict, the cost of his drugs, no matter what he may have to pay for them, seems moderate. He is buying something which he deems a vital necessity, and which, moreover, he places, if a choice be required, before food, drink, family, sleep, pleasures, tobacco—every necessity or indulgence of the ordinary man.

The real cost is not to the drug-taker, but to the world. If a human life be considered merely as a thing of economic value, an estimate may perhaps be made of the total loss due to the habit. But the loss should not be reckoned in any such way. It should rather be reckoned by the great amount of moral usefulness and good that might be rendered to the world if these unfortunates could be freed from their slavery, and by the actual harm being done by them, especially by such of them as are now loosely classed as criminals and degenerates. The retrieving of much of the waste of humanity may be accomplished by adequate treatment of the drug habit.[59]

That Towns wrote the subject of the cost of drugs could be "omitted" seems especially noteworthy. He meant well, but he had no crystal ball. In reality, he had no idea what would happen to the price of narcotics once their use was "restricted" as he desired. He had no idea how "the under-world" would profit from the price rise of these substances. Nor did he realize that in just a few short years, narcotics would not only be restricted, but also they would be

prohibited for any usage besides that related to medical necessity.

7) The Harrison Act – December 1914

The second decade of the twentieth century was a time of huge transition. War and revolution killed millions and overthrew centuries of monarchy. The United States entered the "war to end all wars" in April of 1917, which led to "All Silent on The Western Front" when the Armistice followed eighteen months later. The income tax was passed in 1913.   A Democrat had been elected President of the United States in 1912, Woodrow Wilson, whose career up until then had been much more as an intellectual college professor than a professional politician. The National Prohibition Enforcement Act, otherwise known as the Volstead Act, was vetoed by President Wilson on October 27, 1919, but the House and Senate overrode the veto, which began National Alcohol Prohibition on January 16, 1920.[1] In 1919, the Senate of the United States had crushed a dream of Woodrow Wilson when the Senate refused to allow the country to join the League of Nations. These were but a few of the historic events.

Seemingly lost in these turbulent times, but nevertheless very significant in its impact to this day, was the evolution of national narcotic prohibition in the United States, which evolved in just a five year period commencing in late 1914. Unlike alcohol, no constitutional amendment was required. So turbulent were the times! World War I began in August of 1914. The Lusitania was torpedoed in May of 1915. Those events are easily covered in most any American History book. The Harrison Act was passed in between those historic events, on December 17, 1914. Very few seemed to notice then. Few remember the legislation now. A cursory examination of many history books will make no mention of the law whatsoever unless there is a specific focus on the origins of drug prohibition.

Someone that had been noticing was Charles Barnes Towns. As a matter of fact, he was one of the primary "movers and shakers" that helped publicize a perceived need for the Harrison Act in the first place. But a personal contribution was the Boylan Act in New York State, which had been passed on April 14, 1914 by the New York Legislature and went into effect the following July 1.[2] Later, in 1917, Towns was to claim, in an article written for the Boston College publication *The Sacred Heart Review*, that "he was the author of the Boylan Law of New York State to correct drug abuses."[3]

Early in 1913, he had approached New York State Senator John J. Boylan with his restrictive ideas regarding narcotics. Towns seemed to possess the noblest intentions and wanted New York to set an example for the rest of the country. What became known as the Boylan Act was not to pass until the next year, but those that have documented how the bill became law gave Towns the credit for its passage. As was written in *Medical Review of Reviews* in January of 1916:

The Boylan Bill is named after Senator J.J. Boylan, but everyone knows that it is the work of Charles B. Towns.[4]

David F. Musto described the main facets of the Boylan Act in his book *The American Disease*.

Some elements were legitimate attempts to require that a prescription include the address and legible name of the prescriber, prohibit fraudulent professional credentials, and monitor transactions between wholesalers and retailers. All prescriptions for habit-forming drugs would be filled in on special forms serially numbered and retained for inspection by the pharmacist. Towns claimed that these measures would overcome the problems of fraud in obtaining narcotics and ignorance of the amounts of narcotics sold to physicians and druggists, and keep the continued supply of narcotics to patients under the control of physicians. Such restrictions could not be faulted except on the grounds of excessive paper work for the busy physician and druggist . . . But perhaps the major opposition among physicians was created by his proposed restrictions on narcotic prescribing. For example, he would limit to three weeks the time a physician could freely dispense narcotics to a patient. Continuation thereafter would require approval from a local health department. This constraint was introduced to prevent the practitioner from indefinitely "treating" an addicted patient . . . [5]

According to the *New York Times* in an article published on June 21, 1914:

The law for the time being will hardly affect the drug users of the underworld, who have long known secret channels through which they obtain their drugs. It will fall most heavily on the person who has broken no law in the past in securing habit forming drugs and will drive him—or her, for there are vast numbers of women who have become drug fiends in this manner to seek illicit drug ends if other methods are not speedily provided. The law provides that persons who are found to be habitual users of such drugs shall be committed to a State, County, or city hospital or institution licensed under the State Lunacy Commission.[6]

Towns was to claim the following in *Medical Review of Reviews* in March of 1916:

In drafting the legislation of which I was the author in this State now that this legislation has been found so entirely effective, it is being appreciated by the very men who criticized me, for they realize that I have done the medical profession a great service.[7]

Towns did the medical profession "a great service?" David F. Musto documented how many medical men vehemently disagreed with Towns' legislation to restrict physicians dispensing narcotics as they deemed necessary to treat their patients.

[From] the rank and file [physician] who was then beginning to organize to better his economic and social status, [Towns] evoked hostility and resentment . . . Such an unprecedented legislative restriction on the private physician did not go unnoticed and could not have been more effectively designed to stimulate the fear and enmity of the general practitioner. Although the direct loss of income might not have been great for most, the transfer of service responsibilities to health departments continued what the GP considered a trend of government competition for the patient's dollar. The cure of addicts would be shunted to sanitaria, probably operated by "hospital doctors," the unpopular elite of the profession. By this effort to control the medical care of addiction, Towns set himself up as an enemy of the average physician in New York City. He was called a fraud who sought legislation that would injure the unfortunate addict, to Towns' pecuniary advantage, attacked as practicing medicine without a license, and accused of hiring physicians on control, a high-ranking sin among doctors. Towns' "comrade," Alexander Lambert, was a strong proponent of health insurance, annual licensing of physicians, and the establishment of a standard fee schedule. Towns' antinarcotic law was opposed more for its threat to traditional freedom of medical practice than for its goal of restricting narcotic use.[8]

Even as obnoxious and tedious as most physicians considered these various regulations to be, Towns' immediate goal was not narcotic prohibition as much as it was orderly narcotic supervision. He wanted addicts to be treated with compassion in an organized manner where monetary profit would not lead to corrupt medical practices. He strongly believed in a medical solution to narcotic addiction, and wished to implement a managed system that would ensure the addict would be freed from his slavery, while sanatorium quacks would be eliminated from indefinitely exploiting their victims.[9] He wished for those addicts that were not under medical supervision, before the Boylan Act went into effect in New York, to quickly find themselves a physician to assist them to ensure their legal access to their addictive substance. But he was also introducing a significant third party into the field of medicine in an unprecedented manner, and that third party was government, not least of which was the Treasury Department of the United States.

Violation of the Boylan law was a misdemeanor and was punishable by up to one year in the penitentiary or by a fine of $500 or both.[10] An idea seemed to prevail that the victims of drug addiction would be kept separate from criminals after their arrest, and even after their conviction, but no such provision was provided in the statute.[11] While the law intended to target those distributing narcotics more than those using the substances, the atmosphere of the legislation had the aura of being rational and conciliatory rather than punitive.

New York then became a model for federal legislation passed in its final form in December, 1914. William L. White, in *Slaying The Dragon*, wrote:

[Towns] was one of the most vocal advocates of federal drug-control legislation, and was the author of New York's Boylan Law, upon which the federal Harrison Narcotic Act was based.[12]

With the Boylan Act as a background, Representative Francis Burton Harrison (D-NY), who declared, "We are an opium consuming nation today," had agreed to sponsor the legislation in Congress.[13] The debate concerning the [final] legislation was brief and was more focused on international obligations than a perceived growth of opium addiction in the United States. Besides, the bill was considered to be restrictive only, mainly a revenue measure that would impose a tax on narcotic substances at the time of their distribution to the doctor or pharmacist, and more along the lines of its model legislation advocated by Charles Towns.

David F. Musto described the original significance of the law's passage in this manner:

Finally the American Government had redeemed its international pledges; a federal law brought some control to the traffic in opiates and cocaine. The practical significance of the Harrison Act, however, was still debated among the groups affected. There was no general agreement on what would be the desirable or actual enforcement of the law.[14]

The *Consumers Union Report on Licit and Illicit Drugs* described the hidden surprise embedded in the law that would be used to change the how drugs were legally understood in the United States.

On its face, moreover, the Harrison bill did not appear to be a prohibition law at all. Its official title was 'An Act to provide for the registration of, with collectors of internal revenue, and to impose a special tax upon all persons who produce, import, manufacture, compound, deal in, dispense, sell, distribute, or give away opium or coca leaves, their sales, derivatives, or preparations, and for other purposes.' The law specifically provided that manufacturers, importers, pharmacists, and physicians prescribing narcotics should be licensed to do so, at a moderate fee. The patent-medicine manufacturers were exempted even from the licensing and tax provisions, provided that they limited themselves to 'preparations and remedies which do not contain more than two grains of opium, or more than one-fourth grain of morphine, or more than one-eighth of a grain of heroin in one avoirdupois ounce.' Far from appearing to be a prohibition law, the Harrison Narcotic Act on its face was merely a law for the orderly marketing of opium, morphine, heroin, and other drugs in small quantities over the counter, and in larger quantities on a physician's prescription. Indeed, the right of the physician to prescribe was spelled out in apparently unambiguous terms: 'Nothing contained in this section shall apply . . . to the dispensing or distribution of any of the aforesaid drugs to a patient by a physician, dentist or veterinary surgeon registered under this Act in the course of his professional practice only.' Registered physicians were required only to keep records of drugs dispensed or prescribed. It is unlikely that a single legislator realized that the law Congress was passing in 1914 would later be decreed a prohibition law.[15]

Many southern Senators wanted nothing to do with the legislation because they thought that provisions in the bill involved federal police powers, which they thought were reserved to the states. The federal legislation had become more punitive, as the penalties had risen from the Boylan Act: the maximum fine rose from $500 to 2,000; the maximum prison sentence from one year to five.[16] Many southern Senators considered the legislation to be unconstitutional. A compromise was achieved by convincing opponents of the ability of the federal government to tax, which meant the enforcement of the law would fall under the domain of the Treasury Department. Thus, the history of doctors having to write prescriptions for their patients began through legislation that originated at least in part with Charles Towns, though that requirement applied just for narcotics until 1938.[17] Still, the legislation was perceived by most to be mainly medical in nature that prohibited nothing.[18]

The antivice crusaders, despite their rhetoric and pressure campaigns, appeared to have lost their fight: the law did not reflect their prohibitionist desires, nor did the legislators believe they were passing a prohibition law.[19]

An editorial in the April, 1915 *New York State Journal of Medicine* described the Boylan Law as "a good law" and the Harrison Act to be "the better one of the two." The tone was very conciliatory. "Like all new laws, it will require time and experience and correct its deficiencies" despite the fact that "we at first criticized and were mildly resentful and some of the provisions of the law . . ." But the editorial went on to state "compliance with both laws is more annoying than difficult."[20] There was not the slightest hint of where the "new law" would lead. The brightest in the medical profession remained as unaware of that direction as the congressmen that passed the law.

William L. White, in his book *Slaying The Dragon*, made very clear that if life had been tough for an addict prior to the passage of the Harrison Act, life soon only got very much tougher.[21] For the Treasury Department, under a variety of prohibitionist pressure, began to interpret a particular clause in the law to implement drug prohibition. This interpretation was not a result of a vote by Congress. The words have been provided in the text of this chapter already: an example of just how easily the significance of the phrase can be missed! One may have to be a positive mind-reader to catch how the phrase would be used. Few who helped write and then passed the legislation in 1914 could have imagined how the Treasury Department was to exploit the phrase for prohibitionist purposes.

[There was] a joker hidden in the phrase "in the course of his professional practice only." After passage of the law, this clause was interpreted by law-enforcement officials to mean that a doctor could not prescribe opiates to an addict to maintain his addiction. Since addiction was not a disease, the argument went, an addict was not a patient, and opiates dispensed to or prescribed for him by a physician were therefore not being supplied "in the course of his professional practice." Thus a law apparently intended to ensure the orderly marketing of narcotics was converted into a law prohibiting the supplying of narcotics to addicts, *even on a physician's prescription.*[22]

Two weeks after the Harrison Act went into effect, Charles Towns was already being quoted in the *New York Times* that the law had shortcomings. While some of his provocative ideas can be remembered as being wildly off target, in this case, this prediction that follows here could not have been made better if he had been viewing a crystal ball.

[The Harrison Act cannot] prevent the smuggling of drugs into the United States from Canada and Mexico. The business of smuggling drugs from these countries, Mr. Towns said yesterday, had increased enormously since the two laws went into effect . . . "How can this Government prevent smuggling from these countries as long as Canada and Mexico have little or no regulation of the drug traffic within their own borders and no agreement with the United States? The illicit drug traffic, while it is of course disturbed by the laws, is not stopped; and when illegal drug dealers and users have accustomed themselves to the new conditions, they will be able to sell and receive as much of the drugs as ever."[23]

Towns also predicted due to the exemption clauses contained in both the Boylan Act and the Harrison Act, advertising for various patent medicines that were still legal would greatly increase. As a result, drug users would be able to obtain just as much of their narcotic as before.[24] However, little did he anticipate what actions the U.S. Treasury Department had in mind.

Six weeks after the Harrison Act became law, the Treasury Department was to issue Decision 2200 on May 11, 1915, which required that physicians' prescriptions to addicts for opiates had to specify progressively decreasing doses. Eventually, this led to the Treasury Department treating any prescription made by a physician of an opiate for an addict to be a violation of the law. The Treasury Department successfully chose to prosecute specific court cases, which progressively strengthened their executive authority by rulings of the Supreme Court.[25]

No direct comment by Charles Towns has been found to date that directly addressed the Treasury Department's interpretation of the Harrison Act. Speculation on the reason for his silence on the matter may have to do with how the Treasury Department took advantage of claims made by Towns himself. He insisted his medical cure for opiate addiction was successful almost all the time. He never concerned himself with the relapse rates of drug addicts, which may have influenced the reasoning of the Treasury Department. Why should an opiate be prescribed indefinitely for an addict? Should not the afflicted just take the foolproof remedy for his addiction and be done with it, once and for all? William L. White in *Slaying The Dragon* has observed:

It was through such misrepresentation of success rates that the inebriate asylums and private treatment sanitariums contributed inadvertently to the criminalization of narcotic addiction in the U.S.[26]

Thus, the Treasury Department's interpretation mutated the Harrison Act from being a medical model for opiate and cocaine addiction into predominantly a criminal model, which was what Towns had criticized previously and wished to replace. Towns had wanted to empty prisons and jails of addicts, proclaiming that addiction to morphine could almost become a relic of past mistaken societal ignorance. The Treasury Department ensured that not only would those prisons and jails remain populated, but also the numbers imprisoned for using drugs would substantially increase.[27] What the states had previously declared as being criminal was now enlarged to be a federal criminal issue and responsibility. Despite these unexpected twists of the Treasury Department's enforcement of the Harrison Act, Towns' confidence in the effectiveness of government solutions seemed not diminished one iota. No written criticism by Towns of this ruling has ever been found.

Towns' ally, Dr. Alexander Lambert, may have been a contributing factor to Towns' silence to this unexpected legal implementation by the federal government's executive branch.

Dr. Lambert never believed that medical remedy for addiction was appropriate for "the criminal element. The punitiveness that is associated with the 'police approach' was the policy he espoused for that element or type of addict."[28] Thus, the interpretation of the Harrison Act by the Treasury Department was favored by Dr. Lambert. He was to write an appendix to Towns' upcoming book *Habits That Handicap* that was published in 1915. In 1916, Dr. Lambert became the head of the AMA's judicial council and was elected president in 1919. Dr. Lambert had continuously been Towns' greatest benefactor, thus, Towns was in no position to do anything to jeopardize his standing with Dr. Lambert, a longtime backer of Towns Hospital itself. There was no way that Towns could bite the hand that fed him.

Yet, with the legal interpretation of the Harrison Act still in the future, and with his recent achievements of helping pass legislation in both the New York Legislature and the halls of Congress, Towns thought now was the time for him to write a book that would further capitalize on his recognized influence and further his cause. This book became the only one of his books that is still easily available today.

8) *Habits That Handicap* – August 1915

If a physician was not aware of Towns' opinions of the medical profession from his previous *The Century Magazine* articles, the examination of Towns' book might have caught his attention. Towns made a virtual indictment of a large percentage of doctors as being ignorant of the nature of addiction, even when the doctors were addicts themselves.[1] Towns wrote an indictment and a demand.

Figure 10 - Towns Hospital in New York City

There is only one way by means of which humanity can be relieved of the curse of drug using, and that is to adopt methods putting the entire responsibility upon the doctor. Until the recent legislation was passed in New York State, no one had ever considered the doctor's responsibility; this most valuable medical asset and most terrible potential curse had been virtually without safeguard of any effective kind. Discussion of the drug problem in the press dealt wholly with those phases which make themselves manifest in the underworld or among the Chinese. I am reasonably certain that until recently the world had heard nothing of the blameless men and women who had become drug-users because of illness. This seems strange, since there are in the United States more victims[2] of the drug habit than there are tuberculosis.[3] It is estimated that fifteen percent of the practicing physicians in the country are addicted to the habit,[4] and although I think this is an exaggeration, it is nevertheless true that habit forming drugs demand a heavy toll from the medical profession, wrecking able practitioners in health and reputation, and of course seriously endangering the public.

I have elsewhere explained the fact that the medical man himself is ignorant of the length to which he can safely go to in the administration of drugs to his patients. If he is ignorant of what quantity and manner of dosage constitutes a peril for the patient, is it not reasonable to suppose that similar ignorance exists in his mind to his own relations with the drug habit? As a matter of fact, I know this to be the case; many physicians have come to me for help, and ninety-nine percent of them explained to me that their use of drugs was the direct outgrowth of their ignorance. If the man who practices medicine is unaware of what will bring about the habit, what can be expected of the medically uneducated citizen who is threatened by those in whom he has most confidence—his doctors?[5]

Towns indicted doctors and demanded they recognize their culpability. His claim that drug addiction afflicted more of the American population than tuberculosis was an alarming assertion.[6] Of course, as was standard for Towns, no supporting data was provided to back the claim, nor was any study referenced that affirmed that fifteen percent of physicians were addicts. Towns seemed to extrapolate his opinions almost entirely from his personal experiences from which he always seemed to hold in very high esteem.

Towns continued the introduction with the assertion that the problem of drug addiction in the country was more serious than previously known. The recent Boylan Act in New York and the Harrison Act drove addicts to hospitals, which brought their large numbers to the attention of the public. Towns wrote that these addicts were sufferers that did not come to hospitals before because they believed they would not receive any worthwhile relief. They were very fearful of undergoing the agony of deprivation, which even then, would not remove the craving for their substance, and thus necessitate them returning to their agony of addiction after a futile endeavor to stop their drug slavery.

> No human longing can compare in intensity with that of the drug-user for his drug. Unrelieved, he will let nothing stand between him and it; neither hunger, nakedness, starvation, arson, theft, nor murder will keep him from the substance that he craves. Clearly humanity must be protected against such an evil. And the physician must be saved from it, for saving him will fulfill in a large measure the demand for the protection of the public.[7]

The Introduction concludes with a paragraph extolling the virtues of the Boylan Act and how the legislation set the example for other states. Curiously, there's no mention of the Harrison Act whatsoever, nor is there any mention of the Treasury Department's Decision 2200.

Chapters I-III on Drug Addiction

The first chapter of *Habits That Handicap* was titled "The Peril of The Drug Habit," which may seem rather familiar. This first chapter, word for word, was taken from his *The Century Magazine* article of the same name written three years previously in August, 1912, and discussed in full already in Chapter 4 of *King Charles.*

Chapter II, titled "The Need of Adequate Specific Treatment For The Drug Taker," was extracted from his October, 1912 article in *The Century Magazine* entitled "The Drug-Taker And The Physician." The first two paragraphs of the original article were removed as well as the second to the last section that was named "Conditions of Effective Treatment." Otherwise, the second chapter is identical to the October article and already explored in Chapter 4 of *King Charles*.

The third chapter of the book, "The Drug-Taker And the Physician," took on the title of the October, 1912 *The Century Magazine* article, but no original magazine article is known to have provided the text. Towns' expressed a huge faith in bookkeeping and the creation of a paper trail by government officials. He believed that through the creation of accurate records and the resulting accountability, addiction among physicians could be eliminated once and for all.

Proper restrictive legislation of sufficiently wide scope would very quickly disclose every drug-taking doctor in the nation, and either force him to correct his physical condition or drive him from the profession. An exact accounting for every grain of habit-forming drugs which he purchases, possesses, or administers, must be demanded of every physician in the United States before this evil can be entirely abated; and this accounting among physicians will be impossible until a similar accounting is demanded of every grain imported, manufactured, and dispensed by wholesale and retail druggists . . . Many who have not taken steps in time have reached the irresponsible and hopeless stage. To the medical profession in general, as well as to the public, these men are a dreadful menace. [8]

As was the common assertion of Towns and others, such his benefactor Dr. Alexander Lambert and Dr. Hamilton Wright (who had been a strong force for drug prohibition until falling out of favor with the Wilson administration around 1915), there was no such thing as moderate drug use. That was among the reasons why narcotics were considered evil. Towns also believed the fear of being disgraced had been what had kept most addicted physicians from facing the betrayal of their responsibilities.

Towns had blamed physicians previously for creating much of the drug addiction in the country. He had been highly critical of their lack of knowledge of how they treated addictions: their own and others. He had helped promote regulations that would require large increases in paperwork for most doctors since he insisted they could not be trusted. He had also advocated the creation of public health facilities that may have been a threat to be direct competition for the private physician. However, regarding addicted doctors, Towns proclaimed, "I, a layman, have been greatly surprised that the medical world shows so little sympathy for these unfortunates" as if he had been their best friend all along.[9] Consequently, he made the following recommendation.

> No physician should be permitted to practice who is addicted to the use of habit-forming drugs or who uses alcoholic stimulants to excess; but whatever is done in regard to these men should be accomplished without publicity and without any loss of pride or standing. A doctor who has used either drugs or alcohol is much more to be pitied than blamed.[10]

Towns remained consistent with the belief that an employed member of society had much value, and that every effort should be made to treat his addiction, then quickly return him back to his place of employment as if nothing had gone wrong. He considered pride to be the addict's number one asset. If one carelessly broke a patient's pride in the process of treating him, one would risk breaking his sense of self-worth, which may leave him a permanent mental cripple.

Nevertheless, the addicted physician was a pariah to society, and every effort had to be made to remove such threats from harming the patient, who was more likely to become an addict himself if an addicted physician treated him.

It is a curious fact that this doctor will be more than likely to administer the drug he uses to his patients, not with malicious, but with probably friendly, intent, and that he will feel no scruples whatsoever in acting as a go-between for drug-users in general who find themselves unable to obtain supplies easily. It is a curious and tragic fact that the drug-taking doctor will spread the habit in his own family. There have been many instances in my hospital when I have had a physician and his wife as patients at the same time and on the same floor.[11]

Virtually leaving no stone unturned in his desire to condemn the drug habit, he concluded his third chapter with words regarding another consequence of the behavior that resulted from using cocaine.

It is a curious fact that while in the under-world the drug habit has become a social vice, especially in the case of cocaine, and is frequently a proof of mixed sex-relations, in the upper-world it is accompanied by a secrecy of method and sequestration of administration that characterizes no other form of vice.[12]

Chapter IV – "Psychology and Drugs"

Chapter IV was titled "Psychology and Drugs" and reflected much different times when there was no large illegal drug industry since most drugs had been legal and relatively inexpensive. According to Towns, the sources of addiction first and foremost had been the doctor, and second had been pharmacists and druggists. A third, but smallest, contributor had been from "the tendency of certain persons toward dissipation," or, in other words, those interested in only money and pleasure.[13] Towns seemed totally convinced that regulation of what he called "the upper-world" would inevitably lead to a corresponding result in "the under-world."

Regulation of the upper-world in regard to the distribution of habit-forming drugs will automatically regulate the under-world in its similar activities. The amount which will be smuggled by those of criminal tendencies always will be small as compared with the amount improperly distributed through channels now recognized as legitimate until all the States have passed restrictive legislation founded upon, modeled after, and cooperative with New York State's legislation; and all this must be backed and buttressed by Federal legislation of a special kind before real and general good can be accomplished in the United States.[14]

Towns was an ally of the prohibitionists of the times that truly believed that government regulations could overrule personal desires. Future events were going to have to prove regulation advocates such as Towns wrong. For the time being, he was part of a wave of thought that believed a medical approach could solve addiction. He implied, but never addressed, how government regulation would remain void of corruption.

He also did not spare the trained nurses from what he conceived to be their part in the creation of drug addiction, nor their professional limits when the profit motive interfered with medical ethics.

That the medical world should ever have been so lax in its realization of its proper responsibility as to allow trained nurses to carry hypodermic syringes and to administer habit-forming drugs seems to me to be one of the most amazing things in the world. No physician who has had an extensive experience with drug addiction and who has any conscientious scruples whatsoever will fail to make sure before he leaves a nurse in charge of a patient that the attendant possesses no habit-forming drugs and is without any instrument with which they may be hypodermically administered. If such drugs are to be used, they should be kept in the physician's possession until they are used, and should be administered by means of an instrument which he carries with him. When such drugs are left, the nurse should give an accounting for every fraction of a grain.

I have no desire to convey the impression that in my opinion all nurses are untrustworthy or unscrupulous, but it must be remembered of them, as it must be remembered of the doctor, that they are in the employ of the patient, that their income depends upon giving satisfaction to their employer, and that they are likely to make almost any kind of concession and resort to almost any practice in order to make comfortable and profitable assignments last as long as possible. It is impossible not to admit the truth of this statement, and it must be recognized that if it is true, a nurse is under too great a responsibility when she is in possession of a hypodermic kit, particularly if the patient knows that it is *her* kit, *her* hypodermic, *her* drug, and that she will not be called to account by the physician for such drugs as she may administer.[15]

If any nurses had felt ignored previously by any of Towns' opinions of the medical profession, surely the opinions just expressed would have convinced the nurses that Towns had plenty of suspicion and criticism of their profession as well. While most any nurse would wish to relieve the pain of a patient, the accusation that many nurses were selfishly increasing the profits of the hospital by administering drugs seems rather a low blow. But Towns felt that he had a window on the truth and if that truth offended, that was only because of the failure of the skeptic to have an open mind and free himself of prejudice.

After all, nurses were only human, prone to temptation, just like the rest of us. Towns then wrote a line of reasoning that appears extraordinary in his attempt, while remaining a critic, to be the best friend of the nurse. This reasoning also concluded with a sense of prophesy that predicted a future for the United States.

[The nurse] is frequently under terrific strain, which makes her tend toward the use of stimulants of any kind. That which she can administer to herself by means of the hypodermic is closest to her hand, is easiest to take, and is least likely to be discovered. Again, too, it must be remembered that the nurse is as susceptible to pain as are the rest of us. Suffering, with the means of alleviation at her hand, and, like the doctor, ignorant of its true peril, what is more natural than that she herself should use the hypodermic for her own relief? Thus it comes about that probably a larger proportion of trained nurses than of doctors are habitual drug-users. This is not a statement which is critical of the profession, for if all mankind knew of drugs, had hypodermics, and knew how to use them, a very large proportion of the human race would resort to this quick and effective, if inevitably perilous, means of finding comfort when agony assailed them.[16]

No sense of recreational drug use was revealed in the preceding, only usage to relieve pain, tension and exhaustion. His observations that increased availability of drugs, illegal or otherwise, would increase their use have been born out through the American experience. Towns, however, believed that nurses, along with anyone else, had no idea of what they were risking. He thought the pain of drug withdrawal to be a pain beyond the ability of most to endure.

The world does not, the world cannot, understand that while to the normal human being the worst that can come is pain, the worst pain is vastly less terrible than the horrors which at intervals inevitably afflict the habitual drug user . . . The horror of the pain is not so great as the horror of the drug habit.[17]

Towns considered himself to be a heroic pioneer that discovered how to alleviate the incomparable pain that accompanied narcotic withdrawal, which had kept so many victims prisoners of their addiction. How, then, he would reason, could anyone be critical of his motivations or desires to help his fellow man? He previously stated in Chapter 4 "it is impossible not to admit the truth of this statement" or any other of his statements. The truth was on his side; he reasserted, and if the feelings of his readers were hurt, that was their problem, not his.

Chapters V-VII on Alcoholism

Chapter V was the first of three chapters on alcoholism and was titled "Alcoholics." Again he wished to position himself as a humanitarian who wished to rescue victims that had been rudely and carelessly treated by well-meaning, but ignorant or incompetent, professionals placed in positions of responsibility. So abused were alcoholics that they were being jailed or locked up in insane asylums from abruptly being deprived of alcohol. If only the Towns' solution had been made available to these poor souls! Alcoholics could have been back contributing to society rather than remaining a burden on the productive through the costs of incarceration, or long-term confinement as required for those believed to have been driven insane unnecessarily.

He explained his basic strategy of treating alcoholics, and also relayed the shortcomings of typical hospitals in dealing with this type of patient.

> With the alcoholic, as with the drug-taker, the first thing to be accomplished is the unpoisoning of the body. In order to accomplish this, it is first necessary to keep up the alcoholic medication, with ample sedatives, using great care lest the patient drift into that extreme nervous condition which leads to delirium. If delirium does occur, nothing but sleep can bring about an improvement in the patient's condition. This is the point of development at which physicians not properly informed in regard to such cases are likely to employ large quantities of hypnotics, and frequently this course is followed until the patient is finally "knocked out." In many instances an accumulation of hypnotics in the systems of persons thus under treatment has proved fatal. I am rather proud of my ability to state that from delirium tremens I have never lost a single case.[18]

While he claimed 40 percent of those in insane asylums had alcoholism in their background, there were also other factors that he believed contributed to that population.

My statement of the part which alcohol plays in supplying the population of our mad-houses has never been denied; but it is also true that the use of headache powders and other preparations commonly sold at our drug stores and as yet slightly or not at all restricted by law, and the use of coffee, tea, and tobacco in unrestricted quantity, also contribute their quota to the insane.[19]

Towns concluded the chapter by warning that if an alcoholic seemed chronic, he should not be abruptly deprived of alcohol without risking death or insanity.

Chapter VI, "Help For the Hard Drinker," was taken word for word from June, 1912 *The Century Magazine* article, with one sentence added in the end. This article was examined in full in Chapter 4 of *King Charles*. Possibly he thought that his book would reach readers that were not familiar with the magazine articles written three years before.

Chapter VII has the title "Classification of Alcoholics" and immediately addressed Towns' opinion that while narcotic addiction was the creation of the physician, such was not the case with alcoholics. He then wrote a paragraph that may have as much applicability one hundred years later than it did when it was published in 1915.

In these days all mankind searches for exhilaration. The instinctive demand for it is an inevitable result of the artificial social system which we have built up. We work beyond our strength, and naturally feel the need of stimulants; we play beyond our strength, and as naturally need whips for our vitiated energies. The greatest social disaster of all the ages occurred when first alcoholic stimulation, which is only one step in advance of alcoholic intoxication and narcotization, found its place as an adjunct of good-fellowship. All humanity turns in one way or another to artificial stimulants, and while alcohol and narcotics are the worst among these, we cannot slur the fact that many who would shun these agents as they would a pestilence, turn freely to milder, but not altogether harmless, stimulants, such as tea, coffee, and tobacco.[20]

Who knows how Towns might have written such a paragraph had he the knowledge of amphetamines, which were introduced as a medicine for nasal congestion in the mid-late thirties,[21] or LSD that emerged some years afterwards, or the powerful stimulants such as crack cocaine that became prevalent in the late part of the twentieth century?

He then described the man who could be saved as differentiated from the man who could not be saved from the ravages of alcohol. By and large, he watched to see if the patient was economically self-sufficient and a worker, and with those he had great hope. The ones unlikely to recover were the very rich, where money did not matter, or the very poor who had to rely on charity without any financial stake in the outcome.

The decent and potentially valuable citizen who through overwork, worry, sickness, sorrow, or even through a mistaken conception of social amenities or duties, drifts into excessive alcoholism is a victim of our imperfect social system, and repays remedial effort. Furthermore, such a man is invariably savable if he himself applies for salvation, assists with his own will in its application to his case, and pays his own money for the cure.[22]

Towns considered it was essential that the patient have his money at risk, and that the money be paid in advance. If an employee was sent to Towns, he claimed the patient would be admitted under the following terms.

If, for example, the employee of a person or a corporation is sent to me for relief from alcoholic tendencies by his employer or employers, I invariably refuse to accept the case unless it is agreed that the sum paid for the patient's treatment shall be held against him as an obligation to be repaid as soon as possible to those who have advanced it. [23]

His advocacy regarding the hopeless alcoholic, who was going to have to be colonized, involved some rather strong opinions. Due to some of his most controversial assertions, which in this case involved a proposal for sterilization of certain untreatable alcoholics, his words best reveal his approach to such provocative views.

Among such cases will be found fit subjects for colonization, and these are the only ones who should be treated in this way. No greater social mistake is possible than the colonization and segregation, either in sanatoriums or inebriate farms, of other than utterly hopeless alcoholic cases. The next greatest mistake undoubtedly is society's failure to segregate those who are utterly beyond the pale of hope. These men and women will be less of a burden to their friends and the community after segregation; their segregated existence will not constitute a threat against society of the present and future generations. It is my opinion that these people, men and women, rich and poor, should be sterilized and put at work. It is possible that this plan, if properly carried out, might develop some institutional effort worth while. That at present practice means a waste of time and money.

It should be borne in mind that deprivation never yet removed the underlying cause of the desire for alcohol, no matter over how long a period this deprivation may have extended, nor has it ever removed the desire itself. These things can be brought about only by the elimination of the poison from the victim's system.

All alcoholics, no matter whether they are preferred risks or hopeless cases, whether they are to be returned to society or isolated and sterilized, should be unpoisoned.[24]

Towns believed that any alcoholic that was abruptly stopped, without being medically treated for his condition, was doomed even if he survived the separation and did not become a permanent resident in an insane asylum. The reason for his senseless drinking was because of a physical craving—the unforeseen biproduct of why alcohol should not be consumed in the first place. A residue has accumulated within the victim's body – as if the drugs or alcohol ingested were snake venom requiring an antidote – an anti-venom – for the patient to recover. The memory of this substance or any other stimulant poisoning, had to be purged from the patient's cells—precisely what Towns claimed his remedy accomplished. Even if an alcoholic was hopeless, and would have to be institutionalized for the rest of his life, Towns recommended that he be "unpoisoned" for humanitarian reasons to remove the torture of craving. Afterward, he should be sterilized for the good of humanity. Towns seemed to be able to make such recommendations all the while believing he, before anyone else, was the alcoholic's best friend. Repeatedly he wrote of how the right medical approach, which was his, would prevent the agony of withdrawal, annihilate craving, and stop most all deviant behaviors resulting from addiction.

He claimed that the recovery rate for the Towns Treatment was no less than 75%,[25] but as was later revealed elsewhere by Towns himself, any methodology for supporting the assertion was missing. The remedy worked because Towns said it worked! What more proof did anyone need? If the patient did relapse, that was not because of any shortcoming of Towns' knowledge; it was because the addict made the rather thoughtless mistake of returning to his substance from which he had been liberated.

Towns did write that his solution was not a cure and had limitations, but it was vastly superior to competitive approaches of the times.

> This treatment is not offered as a cure of morphinism or as a cure of delirium tremens or chronic alcoholism . . . It will, however, obliterate the terrible craving that these patients suffer when, unaided, they endeavor to get off their drugs or are made to go through the slow withdrawal without some medication to ease them. Compared with the old methods of either slow withdrawal or rapid withdrawal, it is infinitely superior . . . But neither this combination of drugs nor any other combination known to man can prevent persons, after they are free from their addiction—be it alcohol or morphine— from going out and repoisoning themselves by taking again the drug which has poisoned them and led them on to their habitual intoxication. [26]

This admission that addicts and alcoholics sometimes returned to their poisons that led to their "habitual intoxication" was as close as Towns ever came to examining the subject of relapse. He was not particularly interested in why people failed. More on that subject was explored later in the book.

Rarely did Towns provide any exceptions to his boundless enthusiasm for the full-proof nature of his treatment. However, the hardcore drunks encountered at Bellevue Hospital admittedly were a challenge that often was beyond any medical solution, including his.

No test more exacting than the one made at Bellevue Hospital could be devised. Most of the cases appearing for treatment in the wards of that institution are of the most advanced type, for the nature of the New York hospital system may be said in a general way to select for Bellevue the least hopeful patients coming from the least hopeful classes of society. If, therefore, anything approaching permanent relief was secured for as many as twenty out of every one hundred cases, an extraordinary efficiency was indicated.[27]

But with the worthy, with the responsible, with the employed, Towns proclaimed there was an almost assured solution for recovery that would take not much longer than five days. The approach was not only essential but economical! The capital investment necessary to implement his remedy nationwide would be relatively small.

Properly carried out, my treatment will accomplish exactly this in every instance. It will accomplish it within five days and very likely within three days. I have never known it to require a period of more than seven. When this treatment is properly provided for throughout the country, it will be found that neither large nor costly institutions will be necessary. The stay of every patient is so brief that in the average community a small institution containing only a few beds will be found sufficiently large to meet all local needs.[28]

Thus, the recovery of all but a relatively few alcoholics could take place in hospitals rather than jails. The habitual drunkard was not a criminal.[29] So fundamental was his belief that his approach would remove the cause of the drunkard's continued stupor, that he made an extraordinary proposal. If a bed in a curative institution was not available and the drunkard had to be temporarily housed in a jail, he should be provided with alcohol for humanitarian reasons until he could be admitted to an appropriate hospital.

It would be better for a community to keep a victim upon a steady diet of alcohol for weeks while he was waiting for a bed in a curative institution than to risk causing the man's death or insanity by depriving him of his alcohol until the means for relieving his system's acute demand for it were at hand. By following a similar plan, it will be found that the evil of habit-forming drugs can be exterminated in the United States.[30]

What an extraordinary statement! The domestic evil of habit-forming drugs could be eliminated once and for all! Any concept of what followed in the latter half of the twentieth century, termed "recreational drug use" or "getting high," was never visualized. That the addict might even enjoy his drug habit was not even considered a vague possibility. Towns' thinking came from the medical model: the addict had been carelessly introduced to his substance because of physical pain, the phenomenon of craving resulted, and from then on, the addict was involuntarily enslaved by the poisons contained in his drug. While Towns never was known to be a religious man, the proclamations Towns made throughout his career suggested that he acted as if there was a faint, secular halo above his head, which might be seen if one "changed his mental attitude and observed." In years to come, his humanitarian attempts would be forgotten or ignored. He would become known as a "quack" because of unacceptably high rates of relapse and the eccentric medicines employed.[31]

Towns believed that his leadership could provide the paths to sane and effective healing for alcoholics across the country. If only judges could follow Towns' wisdom and experience in helping the alcoholic! A magistrate, rather than imprison the drunk, could send him to a local public hospital that specialized in handling alcoholics. After all, since society permitted alcohol to be irresponsibly provided, society should be willing to pay for the consequences.

> If the world wishes to be relieved in any measure from the human waste attributable to alcohol, the time must speedily arrive when municipalities will recognize it as their duty to provide definite medical help for every man who wishes to be freed from the craving for alcohol, and who cannot afford to pay for treatment . . . nowhere in the United States or, as far as I know, anywhere else is there a single organization which is effectually working along definite and intelligent lines for the preservation of the endangered man who is still curable . . . In every city must be established emergency hospital wards to which committing magistrates may send persons with excessive alcoholic or drug histories. Treatment in these emergency wards will be neither difficult nor costly.[32]

Towns then came up with a prediction that, sadly, has represented one of those commonly experienced realities of today, which is one of those "secrets" often found in many penal institutions: if inmates wish to continue to use drugs because of their continued cravings while in prison, they will find a way to do so.

> If a drug-user or alcoholic who has been locked up in a prison is in no way relieved of his craving for the substance which is harming him, his efforts to obtain it will be desperate. The class of men who surround him as prison guards is not of a high type. If he has money, they will get it from him if they can; and if he has friends outside, especially if they themselves be drug or liquor addicts, they will attempt to smuggle to him what he craves. Inasmuch as it is much easier to smuggle drugs into a prison than it is alcohol, many alcoholics have been changed in prison to drug-takers, and after this change the metamorphosis for the mere drunkard into an actual criminal has often occurred.[33]

Towns, without any concept that narcotics or any other kind of drug, might be used voluntarily for purposes of entertainment or heightened stimulation, was convinced that his remedy should be used to remove the inmate's craving prior to his incarceration. Towns thought the inmate would be highly unlikely to desire the drug while serving his sentence if the cause for physical craving had been removed. This proposed practice appeared to him to be a humane manner in treating the incarcerated. Otherwise, Towns already had documented that drugs were quite present in prisons, and would remain that way until the prisoners themselves did not demand them.

The next two chapters return to a subject in which Towns considered himself exquisitely qualified to examine, which for him was tobacco.

Chapters VIII-IX on Tobacco

Chapter VIII, titled "The Injuriousness of Tobacco" in the book, and "The Injury of Tobacco" in the original article, was the final time that he used a previously written *The Century Magazine* article as a chapter in *Habits That Handicap*. His original composition was examined already in Chapter 4 of *King Charles*. However, he removed one very large paragraph and the front part of a second from his earlier work and expanded those ideas into Chapter IX, which becomes the focus here.

If there could be any remaining doubt of how much Towns despised cigarettes, by the time one finished Chapter IX "Tobacco And Future of the Race," the condemnation of tobacco could be hardly stronger.[34] Young boys were being introduced to tobacco as their first "poison" with many negative consequences.

[Tobacco's] effects are most immediate and evident upon the young and weak; for they are easier to poison than the mature and strong.[35] It is noteworthy that cigarettes are "doped" expressly to allay nausea, which is the normal effect of tobacco-smoking upon the uninured[sic] human system, and at the same time to quiet that motor unrest which is the first symptom to follow the introduction of nicotine into the human system. The narcotic effect of the adulterant drugs is therefore to ease the smoker's first pang and to make him more quickly the victim of the tobacco habit.[36]

As bad a poison as tobacco was to a young man physically, however, was not the worst of it. Tobacco corrupted the morals of a young boy from the very beginning.

I am convinced that the use of cigarettes is responsible for the undoing of seventy-five per cent of the boys who go wrong. Few boys wait until they are mature and their resistance is at its maximum before they begin the use of tobacco . . . When they begin to smoke, they do so against the wishes and usually against the orders of their parents. This means broken discipline and deception. The boy who endeavors to conceal the fact that he smokes is started along a path that is even more harmful than tobacco. He has to invent excuses for being absent from home, and to explain away the odor of tobacco that is sure to cling to him; and when a boy begins to lie about these things, he will lie about others . . . Boys who spend their time in smoking go where they will find other lads also engaged in the forbidden habit. They find congenial groups in pool-rooms, where they learn to gamble, and in the back rooms of saloons, where they learn to drink. The step from the pool-room or the saloon to other gambling-places and to drinking-places frequented by the unworthy of both sexes is an easy one. Thus the boy whose first wrong-doing was the smoking of cigarettes against the wishes of his parents soon becomes the target for all manner of immoral influences.[37]

Towns found it "astonishing" that there had been so little concern for society to keep the lives of young men, society's most valuable asset, to be "clean" and tobacco free. There was no stronger harmful influence on young men than early smoking. Temptation was everywhere, however because so many men that were supposed to be good examples for young men were themselves tobacco smokers. He then proceeded to write some logic that would hardly make a tobacco-consuming father of a young man feel very good about himself.

Orators and essayists from the beginning of time have found a stumbling-block in preaching to their followers virtues they admire and value, but do not themselves possess. The father who forbids his son to smoke because it is harmful and expensive, while his own person reeks with it, is not likely to impress the lad very vividly with either the force or the honesty of his argument. More than one parent has found himself abashed in such circumstances by a son with logic and intelligence. For such a parent there is only one really honest course—to admit to his son that he himself has been a fool, but that he does not wish his son to follow in his footsteps.[38]

Towns' recommendation for the future was for the education of young men by qualified individuals that were not addicted to any poisons such as tobacco themselves. Also included in this proposal was one of the rare instances that he came close to mentioning anything about the potential for there being a God.

If cleanliness of body is next to godliness, then cleanliness of mind is godliness, and cleanliness of mind, real cleanliness, is impossible while ignorance exists. Nothing in education is more generally neglected than the enlightenment of the young—an enlightenment which can come only from the mouths of elders who are themselves clean— as to the deadly nature of alcohol, habit-forming drugs, and tobacco.[39]

Nevertheless, tobacco seemed omnipresent to Towns. What could non-smoking concerned parents do to help their sons stay away from tobacco while the church and universities were sources of poison and pollution?

Thousands upon thousands of parents in this country feel as I do on this subject; but while they realize the danger which might result from the influence of a teacher who smokes, they utterly neglect the far more dangerous and powerful influence of a father who smokes. To my mind, however, it is essential that parents should seriously consider the personal character of the men to whom they intrust[sic] the education of their boys.

But the use of tobacco reaches far beyond the home circle and the schools and even pollutes the atmosphere of the church itself. There are few clergymen in the United States who do not use tobacco, and so a clean father who rears a clean son is under the tragic necessity of urging his attendance at a dirty church, and later on sending him to be a student in a dirty college, for the simple reason that there are no clean ones.[40]

There can be substantial room for doubt how Towns determined the alleged predominance of clergymen or university professors that smoked tobacco. No tours of such facilities were ever reported. No mention of Towns attending a university or church has been learned. Towns typically, as before, expected the open minded to accept his word as being an authority on the matter.

Then, at the conclusion of the chapter, he included somewhat of a surprise, which was to declare that he was not a "moralist" after lecturing on the decadence of tobacco. Apparently he wished to distance himself from any of the religious temperance movements popular with many at the time. He preferred to be thought of as a "practical student" when he asserted of all the hazardous substances discussed in his book, tobacco was number one.

I have no desire to moralize upon the subject of tobacco. I am not a moralist, but a practical student of cause and effect, urging the elimination of bad causes so that bad effects may be eliminated in turn. A very wide experience in studying the result of the use of narcotics has convinced me that the total harm done by tobacco is greater than that done by alcohol or drugs. Nothing else at the present time is contributing so surely to the degeneration of mankind as tobacco, because, while its damage is less immediately acute than that done by alcohol or habit-forming drugs, it is, aside from its own evil effects, a tremendous contributory factor to the use of both.[41]

He concluded the chapter with reference to the warning about "alcoholic fiends" reproducing and raising children with damaged nervous systems. He implied that so many of these parents never would have become alcoholics without first smoking tobacco.

Chapter X – "The Sanatorium"[M]

In Chapter X "The Sanatorium" he continued his strong criticism of the sanatorium industry for not effectively using the Towns Hospital approach. His criticism seemed to have little to do with the medicines employed or the qualifications of the administrators present at such institutions. Instead, the criticism was focused on the sanatoriums that were charging their patients by the week.

It is certain that the person who makes a weekly charge to such patients is rarely honest with them or tries to shorten their stay. Several years ago I freely and without reservation gave all the details of my treatment to the medical world, and though many institutions have

---

[M] - "Sanatorium" and "sanitarium" are used interchangeably, as seen on Figure 11.

Figure 11 - Representative sanitariums ads of the times that appeared in the December, 1916 *The Modern Hospital*. Please note the two spellings: sanitarium and sanatorium.

Figure 12 - *The Modern Hospital*, December 1916 This sanitarium was a prominent advertiser for the times and was often encountered in the various magazines of the 1910's. In another ad in the *New York State Journal of Medicine* in 1915, they advertised for treating cases of drug addiction.

endeavored to install it as a part of their own curative policy, most have failed. The failure may

be attributed principally, if not wholly, to the fact that few have also adopted the necessary

principle of a fixed charge, without regard to the length of time the patient is under treatment.

The weekly charge, with its attendant temptation to keep the patient as long as possible, has

invariably defeated all possibilities of success.[42]

He also suspected that the sanitarium was using the substance improperly to which the

patient was addicted by indefinitely prolonging its use. Towns never intended the patient to

have been separated abruptly from his substance. He was supplied decreasing dosages of it

periodically in the first days of the treatment. Towns expected the entire experience to last no

longer than seven days. He asserted that the sanitariums were providing the addictive

substances in excessive quantities over too many days, which kept the patient poisoned. In that

state, he had to pay for the next week because the cravings would remain and would have to

stay indefinitely. The beds of the sanitarium stayed occupied, which kept the cash flow of the

institution healthier than many of its patients. Thus, charging by the week was an

overwhelming and distorting design flaw. Sanitarium administrators were but human, and

prone to irresistible temptations to exploit their patients unless the design of their

methodology recognized that reality. Towns' fixed fee concept, in addition to the warning to

the patient that he would get but one chance to recover at Towns Hospital, was considered an

infallible approach.[N] The quicker the patient was treated effectively, the quicker his suffering

would end, and the happier he would be. The quicker the sanitarium could treat and release

[N] There was no record found of any patient that was refused entry for a second treatment as long as he could pay the fee. However, that is not to deny that a second treatment was ever refused. The reputation of Towns being a safe place for the wealthy to sleep off binge after binge evolved as the years passed.

their patient, the more money the fixed-fee sanitarium would make. Towns insisted that his

approach directly recognized a major human frailty that had been overwhelming the

motivations of lesser men: greed.

Towns thought the deprivation of the drug in a typical sanitarium was often hell on

earth. Potential customers would not willingly pay for an approach that would lead to them to

be tortured, either intentionally or otherwise. Fear of traumatic separation from their

substance is what kept most potential patients enslaved. He would only select and then stay in

a sanatorium in which he remained comfortable, so Towns thought.

> [A sanatorium's] main province is to keep its paying guests and to make them comfortable . . .
> The average sanatorium is merely a small colony of drug-users. No one can deny that. Now, no
> man who has been freed from his desire for drugs and no one who is being made uncomfortable
> by deprivation will remain in such surroundings for any length of time.[43]

After all, the patient was the customer in the typical sanitarium design, and if he did not

get what he wanted to feel comfortable, would not he simply just leave? Of course, the

sanitarium would give him what he demanded to stay at the facility, and that would be his

drug! No one was at fault in such a system, according to Towns, and therefore he did not wish

any sanitarium competitor to take his criticism as being too harsh. He wanted the impartial

observer simply to recognize human nature, and realize that the methodologies of the

sanitarium were corrupt even if the sanitarium staff meant well. One could not convincingly

dispute his "truth," Towns would assert, and, therefore, any competitors were mistaken if they found his remarks as insulting. His revelations were to be understood as an advance of common sense.

Successful treatment is brief treatment, and no establishment operating upon a system of a weekly charge to patients will make an earnest effort to release these patients as soon as possible[44] . . . payment in advance may be regarded as the most effective means for inducing the patient to complete the necessary course.[45]

Prolonged exposure to such environments could be hazardous to the health of the patient, for if he was not an incurable addict upon entering the facility, he risked becoming incurable, if not poverty stricken, from exposure to such places.

The constant drugging that conceals the symptoms of organic ailment may permit one of comparative insignificance at the time a patient entered a sanatorium to become incurable before he leaves. Thus the result of his stay may mean in the end a serious or even fatal deterioration. And the prolonged stay becomes a means, intentional or unintentional, of mulcting[o] the patient or his friends of money . . . I have had patients come to me from such institutions to which they had paid sums as large as $10,000. Wealthy people are specially likely to become victims of this form of rapacity,[p] and a mere glance at some of the receipted bills that I have seen in their possession is enough to stagger a modest financial imagination. The ingenuity with which a sanatorium manager devises "extras" is worthy of the name of genius.

---

[o] Mulcting – to deprive someone of money by fraudulent means
[p] Rapacity – given to seizing for plunder or the satisfaction of greed

And the physically incurable patient is often retained in the sanatorium till his money or the money of his friends is exhausted in a needless sacrifice to greed.[46]

From the fact that I know when a patient enters my house that I can get no further money from him or her beyond the advance payment I gain a distinct advantage. I do not feel it necessary to cater to my patient's whims, nor do I feel it necessary to sacrifice any portion of the necessary routine of the treatment because the patient may be rich or influential and may make extraordinary demands upon me. All that I have to do is to go ahead along those lines which I know are effective and which will gain results.[47]

If the sanatorium experiences were so horrifying, so-called "ambulatory" approaches, otherwise known as a home cures, only ensured another kind of horror, which was eventual failure (see figure 50 in the appendix for an example of a $5 home cure). Towns already had expressed that the promises made by an addict or alcoholic were without merit. Without the supervision in a controlled environment by an impartial physician, immune from being influenced by any personal relationship with the patient, the victim of addiction almost always stayed that way. In other words, there was no other approach, that worked, as well as being both economical and humanitarian, other than hospitalization in a facility designed by Towns.[48]

He considered himself an expert on the forces that negatively influenced dealing with addicts. Friendship with a patient would distort the approach of a physician. A surgeon typically would not operate on a family member or close friend. How could anyone think a physician could effectively treat a friend burdened with addiction?

The friendship existing between a physician and his patient must often disarm the former and incapacitate him for the strict dealing that is required in a treatment like mine. The mere fact that in caring for a friend or one of his regular patients the doctor feels unwilling to exact a definite charge in advance is a certain handicap here . . . I find that only when the patient is on premises other than his own, in unfamiliar surroundings where he is subject to a strict and inviolable discipline, can the best results be obtained . . . The advantage of a definite charge, paid in advance, was a discovery that I made early in my work. With a large proportion of my patients it would otherwise have been impossible for me to obtain the definite medical result . . .[49]

Not only should the physician not be a friend of his patient prior to his entry into the hospital, but also no friendship should be permitted to evolve at any time afterward. Strict impartiality without the hint of emotion, along with a clear eye and steady nerves, was required. A bronco rider only cared if he could ride and break the bronco. Who cared what the name of the bronco was? Who cared ever to ride the bronco again when you already broke him in the first place? Furthermore, male stallions, when brought into too close of proximity to each other, had the tendency to fight. Therefore, they should not be allowed to be in contact with each other for the peace of all involved. And, of course, if one allowed the stallions contact with any mares, "everybody knew" what would happen next.

It is also necessary to make an invariable rule that no person entering my institution for treatment shall be permitted to come into contact with any other person who is there for treatment, for there can be nothing psychologically worse than the discussion of symptoms and the exchange of experiences among people under treatment. It is also a rule that in the institution physicians employed in the establishment shall not become intimate with the patients or spend with them any time not necessarily devoted to professional investigation and attendance. Nurses also must be as businesslike as possible in all their relationships with patients, and must do as little hand-holding and sympathizing as possible even in the cases of ultra-nervous women patients.[50]

Regarding aftercare, Towns, himself a very physically fit man that spent as much as two hours a day exercising, recommended that a patient pursue some vigorous physical activity after his release. An efficacious mental and physical change was boosted immensely by the patient's willingness to exercise and take advantage of hydrotherapy and other therapies. Towns wanted his patients to do more than simply be "sitting on a pleasant veranda in an easy-chair exchanging tales of symptoms with other invalids," which was how he visualized the common practices of most sanatoriums.[51]

To conclude this chapter, as if he already had not written enough to insult many a physician, he demanded physicians weed out members of the profession that were addicted themselves but still practicing. A "conference between delegates from medical societies of various States" should be formed, he insisted, to rid the profession of the afflicted.[52] Furthermore, since this was a matter in which self-policing could not be expected to work, he proposed that "every institution under private management in the United States shall by law be held responsible for its method of treatment."[53] Such an emphasis by him seemed to imply that if a medical facility did not employ the state-of-the-art Towns Treatment, they, by law, should be forced to explain why.

And since the title of this chapter was "The Sanatorium," how could he end this chapter without insulting them one more time? Sanatoriums should be required by law to report to a local health board if any patient had been maintained on his addictive drug for more than three weeks. Since Towns did not keep his patients for much longer than a week, and his solution was so effective, he questioned how could any ethical sanatorium keep a patient for longer than three weeks? Was that not proof of their desire to exploit their patient? He positively despised the efforts at colonizing drug-users.

It must not be understood that I attribute all the efforts at colonizing drug-users to unworthy motives. Much of it has been due to the complete ignorance of the medical profession in regard to this form of affliction. Finding itself unable intelligently to cope with conditions, it seeks the line of least resistance and adopts the colonizing sanatorium, with all its evils, as the best plan that can be found . . . I was told by some of the best-known neurologists in the world that out of thousands of patients whom they and their confrères had sent to the best-known and most conscientiously operated institutions in the country not one had really been helped. They assured me that if I had found something which would give actual and material aid in any degree to even five percent of the drug victims who were sent to me for treatment, I would be doing more than any man had ever done before.[54]

Towns considered himself "boldly going where no man had gone before" long before the 1960's TV show Star Trek ever used that phrase in their opening. With such noble goals and lofty ideals, without the slightest monetary motivation, Towns would question how anyone that wanted to rid the world of drug addiction could disagree with his impeccable logic and motives. Only petty, little men that were blind to his proven solutions could disagree.

Chapter XI – "Preventive Measures"

Chapter XI 'Preventive Measures' continued Towns unending recommendations to the medical profession regarding how the drug evil could be eliminated, once and for all. However, as Towns knew many critics would think of him as nothing but an outspoken advocate of his hospital, for him to be accepted by the majority of physicians, his motivations had to be beyond suspicion. He was willing to lead the effort to set up test scenarios where his remedy could become the unquestioned medical approach for addiction. He was willing to set up a clinic "where the professional student may prepare" to learn the Towns Treatment, and Towns considered this was possible "only through some arrangement in which I have no financial interest whatsoever."[55]

I am fully aware that I must first overcome a strong undercurrent of skepticism among the members of the medical profession. The efficacy of the treatment must be proved. Even among the best-informed physicians it is a popular belief that the treatment which I announce as simple is really an impossibility.[56]

He proceeded to use the names of Dr. Richard C. Cabot, who wrote the preface to his book. Towns also referenced Dr. Alexander Lambert, who had written the appendix, which praised the Towns Treatment, sometimes referred to by some as the Towns-Lambert Treatment by some in the medical community. Towns had convinced both of these esteemed doctors. Therefore, he should be able to extend that belief to any opened-minded doctor that was seeking a solution to this previously baffling problem. The need was more urgent than before since the consequences of addiction risked incarceration: the emerging waves of punitive legislation had declared narcotic use without a prescription to be a felony. Society had to protect itself somehow from the danger of what drugs combined with alcohol could produce.

> Modern society presents few spectacles of suffering more acute than that endured by the drunken drug-fiend. Few persons, moreover, are so dangerous to its welfare.[57]

While he had been so generous to offer his methodology to the world at no cost, he had not anticipated that untrained doctors, or at least doctors he considered untrained, might attempt to use it, achieve poor results, and then be so unethical to claim that the remedy did not work. He called them "fakers."[58] Of course, the fakers did not have any better alternative, voiced only criticism, and, therefore, offered nothing in the way of contributions to solving the dilemma of addiction. There were also the "medical buzzards" that were in the profession only to make money.[59] But what seemed to bother Towns more were the doctors that offered no opinion whatsoever regarding his solution. They only offered "general indifference," and were going to continue on their path of ignorance unless new solutions somehow reached them.[60] Towns expressed that he was writing this book in the effort to contact the uninformed.

He was advocating restrictive legislation, and as of the publication of *Habits That Handicap*, the Boylan Law had gone into effect about fifteen months earlier in the State of New York. The Harrison Act had been passed the previous December and had gone into effect the previous March. Decision 2200 from the Treasury Department had been issued only six weeks after that, but there's no evidence that Towns knew of it then or later. However, he continued to write about the need for additional legislation. He repetitively asserted that because society had allowed drug addiction and alcohol consumption to rise near epidemic proportions, society should finance the solution for those who could not afford to rid themselves of their affliction. Intelligent legislation would provide for facilities and staff in every large community so that suffering could be kept to a minimum during the merciful hospitalization required. Nothing less provided a solution to this evil. If such an administration could be created through legislation that would help bring his dream to reality, Towns wrote that he "should be glad to devote my services to it."[61]

For the first time, Towns mentioned that four patients had died in the course of receiving his medications during the "whole fourteen years of my practice."[62] No deaths had been reported among the four thousand Chinese treated during his missionary trip. Since the date his first hospital opened may have been as late as 1909, the vast majority of his domestic patients were probably treated after that date. The news of these four deaths were treated as an insignificant footnote—an inevitable consequence of the serious nature of addiction he was combatting.[63] Later on, he may have forgotten he wrote about these four deaths.[64]

He claimed that his medical approach had been "carefully systematized and made as highly scientific as it has been possible to make it.[65] He insisted his methodology had been proven for any healthy alcoholic or drug addict who did not have severe complications already as a result of his habit. Old methods of treating addiction had proven worthless. He then repeated his assertion that colonization of alcoholics accomplished nothing beyond tending to turn them into convicts. Towns' solution was so proven that he outlined simple options for evaluating patients after their release, which Towns had learned from his vast track record of experience.

> The problem confronting the physiologist after a patient has been relieved of a drug or drink habit is comparatively simple. If this relief makes diagnosis possible and reveals the existence of an unsuspected, but curable, ailment, the course to follow is obvious. With the psychologist the problem is frequently more complicated. The useless citizen who becomes a drug or drink user will remain a useless citizen after the drug or drink habit has been eliminated . . . Thus perhaps the most important query the psychologist interested in this work must ask after the treatment of a patient is, What is left of value, and what can be done with it? . . . No one is so hopeless as the vagrant rich. No man will ever make a reputation in work of this character who deals wholly or even principally with people to whom money has no value.[66]

Once more Towns stressed how important the work ethic and the desire to be self-supporting were to the core of how he evaluated his patients.

He did admit that the week of hospitalization was but the first step in the rehabilitation of the patient. But he considered many physicians to be entirely incapable of making an accurate patient evaluation after he was withdrawn from his substance. Towns asserted "the elimination of drugs or drink from a degenerate will not eliminate degeneracy."[67] Though the evaluation of most patients was simple, there were exceptions. Occasionally he claimed to have consulted as many as six specialists to help determine the potential chances of a certain patient to become a productive citizen once again.

He thought the psychologist should determine if a patient was a victim of drug addiction because of his physician. If so, the prognosis for the patient was very favorable. If, however, the habits were incurred as a result of "the direct or indirect result of alcoholic dissipation or sexual excesses, or is a social vice, the case is extra hazardous. Here lack of morals standards and the loss of pride are serious handicaps."[68]

While Towns often seemed to sympathize with the alcoholic or the addict, he considered himself entirely capable of evaluating a prospective patient prior to his admission. If he thought nothing could be accomplished by a stay at Towns Hospital, despite all the compassion he had expressed previously, he reserved the right to refuse the patient admission. He had learned this lesson the hard way, so he claimed.

> Not long after I began my work I tried to help a man against my better judgment; I felt reasonably sure that he lacked the worthy qualities that would make him cling to and appreciate whatever advantages the treatment might afford. My estimate of his character proved to be correct; the man relapsed, and became a traveling liability on me, a reproach against my institution and my treatment.[69]

He admitted that a percentage of alcoholics and addicts belonged in a "human scrap-heap" and their cases were hopeless. He did not seem to have a great deal of sympathy for them.

> I believe that those among this class who have become public charges and refuse to work should be forced to do so by state or municipal authority. Society or their own families should not bear

the burden of their useless existence. They should be segregated in some place where they will

be physically comfortable, where they may be made industrious and useful, and where a

separation of the sexes will prevent the increase of their worthless kind . . . It is well that where

they are first sequestrated there they should be permanently kept. Through this course alone

society will be spared the periodical havoc they will be sure to work during their intervals of

freedom.[70]

The necessity of making such unpleasant evaluations made an impersonal relationship

with the patient even more essential. The evaluation necessitated the professional diagnosis of

the patient on the basis of what was good for society. Friendship would only distort the

evaluation, according to Towns, and, therefore, should be prohibited without exception.

Chapter XII – "Classification of Habit-Forming Drugs"

Chapter XII has the title "Classification of Habit-Forming Drugs." Discussed here were

morphine, heroin, cocaine, hypnotics, and what he called coal-tar products.

His discussion of morphine and opium was a mild repetition of what he had written already.

Most addicts, he repeated, had been unintentional victims. Regarding cocaine, however, his

judgment was again quite severe.

Unscrupulous chemists and physicians have unloaded upon the world a drug which is beneficial

when taken medicinally, but one that has reaped a harvest of irresponsible victims, in which

murder, all forms of crime, and mental and moral degeneracy have conspicuously figured, and

all for financial gain . . . [Cocaine] relieves the patient from discomfort, making him feel, indeed,

as if there were no nose on his face. Its effect, however, lasts only from twenty to thirty minutes. This is one of the reasons why the cocaine habit is so easily formed. A man taking any

powerful stimulant is sure to feel a corresponding depression when the effect of that stimulant

has died away, and it then becomes necessary for him to take more of the drug in order to buoy

himself up and restore himself to the point of normality . . . No drug so quickly brings about a

mental and physical deterioration. It is virtually certain to be a short cut to one of two public

institutions, the prison or the madhouse. It will send the average person to the prison first

because it is an expensive drug, and the craving for it is more than likely to exhaust his financial

resources and then drive him to theft. It is the most expensive of all drug habits.[71]

Towns was admitting that he no longer thought the way he did about cocaine just three

years previously when he wrote in the October, 1912 issue of *The Century Magazine* that "to

the average addict, the cost of his drugs, no matter what he may have to pay for them, seems

moderate."[72] When Towns evolved to another position, he seemed to write with the same

conviction and fervor that he did before, but without any recognition that he might have

contradicted what he had written before.

His condemnation of hypnotics gave another example of Towns using extremes in his

description of what he considered to the worst kind of drugs.

I wish to put myself on record now as saying that there is no class of drugs so sure in the end to

bring about a deterioration of the physical being as the frequent use of the hypnotic group, or

coal-tar products, the sleep-producers. I have never seen more pitiable cases than those who

have come to me after they had been taking regularly, during a considerable period, some cure

for sleeplessness. This habit not only produces an extreme neurotic condition, but changes the entire temperament of a person. It will turn the most beautiful character into an extreme case of moral degeneracy.[73]

He wished hypnotics and the coal-tar products to which he referred to be regulated in a similar manner to narcotics and cocaine. Despite the intensity of his previous rhetoric, less than two pages were devoted to this subject in the book.

He concluded the chapter outlining the various hazards that could be found at the corner grocery store or pharmacy. Narcotics appeared in diarrhea and cough medicines. Druggists commonly could make up their brews of codeine, morphine, heroin, or a derivative of opium. He condemned this practice of the druggists that made their medicines and that provided them to a customer without a prescription or any proper diagnosis. He concluded the chapter with some words that might be thought of as being, in part, prophetic regarding headache medicines.

Only a very powerful drug can stop a headache as quickly and completely as Americans have come to demand. The preparation must be strong enough to deaden disordered nerves, and being chosen because it will be generally effective, not selectively effective, as in the case of a remedy chosen after an intelligent diagnosis has revealed the nature of the trouble to be treated, it is virtually certain to have no curative qualities whatever. Hundreds of deaths have resulted from unwisely experimenting with such preparations. Most of us have peculiar idiosyncrasies with regard to certain drugs . . . With such people large doses might bring about serious results and even death.[74]

Chapter XIII – "Psychology of Addiction"

Chapter XIII, interestingly titled "Psychology of Addiction," represented a very unexpected, unsympathetic style for Towns, who up to this point, seemed to have been blaming society for providing the temptations far more than he blamed addicts or alcoholics. Here he warned the specialist or psychologist how he was not to fall for the manipulative nature of his patients.

> The common idea that one who is struggling with a drug or alcohol habit needs sympathy and psychological encouragement is totally at variance with the facts. No one has ever accomplished anything worth while by holding the hand of an alcoholic, and any one who is endeavoring to help a case of this sort will find himself instantly and seriously handicapped if he puts himself in intimate personal relationship with his patient . . . I have never made a friend of one my patients . . . "[75]

This impersonal approach was reemphasized when Towns met some social-service workers in Boston that were sharing some ideas that eventually may have had some limited similarities with the reliance of A.A. members on mutual personal experiences.

> Personally, I have never been an excessive alcoholic. It is an interesting fact that many men endeavoring to deal with people of this class use as a bait the statement that they themselves have been victims. Their usual claim is that they first cured themselves, and then took up the work of curing others. I remember a meeting of social-service workers in Boston that I was invited to address. I made a statement to this effect in the course of my talk and greatly

offended a previous speaker who had emitted the usual professional patter concerning his original self-cure. I was quite willing to compare with him the results of our methods of treatment, but had no opportunity so to do.[76]

Towns thought a hereditary predisposition to addiction was a myth though he did consider that a child born to addicted parents might be predisposed to a nervous condition both for physical and environmental reasons. He then turned to a discussion of alcoholism as a disease, which he had claimed in his 1912 *The Century Magazine* article on alcoholism. Now, however, he believed the assertion to be only partially true. Alcoholics always looked for excuses, he thought, and the disease claim simply seemed to provide them just one more.

We hear much sympathetic talk of the "disease of alcoholism." This is only in a sense true. It is not a case of helpless chance, for the difficulty has been manufactured and developed by man himself. The alcoholic, mentally weakened by the reaction of the stimulant, is of all people most likely to exhibit that most striking evidence of weakness—a craving for sympathy rather than for blame. Habitual alcoholics continually plead for sympathy with mothers, fathers, wives, and friends; and too often they are granted not only pity, but, what is worse, toleration. The sanatorium promoters and proprietors of fake cures continually harp on alcoholism as a disease; and even a few scientists, who should know better, have been misled into an acceptance of this theory. Doctors should be the first to knock from under their patients the psychologically harmful props of the heredity theories. The first thing a physician must do when dealing with an alcoholic is to cut every string of excuse which lies between him and his habit. He must leave nothing of this sort to which the drinker may cling. Sickness, worry, unhappy circumstances of whatever sort must immediately be eliminated as excuses for alcoholic indulgence. If they are not, the patient, although he may gain for a time the mastery over his habit, will presently be certain to find an excuse in his own mind to justify a return to it. Then will come a new downfall. There must be no reservations either in the attitude of the doctor or his patient or in the mental attitude of the patient toward himself.[77]

Here he partially moved away from his June, 1912 statements in *The Century Magazine* "Help For The Hard Drinker" when he repeatedly wrote "the disease of alcoholism." Towns then wrote a paragraph regarding alcoholism that has since been accepted by many: he stressed there was no cure for a real alcoholic.

I cannot too strongly emphasize the fact that no cure exists, or ever will exist, for alcoholism. Its effects may be eliminated, and the victim's physical condition become so greatly improved that weakness will not make him yearn for stimulation; but this does not constitute a cure. Nothing except a man's own mind, whether the treatment extends over six weeks, six months, or six years, can ever relieve him of the danger of a relapse into alcoholism. In most cases a definite medical treatment is the intelligent beginning of help, but no medical treatment, no matter how successful, can compass that victory which a man must win by means of his own determination.[78]

Towns then continued his warnings regarding chronic alcoholics in a rather discouraging manner. While he had partially rejected alcoholism as a disease, saying that alcoholics used that claim as an excuse, he now directly addressed "chronic alcoholics" that he had previously termed "hopeless." He documented what was to be done with such unfortunate poor souls.

It is my opinion that among alcoholics, no matter how worthy they may have been before they lost control, not more than twenty-five per cent of those whose addiction has become chronic are curable; that is to say, promise any reward whatever for salvage work. The world must remember that the inflamed brain leads to everything on earth which is not worth while, and therefore that the man whose brain has for any considerable period of time been in this condition must have enormously deteriorated. It must also be remembered that at least one half of the world's chronic alcoholics have syphilitic histories.[79]

Towns, again, does not bother to reference his sources regarding the presence of syphilis among alcoholics across the world. What studies were found that documented an "inflamed brain" were also not mentioned. One legitimately may wonder if Towns was projecting this assertion from his observations of alcoholics in and around Boston and New York City, along with his 1913 trip to Europe. (Of incidental interest: Towns never mentioned in any of his writings found so far that he ever traveled to the west side of the Hudson River).

He then continued a line of stereotypes that further represented his very high opinion of himself. While earlier in his writings, he appeared to be the best friend that alcoholics might ever wish to have, the line of reasoning presented here would intimidate anybody that had had a prolonged difficulty staying sober. If Towns considered the alcoholic's diagnosis to be hopeless, this unfortunate soul was going to be required to give up a good deal more than just drinking.

It is my belief that the hopeless inebriate should be unsexed, not because of the danger that, if left sexually normal, he might transmit his alcoholic tendencies by heredity to his offspring, but because he is a liability at best, and to leave him normal adds to his potentiality for waste and evil . . . If we go one step beyond syphilis and consider other venereal diseases, we shall undoubtedly discover that not twenty-five, but ninety, per cent. of chronic alcoholics, excluding women, have been victims of gonorrhea[80] . . . It is my belief that every community should have an institution in which hopeless inebriates may be kept away from their cups and away from sexual association. There they should be put at useful occupations; full advantage should be taken of whatever productive capacity alcohol may have left in them; and they should be maintained in a state as happy as their capabilities may permit until they mercifully die.[81]

While Charles Towns began his crusade with the desire to limit the incarceration of alcoholics in penal institutions, his fate for those he considered chronic alcoholics now looked essentially identical to the hell from which he had once tried to save them. Implied in these words may have been some past practical failures and frustrations that were not his style to admit.

He concluded this chapter returning to familiar themes that to treat an alcoholic effectively, he must be treated rapidly and allowed to return back to being a productive citizen. Once again, Towns insisted the patient should be required to use his own money to pay for the hospital visit. Once again he stressed how the physician should directly address the self-confidence of the alcoholic because that was the greatest asset of the afflicted. He then provided another specific warning to the chronic alcoholic, something that he had not considered necessary for the drug addict.

> It is specially important for an alcoholic to learn that at a certain point society will have had enough of him. Fathers must break with alcoholic sons and daughters, mothers must break with alcoholic children, wives and husbands must be freed from alcoholic mates, charitable institutions must be rid of alcoholic derelicts. Society itself must be rid of this waste material, after it has ascertained that their cases are hopeless and has provided comfortable sequestration for them.[82]

And if those sentences were not enough to get the attention of any alcoholic deep into his cups, Towns provided an additional warning to those he seemed predisposed to despise: the very rich chronic drinker first, and the very poor chronic drinker second.

> To put a poor man to sober up on a farm where the State will pay his board and expect him not to become an active menace to society as soon as the period of his sequestration comes to an end is no more foolish than to put the rich man's son into a private institution where he will be petted, coddled, and retained at the highest rates as long as possible, and from which he will be eventually permitted to return to his old haunts freed from the immediate physical discomforts of his past alcoholism and therefore provided with a fresh capacity for strong drink and rejuvenated powers for evil-doing.[83]

Towns thought it was potentially insulting contact his patients after they had been treated and released. By prying into their affairs, one might undercut their pride essential to their recovery. In fact, such action could undermine their confidence because even desiring to contact them could be perceived as a lack of trust. Besides, if a patient decided to return to his previous madness, he had no one to blame other than himself.

One must finish with the alcoholic promptly and conclusively. I have found that alcoholics taking treatment at my hospital must understand that I do not wish to hear from them after they have left my care; that I do not wish to know if they have yielded to new madnesses and relapsed into alcoholism.[84]

He then concluded the chapter with one more vehement criticism of older alcoholic men. These were the men who failed to teach young men the value of money and working responsibly.

Nothing can be much more pitiful than the spectacle of a youngster led into an alcoholic addiction through the influence of older men . . . Association with thousands of those who have gone wrong has proved many social facts to me, one of which I mention here despite its apparent irrelevance. The boy who has never known the value of money, on whom the responsibilities of life have never been impressed, is as seriously uneducated as he would be if lack of common schooling had left him illiterate.[85]

Chapter XIV – "Relation of Alcohol and Drugs to Insanity"

Chapter XIV "Relation of Alcohol and Drugs to Insanity" returned to more of a conciliatory tone than the previous chapter. In this concluding chapter, he recommended solutions to prevent sanatoriums and penal institutions from having to receive one-third of their population if proper diagnosis and solutions were applied quickly enough. Even the hopeless he thought should be "unpoisoned" prior to their being colonized permanently, which he thought to be the only choice remaining for them. The hopeless might have avoided becoming that way had alcohol not been so abruptly removed. Towns also covered what he thought to be some subtle differences between alcohol and drug recovery.

There lies a public peril of unappreciated magnitude in the fact that mere deprivation, the only method so far followed, has been, and if it is not corrected, will continue to be, one of the principal feeders of our insane asylums. Alcoholism will lead to insanity eventually even without deprivation. The case is somewhat different with drug victims. Ordinarily they will not become insane unless deprived of their drug, although in the final stages of the habit they are likely to become incompetent and subject to certain hallucinations, imagining the existence of plots against them, suspecting unfairness on every hand, taking easy offense, exhibiting, in fact, a general distorted mental condition. It is true, indeed, that in some instances the drug victim who is deprived of his drug may become definitely insane, but death is the more frequent result.[86]

Towns then went on to continue his dialog for the need of restrictive legislation to discourage drug addiction.

It can scarcely be expected that restrictive legislation will entirely prevent the sale and use of drugs in the under-world any more than restrictive legislation has been able to prevent the practice of burglary or any other type of crime or lawlessness. It is highly probable that the under-world will always be able to get its drugs; but it is nevertheless true that the passage of restrictive legislation and the enforcement of such laws will tend to prevent the descent of many into the criminal class.[87]

He identified the alcoholic disease of denial in the following. In addition, he embarked upon a line of reasoning that he thought applicable to his times, but hardly applies to many drug addicts of today. The addict of Towns' times was perceived predominantly as a victim of his physician, not as a person that might be looking for the recreation or enhanced entertainment. Entirely voluntary self-medication, without perceivable guilt, as practiced by some today, was not even imagined.

The victim of drugs psychologically differs very materially from the victim of drink. Until his trouble has reached an acute stage, the alcoholic feels little interest in any of the methods advertised as remedial for alcoholism. Many men deny to their friends and even to themselves that they are alcoholics until they have reached a point akin to hopelessness in their friends' eyes and their own. The drug-user, on the other hand, knows that he is a victim as soon as he becomes one; in ninety-nine cases out of a hundred he is immediately filled with an intense longing to be relieved of his habit.[88]

Any drug-user will tell you that no punishment recorded in the course of human history, no torture visualized by the most inventive imagination, can compare with the unspeakable agony of deprivation.[89]

A reader of today must be reminded that the drug world of Towns' times mainly consisted of opium, heroin, morphine, and cocaine. Narcotics predominantly led to a sedated condition whereas a cocaine high lasted but thirty minutes. Writers such as Aldous Huxley and Timothy Leary were all to be in the future, as were amphetamines, LSD, and crack cocaine. Thus, Towns wrote about how there were all sorts of writers that glorified alcohol, but none that he knew that praised drugs. Towns then continued his stereotypical descriptions of drug users and alcoholics that he considered so valid for his times.

The drug-victim investigates every hint of hope with eager interest, reading, intelligently questioning, experimenting. He shrinks from publicity with a horror that is backed by an acute consciousness of his condition, while the victim of alcohol becomes so mentally distorted or deadened that he takes no thought of consequences, cares nothing for publicity, and finds himself unable to avoid public exhibitions of a kind that put him into the hands of the police.[90]

He continued his advocacy of restrictive drug legislation. Such laws would force the addict to seek medical help simply out of desperation and craving, and in that way, he could receive a medical relief from his suffering. He considered such laws to be entirely humanitarian and sympathetic to the drug victim.

Among the various assertions Towns was to make regarding the future, very few of his prophecies seem to have carried more weight over the years than his following assessment of prisons and drugs, even though some fine, honest people in the corrections field may feel themselves very abused by this description.

That imprisonment should rarely, if ever, result in freeing a person from the drug habit can mean only one thing: that drugs are obtainable in every prison. Guards and other employees in such institutions are of a low class, for men and women of a high type are unlikely to seek such employment. I fear that this fact will prove one of the most serious stumbling- blocks in the path of those who are endeavoring to make a success of inebriety-farm experiments . . . [Society] has always underrated and still underrates the terrific complications of the task of working for the reclamation of, or even caring for, the down-and-out.[91]

Because prisons would otherwise become infested with drugs, Towns believed that the Towns Treatment must be provided to every drug addict as soon as possible either before or immediately at the beginning of his incarceration. Otherwise, the hell of craving, the incredible suffering of deprivation, would drive the criminal to bribe, cheat, escape—anything to fulfill the demands of his addiction. Again, Towns' advocacy represented a humanitarian attempting to bring sanity where he perceived there was very little.

The intelligent beginning of help in these cases is to unpoison the patient, put him physically on his feet, where he does not want drugs or drink, and where he does not feel the slightest desire or craving for them, and has no dread of ever drifting into these habits again. When you have brought about this definite physical change, you are invariably able to get a definite mental change. You cannot hope to get the mental change until you have first cleared the system of poison, for in this state the patient is in a most responsive condition to deal with.[92]

Then the book concluded with a tone with which it began. Towns considered himself entirely above most mundane human motivations, and surely above any character defects that a profit motive caused. His perception of his benevolence was that of a compassionate king. His advocacy was for the good of society, of the addict, and of the world. After all, if his policies were to be implemented as he recommended, drug addiction and much of alcoholism would no longer exist, and Towns Hospital would go out of business because it had solved the problems for which it was created. What could be nobler than that?

Of course the general reader may think this book merely a clever advertisement. In it I state that it is wrong to stop the use of morphine and alcohol unless the victims can be treated for the habit, and next I condemn doctors and sanatoriums for their useless methods of treatment, while lauding my own. Naturally, my reader may assume that my only motive is the selfish one of money. Well, one may suppose what he likes, but the truth is that I urge every city and State to establish places that will drive me out of business. I urge physicians to take up this treatment and cure their own colleagues. I have no secrets. My methods have been published, and I am now devoting most of my time to legislative work from which I do not profit a cent.[93]

9) *Medical Review of Reviews* December 1914 – July 1917

A special article, "The Most Successful Treatment of Morphinism and Alcoholism Today," appeared in the December, 1914 issue of the monthly *Medical Review of Reviews*[Q] that could not have been more complimentary to Charles B. Towns. Dr. Alexander Lambert's article, which appeared in *The Journal of the American Medical Association* on June 21, 1913, was heavily quoted. The piece included a lot of drama, continued with a vindication of Towns' opinions on sanatoriums, and then praised Towns and his hospital.

> The history of mankind from the earliest dawn to the present day has been one long, incessant struggle against slavery . . . Centuries and centuries of struggle, in which millions of people lost their lives, were waged against tribal slavery, feudal slavery, oligarchical and monarchial slavery, and last but not least chattel slavery; and finally humanity has reached a semblance of liberty. There is one kind of slavery, however that still holds its victims in an iron clutch as relentlessly and as mercilessly as ever before; nay, its victims have of late years been increasing at an alarming rate.

> We are referring, of course, to the slavery of the drug and alcohol habit. And the victims of the drug habit have up to very recently been the most pitiful of human beings, for the broadminded and unbiased physician—and to him alone this article is addressed—will frankly admit that up to a few years ago, there was practically no scientific treatment of the alcohol habit, the opium and morphine habit, and the cocaine habit. The private physician stood helpless before these cases,

---

[Q] The 1915 issues of *Medical Review of Reviews* contained a list of 339 medical periodicals along with prices available for a physician to reference. While this book has provided numerous Towns Hospital advertisements that may have not been seen before by most, no claim can be made that the exhibits provided herein are a complete collection.

while the numerous sanatoria that flourished—the less said about them the better. A few of them conscientiously tried to help the patient, but their methods were crude and unscientific, and—what is more important—inefficient. Most of them, however, were cold blooded money-making affairs, whose sole purpose was to bleed the patient, and they bled him in the last farthing, and he was sent away, often in a worse condition that when he entered. Very few patients improved in those sanitaria, and even improvement was a temporary one, necessitating the patients' returning again and again, while many sank lower and lower, not a few ending their career in a suicide's grave.

The black, somber picture received a brighter, rosier hue when, a few years ago, Mr. Chas. B. Towns, a layman, gave to the medical profession, gratuitously, and without any expectation of reward, his treatment for alcoholism and the drug habit. This treatment received the unqualified endorsement of our foremost physicians . . .[1]

The article described the Towns Treatment in detail, (which will be covered later in Chapter 12). The fixed fee concept was praised as well as the openness of record keeping and the invitation to invite physicians to visit the hospital and learn the methodologies employed. The indictment of the sanatorium industry and differentiation of Towns Hospital from sanitaria[R] could hardly be written more forcefully. Towns Hospital was fulfilling what the *Medical Review of Reviews* Editor considered to be a very real medical need. The article concluded.

[R] Here we have a third word, "sanitaria," to equate with sanatorium and sanitarium already used in the text

Those familiar with the Charles B. Towns Hospital have given it unstinted praise. It is only necessary to bring Mr. Towns' work to the notice of the entire profession to secure for it the profession's generous and undivided support.[2]

The favorable impact this article had for Towns' personal reputation and that of his hospital could not have been clearer. If imitation is flattery, the *Medical Review of Reviews* article was repeated word for word in two parts in the *Maryland Medical Journal* during the months of February and March of 1915, and may have had much wider exposure than that.[3]

This very favorable reputation builder was followed a year later when a very favorable book review of *Habits That Handicap* was written, which appeared in the January, 1916 issue of the *Medical Review of Reviews*. So began more than a two-year relationship of monthly columns authored by Charles Towns in the magazine with the last column appearing in April of 1918. The publication of these columns represented the zenith of Towns' influence. Here he was, a man that had received no more than an eighth-grade education, writing a column in a publication in which was almost entirely the domain of esteemed doctors. He was rubbing elbows with men that were involved in the front lines of medical research, which put Towns precisely where he thought he belonged when addiction and alcoholism were the subjects.

The author of the favorable book review was not named but is assumed to be written by, or approved by, Victor Robinson, the editor of the publication. He listed Towns among great laymen that had made significant achievements to medicine such as Oliver Wendell Holmes for his *Medical Essays*, the sexual psychologist Havelock Elllis, the American reporter on medical education Abraham Flexner, and the original whistleblower on quack patent medicines Samuel

Hopkins Adams.[4] Robinson then turned to Towns with more words of warm praise.

> The most conspicuous figure in narcotics is another layman—Charles B. Towns. We are apt to
>
> regard with suspicion a non-medical man who claims he has a successful treatment for drug
>
> addiction and alcoholism—especially if he has an institute at the same time. Mr. Towns has
>
> both, but he is above suspicion. His treatment has been published in Osler and McCrae's
>
> *Modern Medicine*, is used in hospitals with which Mr. Towns has no connection, and has been
>
> unreservedly recommended by such physicians as Alexander Lambert, of Cornell, who described
>
> it in detail in the *Journal of the American Medical Association*, and by Richard C. Cabot, of
>
> Harvard, whose training and traditions are such as to make him withhold his endorsement until
>
> absolutely convinced.
>
> I come from good old Boston,
>
> The land of the bean and cod,
>
> Where the Cabots speak only to the Lowells,
>
> And the Lowells speak only to God.
>
> But the exclusive Cabot writes: "I do not hesitate to say that Mr. Towns knows more about the
>
> alleviation and cure of drug addiction than any doctor I have ever seen."

> Mr. Towns' recent volume, *Habits That Handicap*, published by the Century Company, is the
>
> most sober and important work that has appeared on the subject.[5]

How could any author not be extremely pleased with such splendid praise? The

complimentary tone continued throughout the four-page article as the virtues of Towns' opinions were acclaimed. Towns' legislative efforts were then spoken of in a most

commendable fashion.

> The author points out the peril of habit-forming drugs in patent-medicines and pleads for
> effective federal control of the deadly traffic. Some of us have lost all faith in legislation, and
> the acts of Congress only bore us, but Mr. Towns is the Solon of narcotics; all the time that he
> can spare from his hospital he spends in legislative efforts. Perhaps there are reasons why he
> should be sanguine; the reason it is not impossible—except on a physician's prescription—to
> purchase a hypodermic syringe or a milligram of morphine anywhere in the State of New York is
> because of Mr. Towns. The Boylan Bill is named after Senator J. J. Boylan, but everyone knows
> that it is the work of Charles B. Towns.[6]

What compliment could have been exceeded by being referred to as "The Solon of

Narcotics?" Clearly this article introduced an author of which the publication held in the highest

esteem. Soon the decision was made though it was not announced here, that Towns was going

to be one of the magazine department editors. The article then concluded in a manner that

might make even the most modest man's ego swell a bit.

> In short, we have nothing but praise for this book. It is the production of a matured, well-poised,
> efficient man, who writes of what he knows. Whoever reads it will see that Mr. Towns is not a
> moralist, but a practical student of cause and effect. His pages are not filled with perorations,
> but they abound in facts. For years he has seen the menace of opium and alcohol and tobacco

growing ever greater, and with earnestness and intelligence he tries to save his fellow-men from habits that handicap.[7]

A table of contents of the twenty-two articles Towns wrote as Editor of the Department of Drug Addictions and Alcoholism for the magazine between March of 1916 and April of 1918 follow. These were written under a standard heading of "Drug Addiction and Alcoholism Under the Direction of Charles B. Towns." As much of this material during the balance of 1916 was previously presented in his *Habits That Handicap* and *The Century Magazine* articles, only highlights and previously unexpressed opinions found in these articles will be examined. Any missing months reflect either Towns did not write an article that month or he included another author's article in his place. The page numbers refer to how they appear in the referenced publication.

DRUG ADDICTIONS AND ALCOHOLISM
UNDER THE DIRECTION OF
CHARLES B. TOWNS

Table of Contents of Towns Medical Review of Review Articles

March 1916   My Relation to the Medical Profession, page 198

April 1916   Government Responsibility for Drug Victims, page 280

May 1916   Alcoholic Reminders, page 366

June 1916   Concerning Heroin, page 439

July 1916   The Cigarette and the Boy, page 520

August 1916   Women and Tobacco, page 599

September 1916   The Man Who Cannot Be Saved, 679

November 1916   Aphorisms on Alcohol, page 832

December 1916   The Future of Addict Legislation, page 905

January 1917   The Present and Future of Narcotive Pathology, Part 1, page 35

February 1917   The Present and Future of Narcotive Pathology, Part 2, page 113

March 1917   The Present and Future of Narcotive Pathology, Part 3, page 195

June 1917   Alcohol and the War, page 429

July 1917   Alcoholism and Degeneration page 507

August 1917   The Necessity of Definite Medical Result, Part 1, page 584

September 1917   The Necessity of Definite Medical Result, Part 2, page 640

October 1917   The Necessity of Definite Medical Result, Part 3, page 702

November 1917   How to Eliminate the Alcoholic as an Insane Problem, page 761

December 1917   Coffee Inebriety, page 825

January 1918   Psychology and Drugs (Chapter 4 of *Habits That Handicap*), page 34

March 1918   Alcohol and Antenatal Welfare, page 156

April 1918   Inebriety and Drug Addiction, page 217

Relatively short summaries of these articles follow in this chapter and chapter 11.

"My Relation to the Medical Profession," March 1916

His first article named "My Relation to the Medical Profession" was in the form of an introduction. He may have thought he had an entirely new audience. In his first articles, very little was included that had Towns had not written previously. He boasted, "I have the right to emphasize the fact that the beginning of this work was the beginning of definite care and treatment for the drug and alcoholic addict."[8] He also spoke as if he was worthy for his critics to reverse their previous criticisms of him since he thought recent events had validated his legislative efforts beyond doubt.

> In drafting the legislation of which I was the author in this State now that this legislation has been found so entirely effective, it is being appreciated by the very men who criticized me, for they realize that I have done the medical profession a great service.[9]

Nothing specific was included regarding what any criticisms were or who congratulated him on the "great service" he did for the medical profession. By now such lack of supporting information comes as no surprise. He reiterated that the sale and purchase of drugs should be entirely in the domain of government monopolies, and the distribution of drugs to end users should be exclusively through physicians. Until his remedy was introduced for alcoholics, no sufferer had been "receiving no more intelligent treatment and care than he did one hundred years ago."[10] He closed the article with an observation that rarely was an alcoholic kept in his hospital for more than one week, and rarely was a drug addict kept for more than two weeks.[11] This reference to keeping a drug addict for as long as two weeks was the first time there was any mention that any patient might be kept at Towns Hospital for beyond ten days.

"Government Responsibility for Drug Victims," April 1916

"Government Responsibility for Drug Victims" asserted once more that because society allowed alcohol to be served indiscriminately, and that most drug addicts were victims of their doctor or druggist, that society should provide the medical resources required for the victims to

Shakespere on Alcohol

DON'T LET ALCOHOL FOOL YOU!

ALCOHOL CAUSES
AT LEAST
FIVE DIFFERENT KINDS OF
INSANITY

From The Survey

Figure 13 - Ad included with May 1916 Article complete with misspelling of Shakespeare

recover when necessary. No one was to be criticized more than "the committing magistrate" who had been judging victims of their habits without "intelligence" using the same reasoning as "one-hundred years ago." Instead of asking for appropriations to house the sad results of the mistreatment of these victims, society should learn that the Towns Treatment was the way to prevent 25 to 35% of addicts and alcoholics from ever having to enter such facilities. The "alcoholic is the greatest sociological problem that confronts us," but established authorities seemed to have no approach other than to building more prisons and sanitariums. One-third of the patients at Bellevue Hospital he claimed were there because of alcoholism. Up to ninety percent of the population of the workhouse was there for the same reason. The time for a new approach was long overdue.[12]

"Alcoholic Reminders," May 1916

"Alcoholic Reminders" reiterated some assertions that are near to the opposite of what a variety of twelve-step programs and many treatment centers do today.

Remember there is nothing which degrades these patients so much as colonization. Whether in a private or public institution, this type of patient should not be brought into contact with his own kind.[13]

There were some other essential points that Towns very much wanted the reader to remember.

> Remember that by simply sobering up the patient, you do not bring about any definite psychological change, and until this is done, you cannot hope to bring about the mental change which is essential before you can hope to benefit a patient of this type.

> Remember that moralizing with a man who wants to drink, or who is under the influence of drink, or exacting resolutions from such a man, or threatening him with penalization and disgrace, has rarely, if ever, saved one of these unfortunates.[14]

He also repeated his assertion that quitting alcohol would be unlikely unless the patient quit smoking tobacco as well. He also insisted the patient must be employed, for if he did not want to work, any attempt to help him would be disastrous.[15]

"Concerning Heroin," June 1916

For the first time, Towns started writing what he understood to be a history with references to actual events and people, which allowed his writing to be validated in the light of resources available today. Towns attributed heroin being invented by a German chemist by the name of Heinrich Dreser in 1898.[16] However, C.R. Alder Wright in 1874 of the United Kingdom has been credited with the discovery, with Dreser becoming involved almost a quarter of a century later in the search for a substance less potent than morphine. Inadvertently the substance derived from Wright's and Dreser's experiments led to a substance much stronger than morphine. Because of its potency, the name "heroin" was chosen from the German word for "strong" by the German Bayer Corporation, the same company that was to bring the household name Bayer Aspirin to the United States soon after the beginning of the twentieth century.[17]

Towns also attributed cocaine being used first by a German named Karl Koller in 1884, who was experimenting with its use in ophthalmology.[18] Coca leaves had been chewed in South America for many centuries, but the cocaine alkaloid was first isolated thirty years before around 1855. Quite a bit of experimentation with the substance took place prior to Koller experimenting with cocaine, but Towns' narrative was accurate for the information he provided.[19]

Otherwise, the article mainly described Towns' first encounter with heroin. His experiments with his first heroin patient, who happened to be female, led him to conclude that this substance was three times stronger than morphine. Not surprisingly, he claimed she was removed from the substance completely after just four days.

"The Cigarette and the Boy," July 1916

Most of this article was taken from his previous writings. After the first paragraph of this July, 1916 article, the majority of the text was almost word for word identical to the first six pages (166-172) of Chapter IX of *Habits That Handicap*. Then, from the preceding chapter VIII of *Handicap,* he used three paragraphs from pages 149-151, two more paragraphs from page 152, and additional paragraphs from pages 156-157 on the subject of why tobacco has done so much harm to young boys. The concluding paragraph then referenced Elbert Hubbard's words from the short article *The Cigarettist* that damned cigarettes with relentless judgment.

Place no confidence in the cigarettist—he is an irresponsible being—a defective. Love him if you can; pity him if you will, but give him no chance to clutch you with his nicotine fingers and drag you beneath the wave."[20]

"Women and Tobacco," August, 1916

"Women and Tobacco" seems to have been an attempt to make up for not previously noting that women smoked tobacco as well as men. Here he examined the subject with all the characteristics of a stereotypical chauvinist. He confessed that when he wrote his first article on the tobacco in 1912, "[he] did not feel that at that time its influence among women of this country was sufficient for [him] to even mention them in connection with its use."[21] The opinions that followed resembled his attempt to praise smoke-free women while harshly condemning female tobacco smokers. In Chapter IX of his recent book, he had denied the label of being "a moralist"—someone who had very strong opinions about what is right or wrong who speaks with an air of superiority. How he could deny that label and write the following, seems incongruous.

The woman who permits herself to drift into habits of this kind soon loses all self-control and goes the limit and it is only a matter of time, which depends entirely upon her physical constitution, on how long she will last. There is nothing on earth she can do that will so surely bring about her mental and moral ruin as the use of tobacco. It changes her entire mental attitude towards life and she lets down the last bar of reason and seeks and courts congenial companionship among other unfortunates of her class and in the end it degrades everything in woman that is worth while, and in a short time the lovely, devoted, clean wife and mother becomes negligent and all her womanly duties and responsibilities, and if an alcoholic history has not previously existed it is only a matter of time when she will also acquire that vice. Can you picture a more disgusting human being than an alcoholic and nicotine poisoned woman? The influence and environment of the home is measured by the mother, not by the father, with few exceptions. We men must all concede that women are very much stronger characters than we are. There are very few successful men but owe their success to their wives. Any man left to himself by women amounts to little. No woman puts herself on a par with a man when she indulges with him in life's vices, she always puts herself beneath him. There is some hope of saving a man who may drift into the taking of drugs and drink but when a woman takes up drugs and drink for the sake of dissipation the moral hazard is far greater than among men, and there are very few of them in the end who are ever restored to normality. When they begin to dissipate they travel faster and further than men do. When a woman with a cigarette history is brought to me for help I invariably throw up both hands and am frank to say that we can hold out little or no hope for her regeneration. There is no real man who, even tho[sic] he uses tobacco himself, looks with favor upon a woman using it, and I have never seen a real man indulging in the use of tobacco with a woman - it has always been a thing in trousers. If the young women who use tobacco to the mental estimate in which men hold them, there would be few tobacco users among them. They are immediately associated with the morally low, it makes no difference what their breeding or social standing may be. They are looked upon with suspicion, and time and place and circumstances permitting, they sooner or later have to defend their virtue or lose it . . . No more pitiful sight on earth could possibly be imagined than the spectacle of some mother who is a cigarette smoker in bringing into the world a poor, pitiful physical and mentally defective child, and besides not wanting to assume any of the responsibilities of motherhood in rearing it. So this type of woman will not contribute, fortunately, to the increase of our population. There is nothing that she can't possibly do that is going to so surely rob her of her good looks, of everything in her life and make up that is pleasing and fascinating to men - and the man who tolerates their smoking are the first to kick them aside for those that are younger and prettier, when tobacco has worked its irreparable havoc.[22]

"The Man Who Cannot Be Saved," September, 1916

"The Man Who Cannot Be Saved" had been almost entirely borrowed from *Habits That Handicap* as well. Because he was now using this material for the third time in five years, possibly he thought he needed to disguise that fact. The article began with what had been the first four sentences of the second paragraph of Chapter VII "Classification of Alcoholics" on pages 113 and 114 of his book. He then skipped to page 115 where another long paragraph was reused. However, this time he added a new twist. He made the first sentence of the *Handicap* version into its own paragraph but preceded it with the remainder of the original paragraph. Almost nothing new was provided in the article. As an additional feature of the magazine column, he included a byline of "Narcotic Aphorisms." The six paragraphs of this section were simply selections from four different chapters of *Habits That Handicap* that he thought could be repeated to his advantage.

"Aphorisms on Alcohol," November, 1916

The November, 1916 article was titled "Aphorisms on Alcohol," after the October column had been written by a Horace M. Simmons, MD titled "The Saturday Evening Post and the Tobacco Traffic." By this time, before Towns' article began, a standard introduction was being included each month. These words had to reflect the legal turmoil impacting physicians through the criminalization of the Harrison Act, passed nearly two years before. The *U.S. v. Jin Fuey Moy* ruling by the Supreme Court had been decided in the previous June, fear of drug addicts was on the rise and the legal liabilities of doctors that treated addicts were becoming plagued with increased risk. (italics in original).

The immense amount of recent legislation on narcotics is naturally bewildering the medical profession and more than one honest physician has unwittingly found himself in the toils of the law. In connection with my work as Editor of the Department of Drug Addictions and Alcoholism in Medical Review of Reviews, *I consider it one of my duties to answer questions concerning State and Federal legislation on the subject. I also want the readers of this magazine to feel at liberty to write to me at any time concerning any phase of the narcotic problem. I know that this subject is not included in the medical curriculum, and that it is unknown land to the average physician. I will be glad to answer questions relating to the diagnosis and treatment of any of the drug-addictions. Correspondents may feel assured of the strictest confidence, for in no case will the writer's name be divulged without consent.*[23]

"Aphorisms on Alcohol" was a book review written by Towns on the writings of Edwin F. Bowers on Alcohol. Towns began the article with some quotes of Bowers, which Towns must have relished.

The Arabs, who gave it its name—al ghole—had the right idea. Alcohol is exactly what its name indicates—an 'evil spirit.'

Darwin records the case of a baboon made drunk with beer. The next morning's keeper found him a picture of dejection and woe, holding his head tightly after the fashion of a repentant roysterer [sic].[S] The simian[T] showed more sense than the average drinker, however, for when he was again offered beer he refused point-blank to touch it.

Alcohol is formed in nature only as an excretion. It is the garbage of vegetation, the discarded elements of decayed plant life. It is food only for the ferment of vinegar, and poisons for everything else.[24]

The manner in which Towns wrote his very short book review made it difficult to determine where the writings of Edwin F. Bowers were being quoted or where Towns had provided his own opinions. In any case, an assertion then appeared that claimed Russia soon would be saving lives. Czar Nicholas II, following the advice of his infamous close advisor Rasputin, had banned the sale of intoxicants just before the start of World War One in July, 1914.[25]

On the basis of their statistics, insurance men calculate that if Russia, for instance, persists in banishing all alcoholic beverages from within its borders 1 million lives will be saved to that awakened country within the next ten years.[U]

[S] Definition of roysterer – "To engage in boisterous merrymaking; revel noisily."
[T] Definition of simian - Relating to, characteristic of, or resembling an ape or a monkey
[U] From Wikipedia: "The **Russian Revolution** is the collective term for a series of revolutions in Russia in 1917, which dismantled the Tsarist autocracy and led to the creation of the Russian SFSR. The Emperor was forced to abdicate and the old regime was replaced by a provisional government during the first revolution of February 1917 (March in the Gregorian calendar; the older Julian calendar was in use in Russia at the time). In the second

This article was written just a few months before the first major upheaval in Russia took place, which was not, so far as historians have reported to date, a war for or against vodka. Towns, nor Bowers, nor Dr. Frank R. Stacey nearly two years earlier,[26] could have had any idea of the horrific turmoil that was to come from the Russian revolution or that the Czar was soon to be overthrown and executed along with his entire family on July 17, 1918. Obviously these opinions did not reflect the top priorities of "that awakened country," not to mention that the article was written as Russia was well into a third year of World War I.

Towns also decided to provide an additional opinion piece that encapsulated the enthusiasms of the times for prohibition, as if the great evil alcohol was to be banished from plaguing the world once and for all. This short article asserted that "king alcohol was dying," that alcohol had been a "diabolical ruler" that was showing "symptoms of senility," and that the "magic spell of alcohol [was] gone, never to return" because "King Alcohol [was] tottering into his grave."[27]

"The Future of Addict Legislation," December, 1916

"The Future of Addict Legislation" provided some original, highly self-congratulatory, new writing. Now he could claim that not only were his views being vindicated, but "the people of the whole country [were] vitally interested."

The people are now waking up to the moral enormity of this whole drug situation, and are beginning to realize the social waste and economic loss that it involves. It will not be long before

revolution, during October, the Provisional Government was removed and replaced with a Bolshevik (Communist) government."

public opinion Is clearly crystalized and will compel the authorities to undertake to do a number of things which I urged the medical and pharmaceutical professions of the State of New York to do four years ago . . . When I took up this work there was no legislative precedent, either State or Federal, restricting the manufacture of sale of such drugs[v] . . . So, my findings on the subject have made medical history and furnish the data for legislative enactment which, for the first time has placed the sale and use of habit-forming drugs on a scientific basis. After making my findings and fixing the medical facts beyond all question, they were given to the medical world to help in meeting the intolerable situation growing out of the practically free and unrestricted use of habit-forming drugs.[28]

He also wrote that "the Commissioner of Internal Revenue realizes also that something further must be done," while reasserting his proposal that there needed to be more "medical care of the drug victim" along with providing legislation "for the legitimate supply of the drug to those who for any reason based on actual physical conditions are eligible for narcotic treatment." However, Decision 2200 of the Treasury Department, made in mid-1915, had criminalized ambulatory treatment of addicts already, and no legislation was forthcoming to change anything for the better. The Harrison Act never declared that ambulatory treatment was illegal. In reality, the United States Congress had as its focus other matters. Drug addicts that continued their habits were to become criminals regardless of receiving a prescription

---

[v] Colorado had laws regarding cocaine as early as 1897. Georgia banned all forms of cocaine sale in 1902. California passed a 1907 law requiring a prescription for the substance. David Musto in *The American Disease* documented that the Tennessee Narcotic Act of 1913 (p. 100) was to feature "the registration of addicts to enable them to have opiate prescriptions refilled 'to minimize suffering among this unfortunate class' and to keep 'the traffic in the drug from getting into underground and hidden channels." Towns' claim that there were no State drug laws prior to his advocacy was not true.

from his doctor, and if the doctor were not careful, he would be considered a criminal as well for supplying the narcotics.

Towns again tried to represent himself as a realist, which was to insist how the narcotic eventually overwhelmed any consumer of it. The slave of drugs, and anyone that used them more than a few times was such a slave, involuntarily would go to whatever length necessary for him to feed the demands resulting from intense craving. If the drug became available anywhere, the addict would find it. Thus, Towns restated an opinion that he had stated before: drugs were an international problem and only an international solution could solve the world crisis.

> [Our] laws alone, no matter how drastic they may be, cannot check the traffic in drugs among these people. This situation can be reached only thru international law by all nations acting in concert in this matter. Not until the situation is cleaned up internationally will it be possible to control the illegal and illegitimate phases of this matter.[29]

Towns never declared any preferences for a political party in any of his writings examined to date, but as said before, he resembled a Woodrow Wilson Democrat on at least one issue. Towns had once again declared his support for the development of any international organization designed to tackle what he insisted was a world drug problem. However, as would be revealed in years to come, a number of countries considered eventual U.S. proposals to control drugs worldwide to be an infringement on their national sovereignty. Very little action resulted regarding American proposals for increased narcotic legislation.[30]

He reiterated his desire to solve the dilemma of drug addiction once and for all time. He wanted his readers to recognize that his motives were beyond criticism: he once again claimed that his pure motives would and should put him out of the drug treatment business!

> I want doctors and druggists both to understand that my only aim and purpose concerning this whole subject is to try to put an end to the unnecessary use of such drugs. If, in view of the nature of my work I am able to bring about this result, it will terminate my financial interest in carrying on a hospital work for the treatment of drug victims. - - - if there are no drug victims my hospital will have no narcotic patients to treat. My aim is to put an end to this horrible drug curse and I want the help of both doctors and druggists in doing it.[31]

He was then to end his first year of writing for *Medical Review of Reviews* with a lot of optimism about the future.

> And so I am willing to say this, and to say it without the slightest effort and exaggeration -- that within the next few years, if better legislation be provided on this subject, as it ought to be, a 'drug case,' made such thru the legitimate medical use of habit-forming drugs, will be considered a medical curiosity in any institution that receives such patients for treatment.[32]

Another optimistic note from Towns probably did not please some in the sanitarium business as nearly as much as it seemed to please him.

Thanks to the co-operation of the medical profession, my success in this work makes it possible for me financially and otherwise to do earnestly whatever I can to wipe out this drug curse. Such conditions as I hope to see legally and actually effective are going to put a great many sanitariums out of existence . . . I will undoubtedly have to depend upon some other source of revenue to take the place of the drug victims I have been treating; but I am going to try, for once and all, to kill the 'drug goose' that has been laying the 'dope egg.'[33]

By 1920, the 'drug goose' and the 'dope egg' had become all but extinct at Towns Hospital. That outcome was not because of the elimination of drug addiction as he had once believed possible. He, as so many other professionals, had to protect himself from the atmosphere of fear resulting from inflamed rhetoric that claimed "drug fiends," friendly to the Germans, were poisoning U.S. school children. The atmosphere, which Towns' rhetoric inadvertently had encouraged, led to the concept of drug treatment hospitals to be feared as containing derelicts and enemies. He had to diminish the perceived risk of just who his hospital treated. The punitive threats of law enforcement soon made the prescription drug maintenance business too hazardous for most respectable physicians or hospital proprietors, and the last drug maintenance clinic went out of business because of government pressures by 1923.[34] The number of drug addicts treated from 1920 forward at Towns Hospital is not known, but presumed to have been a closely guarded secret.

"The Present and Future of Narcotive Pathology," Part 1, January, 1917

The first three months of 1917 had Towns writing a three-part article entitled "The Present and Future of Narcotive Pathology." He began the series by claiming "sixteen years of the closest application to the study of drug and alcoholic addictions" which had led him to believe "that of all the classes to whom society [was] manifestly unfair, the most unfairly

treated [was] the drug and alcoholic addict."[35] (Sixteen years date back, of course, to 1901, and

once more, that number may be a salesman's exaggeration). Once again, he displayed his

fundamental belief that society was largely to blame for ridiculously permissive practices that

were the cause of almost all addiction problems.

> Consider that society long ago actually, if not legally, banished the house of prostitution to the
>
> side streets, as it were. But society in the United States . . . still thrusts tobacco at its members
>
> by all kinds of advertising and display, plants a saloon at practically every street corner, hands
>
> out 'dope remedies' almost without restraint, distributes hypodermic syringes to anyone who
>
> has the price to pay for them and dispenses habit forming drugs with or without reference to
>
> prescriptions, according to the social morality of the dispenser on the one hand and, on the
>
> other, to his ability to escape detection by the authorizes. Almost literally, 'everything goes.'"[36]

In reality, the 'everything goes' slogan could also have been used by the Treasury

Department and their example to others in law enforcement regarding the pursuit of the 'drug

evil.' No law was passed to justify their increasingly punitive practices legally. Law enforcement

had begun treating drugs with more zealotry than the forces leading to alcohol prohibition. The

New York Times included an alarming article on December 5, 1913 which was probably very

much similar to the future thinking of the Treasury Department in justifying their interpretation

of the Harrison Act.

The United States is now second to China and ahead of every other country in the world in the use of opium and the narcotics derived from it, according to a statement today by Dr. B.C. Keister . . . The menace is so great, the speaker said, that there is danger of our 'degenerating back to something worse than monkeydom' . . . Twenty three percent of the medical profession . . . were now victims of the morphine habit. The medical and criminal records of the country indicated that a complete abolition of the manufacture of the habit-forming drugs, including alcohol, would reduce homicides by fifty per cent, suicides by sixty per cent, and lunacy by thirty-three per cent. The loss to medicine, whatever it might be, from the prohibition of morphine, alcohol, opium and cocaine, would be worth while in view of the possible benefits.[37]

World War I gave a particular patriotic boost to the forces fearing the narcotic menace. Rufus King documented the mood of the times in his book *The Drug Hang Up*.

The 1914 Harrison Tax Act was neglected, and even the drive for national prohibition and the suffragette movement were pushed into the background, as America drifted into her first Great War. Long before the United States actually entered the hostilities, Germany's goosestepping legions began to be depicted as Hun, Boche, and Antichrist. German cruelty, German immorality, and the terrifying reach of the German grand design for world conquest emerged as focal points for all of America's fears and fantasies . . . By 1917 increasing numbers of civic leaders and responsible citizens were calling for federal intervention and strict federal controls to stop the drug traffic. In that year the first caches of illegal drugs were seized by Treasury agents (and Treasury then started the deceptive practice, continued ever since by drug-law enforcers, of announcing each seizure in terms of how many millions of dollars the contraband substances might have been worth if they had been sold at maximum prices in the illegal

market). Estimates of the addict population in New York City alone jumped to 300,000 . . .
German agents were actively engaged in smuggling drugs on a large scale into army training
centers.[38]

At this time, however, Towns was still maintaining calm in his approach to drug addicts.
Soon his views were going to be quite impacted by the headlines of impending war. For the
time being, since he believed he held the truth along with the solution to drug addiction, he
would continue his crusade for the medical approach of treating addicts.

He returned to the claims that the success rate at Towns Hospital resulted in an eighty
percent rate of permanent recovery.[39] However, he could not resist making the observation
that many doctors were unconvinced still by his science. According to him, doctors were
approaching the subject of addiction using a narrow mind and wearing professional blinders.
Towns insisted they need to listen to him and broaden their narrow views.

The [solution] to these problems demands of the medical practitioner that he be not only a
competent physician, but an adequately informed sociologist. For the enactment of drug
legislation to safeguard the use of habit forming and life destroying drugs is more than a
'professional' question. It affects the very 'state of the nation' itself; and no merely 'medical'
consideration of it will ever get anywhere. In his dealing with this phase of the 'drug and drink
evil,' the physician must lay aside the mere 'doctor' and put on the enlightened citizen . . . Why,
I ask, should an innately sound and essentially scientific conservatism be permitted to pass over
into a pronounced professional attitude which, judged by manifestations, seems to come so

close to professional prejudice as scarcely be distinguishable from it? . . . The medical practitioner ought to remember that he is not a law unto himself . . .[40]

Towns had indicated he had had enough of what he saw to be professional prejudice. He thought it to be the time to lecture doctors on the virtues of living in a democracy and warn them that it was "the People" that had the power.

In the United States, being a democracy, it is for the people to say what shall be the assumed risks, if any, connected with the use of drugs in a given community; and it is for the people to say in what manner drugs shall be prescribed and in what manner they be dispensed. The State does not approach the matter from a 'professional' standpoint at all. To the People it is a matter of political economy and is, pure and simple, a 'police measure' for its own safeguarding and protection from those elements of disintegration, and even of destruction, which seem to inhere in what is called 'human nature.'[41]

He then announced that in his next two columns, he was going to examine his proposed solutions once more, and do so very carefully to persuade the physician that his approach was scientific and had achieved a "present perfected state."

I believe I am now in a position to sum up the work of sixteen years in the field in which I was pioneer; and I believe that the results of that work are a safe guide to the future of narcotive therapeusis, because they have been tested and demonstrated over and over again. [42]

"The Present and Future of Narcotive Pathology," Part 2, February, 1917

His February, 1917 article was the second in the series and concerned alcoholic addiction. He repeated an assertion that should be more than familiar by now.

[The] alcoholic is a physiologically poisoned and sickened man with a crooked mind and a perverted will, and that the only way to restore him to sanity and soundness [was] to unpoison him physiologically and then set him free psychologically.[43]

He once again asserted that the Towns Treatment quickly and effectively unpoisoned the patient and set him on the course to never physically crave the substance again. There was no need to have been "tapering off" patients as had been done so ineffectively in sanitariums.

Who would dream of 'tapering off' or of 'easing down' and then indefinitely prolonging the minor symptoms of a rattlesnake bite in order to relieve the patient of his poison? The only thing to do with poison cases is to get rid of the poisons physiologically by one or another scientifically demonstrated method.[44]

His assessments of alcoholics in general provided for some of the most severe, degrading descriptions of them one may ever read.

The clinical experience of the physician who has had largely to do with the treatment of alcoholic addiction, will almost certainly confirm the statement that the psychology of the confirmed alcoholic would seem to be that of a wholly irresponsible and irrational creature, utterly self-concerned and absorbed in one desire to the exclusion of all other desires and interests that do not contribute to the rule one: namely, to satisfy the morbid craving of an exacerbated nervous organism. It is hardly too much to say, that in the confirmed alcoholic, the physician is dealing with a sub-human creature.[45]

Towns then began to address what he referred to as "aftercare" for the treated alcoholic. He was learning that effective, sustained recovery from alcoholism required more than just the removal of physical craving. For the first time, he expanded his recovery horizon to "three to six weeks."

After the patient's physiological unpoisoning, he is in a state to be dealt with, if at all, by those processes which might be called moral repair. He is at least 'clothed in his right mind.' He is in possession of those faculties which constitute him a rational being . . . This is preeminently not the time to 'baby' him or treat him as a sadly misunderstood man . . . To mollycoddle them and treat them as neurasthenic invalids means simply to increase the liability of their relapse; but to build them up bodily will do more to build them up mentally for the first three to six weeks than any other method of procedure.[46]

So there was more to recovery than simply "unpoisoning." These words continued his personal evolution at Towns Hospital. The place was becoming to look much more like the sanitariums of which he had been so critical of previously. Towns' patients seemed to benefit staying away from their old playgrounds for longer periods, which had been a previous legitimate role of sanitariums. To give his words more authority, he referenced both Dr.

Alexander Lambert and Dr. Richard Cabot. Towns wrote that the recovery rate observed by those esteemed doctors was in the 75 to 80% range for patients having received the Towns-Lambert Treatment along with the proper aftercare.[47]

He also provided some descriptions of the challenges that were involved in administering the Towns-Lambert Treatment.

> No special skill is required to administer the dosage; but a great deal of skill and patience and finesse and firmness are required to handle the patient during a term in which he usually comes to feel that he is abused because either doctor or nurse are 'at him' every hour or all the time with something to take or something to do.[48]

One might ask how well the medical approach worked at Towns Hospital when Charles Towns himself did not administer it? Quite a number of doctors were listed on the staff of the facility over the years. Still, one may wonder just how much of the successful outcome really depended upon the perseverance of the man in charge. The potential for "patience and finesse and firmness" may have often been essential to keep the patient in the building, that is, if he had a choice to leave.

"The Present and Future of Narcotive Pathology," Part 3, March, 1917

The conclusion of the three-part series, printed in March of 1917, dealt with drug addiction once more. Towns thought that almost all drug addicts, except possibly those on cocaine, were victims entrapped in bondage. He believed almost all wished to be released from their agony. But many were petrified that a so-called solution for their addiction would result in a hell on earth.

> The drug addict . . . is almost invariably an unwilling slave; and he knows he is a slave and detests his slavery. Realizing their slavery, [the drug addicts] grieve over it, they resent it, and they wish to be free of it . . . For it should be remembered that, whereas alcohol is to the alcoholic a source either of sensational pleasure or of escape from an intolerable world, the drug addict's favorite drug, while at first a possible source of lotos dreams[W] or of egotistic expansion, has at length become nothing more nor less than a means of stilling the cries of every exacerbated nerve ending in his organism - that and no more. The drug addict knows no joy; he is pursued by a demon of potential pain that he knows will become a devil of actual anguish if he does not feed it.[49]

Towns considered a typical morphine addict to be relatively a good patient that would and could listen to reason, as long as the horror of his separation from his drug was handled properly. Not so for a typical alcoholic, and especially not so for a cocaine addict.

> I can imagine no creature this side of hell itself to compare with the typical 'coke fiend' in his acutely progressive stages of his addiction or, sometimes, at the crisis of treatment for the elimination of the drug from his system. Likewise in alcoholism, tho[sic] the conditions are not

---

[W] "lotos dreams" is an apparent reference to The Lotus-Eaters, from Wikipedia: The Lotos-Eaters is a poem by Alfred Tennyson published in Tennyson's 1832 collection. It was inspired by his trip to Spain with his close friend Arthur Hallam, where they visited the Pyrenees mountains. The poem describes a group of mariners who, upon eating the lotos, are put into an altered state and isolated from the outside world.

so pronounced, the patient is seldom an angel or anything like one. The morphine patient, on the other hand, compared to the usual 'alcoholic,' is generally a 'good patient.'[50]

Towns once again embarked upon some reasoning that epitomized his nature of making observations for which there was no medical research quoted or studies referenced. These opinions seem to be entirely within the realm of Towns' experiences, which revealed to him unshakeable truths of which most would remain unaltered for the rest of his life.

This difference [in patients] is of course due to the difference in physiological effect of the two classes of narcotics. Whereas the effect of alcohol, and likewise of cocaine, is to break down and to degenerate tissue and thus to subvert physiological function thru the organism—if not in one way, then in another—the effect of the opium derivatives is merely to tie up organic function in the addict and then retain him in this tangled, tied-up state. When the drug is eliminated from his system, his organism takes up its interrupted course, according to the general state of his health and the condition of his viscera[x] aside from addictive causes. But the case of the alcoholic or the 'coke' fiend is not unlike that of the clock into which one may have thrown a brick. The alcoholic system has had a 'smash' and unfortunately it is all too likely to remain in relatively smashed condition even after successful elimination of his craving.[51]

This description seemed to reflect his experiences that cocaine and alcohol often had interfered with the patient's diet over long periods. Such patients were more of a physical wreck upon arrival at Towns than typical morphine addicts. One may be hard-pressed to find

---

[x] Viscera – the internal organs in the main cavities of the body, especially those in the abdomen, e.g. intestines

any additional reference in another medical magazine to Towns' description of such patients as those who resembled "a clock into which one may have thrown a brick."[52]

Towns returned to by now very familiar themes of how most morphine addicts had been victims of their physicians, and that physicians were the only humane solution possible to rescue these victims. He reemphasized that the addict could be safely treated without much discomfort. But in his experiences he did not seem to encounter many alcoholic drug users because, in his patients, he described distinct stereotypes.

[Drug addicts and alcoholics] are different beings living in different worlds—the alcoholic eager to 'hog the stage,' as the actors have it, and the drug addict asking only to be let alone. This leads up to the second point, that while the alcoholic may not wish to undergo treatment and will insist that he is man enough to down his enemy once he gets over his present spree, the drug addict harbors no such delusions, and will usually grasp at any means that he thinks will free him from his bondage.[53]

But then there were the physicians that had reported failure in their attempt to employ Towns' methods. In his defense, Towns listed doctor-authored articles that supported the efficacy of the Towns Treatment. He seemed disappointed that his approach was not yet "made a part of the regular curriculum of any medical school so far as I know . . ."[54] The reluctance for the medical community to accept the remedy, where chances of failure had been eliminated, puzzled him. However, should another approach be discovered that was considered as proven and "scientifically perfect" as his own, he would accept it in a magnanimous way, the same way he hoped his solution deserved acceptance.

I believe [my treatment] is now in a form in which, where it is followed out wholly and in good faith, only success can ensue and never failure. This may seem to be a very 'strong' statement but it is literally true. And if the 'Towns Treatment' be improved upon at any time by those administering it I hope to receive the benefit of the new findings, as I have insured others should receive the benefit of mine . . . My one desire is that not alone the 'Towns Treatment,' but any other successful medical means or method for the physiological elimination of narcotic craving shall be made as scientifically perfect as possible and then made available thru the proper medical channels.[55]

There was only one reason that qualified physicians typically failed to return their patients to "life, liberty and the pursuit of happiness," and that was a lack of firmness by the physician himself. The physician needed to persist in the treatment regardless of the "lamentations or delusions" expressed by their patients. The Towns-Lambert Treatment was "the only treatment in the world . . . [that] set men and women . . . physiologically free from their narcotic cravings."[56]

"Alcohol and War," June 1917

"Alcohol and the War" was the title of Towns' June of 1917 article as the United States had entered the hostilities against Germany two months earlier. He began by condemning the drinking of absinthe in France and vodka in Russia. He was highly critical of Great Britain for their air of indifference regarding their alcohol problems. He considered the actions of the Russian Czar to prohibit alcohol consumption at the beginning of World War One to be highly commendable, but provided no recognition that Czar Nicholas II had been forced to abdicate three months earlier in March, 1917. He continued to use the adjective of "evil" whenever his subject was alcohol. Here he recommended that Great Britain and France follow the example of the Canadian province of Ontario.

But after all, there would seem to be no really valid reason why Great Britain and France should not have cut the Gordian knot at one stroke instead of seeking means to scotch the evil. If the most progressive province of a free country like Canada, the Province of Ontario, can wholly banish drink from its borders by the stroke of its premier's pen, why should not France or Great Britain be able to do the same?[57]

As awful as war might be, however, Towns believed there would be benefits from the conflict as long as the perception of drinking alcohol as being evil was strengthened.

However, with regard to the abatement of the drinking evil, the war in any event has wrought already incalculable good, and would seem to hold out an augury of a still brighter future. The mass of scientific medical opinion is that the mind and body will withstand the tribulations and trials of warfare much better without alcohol than with it, and that when wounded or when an operation is necessary the abstainer will bear the shock with more hope of recovery than the man who drinks alcohol in however small quantities.

Therefore, the war has again shown that out of evil good may come. For it has demonstrated conclusively that a nation to be successful must be a sober nation, and this axiom applies to every branch of human endeavor, and especially to that most strenuous and awful of all, that of war. To win in these days one must be efficient, and to be efficient, one must be strictly temperate in all things.[58]

"Alcoholism and Degeneration," July 1917

"Alcoholism and Degeneration" continued his consistent theme that alcohol was a curse to mankind. He insisted that studies had proven that children of alcoholic parents suffered severely as a result of one or both of their parents drinking. Towns was considered to be an atheist for most of his life, but his abundant use of the adjective "evil" might lead some to think of him in other terms.

Alcohol in addition to the harm it wreaks itself, brings many evils in its train. The man or woman who drinks is on the high road to degeneration, for alcohol injures the faculties, dulling moral restraint, and exciting the lusts. Venereal diseases almost invariably follow in the wake of alcohol, and it is now a matter of common knowledge that maladies of this nature are the most potent cause of mental deterioration and physical degeneration. The argument is frequently advanced that alcohol is not nearly as harmful to the race as its opponents claim it to be, because it weeds out the unfit and that in a drinking race it is a case of survival of the fittest.[59]

Towns very unsurprisingly again concluded that alcohol and degeneracy went hand in hand. While he kept most all of his comments focused on the sphere of medicine and addiction, he had to have been viewing the domestic movement towards alcohol prohibition with much anticipation.

"The Necessity of Definite Medical Result in the Treatment of Drug and Alcoholic Addiction," Part 1, August, 1917

The August, 1917 article began a three-part series with a rather lengthy title of "The Necessity of Definite Medical Result in the Treatment of Drug and Alcoholic Addiction" with the rather equivalent lengthy subtitle of "Medical Treatment Necessary to Procure Obliteration of Craving but Must be Followed by Intelligent Sociological Effort to Secure Effective Mental Attitude." This new three-part series represented his response to how two of his previous magazine articles had been reviewed. One of those three-part articles had appeared in *Medical Review of Reviews*, January through March of 1917, and has been discussed in this chapter already. However, the second article, which also appeared over three months, was written in the medical journal *The Modern Hospital* from December of 1916 through February of 1917. *The Modern Hospital* trio of articles, along with his most controversial brochure, need to be examined before this August, 1917 article. As in this period he was writing in multiple medical magazines, he truly appeared to be at the peak of his career.

10) *The Peak*, December 1916 – December 1917

This brief three month period represented the peak of Towns' career. He was the owner

Figure 14 - Charles Barnes Towns in the October, 1912 *The American Magazine* article

of a nationally acclaimed hospital for treating addiction in the most prestigious city in the United States. He was now a published author. He had become a columnist for *Medical Review of Reviews*, and now, he had become both a writer and an advertiser in the prominent medical magazine *The Modern Hospital* that focused on the administration and advancement of hospitals. He had published an opinion pamphlet in late 1916, "Federal Responsibility in the Solution of the Habit Forming Drug Problem," on the increasing dangers of narcotics. *The New York Times* considered his opinions to be news since Towns had become "an authority on anti-drug legislation." Towns had urged "that the Congress empower President Wilson to appoint a committee to investigate the whole subject of Federal responsibility in the solution of the habit forming drug problem."[1] Towns was a prominent, quoted authority on drugs.

"Care of Alcoholics in the Modern Hospital," December, 1916

His December, 1916 article was titled "Care of Alcoholics In the Modern Hospital" and carried the lengthy subtitle of "Employers, Police, Magistrates, and Social Agencies Must Help if Problem Is to Be Solved—Proper Medical Treatment Applied to the Cause Must Be Given." He claimed to have pioneered an "entirely new field of hospital work" while admitting not having been "a medical man, and never having had, in any way whatsoever, any connection or any experience with any other medical institution . . ."[2] Towns' personality seemed to provide the ability to turn the lack of experience and qualifications to what he considered to be an advantage of his background.

That temperament also allowed him the self-perception to criticize the medical profession, but then transform the criticism, as if his observations were effective, but bad-tasting, medicine containing a sweetener that made it taste good after all.

> It surprises me to note how little the drug and alcoholic patient is understood by the medical world as a whole. This is no reflection, however, on the medical profession.[3]

Towns continued his reflections to assert that the medical profession was not to blame.

> [T]here [was] nothing in their medical education to give them any knowledge whatsoever of this medical problem. I have never yet been able to overcome the surprises which have come to me in finding that my lack of knowledge of medicine has enabled me to establish so many precedents in connection with this work and in dealing with the various phases of this subject. It is part of my makeup to get at causes. It has never made any difference to me whether I was breaking a mule on a farm, struggling with some problem in an accounting house, or in a quandary over some difficulty that has arisen in my present work, no matter where I was or

Figure 15 - Ad for Towns Hospital that appeared in the December, 1916 *The Modern Hospital*

what I was doing, I have always wanted to know the whys and wherefores and to get at the

causes.[4]

Not only was he dealing with causes, his mission was to rid the country of "one of the

biggest economic wastes" through his campaign against alcoholism and addiction, which he

hoped would cause the medical community to give the subject the "serious consideration it

should have." He observed that when many hospitals experienced an increased number of

patients that had relapsed and returned, they did not change their methods, they only

increased the number of beds in the hospital wards. Such a futile approach had become a

severe problem that had gone on for a century.

It may surprise some of my readers when I make the statement that there is no more medical

intelligence being exercised today for the alcoholic - so far as I have been able to learn - than

there was one hundred years ago . . . The alcoholic is either penalized by a fine, reprimanded,

and dismissed with a threat, or disgraced through being subjected to a short term of

imprisonment among the lowest types of human beings . . . I cannot begin to tell how

strenuously I feel the pathos and the pity, and the ignorance and the stupid blundering

inefficiency, of this antiquated way of looking at the problem and of dealing with the alcoholic.

To set state and municipal authorities right as to the best ways and means of dealing with the

matter is, I feel, one of the most important undertakings my entire work has developed.[5]

Once again, Charles Towns had announced that he considered himself a best friend of

suffering alcoholics and of those professionals previously baffled about how to treat them.

Towns had arrived to end the pathos of almost barbaric practices of handling alcoholics. Through his pioneering work, which had not yet been fully appreciated by the world of medicine, wonderful changes could evolve for the betterment of all mankind if only the medical world opened their minds.

He returned to what have become, by now, familiar themes of how the effective medical remedy would return at last 75 percent of "worth while" patients back to their useful lives. He again stressed how his effective approach could be accomplished in "five days to one week," but there was an obstacle.

> [The] very medical men who are in charge of this work are not big enough or broad enough to realize the importance of the definite medical treatment and care of this type of patient. They are traveling along in the same old medical rut they have been following ever since medical history began.[6]

He repeated his call to save the effective employee from being removed from his job, and hoped that the state and municipal authorities would move to educate employers of their special responsibilities to their addicted employees. They needed to help employees to recover from the results of temptations that they should never have had to face in the first place. Now that a definite medical solution existed to the problem, it was high time the employer took advantage of what science had to offer for the good of everyone involved.

Towns concluded the article with "It can be done and it is going to be done, and I am going to do what I can to have it done."[7]

"Federal Responsibility in the Solution of the Habit-Forming Drug Problem."

This 22-page pamphlet has had only one remaining readable copy in the United States within the public domain.[8] One may surmise that Towns, in the years that followed the December, 1916 publication of this pamphlet, may have attempted to re-purchase all of the distributed copies so he could have them destroyed. His writing contained in this pamphlet revealed anger and frustration. His sympathy for addicts seems to have disappeared. Whereas he mainly addressed the medical community throughout most of his writing, the audience for this pamphlet was the U.S. Congress. He wanted their attention, and he wanted suppliers of illegal narcotics punished with as severe penalties as possible.

The pamphlet had a rather lengthy subtitle: "A Proposed Governmental Solution of the Habit-Forming Drug Question, Considered in Its Medical, Pharmacal and Sociological Phases and with Reference to Its State, National, and International Aspects; and Showing the Inadequacy of the Existing Laws on the Subject." As a preface to the pamphlet, Towns listed the specific amendments and revisions he proposed were necessary to make the Harrison Act a better law. However, as Congress never addressed any of these recommendations, Town's recommendations appear quite forgettable. Besides, the U.S. Treasury was to require no action by Congress to implement narcotic prohibition in the next three years.

The early pages of the pamphlet contained very little that was new. But then he began to make some unusual boasts. He wrote that "little or no cocaine evil" in the early days of his career existed and that heroin was "the worst drug curse of to-day, [which] was created and developed since he began his work."[9] He had made no such claim about heroin when he had written the "Concerning Heroin" article in the *Medical Review of Reviews* the previous June just six months before. He also wrote about himself in the third person when he claimed to have

been "the author of the Boylan law of New York State," which he claimed had been the model

for the Harrison Narcotic Act.[10] He repeated his warnings about the need to regulate the

syringe and to keep it an unknown device to as many as possible. Still, there was nothing

unprecedented or unusual about the proposals in his pamphlet until he once again insisted that

mankind would be better off if morphine, cocaine and heroin were no longer manufactured.

Whereas he had said that before, he had not insisted the patients experiencing agonizing pain

would be better off dead rather than risk becoming drug addicts.

Our own country and the whole world would be better off without such drugs. It would be

better for people to suffer untold agonies temporarily than to become afflicted with the drug

habit. Those who must have the drug to alleviate the pain caused by permanent illness or

injury—who must practically live on it—would be in the end much better off dead than to have

to deal with them as drug addicts. Considering the few human beings who are now taking the

drug for the last reason stated, and considering the great army of drug victims the illicit traffic in

such drugs has created, it is a fair question whether the alleviation of pain for the few is worth

the awful price paid for it by the curse to the many. My findings have shown that not more than

ten per cent of those afflicted with the drug habit are entitled to use it continuously because of

physical disability. This means that we are sacrificing ninety percent of those who could be well

and normal without the drug to alleviate the suffering of some few incurable persons.

The moral degeneracy, mental impairment and physical deterioration brought about by the

unnecessary use of these drugs make it impossible to calculate the harm and injury that have grown out of the illicit traffic in them. This traffic is filling our prisons, our insane asylums, our madhouses and our houses of correction, taxing them to their limits with grown men and women, and, saddest of all, with young boys and young women who have drifted into the lowest strata of life from the use of such drugs, none of these people knowing in the beginning what it all meant in the end.[11]

Towns continued to stress that he considered most drug users to be victims. However, if addicts could not get their drugs from legitimate sources, Towns noted they would turn to illegal dealers, which he wrote were equivalent to murderers. Because of the severity of their crimes, American law should be written to execute them. Society would be better off without such vermin.

There are two things we can do now. One of these is to restrict the medical practitioner in prescribing and administering these drugs. The other is to impose the heaviest penalty possible upon illicit drug traffic. The man who knowingly creates a drug habit should be put in the same class with the murderer or worse. Twenty years at hard labor should be the minimum penalty. I would like personally to see the same treatment meted out to such cold-blooded beings in the United States as would be meted out to them in China: make the punishment capital! A few heads would put an end to this damnable business—and the heads would be heads we could easily do without.[12]

Towns had written "The Future of Addict Legislation" in the *Medical Review of Reviews* during the very same month as this pamphlet, but without any of the punitive recommendations or claims that anyone would be better off dead. The reasons for him to have expressed such recommendations remain unexplained. But he was not yet done in expressing opinions in this pamphlet that he would not write again.

Charles Towns seemed to take a page out of King George III of England and proposed a stamp act. As he had insisted four years before in "The Peril of the Drug Habit" written in *The Century Magazine* in August of 1912, narcotics should become under a government monopoly internationally for both production and distribution. Stamps would be used to record shipments legally as they entered countries and buyers of the substances would be documented for every transaction related to their distribution.[13]

His faith in rational, incorruptible government seemed without limit. He concluded this pamphlet with a passion that Congress had the solution for narcotics within their grasp if only they would realize the crisis at hand.

> With the united wisdom of Congress applied to the matter, there can be no doubt that such an investigation as is proposed would lay the foundation for Federal legislation that would once and for all solve this monstrous problem.

> As a conclusion of this whole matter, I renew my suggestion that Congress empower the President to appoint a Committee of able men to investigate this whole subject in all its phases, making such appropriation for this purpose as in the wisdom of Congress may be necessary. Such action of Congress would mean not only a solution of this subject as far as the Federal Government is concerned; it would mean also a solution for the States. And it would establish a legislative, medical and sociological precedent that would give this country for the first time the

primacy it ought to have in asking other countries to join with us once and for all in terminating this evil—an evil which has now become not merely a series of isolated national problems but a united world problem.[14]

"Successful Medical Treatment in Chronic Alcoholism," January, 1917

The January, 1917 article in *The Modern Hospital* seemed to return him back to a less pugilistic character while continuing his practice of verbose titles: "Successful Medical Treatment in Chronic Alcoholism" was the banner accompanied by a subtitle of "An Outline of Practical Procedure as Developed in the Work of a Hospital for Drug and Alcoholic Addictions—Necessity of Intelligent Sociology in Solving the Alcoholic Problem." He wrote that the editor of *The Modern Hospital* had asked him to be more specific regarding the Towns Treatment, but before he began, he revealed something about himself.

> While I do not belong, and never expect to belong, to any humanitarian society or any prohibition organization, I here put myself on record as saying that I think that society, in one way or another, is wholly to blame for this alcoholic problem, and that it is directly responsible to those unfortunates who for any reason lose control of themselves from the use of alcoholic stimulants.[15]

For whatever reason, he had deemed it necessary to make clear that his assertions were from the medical arena, and not from a temperance or religious perspective. Towns believed addiction and alcoholism resulted not so much from sin as from temptation, ignorance, or

An Outline

of the

Regular Work

of the

CHARLES B. TOWNS HOSPITAL

for

Drug and Alcoholic Addiction

HOSPITAL HEADS and the medical profession generally do not fully realise the nature of the special work we are carrying out here. Our experience has been that they are not fully informed as to the definite hospital way in which our work is done. We feel they cannot, therefore, fully appreciate either the magnitude of our work or its individual importance as an institutional basis for dealing with the various phases of drug and alcoholic habit. On this account I want to outline here some of the details of our regular, every-day hospital work.

THIS HOSPITAL is open to all physicians. Any physician communicating with us in regard to a patient is always invited to bring his patient to us and remain in attendance at least while his patient is undergoing definite medical treatment. This is very generally the practice of physicians in nearby states, and quite frequently of those in even far distant parts of the country. Three days to a week is ample time to observe all of the definite medical treatment required in both drug and alcoholic cases.

IT HAS ALWAYS been a policy of this Hospital to preserve a careful bedside history of all cases under treatment, and it may interest you to know that we have nearly eight thousand such charts alphabetically arranged and filed for immediate reference.

AS THERE IS no secret medication in OUR treatment, and as the physician visiting his patient here has access to his patient's complete bedside record, the physician is able to follow intelligently every detail of the work from beginning to end. Physicians who make such observations soon realize that it is definite and important work, that can be carried out successfully only in an institutional way. Only those who are thoroughly familiar with the various types of addict patient, who have had ample opportunity for clinical observation in the treatment and care of such patients, and who can devote their time exclusively to the work, are in position to carry treatment to a successful issue. Treatment on any other plan will in most instances prove a failure, with no possible

Figure 16 - Page 1 of a two-page ad appearing in the January, 1917 *The Modern Hospital*

THE MODERN HOSPITAL—ADVERTISEMENTS

benefit to the patient and nothing but discredit to the physician. The effect of failure on the patient is especially unfortunate, for it effectually prejudices him against all future efforts in his behalf—and it discourages as well his family and friends in their efforts to help him.

EACH ADDICT CASE under treatment must be dealt with individually. There is no such thing as a medical mill through which the patient may be put and come out "cured" as a result of the process. Meeting the various abnormal conditions that nearly always grow out of such cases under treatment, both drug and alcoholic, is of extreme importance. In every instance any unfavorable condition must be avoided that might develop from lack of intimate knowledge of clinical detail in dealing with this special class of sick person. Only by the exercise of an exactly clinical technic and a skillful personal handling of the patient can a definite medical result be assured. When we have obtained this definite medical result in our work here, we feel that it is in most instances only the intelligent beginning of help for the patient. We are then in a position to determine the next best thing for the patient to do.

IN MOST INSTANCES some recuperative means should be resorted to, and, as this Hospital has no relation to or connection with any other institution, either directly or indirectly, and as practically nine-tenths of the patients who enter this Hospital come to us through their own physicians, there is no suggestion of any kind going beyond definite medical help made in any way to the patient without first having an understanding with his physician. Our policy of referring patients back to their physicians, with such recommendations, whether medical or sociological, as we know would be of value in the after-treatment of the patient has always been adhered to without exception. However, we find that, with few exceptions, in the case of this special type of patient, there is no form of treatment that will so quickly and successfully pull these patients together after successful medical elimination of their accumulated poison as the intelligent prescribing and administering of various features of hydro-, electro-, masso-, and mechano-therapy.

FOR THIS REASON this Hospital has equipped the most modern unit of its kind that has ever been established in this country. This special branch of the work is under the direction of two of the best medical men that we could find, who specialize in this special line of work. The results we are obtaining in this respect are remarkable. I consider this one of the most important developments of this Hospital's work since its organization. We are able to send a patient away from here within a period of from two to four weeks—unless his physical condition is a desperate one—in such shape that he, or she, is able to go back to his, or her, own environment prepared to take up the duties of life in the best possible condition. The advantage that comes to us through first scientifically unpoisoning these people is a marked one. We not only have, first, a physical advantage as far as the patient is concerned, but, second, we have in most cases a marked mental advantage as well. The usual methods of deprivation, salines, sweats, baths, and packs, in the end never bring about the definite physiological change that is indicated in the medical treatment of alcoholism and morphinism, and that always and invariably should be had.

WE ACCEPT NO PATIENT here for treatment without first having a full history from the physician. This means that we do not accept any patients except those who we think will be benefited by the treatment administered here. When the doctor knows beyond any question that it is up to him to determine what is to be done for his patient here, and the length of time the patient shall stay for treatment, and when he knows that his patient is going to be referred back to him beyond question, and that, if it is convenient to him, we want his personal co-operation while his patient is under our treatment, this class of work is placed on just as nearly a perfect institutional basis as it is possible to place it.

IT IS THE POLICY of this Hospital to make definite fee, payable in advance, which covers all hospital treatment of every sort. Every feature of this work is just as high-class and important as it is possible to make it. We avoid colonization and the long periods of stay, with the usual weekly charges which such a course nearly always incurs. Individual day and night nursing and exclusive accommodation en suite, with bath, private telephone, and individual personal service, may be had if desired. Where patients are fearful of publicity, they may enter the Hospital under assumed names, many patients coming here without even the Hospital staff knowing who they are, and, we assure you, with not the slightest curiosity to find out.

Descriptive matter of the work of this Hospital in all its details will be gladly sent to the heads of hospitals or to any practicing physician, and correspondence relative to the treatment of any particular case is invited.

THE CHARLES B. TOWNS HOSPITAL

for Drug and Alcoholic Addiction

293 Central Park West **NEW YORK CITY**

It is our plan to use a page in The Modern Hospital monthly, and from time to time we are going to bring to the reader's attention the different important features connected with this special line of work.

Figure 17 - Part two of a two page ad appearing in the January, 1917 *The Modern Hospital* stupidity. Most of the fault did not lie with individuals, but from a mistaken society that needed to change.

He relentlessly held to his belief that medical treatment was mandatory for the effective separation of an addict from his substance.

Medical treatment of a definite sort is absolutely required. It has been, and it still is, a struggle to get the physician to understand that deprivation never removes the cause of alcoholism, or the desire or craving for stimulants . . . This means that carrying out this work as I have been doing has eliminated the hazard of alcoholic insanity, and we all know that the chronic alcoholic has been the chief source of population of the asylums for the insane. And so far as the hazard of death is concerned, it should be interesting for the reader to know that for the first twelve years of this work . . . we did not have a single death.[16]

Towns then went on to explain the three basic ingredients of the treatment to be tincture of belladonna, fluid extract of xanthoxylum, and fluid extract of hyoscyamus. He asserted these substances were commonly found at the corner drugstore. But without going into great detail regarding his methodology at this time, he had strong advice for the practicing physician in recognizing delirium tremens.

The physician who is not thoroughly familiar with the alcoholic would find it most difficult to differentiate between the alcoholic delirium and the belladonna delirium. He may distinguish between them by the fact that the alcoholic delirium is always preceded by extreme tremor, while belladonna delirium is not.[17]

Towns believed that delirium tremens could be avoided in almost all cases and that a common practice of using physical restraints for such patients was a mark of just how cruelly alcoholics had been handled.

No man objects to the use of physical restraint in a case of delirium tremens more than I, and in my opinion, it shows medical ignorance and cowardice when it is done.[18]

Much of the balance of the article concerned the length of the Towns Treatment and the nature of sedation that might be employed depending upon the health and evaluation of the patient. (The details of the treatment will be relayed in much greater detail in chapter 12 to follow).

He strongly concluded the January, 1917 article with some arguments that he never seemed to mind repeating. First, he expressed his contempt for sanitariums in favor of what he called "alcoholic clearing houses" and stressed once more how important employment was to the recovery of the patient.

I hope to see the time when each one of our big hospitals will have an alcoholic clearing house - not an alcoholic boarding house. When this work is taken up in this positive, definite way, the authorities are going to dispose finally of the alcoholic in one way or another . . . A sociological department should see that such a man either gets back his old job after his treatment is completed, or that some other employment is provided for him. If the man is physically able to work and won't work, he should be made to work by the state and municipal authorities.[19]

He once again repeated the theme that the education of physicians would save the lives of alcoholics.

> There are more fatalities in alcoholic wards from alcoholic delirium in pneumonia than from pneumonia itself. Unless physicians have a thorough and perfect knowledge of dealing with the alcoholic, ninety-nine chronic alcoholic patients who develop pneumonia will die of delirium tremens if they do not die of pneumonia. To organize this work as it should be organized would lessen the usual number of such cases in these institutions about 75 percent.[20]

Then he concluded with his insistence that just the detoxification of most alcoholics was futile and would only lead to their eventual relapse.

> To sum up, the situation as far as we have gone means this—that no alcoholic has a fair chance when he is simply sobered up. Unless something medically definite is done for the chronic alcoholic, his end is either the madhouse or the morgue . . . The alcoholic is humiliated, punished, and still further degraded, and society is doing everything it possibly can to destroy him utterly. This is all wrong.[21]

"The Sociological Aspect of the Treatment of Alcoholism," February, 1917

The third and concluding article of this series appeared in *The Modern Hospital* in the February, 1917 issue with the title "The Sociological Aspect of the Treatment of Alcoholism" with the additional lengthy subtitle of "Fallacy of the Belief That Alcoholism is Hereditary—Help

Effective Only for the Man Who Wants to Be Helped—Tobacco an Unfavorable Factor." He

began the article by lambasting the idea that alcoholism was a disease.

> Medical men have been largely responsible for making the alcoholic believe that alcoholism is a
>
> disease. Stop and think for a moment and you will see how absolutely absurd that is![22]

He had moved on from his own previous writings in June of 1912 when in "Help For the

Hard Drinker" in *The Century Magazine* when he had written "victims of this serious disease"

and "the definite disease of alcoholism." No record has yet been found that has provided a

record of Towns reconciling his contradictions. He continued to write how alcohol had poisoned

the patient, and the only solution was the medical unpoisoning of the victim. If the patient had

relapsed and was present again needing hospitalization, this failure was not because his

previous recovery visit did not work. Towns had another explanation.

> I can show from our case records and clinical notes that in the cases in which such a patient
>
> through weakness relapses into taking stimulants, he never charges that the source of his
>
> weakness was a craving for them. The cause may have been psychic - business troubles, a
>
> quarrel with his wife or what not!—but it was not alcoholic craving as such.[23]

Next he made an observation that can often be heard to this day: "There is no such

thing as 'curing' a case of alcoholism." However, he also gave himself the majority of the credit

for first giving this observation to the world.[24] He repeated his assertion that the most difficult

alcoholic cases almost always involved the "vagrant rich" or the "vagrant poor," while lack of

Figure 18 - Towns Hospital ad that appeared in the February, 1917 The Modern Hospital

occupation was the great destroyer of men. Interestingly enough, he also repeated the

assertion he had made the previous month regarding his background.

I am not a member of any organization of any kind, either religious or otherwise, that stands for

prohibition. For that reason I am able to express myself as freely as I please. So I now want to

put myself on record as saying the world would be better off if there was never another drop of

alcoholic stimulant made, sold, administered or taken.[25]

He never explained why he thought that being a member of a religion would have

restricted his freedom to express himself. He then appeared to enlarge the movement towards

prohibition in the United States as if it included the rest of the world.

It looks as if we are going to have world-wide prohibition; but unfortunately, as conditions now

exist, the problem of dealing with the now-alcoholic is not going to be solved merely by

"prohibition." He is going to seek harmful stimulants in some way.[26]

He firmly believed that while progress might be slow in ridding the country of this

menace of alcohol, that education was the eventual answer for creation of men of a "better

class" that would recognize the foolishness of the past.

Start a campaign of education—not one of abuse, not one of penalization, not one that is going

to create resentment, but a campaign of enlightenment. Then you are going to solve the

problem among the better class of working men.[27]

He repeated his view that because state and municipal authorities were to blame for allowing alcohol to become such a public menace, laws should be passed which would "for the first time require them to deal with this subject intelligently." What Towns had previously called "alcoholic clearing-houses" should become a matter-of-fact reality in most any large municipality. Once and for all, if society were willing to leave their prejudices against the alcoholic behind and follow Towns' leadership, the insanity surrounding this historical enigma would slowly disappear. But this solution would take time and come from the next generation that would not think of poisoning their bodies with foreign substances and lead clean lives.

Any progress toward real result on this subject is going to come from the younger class of human beings who do not know what the taste of an alcoholic drink means or personally what "drunk" means. I would like to see as part of the curriculum of every public and private school in this country, enforced study of what drugs, alcohol, and tobacco really mean in their effects on the human system . . . Clean men and women who believe in the clean things of life should be the only ones eligible to teach such principles. Not until such education has been given will there be any real progress made in removing this curse.[28]

Towns had much faith that Federal legislation contained the solution to American alcoholism. Nevertheless, the Federal Government had been abusing alcoholics through ignorance too. No one had been treated worse than the alcoholic American soldier.

Figure 19 - Part I, Page 1 of *The Modern Hospital* ad that began in March, 1917, which covered three months.

as capacity to inspire enthusiasm, interest in the personal welfare of those who come under his direction, and so on.

This is practically outdoor work, as it is done in our roof establishment, which is open as a roof garden in the summer and inclosed as a properly ventilated solarium in the winter. It overlooks Central Park and a great stretch of the city north and south, and the whole effect of the place is to interest and inspire those who resort to it. At the same time the whole area of Central Park is at our disposal, and we make good use of it as a recreation ground for those whose progress makes such a course advisable and possible.

NO SECRETS FROM PROFESSION

I wish every medical practitioner would understand that this hospital has no policy of secrecy about treatment and so on. I wish I could make him know without doubt that, when he visits us or brings or sends his patient here for treatment, all our hospital facilities are at his disposal and that his patient is just as accessible to him as he is to the resident staff physician in whose charge he may be.

We have no secrets about medical treatment or about anything else that is professional matter, and everything we do is done in the spirit of absolute straight-out co-operation with the visiting doctor who brings his patient here or who sends his patient to us. Where the physician cannot come with his patient for treatment, we are glad to send full and frequent reports by mail or wire, as directed—every day if so desired.

It must be of interest to medical men to know that at least three-fourths of the patients who come to us come through physicians, either directly or indirectly, and that during the past three years alone—not taking into account the thousands so directed to us before that time—we received nearly three thousand (3,000) patients (of whom about one-fourth were women) directly through sixteen hundred (1,600) physicians.

DEALING WITH THE MEDICAL MAN

I have proved beyond any and all question of doubt that it pays to deal fairly and squarely with the medical man and with his patient, upholding always the highest principles of medical ethics, and establishing it as an unquestionable fact that no medical man has to speculate as to what he may expect from this institution when he brings a patient here for treatment or refers a patient to us for that purpose.

This Hospital has no connection of any kind whatsoever with any other institution, and does not undertake to refer patients to other institutions for after-treatment and care. No member of the medical profession has any financial interest in the Hospital, and the medical men who give it their valued co-operation as consultants do so without pecuniary consideration of any kind whatsoever. The Hospital splits no fees, pays no commissions, and divides no profits. It stands straight with the profession and the world, and those medical men who know the Hospital most intimately are, of all men, most absolutely convinced that this is so.

PATIENT BACK TO PHYSICIAN

In conclusion: I have tried to make just as plain as I can make them these several principles —that this Hospital is at the disposal of the medical profession; that it employs no secret remedies; that it has no other object but to do the best it can medically for the patient and professionally for the patient's physician; that it means always to bring the physician into closer and more permanent relationship with his patient.

When our work is done, we return the patient to the care of the medical practitioner, so that the advantage of such a relationship may accrue to the patient through the physician's further medical counsel and aid. If you will come and visit us, or if you will write us, I believe we can show you that what I have here laid down as governing principles are actually carried out in our everyday work as a genuine modern hospital standard of practice.

OUR EXPERIENCE AT YOUR SERVICE

I regret that more physicians are not personally acquainted with us. Not only do I now, as always, extend the heartiest invitation to the profession to visit the institution and see it for themselves, but I would also like them to know that, beyond the matter of acquainting them with our hospital work, I would be glad personally to give them any information I can that would be of interest or value, whether their patient enters this Hospital or not.

My experience in this work has in many instances enabled me to render service by suggestion as to the best course to pursue in a given case, and there is no obligation whatsoever on any physician whom I may be able to serve in this way. I am glad to be of what service I can—be that service great or small.

The CHARLES B. TOWNS HOSPITAL
293 Central Park, West, NEW YORK CITY

This is the third of a series of three advertisements to appear consecutively in THE MODERN HOSPITAL describing in detail the work of the Charles B. Towns Hospital for Drug and Alcoholic Addictions. Medical reprints and booklets about the hospital mailed upon request.

Figure 20 - Part I, page 2 of *The Modern Hospital* ad that began in March, 1917, which covered three months.

a CLEARING HOUSE *for* ALCOHOLIC *and* DRUG CASES

The Work of the Charles B. Towns Hospital—

What it does for the Patient—

How it cooperates with the Medical Practitioner and with the Hospital in the Treatment of Patients of Addict Type.

By CHARLES B. TOWNS, CHARLES B. TOWNS HOSPITAL, NEW YORK CITY

PART II

UNUSUAL HOSPITAL FACILITIES

First of all, to give you some idea of the unusual situation of this Hospital and of the advantages it has for carrying on a helpful personal work for its patients, let me point out that the Hospital building itself faces Central Park, overlooking it at its highest point, with the fashionable residence section of Fifth Avenue in the distance. There is no more beautiful view of the Park to be had anywhere. There is a park entrance immediately at our door, and we are within two minutes' walk of the great Croton Reservoir, which has a one and three-fourths miles' walk around it, while the Drive and Bridle Path are right in front of us.

The Metropolitan Museum of Art is within sight, and can be reached by a ten minutes' walk across the Park. The American Museum of Natural History stands on the same street with ourselves (Central Park West), and is only a few blocks away. Within a ten minutes' walk is Riverside Drive and the Hudson River. Subway, elevated, and street car lines are at hand to carry one quickly to the centers of amusement and business, uptown and downtown, respectively. I would not exchange the situation of this hospital or its equipment and facilities for those of any other institution that I know anything about, city or country.

RESIDENT AND CONSULTING STAFF

The Hospital building itself is a modern apartment house of the best New York City type, prac-

tically reconstructed for its present purpose. The work of reconstruction was done under the supervision of specialists, and has been approved by the New York City Building, Fire, and Health Departments after rigid inspection.

A feature of the structure as it now stands is a roof garden and solarium, which provide open-air recreation the year around, being open and shaded in summer and inclosed and warmed in winter. The view of the Park from this point, or from our front windows, is unexcelled, and affords an interesting outlook every day of every season in the year.

The Hospital work is directed by a staff of five physicians, who are resident in the house or continuously in attendance, and is carried out under the most exacting standards of modern hospital practice. The consulting staff is composed of a group of practitioners known to the medical profession throughout the country.

A complete bedside history of every case is carefully kept, with such clinical notes and observations as may assist both our staff and the patient's own physician in their study of the case in its sociological relations, as well as its solely medical aspects.

PATIENT'S PHYSICIAN WELCOME

All doctor's orders are written, and there is a careful clinical checking up of each case every day. As there are no secret remedies employed in our treatment, the physician, when visiting his patient, is thus in a position to follow the patient's treat-

Figure 21 - Part II, Page 1 of *The Modern Hospital* ad, which appeared in April, 1917.

THE MODERN HOSPITAL—ADVERTISEMENTS 77

DESTRUCTIVENESS OF IDLENESS

One of the worst features of these colonizing resorts is the idleness in which the patient passes his days and the resultant boredom that besets him. Truly it is "enough to drive a man to drink!" But, on the other hand, always remember that you can't keep in an institution for any length of time a man who has had definite, medical treatment for a habit or addiction. He declares he is losing time. He wants to begin life over again, to get back to work, to do something! And he is right. A man who has been freed from a habit or addiction and is now able to work, can work, and wants to work, should have employment at the earliest possible day. Long and enforced periods of idleness are destructive. The question of colonization resolves itself down to this: that commitments to institutions, long periods of stay, and indiscriminate colonization should be limited in application only to those who show themselves to be defective or who, for one reason or another, have become helpless and hopeless human derelicts.

CHANGE OF ATTITUDE NEEDED

There must be a marked reform in the general attitude of those who are in any way whatsoever attempting to deal with this type of patient. Some day the authorities and all others concerned in the matter are going to wake up to the fact that the usual commitment methods of dealing with drug and alcoholic patients are all wrong. I found early in my development of work for the addict type of patient that it was not a sanatorium work in any sense of the word, but that it was essentially a hospital work.

I have sometimes been amused to note certain of the old type of sanatoriums that accept alcoholic patients, trying to pattern after my work simply by calling their institutions "hospitals" instead of "sanatoriums," when, as a matter of fact, they still pursue the old sanatorium methods, and the atmosphere of their places remains today the same old atmosphere of yesterday. More than a change of name is needed. What is needed is a change from policy to principle!

In the course of my fifteen years of specialized experience, I have been able to eliminate practically all the disadvantages that formerly marked the treatment and care of this type of patient. I have established an intelligent classification of addict types as the basis of a comprehensive plan of treatment—not only medical, but moral and mental as well. I have thus been able to "cut out" most of the hazards which have grown out of the lack of definite institutional treatment for and care of patients of alcoholic and drug type.

MAKING MEDICAL HISTORY

From the very beginning of this work we have had to establish an entirely new precedent—institutional, medical, and sociological—for there was none we could find to guide us; and from that day to this we have had to carry on an educational campaign, not only for the enlightenment of the lay world, but for the information of the medical world as well.

The brief period of time in which we have found it not only possible, but actually necessary, to get definite medical results, was for a long time prejudicial to our work. Physicians, relatives, friends, and patients themselves could not believe it possible to get definite and satisfactory medical results within so short a time; and many of them —the doctors especially—still seem to think so in spite of all demonstrated proof.

Alcoholic and drug patients who had been accustomed to long periods of stay in institutions, but who nevertheless had not been benefited by these long periods of residence, considered it worse than useless to come to a place where the treatment was in general limited to a few days, or at most a few weeks, while relatives and interested friends thought it sheer folly to send the patient to a hospital where a procedure of such brevity was carried out.

DEVELOPMENT ON PRINCIPLE

From the beginning, however, I have adhered strictly to my principle and have never deviated from it. So, from a modest beginning, my work has developed until I now have the best situated hospital and the most adequately equipped institution that I know of to carry on a work such as ours.

The plant and equipment of the hospital comprises every feature that can possibly be of any value or profit or worth in doing anything and everything whatsoever for such patients of this type as we accept—for, remember that we accept only those patients whom we are reasonably certain we can help.

The patient who has "stayed put" has established this undertaking and assured its success. We consider the relapsed patient a liability, and for that reason we select our patients carefully. Consequently we have only a small percentage of relapses. We are trying to create assets of permanent character—and the man we have helped to "make good" permanently is the only man to whom we can "point with pride."

The CHARLES B. TOWNS HOSPITAL

NEW YORK CITY

This is the first of a series of three advertisements to appear consecutively in THE MODERN HOSPITAL describing in detail the work of the Charles B. Towns Hospital for Drug and Alcoholic Addictions. Medical reprints and booklets about the hospital on request.

Figure 22 - Part II, Page 2 of *The Modern Hospital* ad, which appeared in April, 1917.

a CLEARING HOUSE for ALCOHOLIC and DRUG CASES

The Work of the Charles B. Towns Hospital— What it does for the Patient—

How it cooperates with the Medical Practitioner and with the Hospital in the Treatment of Patients of Addict Type.

By CHARLES B. TOWNS, CHARLES B. TOWNS HOSPITAL, NEW YORK CITY

PART III

COMPLETE PHYSICAL DEPARTMENT

Now, I want to include in what I have said about the details of our hospital work a few words on the work of what I consider to be one of its most important departments. This is the work of our Physical Department, in which the results accomplished by definite medical treatment in the hospital are re-enforced and "clinched," as it were, by hydro-electric therapy and other forms of physical therapeutics.

The establishment was planned and equipped in advisement with the best medical authorities in this field and has been declared by competent authorities who have inspected it to be the most complete unit of its kind, so far as known, either in this country or abroad. It offers facilities for the administration of every approved form of hydro-, electro-, masso-, and mechano-therapy.

The hydriatic apparatus is that which was shown at the Panama-Pacific Exposition by the largest manufacturers in the world of such equipment and which was awarded the gold medal. This has been supplemented by electrical and mechanical equipment furnished by one of the best known houses in this country, so that the department is as completely equipped as scientific knowledge and the progress of invention can make it.

NO CONTACT WITH HOSPITAL WORK

The Physical Department is under the special medical direction of two medical practitioners of long experience in this field. One of them has for many years been associated with the leading physiologic therapeutist in New York city and the other has for a number of years been connected with one of the largest institutions of this kind in the world.

Our specialists are thus in a position to advise with the medical practitioner who sends a patient to us as to the best course to be pursued in the treatment of his patient, and are in every way competent to do the best that can be done, not alone for patients of the type treated here, but for anyone suffering from chronic ailments. As the patients of this department do not come in contact with our regular hospital work, the department's facilities are available to anyone suffering from diseases of chronic character who may come to us as an ambulant patient.

WORK DESCRIBED IN BOOKLET

It is needless to say that the attendants of this department have been carefully selected and that they are exceptionally competent to administer the treatment prescribed by the medical staff. If there is anything further required to make this department absolutely competent and self-contained, we do not know what it is, and shall be glad to learn of it. We have taken professional advice in the matter, and have thoroughly sifted the whole known field of means and methods for the administration of physical therapy for the best to be had, and have then installed it.

We have prepared a special booklet covering this branch of our work, and would be glad to send it to you on request. It will inform you thoroughly as to what we are doing in this department, and will, we believe, convince you of the thorough scientific way in which we are doing it.

OUTDOOR EXERCISE AND RECREATION

To reinforce the efficiency of the Physical Department, a portion of the establishment on the roof has been set apart for health culture under the general direction of an able physical culturist connected with one of the best known athletic clubs in the country. The actual work with the patient is carried out by a competent physical director, chosen not only for his professional ability, but also for personal characteristics such

Figure 23 - Part III, Page 1 of *The Modern Hospital* ad. This part appeared in May, 1917.

ment in every detail as recorded by a study of the bedside chart and the staff doctor's orders.

The utmost care is given to diet, but the diet provided is of a sort dictated by long experience and common sense rather than over-insistence on any ideas of "scientific nutrition." All meals are served in the patients' rooms and every care is taken to make the service as inviting as possible.

Patients are afforded the utmost privacy. They are secluded almost to the point of isolation, and during their stay come in contact only with their physician, nurse, and attendant, and are visited by such of their friends as they may desire to see—though needless sociability that would unduly distract or disquiet the patient is discouraged or even forbidden. The patient's presence in the Hospital is thus known only to a few, and the Hospital has no desire whatsoever to discover the identity of those who (as sometimes happens) may choose to enter the institution under assumed names.

"INSTITUTIONALISM" BANISHED

Every effort is made—and, be it said, with success—to banish all taint of institutionalism from the Hospital and to maintain for it the character of a well-conducted club or a hotel of exclusive character. Gratuities to attendants are forbidden, and it will not be found necessary to dispense "tips" to secure whole-hearted service from every one connected with the establishment.

The accommodations of the Hospital are varied, so that arrangements may be made according to the means of the patient or as demanded by his personal tastes, however exclusive these may be. A number of suites with private bath, extension telephone at bedside, and individual nurse are provided and may be had at prices proportionate to the character of their accommodation.

On the other hand, the patient of moderate means can always be accommodated; this only, however, after our advisement with his physician

in regard to the matter and on his physician's recommendation. But, rich or poor, well-to-do or of moderate means, medical treatment and hospital service are wholly and unreservedly the same for all.

ONE FEE COVERS ALL CHARGES

The definite character of our medical treatment and the known period of time in which the definite results of medication are obtained make it possible to make a flat and all-inclusive fee for the Hospital work, so that the expense to be incurred is ascertainable in advance, and thus may be controlled by the patient or his sponsors. This fee covers all charges, with no "extras" of any kind whatsoever.

When the patient leaves this Hospital he is not confronted by a bill of extras long enough to remind him of a summer resort experience, where everything was "extra," from calling for a pitcher of ice-water to saying "good morning" to his waiter at the breakfast table. As stated, there is no tipping permitted here—every service is cheerfully done without the everlasting hand out for a gratuity. There is one, but one and *only* one, fee to pay, and it covers everything in treatment, entertainment, and attendance.

ADVANTAGES OF "FLAT FEE" PLAN

The charge for institutional treatment in the Physical Department, following medical treatment in Hospital, will of course vary with the length of stay, depending on the requirements of each case; but these requirements and the length of the patient's stay for treatment by physical therapy are invariably determined in counsel with the patient's physician.

As there can be no profit to the Hospital in prolonging a patient's residence beyond the period of medical treatment and adequate physical recuperation, the advantages of the Hospital's "flat fee" system must be apparent.

The CHARLES B. TOWNS HOSPITAL

NEW YORK CITY

This is the second of a series of three advertisements to appear consecutively in THE MODERN HOSPITAL describing in detail the work of the Charles B. Towns Hospital for Drug and Alcoholic Addictions. Medical reprints and booklets about the hospital mailed upon request.

Figure 24 Part III, Page 2 of *The Modern Hospital* ad. This part appeared in May, 1917

I cannot conclude this article without paying my respects to the Federal Government in connection with this subject. I have been in the position to observe the treatment accorded soldiers and sailors who have for any reason lost self-control from drink and drugs. A more heartless, cold-blooded, unreasonable lot for human beings never existed than in that dealt out as treatment by a system of court-martial! Every step in such investigations is apparently taken with a view to destroy the man instead of to save him . . . If these unfortunates had the treatment and care that should be given them, if there could be a campaign of education among the men enlisted in the army and navy, what a difference there would be![29]

Education was the answer! He had provided a textbook when he wrote *Habits That Handicap*. One can imagine that he considered himself qualified to teach his solution at any university that included clean living as a desirable part of their curriculum.

Though he had concluded writing articles for *The Modern Hospital*, he continued advertising in the medical publication. He was among the very few, if not the only, advertisers that paid for two-page ads, which tell a story all by themselves.

His final ad placed in *The Modern Hospital* magazine in June, 1917 contained some of the most fascinating numbers that Towns ever claimed in any of his ads or writings. The June ad featured Towns Hospital as having treated over a thousand patients a year (over 80 a month). He proclaimed he had patient referrals from 1,600 physicians and hospital officers some of which were located in Europe and Latin America. One fourth of his patients he wrote were women. In this ad, he also claimed that Towns Hospital had nine physicians as residents and

Figure 25 - The Towns Hospital *The Modern Hospital* ad for June, 1917.

Figure 26 - The American Journal of The Medical Sciences Ad by Towns Hospital in the December 6, 1917 issue

consultants. At no other time in his career were numbers like these so proudly proclaimed. The year 1917 was truly at the peak of Charles Towns' career.

His confidence was never greater than during this year, which led him to make an extraordinary assertion in an ad in *The American Journal of The Medical Sciences* within the December 6, 1917 issue. Any alcohol or drug user was eventually going to require medical treatment. The question was not an "if;" the question was a "when." The only chance for "restoration" of these wayward souls was through a definite medical treatment. In this ad to attract physicians, he appeared to beg them to let him "know your drug and alcohol problems. Their relation to permanent insanity is much closer and more intimate than many realize." Thus, Towns lost any distinction between alcohol and drugs—there was no such thing as long-term recreational use of any of these substances. The prestigious magazine in which he published the ad thought it to be appropriate for publication in their magazine. Towns may not have considered himself a missionary, but he was surely on a mission that appeared entirely appropriate to the upcoming era of alcohol and drug prohibition.

11) *Medical Review of Reviews* August 1917 – April 1918

"The Necessity of Definite Medical Result in The Treatment of Alcoholic Addiction," Part 1, August, 1917

The August, 1917 article in *Medical Review of Reviews* began with an air of self-congratulation and reflected that Towns' science had evolved through times of discovery and times of war. He implied that there was more to recovery from addiction than simply being "unpoisoned" over a few days and sent back to home and work as completely healed. The title of the article was "The Necessity of Definite Medical Result in the Treatment of Drug and Alcoholic Addiction" with the rather lengthy subtitle of "Medical Treatment Necessary to Procure Obliteration of Craving but Must be Followed by Intelligent Sociological Effect to Secure Mental Attitude." He had congratulated himself with regards to how two of his articles, both of which were printed in three parts, had "aroused a good deal of interest and inquiry."[1] These two sets of articles had appeared in *Medical Review of Reviews* in the first three months of 1917 (reviewed in Chapter 9) and *The Modern Hospital* from December, 1916 through February, 1917 (reviewed in Chapter 10). He was very gratified with the responses to these two sets of articles though he did not include any specific quotations or any names of any correspondents. One can suppose, as with so much else regarding Towns, that we simply were to take his word for it.

The successful medical treatment of alcoholism, drug addiction, and tobacco habit is exclusively an institutional work of highly specialized character. This has been my ever-growing conviction for a long time. I have hesitated to express it too often or too emphatically, because I am conducting an institutional work of exactly that character! But my view has lately been

confirmed by the results of two series of articles contributed by me to professional journals.

These articles have aroused a good deal of interest and inquiry . . . So I believe it will be a good

thing if at this time I go further into this subject in a sociological, or perhaps better, medico-

social way as related to the doctor and his patient. My recent correspondence certainly

indicates it as being much needed.[2]

He congratulated himself for his hesitation! Any reluctance for Towns to express his

opinion on alcoholism or drugs may come as large of a surprise as when he was called "the

humblest man from Georgia" by Macfarlane back in 1913.[3] Rarely had he seemed to hesitate or

be concerned with how his opinions may have hurt others. Now, however, times had changed.

While Towns continued to include drugs within his titles and subtitles, he began to reduce his

focus on opium, morphine, cocaine, and heroin in comparison to his past writings. His

advertising and his articles were becoming much more centered around alcoholism because the

changing business climate demanded it. Drug addicts were being perceived as being much more

desperate for their substances, and therefore viewed as dangerous and undesirable. Most

doctors and druggists, rather than risk law enforcement officers invading their practices, were

increasingly avoiding addicts altogether. Many addicts already had been driven to the

"underworld." Soon such perceived dangers of drug addicts, being from dark places where the

lower classes lived, would lead Towns Hospital to avoid featuring its history of treating addicts

at the prestigious Central Park West address. Such a claim would have been bad for the

neighborhood and, therefore, bad for business.

Towns had also been heavily quoted in an article that appeared weekly magazine *The Literary Digest* on June 19, 1917. It was titled "The War and the Dope Habit" and added to the fearful and serious mood of the times.

That the war has resulted in a tremendous and unnecessary increase in the use of habit-forming drugs is the opinion of Mr. Charles B. Towns of New York . . . According to Mr. Towns, who is an expert on the phenomena and alleviation of the drug habits, the great need in this country at the present moment is the appointment of a committee to investigate this whole matter . . . To protect our soldiers from the insidious evil that is doing its work abroad. [Towns] hopes to bring forcefully to the attention of President Wilson certain facts concerning the growth of the drug habit among the troops in Europe . . . "With the united wisdom of Congress applied to the matter there can be no doubt that such an investigation as I have in mind would lay the foundation for Federal legislation that would once and for all solve this monstrous problem . . . [Federal action] would establish a legislative, medical and sociological precedent that would give this country for the first time the primacy it ought to have in asking other countries to join with us once and for all in terminating this evil—an evil which has now become not merely a series of isolated national problems, but a united world-problem."[4]

Such rhetoric increasingly scared people in a time of war when the Germans already had been accused of attempting to sabotage the will of their enemies by hooking large segments of their populations on drugs.

Press stories circulated about drugs being smuggled into U.S. Army training centers by Germans and about Germans 'exporting drugs in toothpaste and patent medicines in order to hook innocent citizens of other countries on drugs.'[5]

Vague warnings of danger of national enslavement by drugs, blended with fuzzy notions about spies, saboteurs, and an imminent German invasion of the New World - and suddenly the harmless, pitied victim of the drug habit emerged as the menacing dope fiend, tool of German malevolence. The campaign to reduce trafficking in drugs rapidly picked up overtones of patriotic fervor.[6]

Towns needed to change with the times. So he claimed that he had been dealing with alcoholics for "nearly twenty years" in his *Medical Review of Review* article, despite the fact he had arrived in New York only sixteen years earlier as a partner in a brokerage firm, and may have treated his first opium volunteer as little as thirteen years before. He had journeyed to China to perfect his use of belladonna just nine years before in 1908 when his mission was to treat 4,000 opium addicts there. His opium solution had built Towns Hospital and earned him his reputation. Treating alcoholics had been only an afterthought following his return to the United States in 1909. Regardless of these facts, he would rather have any doubter heed his word, and disregard petty details. He had a much bigger picture in mind!

Part of that big picture included the difficulty of determining if a chronic alcoholic could recover, and consequently was worth treating.

But whether a chronic alcoholic is an 'incurable' is an individual question that cannot be decided until the man has been relieved medically of the accumulated toxins that perpetuate his physical craving, and his brain cleared up so that he can think straight and act with resolution. You can't tell whether he had either mind or will left until this is done, so no case of chronic alcoholism should ever be pronounced 'incurable' until the man has had definite medical treatment.[7]

He described how many alcoholics became hooked by gradually increasing their intake, at what soon became decreasing intervals, until they were trapped.

[He starts] taking more as the need grows greater, physically unable to tolerate the increase and wondering why he 'can't stand to carry what he used to carry easily'—and then the climax when he can't do without it! Any man who can't keep his promises, to himself or to another, not to drink, will develop chronic alcoholism sooner or later. *And any man who can't do without his drink is a chronic alcoholic.*[8]

Towns then went on to assert that one needed to get to the real causes of a man's drinking. There was a need to discover if there was any hope of undoing the mental causes that led the man to become an alcoholic in the first place. According to him, however, this was a matter of "human arithmetic."

Now, after all is said that can be said about 'saving the man' and all that sort of thing—whether it be religion or ethics or philosophy or humanitarianism is nothing to me—the matter of what you can do for a drug or alcoholic addict boils itself down to a matter of human arithmetic. The 'saving' of the drug addict or alcoholic is generally nothing more nor less than a problem in personal equation, with birth and bringing up and habit and character and occupation and achievement as the factors. And the problem is seldom a simple one![9]

So he desired to learn the facts about his patient, and having acquired that knowledge, Towns figured the problem then "resolves itself into a simple process of addition and subtraction." He then went on to outline a pragmatic methodology that cannot be ascribed to anyone else.

Reduced to its simplest terms and disclaiming all endeavor in the man's behalf that could be called 'religious' in the sense of super-natural aid and so on, the problem consists in investigating the man's record, looking ahead to the man's future, examining the man himself, setting down his positive characteristics and personal achievements on the one hand and his negative disabilities and personal do-nothingness on the other, adding them up, striking off the difference between them and sizing up the index afforded by the remainder . . . Now when you come to gather up your forces to help save a human being from the ultimate hell either of drug addiction or alcoholism pursued to its logical conclusion, you have a job on your hands that not only demands all the medical and other therapeutic aid you can find for him, but it makes some claim upon your heart—or at any rate demands some notice from it. And the hardest part of the whole job of dealing with the man—or the woman—who is losing out from drink or drugs is fairly and squarely and honestly to answer the question: *After we straighten up the physical man and straighten out the crooked mind, what will we have to build on for the future?*[10]

To a discerning mind, does the above logic resolve "itself into a simple process of addition and subtraction?" Rather, do not his methods above involve a mystery of dealing with, however, a "crooked mind" was defined? Rather than simple logic, was not a lot of substantial guesswork and emotional sensitivity required? Just two years before he had written in his book *Habits That Handicap* that anyone endeavoring to help an alcoholic "will find himself instantly and seriously handicapped if he puts himself in intimate personal relationship with his patient."[11] Arithmetic or not, and despite his claim of only pursuing facts, he now wrote that an "intimate personal relationship" with each patient was required to deal effectively with his alcoholism. He felt that he had to learn the patient's personal history to learn of the causes that made him drink. If possible, the patient's family and doctor needed to be consulted and their information analyzed. Furthermore, he believed there were critical differences present between the alcoholic and the addict.

> [A]lcoholic addiction has its origin in some sort of personal disappointment, social, domestic, commercial or other, whereas drug addiction for the most part originates in a siege of sickness, the burden of responsibility or despair of fatigue. Both of these conclusions the doctor's testimony will 'clinch,' and the indication of what to do for the man or woman becomes correspondingly plain.[12]

The qualifications for the physician or "qualified worker" in dealing with these cases of addiction continued to demand special characteristics and personality.

[The] worker has to combine the personal qualifications of doctor, lawyer, and father confessor—and often bosom friend—to get to the bottom of the sad, bad business. The doctor who has won his patient's personal confidence[Y] as well as his confidence in the doctor's professional skill is ideally placed to handle this type of case most successfully.[13]

Towns wanted the physician to proceed with a clinical methodology and proven deductive techniques derived from his years of experience. Sympathy, however, was rarely effective, might be counterproductive. Persistence, patience, and common sense were considered essential. If the final consequences of the addict's ways were made clear, the common sense of the patient would lead to change.

But this is not to say that he is to be treated by holding his hand or coddling him or even praying over him—though I have no objection to any one praying for him. What he more often needs as 'treatment,' following mere medication to unpoison him and get him back to something like a normal physiological creature, is to bring him straight upstanding by a 'mental kick,' show him how he is harming himself, and bringing him to see where he is bound to land if he keeps on.[14]

He concluded the August article with a challenge to the reader to emphasize his approach had been proven over the years. Once again, he stressed that home treatment was doomed. The patient had to be convinced he could never drink again. He needed to achieve a state of mind where he was not fighting alcohol, rather, he would not drink because that idea had been removed.

[Y] Could this be interpreted as a premonition of how Dr. Silkworth treated Bill Wilson many years later?

"The Necessity of Definite Medical Result in The Treatment of Alcoholic Addiction," Part 2, September, 1917

He began the September, 1917 second part of "The Necessity of Definite Medical Result" article with a pair of questions: *What is the matter with the man who drinks? Why does he drink?"*

He indicated that finding the answer might be "as difficult as threading the maze in a mythical story," but indicated that sooner or later the question could be answered. However, one was not to be surprised if "the reason, when you get to it, will very probably be one that lies altogether outside the field of medical inquiry."[15] Of interest, however, was that Towns maintained that it was a question of "when" one would find an answer, not "if."

He was again stressing the need for a personal relationship to be built with the patient so one could get to the bottom of his personality, reveal that background to the victim, and have the newly freed man take advantage of this new knowledge so that he would not repeat the errors of the past. For sustained recovery to follow unpoisoning, simply the man had to stay away from the substance to which he had been addicted. A man's willpower was irrelevant to the outcome.

> I have dealt with many an individual who had no chance, according to a phrenologist or any of the people who size up mentality by bumps on the head and that kind of thing, and I find that when these same so-called 'weak-willed' people were once freed of the accumulated poisons that were ruining everything about them they had 'will power' to spare. After this cleaning out is

done, the man has a new start, a clean start, and all he needs to do is simply to let poison alone.

If he starts out to 'fight booze,' he'll lose. If he leaves it alone, he'll win.[16]

He concluded the September commentary with additional remarks on a very familiar topic of his: he believed that an alcoholic must stop smoking tobacco if he wished a permanent release from his drinking habit.

"The Necessity of Definite Medical Result in The Treatment of Alcoholic Addiction," Part 3, October, 1917

The third and concluding part of "The Necessity of Definite Medical Result" article, begun in August, appeared in the October, 1917 issue of *Medical Review of Reviews*. He reasserted the fundamentals of how a patient could defeat his addiction. A strong, pragmatic, work-ethic was at the core of his beliefs. Work was so very important to Towns; work formed the basis to all of his observations centered on character.

[His most difficult cases involved] one of those unfortunate individuals who did not have to work, never had worked at anything regularly, and with a mother who has means to pay his bills; one of those unfortunate ones who had never received any encouragement to make good even from his own people; had never known what real responsibility meant. Instead of this being a curse upon the man, the curse under such conditions should be upon the parents for their neglect in the bringing up of a child in such a way . . . he had not had the business training and training for responsibility which every normal human being should have.[17]

A chance encounter with this unfortunate individual occurred when Towns met him on a train sometime after he had been released. The encounter truly was accidental.

I say 'by accident' because it is one of the principles of the hospital not to follow up patients, believing that is the wrong thing to do. We want them to forget the hospital, but to remember to live right. The man looked in splendid health, assured the writer he had never had the slightest inclination to take a drink since he left us, never expected to take another, and that it was the first time since he first began to drink that he had never had the slightest craving for liquor and had never felt the inclination to take it; and above all, he was determined to take up business and make a man of himself.[18]

Once again, he stressed that the nature of recovery demanded individual responsibility. Without that basic ingredient, "we are limited in the things which we can do for these patients."[19] He repeated the assertion that there were truly only two hopeless classes of alcoholic: "One of these two classes is that of the vagrant poor man. The other class is that of the vagrant rich man." Vocation was always a key: the sense of self-respect that came from earning one's way was irreplaceable.

If he be an employee whose employer is 'standing for' his help, let him pay back as he can; but rich or poor, professional man or laborer, make him pay: according to his ability to pay. What costs nothing counts for little, in this or any other case.[20]

If the man had previously been a vagrant or unemployed, then farming or some shop trade was recommended. Improved work habits would prove to the man that he could stand on his own two feet and beat his old life-style with the pride of his achievements.

He concluded this three part article with some unexpected observations about his adopted home city. As part of a patient's sociological and psychological recovery, he recommended that the patient spend time taking advantage of "all the clean constructive influence that New York City has to offer."

Nowhere in the world is there so much to interest one and to furnish a mind with new, constructive and helpful ideas to arouse and stimulate the will. The usual outside view of this greatest city in the world is that it is all glitter and glamour and cabarets and 'great white way,' and that no one can escape the contamination of all this. In reality New York is clean and as educative as a university; and that is what I want to make it for the boy or man—or a woman— who wants to make good.[21]

"How To Eliminate the Alcoholic as an Insane Problem," November, 1917

His November, 1917 article was titled "How to Eliminate the Alcoholic as an Insane Problem" and covered very little new ground. The key to treating the alcoholic was to have him avoid going into delirium tremens, and if this were done properly, alcoholic insanity could be avoided, and if the man were found worthy, he could be returned to society better than he was before.

However, Towns once more challenged the medical community to recognize their culpability in failing to educate themselves about modern medical techniques. Lives could be saved. The damage that alcohol had been causing society could be diminished substantially.

I realize that medical men have been greatly handicapped by politics and other influences in trying to do some of the things they wanted to do, but I hope they will fully realize their great responsibility in connection with this whole subject and that they will strip the matter bare to the bone, and will spare no one in cleaning their skirts of the filth that surrounds this whole insane problem.[22]

"Coffee Inebriety," December, 1917

By the time Towns got around to writing his December, 1917 article, he may have exhausted his focus on the topic of alcohol, at least for the time being. He had recently lambasted tobacco as well. He seemed to be in need of additional topic, so he chose to write a warning about a beverage that many Americans have used in the morning to begin their day, both then and now. Thus, he wrote the article "Coffee Inebriety." Because coffee contained caffeine, to Towns that meant it was potentially dangerous. No legislation to correct the problem was suggested, in this case, however.

Perhaps the most conspicuous symptoms of coffee addiction are the eyes and ears are affected. . . Vision or hearing is not destroyed, but the functional troubles are extremely disagreeable and annoying. As I said before, chronic caffeism [sic] is much more frequent in women than in men, and this may attributed partly to the fact that the women, as a rule, lead a more sedentary life than men . . . Anorexia, disturbance of sleep, and attacks of gastralgia,[Z] different kinds of neuralgia, dyspepsia and often profuse leucorrhea.[AA] Obstinate constipation is often a marked symptom, and in all cases in which a large amount of coffee is taken the digestive functions are greatly interfered with, dyspepsia being almost constantly present. The persistent coffee drinker, or eater, for many become so addicted to the habit that they carry coffee in their pockets and eat it continually, have pinched, pale, wrinkled faces, a weak and rapid pulse and suffer a good deal from nightmare . . . . The pronounced coffee drinker becomes thin almost to emaciation and is in a highly nervous condition. Drinking coffee to excess often marks the commencement of alcohol inebriety and opium addiction . . . As with all stimulants, a renewed dose of the poison gives temporary relief, but at the cost of greater misery . . . In short it may be dogmatically affirmed that if less coffee were drunk in America, and especially by the female population, digestive and nervous troubles would be fewer and the general health would be better.[23]

Towns had written in previous years that he was not a doctor. He had written that fact had allowed him to have an open mind unlike many in the medical profession. However, his preceding opinion on coffee began to reveal a tendency for Towns to venture into subjects that doctors were vastly more qualified to address. This tendency to wander far afield from the original mandate given to him may have cost him this editorship a few months later.

"Psychology and Drugs," January, 1918

The January, 1918 article was simply a reprint of chapter 4 of *Habits That Handicap* and was titled "Psychology and Drugs" and has been examined already. Might the editor of the

---

[Z] Gastralgia – pain in the stomach, neuralgia – a stabbing, burning pain
[AA] Leucorrhea - a medical term that denotes a thick, whitish or yellowish vaginal discharge

magazine that hired Towns been perturbed by Towns copying his writings first published elsewhere? The February, 1918 article titled "Morphinism" was written by another author.

"Alcohol and Antenatal Warfare," March, 1918

Towns returned to what first appeared to be his professional domain for the March, 1918 article in *Medical Review of Reviews* with an article titled "Alcohol and Antenatal Welfare." It was the second to the last article authored by him for the magazine. However, in his efforts to explore new ground in the subject of alcohol consumption, he wandered again into an area that he had very few qualifications.

He probably was led to this mistake by the fact that Americans were starting to be killed in substantial numbers in Europe. The next eight months of 1918 would be when the vast majority of American casualties were suffered during "the war to end all wars."[24] Dreadful Allied casualty figures from Europe had regularly been publicized for three and a half years. The war had been depleting the ranks of healthy men of marriage age in Europe.[25] The conservation of males, and the continuation of a healthy American population, therefore, was considered by Towns to be an important topic. If the consumption of alcohol contributed to an unnecessarily high rate of birth defects, now as the time to issue a warning.

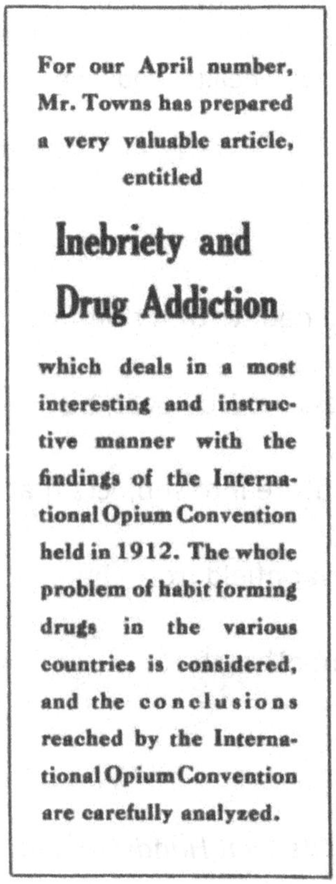

For our April number, Mr. Towns has prepared a very valuable article, entitled

Inebriety and Drug Addiction

which deals in a most interesting and instructive manner with the findings of the International Opium Convention held in 1912. The whole problem of habit forming drugs in the various countries is considered, and the conclusions reached by the International Opium Convention are carefully analyzed.

Figure 27 - Ad that may have led to Towns dismissal from writing for the Medical Review of Reviews

To his credit, he correctly reported that the consumption of alcohol during a woman's pregnancy was hazardous to the fetus.

However, as he was a layman and not a physician, he could not stop himself from crossing boundaries into rather dubious observations. Most doctors would at least know to mention where research on the topic was taking place and the names of the researchers. Towns was not inclined to be restrained by such practices.

> The great and outstanding fact appears to be that alcohol produces an injurious effect upon the so-called carriers of heredity in the germ cells of one generation, which can be seen not in less but in more marked degree in the great grandchildren of the original pair of animals. The embryonic period fills some six or seven early weeks, beginning about two weeks after impregnation. Most of the experimental work in connection with alcohol and the embryonic period has been with birds.[26]

So it would not have been out of line for a reader of Towns' words to think his opinions might have been for the birds! But he continued.

> It would strengthen the crusade against alcohol, if the medical profession were to come out and plainly say that alcohol produces effects upon the unborn infant, the embryo and the germ similar to and not less harmful than those arising from lead, from the typhoid germ or tubercle bacillus. The only poison that affects the unborn child to a more harmful extent than alcohol in its immediate effect is that of syphilis.[27]

Once more, as we see with Towns' remark about syphilis, how impressed he could be with his own ideas. No study or author is quoted regarding that rather provocative assertion. Once again, the reader simply was to take Towns' word for it.

The March article included an addition that may have been added by the editor of *Medical Review of Reviews.* For the first time, an ad was featured for what Towns was going to be covering in the next issue. The ad proclaimed that Towns was going to be writing a "very valuable article," which seemed to set very high expectations for an in-depth analysis. One may surmise that whatever the expectations were of his editor, Towns failed to meet them.

"Inebriety and Drug Addiction," April, 1918

The April, 1918 article titled "Inebriety and Drug Addiction" was Towns' final column for the magazine. He wrote just a two-page article – hardly the length to have "carefully analyzed" almost anything, as had been promised. The first paragraph contained five principles that he claimed at been "enunciated" at the 1912 Hague International Opium Convention, but contained nothing "very valuable," or for that matter, very accurate. Towns did not bother to state the countries that were parties to the convention, nor that the convention output included six chapters and twenty-five articles.[28] Towns only inferred that the convention had concluded that international control of these "noxious agents" was a good idea, and the use of such substances should be restricted to medical purposes throughout the world. He claimed that the French had advocated treating alcohol the same as narcotics "because it had been found that the suppression of the opium evil was leading to the substitution of alcohol."[29] However, regardless of the validity of this view, it had nothing to do with the 1912 Convention, which focused on opium, cocaine, and Heroin.[30] Towns was not writing a piece of scholarship

REAL
PREPAREDNESS
MEANS NO ALCOHOL
ACCURATE SHOOTING
DECREASED 30%
BY ENGLISH RUM RATION

PROHIBITION IS
PART OF PREPAREDNESS
19 STATES HAVE IT!

—*The Barccs*

THE SIDE SHOW

While Boston's big prepared-ness parade filled the streets, this sandwich-man and a com-panion similarly placarded marched around for the Uni-tarian Temperance Society.

Figure 28 – An ad in the *Boston Medical and Surgical Journal* capturing the mood towards prohibition in the times of World War I.

that he had researched. Rather, the article was another opinion piece that had him relying upon himself as the main authority.

He remembered that the American delegation had advocated including "hasheesh"[sic] among the "evil" substances because of what appeared to him to be obvious reasons: if one could not get his drug of choice, almost any other drug might do.

It is evident then that several of the more clear sighted of the high contracting parties to the convention of 1912 recognized that the principles embodied therein are capable of extension by far than that for which provision was made, and that true consistency calls for regulations restricting the use of all noxious agencies endowed with like destructive potentialities. The repression of the few will lead only to the substitution of others. When a drug habit is established, if the victim cannot obtain the drug to which he has become accustomed he will endeavor to satisfy his craving by the drug which he is able to procure. Thus if he is not able to get alcohol, he will procure cocaine, for instance, and if he cannot get morphine he will fly to alcohol.[31]

He then seemed to abandon any desire to discuss the events of 1912 further, but instead, provided his assertions of how alcohol should be perceived.

The point at which the writer is attempting to arrive and to impress upon his readers is that alcohol and other narcotic drugs should be placed upon the same plane, and that the terms inebriate and drug addiction is in some respects synonymous. Referring to alcoholic beverages Dr. Norman Kerr, the well known British authority, very truly remarked that 'all the alcohols are poisons, are irritant narcotic anesthetic poisons; alcohol is a poison in the same sense as arsenic or prussic acid.' A close relationship exists between drinks, drugs and poisons, and there is a distinct and intimate relationship between insanity and inebriety.[32]

To the reader that had been expecting to learn more about the 1912 Hague International Opium Convention, he was to be sadly disappointed because Towns was on a roll! His following observation regarding opium indulgence did not name a source. How he derived the following opinion was never qualified, nor did the words carry any result of any international conference.

What is commonly called the opium habit is a true inebriety, and one feature of this kind of inebriety which distinguishes it from the condition ordinarily known as drunkenness, is that unlike alcohol indulgence, it is never a social, but always a solitary indulgence.[33]

He proceeded to provide a rather haphazard geographical lesson regarding consumption of stimulants by some of the countries he chose to mention, but he intermixed alcohol and drugs in a manner that obviously reflected his views.

In China opium, in the near East hasheesh, Russia vodka, in France absinthe, and in Great Britain whiskey may be placed almost in the same category. If opium were as easily obtainable and as freely indulged in as are strong preparations of alcohol, many morphomaniacs[sic] would be shut up for the benefit of themselves and the community at large. Where one person takes drugs, a thousand take alcohol, and although views have altered, and it is no longer considered the sign of a gentleman to drink to excess, there is not even now the stigma attached to the habitual drinking of alcohol as to drug addiction. If the war had done nothing else, it has demonstrated the alcohol and efficiency are not compatible and, in consequence, all nations at war have to a very large degree tabooed alcohol.[34]

As if World War I provided support for alcohol abstention as a benefit amid the destruction and death? He went on to report that France had abolished absinthe in 1915[BB]. He wrote the French had been consuming the "most deleterious of all intoxicating drinks" in quantities that were endangering the future of the country.

The direct effect of the consumption of some 55,000,000 gallons of absinthe in France yearly was that whereas lunacy, degeneracy, crime, especially crimes of violence, and the number of tuberculous, mentally deficient, and otherwise defective children, were increasing at an alarming rate, the birthrate was fast declining. The war has saved France from ruin from this source by rendering the prohibition of absinthe practicable.

However, the aim of this article is to emphasize the fact that alcohol is a poison, narcotic and anesthetic, and comes to some extent with the same category as the habit forming drugs. Further, the prevention of alcohol to excess and its successful treatment when the habit is formed is one of the most important problems of the age.[35]

[BB] BBC New Europe reported on May 4, 2011 that after almost one hundred years of absinthe being banned in France, the ban was to be lifted. www.bbc.co.uk/news/world-europe-13159863

His last paragraph contained no less a controversial assertion that, again, had nothing to do with the advertised intent of the article. Instead, what was provided was one more classic example of how Towns could write an opinion without stating any source.

It must be borne in mind that while in this article stress is laid upon the point that alcohol is a narcotic, and that so far as this is concerned it may be classed with other habit forming drugs, the effects of alcohol differ, somewhat widely, from those of opium and its derivatives. The effects of alcohol resemble rather those of cocaine.[36]

Why his career at *Medical Review of Reviews* ended remains only a conjecture. One can suspect that Towns' journalism proved to possess substantial shortcomings in research and accountability, at least in the eyes of his editor. The March promotional ad had promised a "careful analysis;" his editor might have found Towns' work not at all "careful or valuable." Regardless, with this article, his medical journalism career was over. He would write two more books and quite a few advertising pamphlets, but not appear again as an authority or editor in any medical publication. His record of influencing legislation ended as well.

Articles by C. B. Pearson M.D., a Hillsdale, Maryland doctor with an acknowledged track record of treating morphine in a facility named after him, the Pearson Home[37] (similar to the Charles B. Towns Hospital), wrote in the May and July issues on the topic of morphine addiction as a disease. The subjects of addiction and alcoholism in the magazine appear to have been in the hands of a physician from that point forward.

12) The Towns Treatment

What was the Towns Treatment? How could it have been proclaimed to be the world's only known cure for opium addiction when it was introduced to the world in Shanghai in early 1909? How could the esteemed Dr. Alexander Lambert declare this medicine to be a state-of-the-art opium solution in the September, 1909 issue of the *Journal of the American Medical Association*?

The Towns Treatment, which was sometimes known as the belladonna treatment,[CC] or the Towns-Lambert treatment, has been described, including detailed chemical names and quantitles, by Bill Pittman in his book *AA The Way It Began* in 1988.[DD] Rather than repeat Pittman's research, which included detailed quantities and chemical descriptions, the administration of the medicines will be more of a concentration here. Dr. Lambert described the procedure.

Briefly stated, it consists in the hourly dosage of a mixture of belladonna, hyoscyamus and xanthoxylum. The mixture is given every hour, day and night, for about fifty hours. There is also given about every twelve hours a vigorous catharsis[EE] of C.C.[FF] pills and blue mass. At the end of the treatment when it is evident that there are abundant bilious stools, castor oil is given to clean out thoroughly the intestinal tract. If you leave any of the ingredients out, the reaction of the cessation of the desire is not as clear cut as when the three are mixed together. The amount

---

[CC] On page 7 of *Alcoholics Anonymous*, Bill Wilson wrote, "Under the so-called belladonna treatment my brain cleared."
[DD] -*AA The Way It Began* was first published by Glen Abbey Books in 1988. It was republished by Hazelden as *The Roots of Alcoholics Anonymous* in 1999. The books appear identical except for their titles.
[EE] Catharsis is used in the context to encourage bowel movements.
[FF] C.C. an abbreviation for "compound cathartic"—assistance in bowel movements.

necessary to give is judged by the physiologic action of the belladonna it contains. When the

face becomes flushed, the throat dry, and the pupils of the eyes dilated, you must cut down

your mixture or cease giving it altogether until these symptoms pass. You must, however, push

this mixture until these symptoms appear, or you will not obtain a clear cut cessation of the

desire for the narcotic . . . [1]

Pittman in his book *AA The Way It Began* listed the specific amounts of the three main

ingredients given to the patient. These chemicals may appear to be ingredients of some

witches' brew created for mesmerizing the senses. Belladonna, otherwise known as Atropa

Belladonna or "deadly nightshade," is a plant native to Europe, Canada and parts of the United

States.

The foliage and berries are extremely toxic, containing tropane alkaloids. These toxins include

scopolamine and hyoscyamine, which cause a bizarre delirium and hallucinations, and are also

used as pharmaceutical anticholinergics.[GG] The drug atropine is derived from the plant.

It has a long history of use as a medicine, cosmetic, and poison. Before the Middle Ages, it was

used as an anesthetic for surgery, the ancient Romans used it as a poison . . . and, predating this,

it was used to make poison-tipped arrows. The genus name Atropa comes from Atropos, one of

the three Fates in Greek Mythology, and the name 'bella donna' is derived from Italian and

---

[GG] Anticholinergic – from http://en.wikipedia.org/wiki/Anticholinergic, - An anticholinergic agent is a substance that blocks the neurotransmitter acetylcholine in the central and the peripheral nervous system. Anticholinergics inhibit parasympathetic nerve impulses by selectively blocking the binding of the neurotransmitter acetylcholine to its receptor in nerve cells. The nerve fibers of the parasympathetic system are responsible for the involuntary movement of smooth muscles present in the gastrointestinal tract, urinary tract, lungs, etc.

means 'beautiful woman' because the herb was used in eye-drops by women to dilate the pupils of the eyes to make them appear seductive.[2]

Xanthoxylum (Zanthoxylum americanum) is the dried bark or berries of a prickly ash tree, which is native to the central and eastern portions of the United States and Canada. Extracts from the bark have been used in traditional and alternative medicine. "The extract may act as a stimulant, and historic medicinal use has included use for 'chronic rheumatism, typhoid, and skin diseases and impurity of the blood . . .' as well as for digestive ailments."[3]

Hyoscyamus Niger, commonly known as henbane as well as stinking nightshade or black henbane, is a plant of the family Solanaceae, the same as belladonna. It is said to have originated in Eurasia. It has been historically used in combination with other plants, including belladonna, as an anesthetic potion, as well as for its psychoactive properties, which include visual hallucinations and a sensation of flight.[4]

Additional chemicals could be employed depending upon the condition and age of the patient. If an alcoholic were admitted while still drunk, first the patient would be put to sleep. A hypnotic, a mixture including chloral hydrate, could be used to sedate the patient. The regular regimen was not begun until after the patient slept it off. If the patient were "the furious, thrashing, motor type," a hypodermic injection that contained strychnine[HH] as its main ingredient could be used that was effective it quieting the patient.[5]

[HH] www.encyclopedia.com/topic/strychnine.aspx - Strychnine comes from the nux vomina that grows in India . . . Although strychnine is a poison, it has been used in the past as a medicine.
www.herbs2000.com/herbs/herbs_strychnine.htm - The strychnine is an evergreen tree indigenous to the tropical and sub-tropical climactic regions and grows in abundance in southeastern Asia and Australia . . . History has it that when the legendary Cleopatra made up her mind to commit suicide, the brutal sovereign utilized her slaves as guinea pigs to experiment the consequences of the different plans on humans. It is said that belladonna, henbane

Bill Pittman referenced Dr. Alexander Lambert's descriptions of the various interpretations of hallucinations that could be expected, and the manner in which the specialist could differentiate alcoholic delirium from belladonna reactions. A requirement was to await the patient creating the expected bowel elimination, which would be assisted by "compound cathartic pills," before commencing with the belladonna. A particular "dark, thick, green mucous stool" was desired.[6] Withdrawal from opium often involved "sweating, diarrhea, and vomiting."[7] No wonder that the book *Pass It On* described that the patient was "puked and purged" at Towns Hospital![8]

One of the cure's detractors later labeled it as "diarrhea, delirium and damnation," but it seemed very neat and scientific when presented in 1909 under the auspices of the federal government, Dr. Lambert, and the *Journal of the American Medical Association.*[9]

Knowledge of what addictive substance was being used by the patient was considered essential. Reduced amounts of that addictive substance would be provided to the patient at prescribed intervals, and in this manner, the theory was that the patient would be removed from his substance with the least amount of discomfort possible. Towns had repetitively condemned the immediate deprivation of the addictive substance from the patient as being cruel and inhumane. An article in the *British Medical Journal* in 1910 described how Dr. Alexander Lambert handled drug addicts and alcoholics by gradually removing them from their addictive substance.

and even the strychnine seeds were among the venomous plant sources Cleopatra experimented with . . . [But in the end, instead] she preferred the asp, a small poisonous snake . . . to commit suicide.

At the beginning of the treatment with the compound tincture he gives, in three doses, at half-hour intervals, from half to two-thirds of the total daily dose of opium, morphine, or cocaine usually taken by the patient . . . After the bowels have acted, but not before, one-third or half of the narcotic may be given . . . In the case of alcoholics the same plan is followed, but it doesn't need to be continued so long. Much closer observation necessary to recognize the early symptoms of is required to avoid the early symptoms of belladonna poisoning . . . At this stage the young, full blooded alcoholic may need a further does of hypnotic, but need not be given alcohol; the older alcoholics and those in a weak and poor condition should have 1 to 2 oz. of whisky about four times a day with milk during the first twenty-four hours, during the second twenty-four hours two doses will probably suffice.[10]

David F. Musto in his book *The American Disease* described the administration of the belladonna treatment in this manner.

[The formula was] was given in 1/2 cc doses at half-hour intervals to an addict until signs of atropine effect were noted: dilation of the pupil, slight dryness of the throat, and redness of the skin. But before beginning with the specific, a 'complete evacuation of the bowels' must have been accomplished, and a half an hour before beginning the formula administration, the largest tolerable dose of the addicting substance was given 'to bridge the patient over as long a period as possible without having to use the drug again.'

About 24 hours later, after a second cathartic had worked its effect, another does of the addicting drug, but this time only one-half or one-third of the previous amount, was given.

Allegedly this left the patient as comfortable as the previous maximum dose. Twelve hours later a third cathartic was given, and 6 to 8 hours later this was followed by 1 to 2 ounces of castor oil, [which] should produce 'a stool that consists of green mucous matter.' When Dr. Lambert announced the treatment . . . he wrote that 'when this stool occurs, or shortly afterward, the patients often will feel suddenly relaxed and comfortable, and their previous discomfort ceases,' bringing the entire treatment to an end.

This outline is drastically condensed from the original elaboration. Not mentioned, for example, is strychnine in small doses, which was necessary to combat the patient's exhaustion after the first day or so.[11]

Towns believed his approach to have the ability completely to purge the body of whatever poisons had previously held the patient in physical bondage. Towns would assure the patient that his recovery could be accomplished with almost no suffering.[12]

He assured the physician to follow his instructions exactly as he provided them without any modification whatsoever. Any negative outcome was because the doctor's ego did not allow him to follow instructions.

And the reason for the failure [of the Towns Treatment] is not far to seek. The administering physician has undertaken to 'modify' the treatment as published - only Heaven knows why, unless it be that he must by all odds and costs be 'original' and free of debt to a 'layman' . . . When any treatment is a failure it means intense suffering for that patient, and he should not be condemned if, in the intensity of his unrelieved suffering, he is able to obtain by some means a soothing drug which will relieve his agony. Great nicety of judgment has to be used in deciding how much the patient is really suffering and how desirous he is of obtaining some alleviation of the fear that he may suffer. *The real suffering should and can always be relieved, and the fear of what may come can always be alleviated.*[13]

Upon completion of the roughly fifty hours of being administered the medicines, the balance of the time spent at Towns Hospital involved nursing the patient back to physical health through a good diet, exercise, massage, and a variety of physical therapies including hydrotherapy. In this era, the privacy of the patient was ensured, and most every comfort was made available. William L. White described Towns Hospital in this manner.

> The Charles B. Towns Hospital operated across from New York City's Central Park and boasted of its exclusive view of "Millionaire's Row" on Fifth Avenue . . . Entering the building gave one the feeling of entering, not a hospital, but a private and quite exclusive hotel . . . The promotional literature promised individual rooms or suites, absolute privacy, individualized meal service, private telephones, and—if the patient so desired—the services nursing attendant, valet, or florist. All of this could be theirs, along with relaxation in a heated solarium that boasted of easy chairs and couches, singing birds, a library and a billiards table . . .[14]

The average stay for an alcoholic was considered to be within the five to seven-day range while a drug addict might stay as long as two weeks depending upon his physical condition. Also, the drug addict was expected to be in worse physical shape than the alcoholic upon entering the hospital. He was expected to have resisted the alleviation of his habit for a longer period because of the associated shame of being identified as a "drug fiend."

What was the claimed recovery rate this time? According to Bill Pittman in *AA The Way It Began*, "Towns claimed a cure rate at 75 to 90 percent, based on the reasoning that if you never heard from a patient again, he no longer needed your services."[15] As has been previously detailed, Towns considered contacting patients after their release to be unwise if not dangerous. Towns had unbounded confidence in the validity of his approach. Consequently, he seemed to reason that his patients would transform his confidence into a heartfelt gratitude resulting from an escape from their drug demons. Any questioning if they were still clean and sober would be counterproductive—even insulting! Of course the treatment worked![16]

One had Towns' word for it, after all. What more proof did you need?

13)The Fall from Grace

A variety of influences began to emerge that began to diminish Towns' reputation before the second decade of the twentieth century ended.

Towns asserted repetitively how his methodology purged the poisons from the body of the patient. But how did this process actually take place? Did the chemicals in the medicine single out the undesirable "poisons" in the blood stream, bind to them somehow or break them down, and cause them to be eliminated? Towns, being a layman, had no qualifications to provide such an explanation, nor did there appear to be any clinical explanations offered by medical men of the times towards why the outcome seemed to work. When Dr. Cabot claimed that Towns knew more about solving the problem of addiction than anyone else he knew, sadly Dr. Cabot had admitted a truth. Somehow, the administration of the Towns Treatment, through the powers of external observation, had the appearance of convincing some rather intelligent medical men that the "unpoisoning" was effective. How Dr. Cabot and Dr. Alexander Lambert, among others, became convinced of the efficacy of the remedy stood as testimony that, for a time, it was considered legitimate, if not state-of-the-art. Dr. Cabot had also previously mentioned that Charles Towns was one of the most persuasive men he had ever met. Dr. Cabot's name was still being used by Towns as a reference as late as 1931.[1] By then, however, Towns' writings were no longer much more than advertisements for his establishment.

Towns Hospital was founded almost entirely because of opium addiction and the derivatives heroin and morphine. Cocaine was included as treatable by the procedure, as was alcohol. However, by 1920 the fear of "drug fiends" had become a very real presence, and most drug addicts had become criminals according to law enforcement and much of society. Towns

Hospital advertising had to change with that reality in mind. While the 1916-1917 advertisements were quite open about solutions for narcotics, by 1921, the mention of narcotics was relatively rare (see Figures 29 through 35 contained in this chapter for seven examples of 1921 advertising). So, in the attempt to keep his hospital's beds occupied, he expanded the range of substances and conditions for which his hospital could claim to provide relief.

After 1920, Towns' standing in the medical world fell while his claims became more and more extravagant. The substances he claimed he could help people with included tobacco, coffee, tea, bromides, marijuana, cocaine, and paraldehyde in addition to opiates and alcohol.[2]

Even the esteemed Dr. Lambert, who had been among Towns' greatest advocates for a number of years, began to lose his enthusiasm.

While the treatment had credibility, even Dr. Lambert did not closely question this logic and in fact employed it himself, but when evidence accumulated that the Towns Treatment was ineffective, the weakness of such claims for cure seemed evident to all. Eleven years after his initial research on the Towns treatment, Dr. Lambert had lost his faith in merely withdrawing the drug. "I tried it," he said "in about 200 patients at Bellevue . . . and I had looked them up afterwards. I found that about four or five percent really stayed off."

Towns continued operating the hospital and claiming to administer the same methods despite the winds of changing times as described by Dr. David F. Musto M.D.

Prevailing concepts of control of addiction in the United States abandoned the medical approach, which Towns sold as avidly as life insurance or stocks, and he faded from the national scene to become the proprietor of just one more sanitarium in New York City. Towns did not change his medical theories, his treatment, or his style of presentation, but the nation discarded specific treatments and was soured on the fantastic claims from their proponents. Towns' story reveals the deep belief among many leading Americans that a cure existed for addiction and that Towns had it. The flaws in his statistics were overlooked as both physicians and statements persuaded themselves that a simple cure existed for this difficult social problem. Towns' own confidence and his bearing must have been part of his triumph; Dr. Richard C. Cabot of Boston knew him as "one of the most persuasive and dominating personalities in the world." But the chief factor of his success was the confidence Americans had in the progress of medicine and its ability to solve by such therapeutic inventions a complex social and personal ailment.[3]

How could so many intelligent men of the times be so mistaken? Dr. Musto provided a very plausible medical explanation regarding the knowledge available to the best medical minds around when Towns' reputation was at its peak.

Perhaps it would be worthwhile to consider the cure as a type of medical cure in general. The physiological basis for the treatment was quite reasonable: Opiate withdrawal usually produces sweating, diarrhea, and vomiting. The atropine-line action of the formula was thought pharmacologically to counteract those symptoms, thereby aiding the patient in lasting out the withdrawal. Atropine also had the effect of causing a delirium confusion, a kind of twilight sleep which erased memory of the withdrawal. In an age of belief in various potent intestinal autotoxins and antitoxins, the wisdom of complete evacuation of the intestinal tract before treatment was quite understandable, as was the continued evacuation of the bowels during therapy. Cathartics[II] rid the body of the poisons that might be causing withdrawal symptoms as well as of any opiates lurking in the intestinal tract that might stimulate antitoxins later on. Therefore, what might now seem a bizarre treatment without rationale was in reality a harmful regimen[JJ] within an accepted set of beliefs.

The way in which the cure was presented by leading medical authorities also conveys a sense of the science as well as the art of medicine. There were endpoints to be looked for—atropine toxicity in the administration of the specific, and the characteristic "green, mucous stool" which meant the treatment was completed . . . Now forgotten, the Towns cure is an example of some of the classical medical "cures" of the past that have combined arcane scientific knowledge, elaborate detail, and professional expertise . . . It will suffice to note that the Towns method had so many social and political pressures favoring it that refutation was difficult for a decade after its publication. It seemed to succeed because the alternatives—no effective medical cure for addiction, and the inaccuracy of some medical theories of the time—were unacceptable.[4]

The reader should recall that it was not humanitarian motives, but political concerns, that had sent Towns to treat 4,000 opium addicts in China by the Roosevelt administration. The

---

[II] Cathartics are medicines that accelerate defecation
[JJ] Regimen – a prescribed course of medical treatment

motives behind the trip originated from a desire to combat an embargo that had been limiting

Figure 29 - A January, 1921 in *The Medical Times* on Insomnia. A curiosity: Towns Hospital is listed as 292 Central Park West A previous December, 1920 ad in the same magazine carried the 292 address.

February, 1921   'SANITARIA and HOSPITALS   29

Use and Abuse of Hypnotics

In all the eighteen years of its service, this hospital has had no more pitiable cases for treatment than those of patients who have been accustomed to taking some hypnotic or sleep-producing drug. Our case records show that there is no other class of drugs so certain to bring about an entire change of temperament and inevitably produce physical, mental, and moral deterioration.

It cannot be too strongly emphasized that sleeping powders do not produce natural sleep; that headache tablets do not cure or remove the cause of headaches; that nerve sedatives act only as a "knock out" to some bodily function, running riot because of an underlying physical defect. Habitual dependence upon the daily use of such drugs is responsible for a large proportion of life boarders in sanitariums and state institutions.

In all good faith the physician may prescribe a hypnotic to be taken at certain intervals—the patient notes the desirable effect—finds out what he is taking—learns that without restriction it may be readily bought over the drug counter—the physician loses control of his patient—and a secret habituation begins.

It is not the quantity of the drug taken but the regularity of dosage that creates addiction. A confirmed addiction in any form tends inevitably to become progressively worse. When an extreme tolerance has been established for any drug which affects the nervous system, neither sudden deprivation nor substitution will remove the craving, but are more likely to be harmful and often fatal.

Obviously there should be just as stringent laws regulating the sale and disposition of the hypnotic group of drugs as of opiates or cocaine. Pending their enactment physicians can do a great service by safeguarding their patients from the hypnotic group of drugs.

Moreover it should be remembered that those persons who are already in the addict class are not without hope. With the definite methods followed at the Towns Hospital it is possible to obliterate any drug craving in a very brief period. This accomplished, the way is paved for a more intelligent diagnosis and treatment of any underlying physical or mental trouble.

With national prohibition in force and further restrictive narcotic legislation pending, new phases of the addiction problem are introduced. Many practitioners will be confronted with the problem of treating drug patients. In all such cases, the facilities of this Hospital are at their disposal.

A "Symposium of Medical Opinion," together with the following reprints, will be sent to physicians on request: "Hope for the Victims of Narcotics," by Alexander Lambert, M.D., New York; "The Drug-Taker and the Physician," "The Future of Addict Legislation," by Charles B. Towns.

Any physician may feel free to consult or confer on any problems arising in his practice within the field of the special work of this hospital.

CHARLES B. TOWNS HOSPITAL, 292 Central Park West NEW YORK

Figure 30 - February, 1921 Towns Hospital ad on Hypnotics in *The Medical Times*

American commercial interests there. Towns returned from China with the apparent credentials of a magnanimous philanthropist, which superseded petty economic trivialities with grand visions of healing all of humanity from the terrible curse of addiction. Towns himself seemed to fall for the legend created about him. He had lectured vastly more educated men than himself. He thought he had what they did not: successful experience in defeating addiction.

Towns' criticisms that held physicians and druggists responsible for the vast majority of U.S. morphine addicts were not trivial accusations. According to him, because society had been foolish, society was also culpable. Towns' proposal for the creation of special hospitals, known as "Alcohol Clearing Houses," for the treatment of alcoholic and drug cases was a means of society taking responsibility for past errors. However, owners of privately funded hospitals thought such advocacy for public medical facilities to represent outright competition for the medical dollar. Claims of unfair competition and potential governmental favoritism within the medical community, resulted. Towns "invoked hostility and resentment" from "the rank and file medical man," not for the specifics of the Towns Treatment but for his politics.[5] His calls for an international tribunal to be formed to solve the drug problem proved contrary to a prevailing mood following World War I that desired to avoid further foreign entanglements, which might have violated the Monroe Doctrine.[6]

While Towns had insisted that experience was the ultimate judge regarding the efficacy of his approach, his claims of success vanished the moment the patient left 293 Central Park West. With regards to his claimed permanent recovery rate, Towns could only guess, and as some salesmen are prone to do, the truth became stretched if not completely distorted. His claims were not based on science after all but on a great deal of wishful thinking.

Figure 31 - March, 1921 Towns Hospital Ad in *The Medical Times* again on Insomnia

Figure 32 - April, 1921 Towns Hospital Ad in *The Medical Times* on Prohibition

Some of Towns Hospital's reputation rested on an almost comical hypothesis that if the patient did not return and was never heard from again, the treatment had worked.[7]

The end of this second decade of the twentieth century ushered in the 18th Amendment and the associated Volstead Act that implemented alcohol prohibition. As already presented in Chapter 7, the end of this very same decade began outright narcotic prohibition, even though no Constitutional Amendment had been required or contemplated for this new arena of Federal law.

William L. White described the progression of events that followed Decision 2200 in May, 1915 by the Treasury Department. This executive branch decision declared indefinite maintenance of drug addicts by doctors through prescriptions to be a violation of the Harrison Act, and, therefore, illegal.

Lacking any substantive knowledge of the relapse phenomenon in opiate addiction, the Treasury Department took a stand against what was called "ambulatory treatment." Ambulatory treatment consisted of the addicted patient's arriving each day at his or her physician's office or clinic to receive a prescription for morphine that was, in theory, progressively reduced until the patient was weaned from the drug.

The Treasury Department opposed ambulatory treatment because, for many patients, it turned into sustained maintenance, and also because the remaining inebriate hospitals and asylums of the day [such as the Charles B Towns Hospital] were still boasting 95% success rates. After all, leaders of the Treasury Department argued, why should someone be maintained on morphine when all he or she had to do was to take the cure? It was through such misrepresentation of success rates that the inebriate asylums and private treatment sanitariums contributed inadvertently to the criminalization of narcotic addiction in the U.S.[8]

Towns had repeatedly criticized magistrates and society for the cruel manner in which drug addicts had been treated. Inadvertently, and apparently quite innocently, the dangers he claimed of "the drug curse," along with his claims of very high recovery rates, were among the voices that helped to federally criminalize narcotics in the United States. His intent was to treat the addict humanely in hospitals rather than having them sentenced to jails or prisons. By around 1920, more addicts ended up in penal institutions than before, and sadly, joined some of their doctors there.

The enforcement of the Harrison Tax Act altered the relationship between physicians and their addicted patients for more than a half century. Doctors who treated addicts risked losing their medical practice through arbitrary interpretations of "good faith" and "proper treatment." If one were to inquire why the modern physician is so ambivalent about the addicted patient, one would only have to look at the history of 20th-century medicine. More than 25,000 physicians were indicted under the Harrison Act between 1914 and 1938. Some 3,000 actually went to jail, while another 20,000 paid substantial fines. The practical effect of such enforcement was that physicians stopped treating their addicted patients.[9]

Towns had repeatedly written about how effective legislation was the solution so that the drug problem could be eliminated once and for all. The Treasury Department approved the goal of Charles Towns to eliminate the drug problem, but not by his means. Towns' advocacy of

Figure 33 - May, 1921 Towns Hospital ad in *The Medical Times* on treating tobacco as a poison

June, 1921   *THE MEDICAL TIMES*   29

CHARLES B. TOWNS HOSPITAL

FRONTING ON CENTRAL PARK

For Medical Treatment by Hospital Methods, of Addictions, Mental and Nervous Disturbances of Functional Type and All Conditions Wherein Complete Elimination of Toxins Is Indicated.

THIS Hospital provides a definite medical treatment for eliminating those toxins always present in addictions, and very frequently the underlying cause of nervous and mental disturbances of functional type.

In addition to providing definite medical treatment, the Hospital also has every facility for Hydro and Electro Therapy that may be useful in restoring the patient to normal tone.

Physical training and outdoor exercise are given under the direction of a special physical director. For this work, the Hospital has not only the advantages of its roof-garden solarium and gymnasium, but the whole area of Central Park with its walks, drives and recreational facilities is accessible from the Hospital's very door. This, together with the wonderful diversity of interests to be found in New York City, are valuable factors in giving patients a new mental outlook.

Patients are received only upon a basis of a fixed fee charge agreed upon in advance and covering all service that the Hospital can render, thus eliminating all extra and special items of treatment and care.

Correspondence or calls are invited. Medical Reprints and Hospital Literature sent on request.

CHARLES B. TOWNS HOSPITAL, 292 Central Park West, New York City

Figure 34 - June, 1921 Towns Hospital Ad in *The Medical Times* on nervous disturbances

Figure 35 - July, 1921 Towns Hospital Ad in The Medical Times on "The Pathological Aspect of Prohibition." The address of 292 Central Park West appears in all the Towns ads in this magazine.

"appropriate legislation" kept promising reasonable and logical solutions to the drug problem that would eliminate punitive solutions for all but the incurable. Instead, the resulting government enforcement of drug legislation led to punitive measures against almost anyone who the Treasury Department thought was breaking their regulations.[KK]

Most of the publicity given "drug fiends" during this decade resulted in a climate of fear. Crime was thought to be an inevitable result of narcotic addiction. While Towns had begun his business by openly recruiting men from "the underworld," such claims proved counterproductive to a hospital address of 293 Central Park West—among some of the most prestigious and expensive properties in the entire country. Attracting "drug fiends" to such an address reserved for the wealthy became bad for the reputation of his hospital. While nothing is currently known about any law enforcement consequences actually experienced at Towns Hospital as a result of narcotic prohibition, what is known is how the advertising of Towns Hospital changed (See the preceding Figures 29 through 35 for the 1921 advertisements). While Towns previously insisted that his hospital was significantly different than sanitariums that he repetitively had so caustically condemned, Towns Hospital began to look very similar. Towns Hospital had become just one more sanitarium—one for the rather wealthy or well-connected that could still afford the upfront fee that Towns considered so essential to initiate the basic motivations necessary for recovery to take place. Over the years, Towns Hospital was to attract the likes of Lillian Russell,[10] John Barrymore, and W.C. Fields.[11] Surely these

---

[KK] No direct response by Towns regarding the Harrison Act, as the Treasury Department enforced it, has ever been found. One wonders what he might have said.

celebrities would not attend just any old place, or one that unnecessarily might jeopardize their career by being associated with dangerous drug fiends.

If a morphine addict was treated at Towns Hospital after 1919, was he stepped down using his substance as had been practiced before? Was any opium present there or heroin, or cocaine? If so, then Towns, and his surrogate physicians or nurses may have become law breakers themselves, which would have provided an ultimate irony of unintended consequences. Towns had unwittingly helped to criminalize narcotics when his original intent had been precisely the opposite. How could any man remain an authority when he did not know where he was headed, nor explain from where he had arrived?

14) Four Brochures to Attract Physicians

When it came to Towns Hospital, Charles Towns had been and would continue to be, his own boldest promoter. Four examples of his advertising skills were represented in these brochures. The first was created in January, 1918, the second sometime around the end of the First World War, the third in June, 1922, and the fourth in March of 1928.

"The Work of the Charles B. Towns Hospital and its Relation to the Medical Profession," January 1918

This sixteen-page brochure, which included only ten pages of text, was a rather unsophisticated effort to encourage physicians to bring their addicted or alcoholic patients to Towns Hospital. One of the most significant shortcomings of this brochure was that he, in effect, "buried the lead." His professional references, among his most valuable assets, did not appear until the middle of the brochure. How long this brochure represented the hospital is not known, but one may surmise that it was replaced rather rapidly.[1]

He advertised that addiction could not be treated effectively in private practice.[2] The brochure repetitively stressed there must be a "definite medical result" from a "definite medical treatment,"[3] which suggested he had borrowed familiar language from his three-part *Medical Review of Reviews* series, which featured "definite medical result" in the title just written the previous October.

Towns had advertised that a patient's stay at Towns Hospital would be in the five to seven-day range. However, he had since realized that this claim had a significant shortcoming: it might repel the physician in private practice he was trying to attract. Should not the outside physician be allowed to determine the duration of treatment that his patient would receive? As long as a fixed fee was set upon admittance of the patient, he no longer limited the duration of the patient's visit. Towns promised these terms would be arranged to the satisfaction of the visiting physician.

There was a time when this hospital did not deal with these patients beyond the brief period of definite medical treatment, but referred patients back to their own physicians for such after treatment and care as the physician might deem advisable in the case. But we have at last been brought to realize that the physician in private practice is rarely ever in a position to provide the definite physical after treatment and care that this type of patient should have after completing the definite medical treatment here.[4]

Towns proclaimed that the aftercare facilities at Towns Hospital were second to none. The physical trainer hired had been employed previously by the YMCA and had carried a recommendation from Theodore Roosevelt in his resume.[5] Four physicians were claimed to be on staff full time, and they were fully in charge of the medical treatments but knew not to interfere with a visiting physician's priorities. None of those four physicians had a financial interest in Towns Hospital.[6]

He also included the following important qualification.

The hospital has never claimed to secure any more than a definite medical result in the treatment of this special type of patient. Those who have read the Hospital literature sent out from time to time know that we have eliminated from it the word "cure," the word "disease" and the words "inherited" and "heredity" as applied to habit and addiction.[7]

Four classes of patients were identified as being suitable for treatment at Towns Hospital. The first class covered the victims of neurasthenia of certain types including "insomnia, nerve exhaustion, and certain types of incipient mental disorders . . ." The second type were those addicted to hypnotics. The third included the drug addict and alcoholic. The fourth class was for the tobacco addict.[8]

Compared to Towns' next advertising brochure, this one becomes rather forgettable.

"The Special Work of The Charles B. Towns Hospital"

This publication date of this brochure is not known, but its contents appeared very similar to the brochure that followed it. Certain references in the text suggest it was printed near the end of, or after, the First World War. Where he had referred to addiction and alcoholism in the previous brochure as a "social menace," the rhetoric employed here had a much greater flair for the dramatic.

> Never in the history of this country has the disorganizing influence of alcohol and all habit-forming drugs been in greater evidence than at the present time. And never was there a time when its menace was more palpable.[LL][9]

The brochure also carried the names of five of his most prominent supporters featured right underneath his own name: three medical professors (Samuel Lambert, Alexander Lambert, Smith Ely Jelliffe and two physicians (George M. Swift and James W. Fleming on the

---

[LL] Palpable – able to be touched or felt.

title page of the brochure rather than burying these influential references in the middle of the text, as he had done before. These five were impressive references for any medical facility of the times. Doctor Smith Ely Jelliffe was a co-author of the prestigious *Diseases of the Nervous System* published in 1917. George M. Swift was on the staff of the College of Physicians and Surgeons at Columbia University.[10] James W. Fleming was listed as an influential physician in the *Brooklyn Medical Journal*.[11]

Towns attributed the rise of narcotic use perhaps to have been from the rise of tensions during the war. He also noted a corresponding rise in tobacco usage for much the same reasons, and this was a "most serious social problem."[12]

Fine Clean boys who had never smoked a cigarette in their lives have been initiated into the habit almost from the day they joined the Colors. Many have since become "fiends" in their insistent demand for this particular brand of poison.

So thousands of soldiers are suffering from the effects of the continuous absorption of furfurol[sic][MM] and the aldehyde products of tobacco combustion—the results of which are evidenced in irritable, irregular heart action, nervous irritability, impaired metabolism, increased arterial tension, and not infrequently, nephritic[NN] degeneration.[13]

From this point forward, the brochure contained not much out of the ordinary for a twenty page Towns advertisement. Cooperation with the outside physician was promised. A

[MM] Furfurol – from the Free Dictionary: A colorless oily liquid, $C_4H_3O.CHO$, of a pleasant odor, obtained by the distillation of bran, sugar, etc., and regarded as an aldehyde derivative of furfuran; - called also furfural.
[NN] Nephretic – from the Free Dictionary: relating to the kidneys

definite medical treatment would be made available to the patient over the prearranged period agreed to by the patient and the physician. The aftercare facilities of the hospital were praised. Absolute privacy was promised. The pleasant environment was described to include the presence "canaries in their cages."[14] There also was an expansion of services to include the treatment of all forms of mild nervous disorders.[15] An additional attractive feature for the male patient was claimed.

We employ no male attendants or male nurses.[16] We use no padded cells, no straitjackets, nor any form of physical restraint. In our institution these antiquated methods have never been necessary.[17]

Three full-time physicians, down from four, were claimed to be employed, The four classes of patient treated were identical to the previous brochure. All things considered, the brochure was a marked improvement over its predecessor.

"Hospital Treatment for Alcohol and Drug Addiction," June, 1922

This twenty-eight page brochure intended for physicians reflected some significant improvements in technique. This 1922 version contained everything of the previous brochure with some significant additions, and one significant subtraction: the evils of American doughboys smoking tobacco were not nearly as prominent as before as four years had passed since the end of the war. In the preface to the brochure, Towns provided his signature as almost to sanctify the work with his good name. For additional authenticity, near the end of the brochure, he included four pages, which contained brief testimonials written by twenty-eight different doctors.

The first two of the twenty-eight testimonials were from names that Towns had used as references quite often in the past: Dr. Alexander Lambert and Dr. Richard C. Cabot. Dr. Lambert's referenced words originated in the June 21, 1913 article that appeared in the *Journal of the American Medical Association*. Dr. Cabot's reference originally appeared on May 11, 1911 in an article in the *Boston Medical and Surgical Journal*. But neither of those two references was dated by Towns in his brochure. None of the twenty-six additional doctor references that followed were dated either. Towns may have had a specific reason for omitting them, since most references may have been written years earlier when he was at the peak of his career.

The brochure was written to make Towns Hospital look like an attractive resource for any physician who thought his patient was in need of hospitalization because of almost any compulsion. Contrary to his previous writings, Towns recognized the pain was a legitimate ongoing reason some patients had become addicted.

> This might well be called a "health hospital" devoted to the administration of a definite medication to patients of both sexes, for the elimination of toxemias[oo], whether involuntarily induced through the necessity for the administration of narcotics to relieve pain, or self-induced by drug or alcoholic habit, or from the use of bromides, veronal, trigonal, sulphonal, and other "hypnotics," or somnifics.[18]

[oo] Toxemia – blood poisoning resulting from the presence of toxins

This paragraph is significant for a number of reasons. As in the previous two brochures, the word belladonna was not found. In this brochure, the Towns-Lambert Treatment was mentioned once but was not explained. A suggestion was made to the inquisitive reader that desired more information about the specifics of treatment available at the hospital.

> The whole subject has been covered in a series of medical reprints available to anyone requesting them; and may besides be found in various standard medical text books and medical encyclopedias.[19]

For Towns, there was a notable addition to his original text: footnotes! There were lists of medical textbooks and medical encyclopedias that appeared near the end of the brochure on pages 21 and 22. Footnotes were a relatively rare occurrence for Towns. The practice was not often repeated in the future. Second, the four major addictive drugs, from which Towns Hospital originated, were not mentioned anywhere in the brochure. Third, he started using medical terms such as "toxemias" and "asthenic,"[PP] which reflected an apparent desire to show a vocabulary worthy of his physician target audience.

Patients at Towns were once again described as falling into four main groups, but these four varied significantly from the previous brochures. There was the addict who used drugs to keep up with the frantic American pace of life and ways of doing business. This group encompassed the World War I veterans of the previous brochure. The second group consisted of involuntary addicts who were introduced to drugs by their physician for a condition of pain

---

[PP] Asthenic – lacking strength or vigor

that long since had disappeared, but the addiction had remained. This group included the vast majority of the drug addicts, as he had written previously. The third group consisted of patients who used drugs for the management of pain, and, in this case, their narcotic use was considered understandable. For these patients, the physician needed to be held blameless for his continued administration of the pain killing substance to outpatients, if that was considered necessary. The fourth group was considered to be the voluntary drug type who began using the substances for recreation and was not particularly eager to be separated from his substance. Alcoholics were all considered to be in the fourth group.[20]

Some of the triumphs that Towns claimed to achieve at Towns Hospital can only be accurately portrayed by using his own words. Besides, any attempt to paraphrase some of his sentences may be as inappropriate as it may be impossible.

> In the progress of the Hospital's clinical experience it was long ago found that, correlatively with the elimination of narcotic poisons from the patient's system, came the freeing of many patients from long standing neurosis—insomnia among the chief of these, hypochrondria [sic], nervous breakdown, abnormal blood pressure, and even incipient mental derangement of strictly functional character; and also from such of the usual manifestations of uric acid diathesis[QQ] as gout and rheumatism.[21]

His desire to impress the medical community with his lofty vocabulary and self-taught wisdom was also displayed in the following near run-on-sentence of how the blood stream was relieved of impurities caused by the use of toxic drugs.

[QQ] Diathesis – a hereditary or constitutions predisposition to a disease or other disorder

For such untoward conditions, our experience shows that logical clinical procedure is, first of all, to free the blood stream of these systemic sources of toxic disturbance, to remove from the tissues, by definite medication, those accretions of whatever sort, whether from narcotism, mal-assimilation, sub-oxidation or what-not-else, that are tainting the stream at its source, and when this unpoisoning of the patient has been accomplished by the processes indicated, he is ready for new courses, medical, hygienic, and other.[22]

Did anyone claim to have understood this paragraph back then? Had a reader claimed to have comprehended the above, might he have been passing an admission test to become a patient of Towns Hospital without knowing it?

Next, he stressed that Towns Hospital featured an extensive "rational after-treatment" capabilities using "the most essentially complete unit of its kind in the East."[23] He was very proud that the five-story building[RR] that housed the hospital had no identifiable markers "to distinguish it from its purely residential neighbors . . . in one of New York's most desirable residential neighborhoods . . . Extra service such as that of a special nurse, valet or companion, florist, library, and so on, may be arranged for at the patient's desire . . . Every form of physical therapy as approved by modern clinical authority is administered in the physical department . . . The electrical department is equally well equipped . . ."[24]

[RR] The building at 293 Central Park West has had a sixth story added to it, which architecturally does not match the elegant appearance of the lower five floors. It now is as tall as the building pictured to its left in various pictures included here.

The description of the solarium roof best described the atmosphere of comfort and relaxation available for the patient. Of course, the recommending physician was welcome to have enjoyed the same luxuries whenever he had felt them to be appropriate.

> The Hospital's roof is one of the most valued features of the establishment. It is enclosed under glass and provided with every useful adjunct to the patient's recreation and comfort. There are easy chairs and couches, singing birds in cages, books and magazines, and a billiard table. The view commands practically the whole of Central Park, the fashionable residence section of Fifth Avenue, the picturesque skyline of the city below the park, and on clear days, Long Island in the distance . . . The roof garden is open to the summer breezes but shaded from the summer sun by a system of awnings. In winter it is steam heated to afford a Palm Beach temperature in the bleakest weather.[25]

Though in the past decade he had desired no personal contact with any of his patients, both during and after the hospital visit, this reasoning did not apply for any physician that was willing to bring himself and his patient to Towns Hospital. Towns repetitively emphasized that the hospital staff would do nothing to interfere with the "intimate relationship" the doctor had with his patient.[26] The financial arrangements of how the patient was supposed to afford both his personal physician on top of the expenses of the fixed Towns Hospital fee was not explained.

Towns may have been a native Georgian, but he now thought that New York's Central Park was among the most desirable hospital locations in the country. Consequently, his location was better suited for satisfactory results than just about anywhere else—especially the boring

country!

It is sometimes held that the class of patients received by this Hospital should be sent to the

country for treatment. The Hospital's experience is directly to the contrary. Nothing is more

fatal to the successful treatment of addictions, however induced, than the dullness and

boredom of the usual country environment.

The Hospital is ideally situated to give effect to this principle both by its proximity to Central

Park and by the numerous advantages of New York City as a centre of business, professional,

educational and social life. There can be no question of the benefit to the patient of rational and

constructive diversion, such as furnished in abundance by the Hospital's situation.[27]

Towns then provided a list of attractions, many of which were in easy walking distance

of the hospital, which could have been mistaken for having been written by the New York

Chamber of Commerce to attract tourism.

He concluded the brochure with the three guiding principles that he claimed for his

institution:

1) Co-operation with the Physician

2) Only Voluntary Patients Admitted

3) Positive Effort for the Patient[28]

First, he wanted to emphasize that his hospital was a physician's hospital as a means of

increasing the chances of attracting referrals. Second, if the courts had dictated a defendant must seek hospitalization, he wanted nothing to do with them! He wanted his client base to be sure that the nearby rooms in the hospital would be free of undesirables. Third, he wished to emphasize once more that this location was a hospital, not a sanitarium; that definite, proven medicine was used; and that full and complete rehabilitation was the reasonable expectation for any patient that was willing to make an investment in his future.

"The Medical Treatment of Alcohol and Drug Addictions by Modern Hospital Methods," March, 1928

Six years after the publication of *Hospital Treatment for Alcohol and Drug Addiction,* Towns essentially reprinted this previous brochure but gave it a new title and some relatively minor edits and updates. Only the three names of the supportive professors remained on the title page as the two supportive doctors' names were not present. His signature no longer appeared as well. Some of the rather confusing sentences were removed, and his over-extended vocabulary somewhat reduced. The same twenty-eight doctors were listed as testimonials, which implied that not a single new testimonial had been received in the previous six years. Of the selections of Towns' literature, this brochure added nothing new and deserves no further mention.

15) *Reclaiming The Drinker* - 1931

By 1931, Charles Towns was turning 69 years old. He decided to create some of his most opinionated writing of his career, some of which can appear pretty funny when read today. He had to have been aware of a potential end to alcohol prohibition, which was one of the immediate first term actions taken by Congress even before FDR took office in 1933.[1] The tone of this short 77-page booklet suggested that his age may have added some grumpiness on top of his already substantial high self-esteem. He seemed to have not mellowed one iota over the years.

Here he added to his long list of reasons why a sensible man would not think of drinking alcohol.

Internists and pathologists have emphasized the cause-and-effect relations between indulgence in alcohol and diseases due to, or complicated by, under oxidation. They realize the difficulty of successfully treating such disorders as gastritis, gastric or intestinal ulcer, rheumatism, lumbago, neuritis, neuralgia, chronic headaches, nephritis (Bright's disease) and diabetes . . . Also they confess their difficulty in correcting or overcoming the hundred and one conditions, in which resistance is lowered to infection, and convalescence is retarded because of the reduction in the number and in the fighting efficiency of the leucocytes—the defensive corpuscles of the blood . . .

Sociologists and criminologists have proved by horrible example and rule of thumb, the intimate connection between prostitution, libertinism, sadism, rape and seduction, crimes of violence and all forms of perversion, and show why these deteriorations have their preponderating cause in alcoholic addiction.[2]

His first chapter provided a reminder of what Towns thought every drinker should know.

Every drinker knows that alcohol, when drunk to excess, has caused more death and destruction, more financial, physical, moral and domestic deterioration than any ten causes put together.[3]

Towns, who surely could embellish his ideas to emphasize a point, then asserted that men of all economic classes had consumed "the white poison" alcohol for three hundred centuries—or thirty thousand years![4] We do not know where he derived this information. But, in this case, he may have been more right than wrong in how long humans had been drinking alcohol.[5] Next, Towns compared alcohol consumers to lesser life forms, with highly uncomplimentary results: drinkers were not given the brains to know any better.

This impulse towards intoxicants is not confined to human beings. Insects frequently get drunk by indulgence in over-ripe fruit juices, returning again and again to their Dionysian feast. Wasps and bees often become wildly excited and quarrelsome, finally ending their orgy by crawling away in a semi-somnolent condition to sleep until the effect passes. Hens and chicks eagerly devour bread soaked whiskey or brandy.

Elephants and dogs frequently acquire fondness for liquors. Some degenerate dogs drink beer and refuse meat when both are offered at the same time. Darwin records the case of a baboon make drunk with beer. The next morning his keeper found him a picture of dejection and woe, holding his head tightly after the fashion of a repentant roisterer. The simian showed more

sense than the average drinker, however, for when he was again offered beer, he refused point-

blank to touch it.[6]

Why then did humans continue to consume a liquid that a baboon would not touch?

Did the baboon realize something that the human did not? According to Towns, the answer was

quite likely yes because the baboon knew that he had been drinking an excretion![ss]

While the impulse of intoxicants may be natural, there is not a drop of alcohol in nature. It is

not, and never was a "natural product." Alcohol is formed in nature only as an excretion. It is the

garbage of vegetation, the discarded elements of decayed plant life. It is a food only for the

ferment of vinegar, and poison for everything else.[7]

Chapter II examined titled "When is a Man Drunk" mainly repeated themes that Towns

had written before. He still held that alcohol was a narcotic, "first, last, and always" and since

alcohol impeded one's ability to work, it was a futile endeavor.[8] In the years prior to the

modern technique of determining a blood alcohol level, his reasoning employed here appears

tedious.

Chapter III carried the title "The Mental Effects of Alcohol" and concentrated on the

state of getting and being drunk. He figured that he, a layman and one who had never taken a

drink himself, was better qualified to study the subject conclusively because the drunk himself

had a handicap.

[ss] Excretion – from Webster's: "the act or process of passing waste from the body: the process of excreting waste

[It] is doubtful if one person in ten thousand has ever analyzed the various reactions of one undergoing the process of getting drunk, or if the drinker himself could describe, with any degree of accuracy, his sensations and reactions while achieving unconsciousness . . . Now the aspect of drunkenness that first impresses the observer—apart from the curiosity as to why the particular individual under observation should want to get drunk at all—is the boisterousness, disorder and often violent activity of the body and mind which frequently manifests itself in the initial stages of intoxication.[9]

This process of getting drunk according to Towns had its humorous moments, but those moments did not last very long. The drunk got louder, more obnoxious, and dissolved into nonsensical, semi-conscious chaos.

The drinker becomes more raucous-voiced, blatant and boastful. He wants to organize a "barber-shop quartet" and keeps the neighbors awake by repeated renditions of that drunkard's class, "Sweet Adeline."

He laughs boisterously at anything, or at nothing at all. His emotions are nearer the surface. He will make ardent love to a woman he met only a half hour before. He may run the emotional gamut. He may be elated or melancholy, scornful or sympathetic. His sexual desires may be easily aroused. He will "take chances" that never, in his sober senses, would he dare to take—both with respect to the possibility of venereal infection and the possibility of robbery or blackmail by the woman or her accomplices.

If the man suffers from psychic impotence, the inhibition may often be completely overcome, and libido and potency temporarily restored.

Also, the man's sense of fear will be blunted. He will rush in precipitately "where angels fear to tread." Many men become bellicose during certain stages of drunkenness. They will pick a quarrel with anything smaller than an elephant. They may become badly battered up, as a result of this, yet they appear to be thoroughly insensible to the blows and bruises they sustain.[10]

The process of getting drunk most likely will end with "profound melancholy and gushing tears" while any mention of someone's mother could be depended upon to "cause a lachrymose[TT] leakage among men, otherwise 'hard-boiled' and self-sufficient." By this time, all intellectual capacity of the man would be entirely suspended. His fate ends with a collapse into unconsciousness—"sans purpose, sans movement, sans sense, sans anything."[11] As best as Towns could tell, consuming alcohol was contrary to human decency. The risks far outweighed any possible benefits.

Chapter IV had the title "Alcohol as a Racial Deteriorator." In our times, it is best to stress that the race he was addressing was the human race. The idea was stressed that drinking during pregnancy was extremely risky, but drinking during conception by either sex was risky as well. He wished to ensure that lactating women would not drink during the months of breast-feeding. Failure to follow these rather simple rules could have them most serious consequences.

[TT] Lachrymose – crying or tending to cry easily and often

Indeed, I am convinced that our morons—grown women, whom the Binet[UU] psychological tests prove to have only the mental capacity of 12 or 13 year-old girls, and from whose ranks prostitutes are largely recruited—are thus cursed because of an alcoholized parentage. This also applies to our gunmen and gangsters, many of whom show similar traits of mental decadence and moron incapacity.[12]

Towns then repeated an unfortunately written commentary: he expounded about a country's drinking policies at a time when history would make his assertions look profoundly naïve after events unfolded. In his November, 1916 *Medical Review of Reviews* article, he had complimented the Russians on their prohibition on the sale of vodka, which had been announced as the Russian troops were being mobilized in July, 1914.[13] Of course, vastly more powerful forces of revolution were about to erupt that made the subject of alcohol prohibition in Russia appear as a rather trivial footnote. This time, he complimented an alcohol policy in parts of Germany two years prior to Hitler taking power.

In Germany, a beginning has been made in the "New Education." There the school children learn, as a lesson in composition that "Alcohol is a poison, with whatsoever name it is baptized—with whatever adjectives it is decorated. However taken, in winter in little glasses to warm one, or in large glasses in summer to refresh one, it is always a poison, as morphine, nicotine, cocaine, and opium. It neither warms nor nourishes. It does not strengthen. It kills. It assassinates."[14]

[UU] Alfred Binet, from The New World Encyclopedia: **Alfred Binet** (July 8, 1857 – October 18, 1911) was a French psychologist and inventor of the first usable intelligence test. Together with his collaborator, Theodore Simon, Binet began his investigations attempting to identify children with special needs in education. They developed their first Binet-Simon intelligence scale in 1905, completing two revisions before Binet's death

The "New Education" referenced by Towns apparently had little effect on the malicious education techniques evolving in the beer halls of Munich at the time.

Chapter VI dealt with experiments of feeding alcohol to animals and was of very little value except for one more description by him of the poison he so despised. Alcohol was declared "the Emperor of lethal drugs."[15]

Chapter VII was titled "The Medical Verdict" and condemned alcohol as making a typical drinker must less resistant to disease. Towns provided quite a few references to outside sources in this short chapter. Towns referenced a French doctor who provided statistics that indicated that alcohol was the principal contributing cause of tuberculosis, and then quoted the results of an international congress.

> The International Tuberculosis Congress, meeting in Paris, affirmed the relationship of alcohol and tuberculosis when it officially proclaimed the necessity of proceeding against both, if tuberculosis were to be vanquished.[16]

Alcohol contributed to a variety of unhealthy consequences, which according to Towns led to an increased susceptibility to diseases such as pneumonia. Studies conducted by the Anti-Alcoholic Congress in London and from "two large cities in the East" were used to support his assertion.[17] Alcohol hardened and toughened delicate mucous membranes that led the drinker to experience hoarseness the morning after a binge. The substance "makes the breasts flabby, by robbing the supporting muscles of their normal vigor and tone."[18] And as if to conclusively clinch his line of thinking, he made the assertion that alcohol robbed women of their beauty.

[Alcohol] seriously mars beauty in women. It roughens the skin, and produces discolorations and pimples. By inhibiting the action of the vasomotor nerves—which regulate the expansion and contraction of blood-vessels—it causes a chronic congestion in the tiny capillaries underlying the skin. This dilation, if long enough continued, becomes permanent, because the "elastic' will have gone out of the blood vessels. This causes the skin to become red and flushed, or, in cold weather, leaden or dull purple, and produced the characteristic bulbous nose associated with alcohol drinking.[19]

The number of decayed teeth found in women that drank was from two to four times the number that were found in women that did not drink, according to a referenced study.[20] Drinking women could not nurse as effectively. He then quoted a past president of the American Medical Association and another doctor.

Dr. William H. Welch, Ex-President of the American Medical Association, says: "Alcohol in sufficient quantities is a poison to all living organisms, both animal and vegetable." Dr. Howard A. Kelley adds: "It is clear, in the light of experience and of recent research work, that alcohol should be classed in the list of dangerous drugs, along with morphine, cocaine, and chloral. On the basis of experience I appeal to my colleagues everywhere to abjure its use."[21]

Quite a few additional medical opinions were referenced of the negative effects of alcohol before he concluded the chapter with one more vehement criticism of the substance.

So twentieth century expert medical testimony renders its final verdict in this: Alcohol has no helpful functions to perform in the human system, either in health of disease, as a beverage or as a medicine, under any circumstances, in any form or quantity, or under any condition. It is the most deadly and far-reaching, in its deleterious results, of all epidemics.[22]

Chapter VII had the title "Is Alcohol a Food?" By now, one would not be surprised for his answer to have been in the negative. "In short, it is a poison, which is the direct opposite of a food."[23] He did come up with another colorful title for the substance in the chapter, and that was to call it "The White Water of Death."[24] He concluded this chapter with what can only be described as a "classic Towns conclusion."

We are quite certain that alcohol, because it destroys all organic life, is a splendid medium in which to preserve a man, after he is dead. But to use it during life—either as a food or drink—is incompatible with scientific thought, or even good common sense.[25]

Chapter VIII concerned "The Truth About Beer." Some of these alleged truths may be rather obscure to a most experienced beer connoisseur. Where Towns got his research accomplished for his conclusions were not stated, which comes as no surprise. However, he boldly goes where few went before almost as if he was describing future Looney Tune cartoon characters.

Contrary to generally accepted belief beer is proportionately much more noxious than are wines or liquors. While liquor makes a man brutal and dulls his judgment, beer makes him slow-witted and abolishes judgment. And, while wine or brandy, in sufficient quantity, makes a man crazy, beer, in corresponding quantity makes him stupid. And between insanity and stupidity there is merely a question of choice. Some of us prefer an interesting maniac to a brutalized idiot.[26]

There was a specific reason that beer made the drinker so idiotic, according to Towns while other forms of alcohol did not: beer also contained a varying percentage of lupulin[vv]—the active ingredient of hops. Towns began to build some rather ludicrous observations with this information.

[The] so-called lupulin glands of the hops secrete an ethereal oil consisting of various terpenes[ww] . . . these terpenes act powerfully and disastrously upon the nervous system as well as upon the kidneys. The alkaloids, too, have a stupefying action on the nerves. For the hop belongs to the hemp group, and is closely related to Indian hemp. On the female blossoms of Indian hemp, as on the female blossoms of hops, we find glands holding a narcotic, sticky, bitter tasting substance, which is the active element in hashish.[27]

No empirical evidence is offered to equate how many beers might need to be consumed to equate to the effects of inhaling hashish smoke. He thought no such investigation pertinent.

[vv] Lupulin –from http://azarius.net/smartshop/herbs/herbs-relax/lupulin/ – Lupulin is the glandular powder separated from the strobiles of the Humulus lupulous (hops) plant. It has sedative effects on the body and mind and stimulates sleep . . . The powder is bright brownish-yellow and become resinous. Lupulin is chemically related to THC.

[ww] Terpenes – from http://terpenes.weebly.com/ - **In Cannabis:** -over 120 different terpenes can be manufactured by Cannabis, some only in trace amounts with others in double-digit percentage - produced in the Trichomes, the same glands where THC is produced, comprising between 10 and 20 percent of the total oils produced by the glands - about 10-29 percent of marijuana smoke resin is composed of terpenes/terpenoids

He was on a roll, however, which led to some of his most bizarre, but colorful, conclusions encountered in all his literature.

Hashish is used largely by the various Mohammedan peoples of West and South Africa and in the Malay Archipelago, for narcotic purposes. In the intermediary stage—before complete stupefaction sets in—these hemp habitués' become dangerously violent—even to running amuck with a huge creese,[XX] or crooked-bladed dagger—stabbing and slashing, until they are mercifully killed in their tracks.

Now, hashish contains exactly the same elements as are found in the lupulin glands of hops— bitter tasting resins, an ethereal oil, and one or more alkaloids. Therefore, hops exert the same effect on the human body as does hashish—differing only in degree.[28]

Here Towns provided his explanation for the phenomena of American bar fights and related violence resulting from thoughtlessly over-served beer drinkers! "Brutishness" resulted inevitably from the consumption of too much beer!

Here we have rational and scientific explanations as to why excessive beer drinking is accompanied by that stupidity and clumsy heaviness of mind peculiar to those who indulge unwisely and unwell in the beverage of Gambrinus[YY] . . . We have just seen that alcohol plus lupulin equals brutishness.[29]

[XX] Creese – a variant spelling of kris – a Malay or Indonesian dagger with a ridged serpentine blade
[YY] Gambrinus – the European patron of beer

Towns concluded this chapter with more denunciations of beer, including "the most sinister thing about beer is this apparently harmlessness."[30] For Towns, beer drove the man into a world of stupidity and delusion.

> The man who drinks ale or beer or stout drinks it because he likes its narcotic and stupefying effects. If he thinks he gets any other effects from it, he is deluding himself.[31]

In Chapter IX, titled "Prevention of Alcoholic Insanity," Towns returned to a subject that he had written about in detail when he was near his career peak. He had written Chapter XIV "Relation of Alcohol and Drugs To Insanity" in *Habits That Handicap* sixteen years before. He had written "How to Eliminate the Alcoholic as an Insane Problem" in *Medical Review of Reviews* back in November of 1917. Here he quoted statistics regarding the percentages of alcoholics that inhabited insane asylums to be roughly the same in 1931 as before prohibition. The 18th amendment, by Towns reckoning, had done nothing to diminish the negative consequences of alcoholism.

He did employ a term that was previously absent in his published literature, and that was "dipsomania." He also used "oinomania"[zz] as a term to describe delirium tremens. The consequences of dipsomania were so serious because crime was a byproduct.

> Perhaps the worst feature of dipsomania is the fact that it predispose to irresistible desires of an impulsive character, such as may lead to unnatural criminal actions, the gratification of depraved appetites, or the committing of robbery, or even murder.[32]

[zz] Oinomania – correctly spelled as oenomania today, from the ancient Greek: oino = wine + mania = insanity

He repeated a consistent theme that much of the medical community abruptly had been depriving alcohol from the alcoholic, causing delirium tremens, and from that, permanent wet brain victims resulted that only could live in supervised surroundings. Further, he alleged that society continued to treat most alcoholics no better than they had a hundred years ago, despite his near twenty-year crusade of revealing those shortcomings.

The final chapter of *Reclaiming The Drinker* was identical to the title of the book in which it appeared. He continued to insist "self-respecting pride is the main hope for the alcoholic."[33] He described friends of an alcoholic in a manner worthy of the sister-fellowship to A.A., Al-Anon, which would not be formed until about twenty years later.

Friends may assist, but while the importance of such friendly service cannot be overestimated, it must be of the right kind, or it will be worse than useless. For friends of alcoholics too often either sentimentalize or bully, when they should go about the task of helping, or else they allow too little time for the accomplishment of the reform.[34]

[The alcoholic] must first be robbed of all of his alcoholic crutches. He must not be left with some makeshift to lean on. There must be no strings fastened to him that can be pulled in. Nor must he be restricted, kept track of, and followed up for some indefinite period of time.[35]

The well-known American essayist and lecturer Ralph Waldo Emerson wrote these words in 1841, which may be helpful in regarding an episode of Towns contradicting himself.

A foolish consistency is the hobgoblin[AAA] of little minds, adored by little statesmen and philosophers and divines. With consistency a great soul has simply nothing to do. He may as well concern himself with a shadow on the wall. Out upon your guarded lips! Sew them up with packthread, do. Else if you would be a man speak what you think to-day in words as hard as cannon balls, and tomorrow speak what to-morrow thinks in hard words again, though it contradict every thing you said to-day. Ah, then, exclaim the aged ladies, you shall be sure to be misunderstood! Misunderstood! It is a right fool's word. Is it so bad then to be misunderstood? Pythagoras was misunderstood, and Socrates, and Jesus, and Luther, and Copernicus, and Galileo, and Newton, and every pure and wise spirit that ever took flesh. To be great is to be misunderstood.[36]

Probably the only one that might have considered Towns to be worthy of being included among some of those great names might have been Towns himself. But these words of Emerson can come to mind whenever Towns wrote about the word "disease." In this 1931 booklet he had written (italics added for emphasis).

Nor do I believe that there is anything to be gained by the purely mental treatment of this disease—except in very rare instances. For alcoholism *is a disease*, with a very definite pathology.[37]

But in *The Modern Hospital* article in February, 1917, he had written the opposite.

[AAA] Hobgoblin – an ugly or evil creature that plays tricks in children's stories

Medical men have been largely responsible for making the alcoholic believe *that alcoholism is a disease. Stop and think for a moment and you will see how absolutely absurd that is!*[38]

But in the June, 1912 in *The Century Magazine* article "Help for the Hard Drinker," he had written another opinion.

The man whose drinking has so disarranged him physically or mentally that he is obviously ill is, it is true, taken to the alcoholic ward of some hospital, but even there no effort is made to treat the *definite disease of alcoholism.*[39]

One can legitimately wonder if Towns should have kept a catalog of his own opinions after he wrote them so he could have avoided being misunderstood. Surely he had episodes of writing as if his words were "cannon balls." How, if he had ever been asked, could he have reconciled his varying written opinions regarding alcoholism as a disease? A likely answer: he abruptly would have changed the subject somehow. He would insist on discussing more important matters, such as how Towns had contributed so much to putting alcoholics back into their "right frame of mind."

For the drinker cannot look back over his drinking history and find anything there that is really worth while. He can find only rottenness and filth, sorrow, disappointment and self-destruction. No one need paint any dark pictures to such a man, when he is in his right frame of mind, because he sees it all, and more vividly than anyone could hope to have emphasized.

In many cases there is established immediately a mental disgust for the old drinking life.

It is futile to try to safeguard against exposure the man who has been drinking, for he is going to come in contact with alcohol in all walks of life. Yet, after he has been medically unpoisoned he has no desire for alcohol.[40]

The reference to the word "unpoisoned" represents evidence that many of Towns' opinions had remained unaltered. Once again, there was no mention of the Towns Treatment or belladonna anywhere in this short book. But Towns did relate "we were always able to destroy the craving and the desire for alcohol," which suggested his traditional medicines were being employed as before.

Towns did not seem to acknowledge that an alcoholic, upon being separated from his booze, was about to face a living problem for which he may have been entirely unprepared. Emotional trauma could lead to relapse. The newly sober drunk may have alienated all those he loved, worn out his welcome with his wife, be permanently separated from his children, job, house, office and familiar surroundings. He may have been facing serious legal consequences. The alcoholic might have felt more in need of his familiar medication, his former best friend, more than ever in order to cope! Anything to drown out the wreckage of the past! To face the real world without alcohol might have appeared entirely impossible—overwhelming—out of reach! The pain of failure, the weight of regret, the new address, enforced isolation, the financial consequences, and the legal penalties, could combine to crush the newly sober individual underneath his own fear, shame, and guilt. Towns seemed quite oblivious to the potential remaining chaos that resulted from years of irrational alcoholic behavior, as if the newly sober man could regain a new life as if everyone involved simultaneously benefitted from a mutual amnesia, which allowed for a full pocketbook and a stable and healthy home.

He seemed too focused on the physiological symptoms of alcoholism without adequately perceiving the possibility of obsessions, resentment, anger, and related fears that were once medicated through booze. Yes, the body could be relatively quickly purged of the phenomena of physical craving. So he would be correct in his assertion that "the *craving for a drink never comes back of itself* (italics in original).[41] The relief from physical craving becomes just the first serious milestone of recovery. Towns recommended isolation from the causes of the person's alcoholism for as long as necessary.

The alcoholic who has completed his course of treatment must do everything in his power to place himself beyond temptation. In respect to this imperative necessity of avoiding his old haunts and his former boon companions, if a patient is to remain free from his alcoholic craving, Drs. Jelliffe[BBB] and White[CCC], in "Diseases of the Nervous System" . . . have this to say:

"The matter of isolation is the important one. In cases in which the habit is firmly fixed isolation is highly desirable, if not imperative, as in these cases the patient is unable to resist temptation and as soon as opportunity presents itself, will lapse. After confinement for a few months, during which the patient is restored as far as possible to physical health, he is in condition to

---

[BBB]Smith Ely Jelliffe (1866-1945) received a Ph. D. from Columbia in 1900 where for a time he was a professor. Later "he was clinical professor of mental diseases at Fordham University, president of the New York Psychiatric Society, The New York Neurological Society, and the American Psychopathological Association, and editor-in-chief of the *Journal of Nervous and Mental Disease*. . . He was author of more than four hundred articles. " From Wikipedia. Clearly Towns was referencing a pioneer in the field of "psychiatry, neuropsychiatry, and ultimately to psychoanalysis."
[CCC] William A. White, M.D., Superintendent of the Government Hospital for the Insane, Washington D.C.

abstain if he wants to and is able; if he does not wish to or if he suffers from too great weakness of will, he will return to his old practices. If he does wish to stop drinking, however, he has been given the best possible opportunity, an opportunity which should be early extended in all cases and not delayed until by long-continued indulgences the case is necessary hopeless."[42]

Entirely absent from the preceding is the participation of the patient in any post-treatment activity that involved current or former patients. Isolation from the alcoholic's past temptations was considered mandatory, but no firm suggestions were provided regarding how this goal was to be accomplished. Also, the pronouns, employed in the solution for the patient, were almost always in the singular. Then, of course, Towns also had an additional significant recommendation for the patient after he left Towns Hospital and entered the world of temptation.

I would like also to emphasize the necessity for the alcoholic to avoid the company of women of easy virtue I have found that these women exert a most Insidious and pernicious influence upon men who have been excessive drinkers.

Bacchus and Venus have always been the most intimate of companions, all through the ages, and always will be. And while there are any number of men who can say "no" to a man's invitation to drink, there are relatively few men who can say "no" when a woman cajoles him to take "just one."[43]

Heaven help the poor man that returned to a wife that drank! How mistaken Towns was to concentrate on just male alcoholics when the admissions at nearby Bellevue Hospital included so many female alcoholics![44] Yet, Towns next demanded of the poor patients a requirement that legitimately may have been then, and may be now, beyond the capabilities of a mere mortals, fresh from the wreckage of their past and without their best friend alcohol. If they had problems (and what alcoholic did not?), Towns wanted no attention to be paid to them! "Complications" must be avoided!

> If his wife is about to sue him for divorce he had better put all his matters in his lawyer's hand, outline his policy or issue his instructions, and then dismiss the matter from his mind—or come as near toward doing so as he can. If his boy is raising Cain at school, or his girl is proving herself a problem, he had better postpone the solution of these questions after his own personal problem is successfully solved . . . In other words, the patient who wishes to get the best results from treatment should do all in his power to concentrate on one thing at a time. And, while he is under treatment, this thing should be *his treatment* (italics in original).[45]

He also took one more shot at tobacco users, as he had done with his very first magazine article in 1912. They needed to quit smoking to enhance their chances of quitting alcohol.

Just before the conclusion of the book, Towns described what kind relationship could be expected between Towns Hospital and the patient after he had been released. He described his approach as being "a unique point of view."

I tell these doctors that when a patient leaves this hospital we are through with him. We never communicate with a patient, either directly or indirectly. The patient is given to understand when he leaves this hospital, that we are through with him, and that we have done all we can; that as far as he is concerned, he is to forget our number.

Our psychology in this particular line, I believe, is sound. You can hardly expect to establish confidence in a drinker by constantly communicating with him, or by having him report regularly to you. This would immediately establish in his mind a doubt as whether or not he was going to make good. I have often said to a patient: "there are two reasons why we do not want to hear from a patient when he leaves our hospital. One is, if he makes good he does not want to be billboarding the fact and parading it around. And if he does not make good, we do not want to know about it."[46]

Finally, he concluded the book with the following:

I know that no good booze was ever manufactured; nor will there ever be any manufactured. In fact, I have yet to find, in all the years of experience I have had in dealing with the alcoholic, one single thing to be said in favor of liquor.[47]

Reclaiming The Drinker was reviewed in the *Journal of the American Medical Association* in the April 30, 1932 issue. The rather dry, short review included the following:

This is a written as an advertisement of the Towns treatment and hospital. Mr. Towns is against alcohol in any form internally and says that "the time may come in the not-distant future when to prescribe alcohol in sickness may be considered malpractice." . . . He quotes many medical men and professors in their arguments against alcohol, presenting nothing new or of scientific interest; but evidently Mr. Towns had not read or does not approve of Starling's work *The Action of Alcohol on Man*.[48]

The Action of Alcohol on Man was written in 1923 in Great Britain by Ernest H. Starling, "C.M.G., M.D., Sc.D., F.R.C.P., F.R.S.,[DDD] Foulerton Professor, late Jodrell Professor of Physiology, University College, London."[49] The book provided a scholarly, world-wide treatise on the consumption of alcohol since human history began to be recorded. Since the beginning of civilization, the author documented that there had been no demand to prohibit alcohol consumption until very recent times. What appeared to be an innocent remark by the book reviewer, that easily might be overlooked, was in fact, a huge insult to Towns. Dr. Starling had written in the preface of his work.

I cannot pretend to foretell what will be the effect on the unbiased reader of the evidence here presented. As regards myself, it has convinced me that in a civilized society such as ours the abolition of all alcoholic beverages from among our midst, even if carried out by universal consent, would be a mistake and contrary to the permanent interest of the race. If it were

---

[DDD] These are the actual abbreviations used to describe Ernest H. Starling on the book's title page. No claim is made to comprehend what all those abbreviations mean.

enforced by legislation against the wishes and convictions of a large proportion of the members of the community, I believe it would be little short of a calamity. While it would not result in the long run in the improvement of national health and efficiency, it would diminish that respect for Law and that identification of self with the Law which are essential for the stability and welfare of a democracy.[50]

Towns had claimed he had not found "one single thing to be said in favor of liquor." The JAMA book reviewer decided to provide Towns needed assistance: here was a rather well-known resource that did say something favorable about liquor. Towns could have easily found this scholarly resource had he not been so myopic concerning his own opinions.

16) Drug and Alcohol Sickness - 1932

One would never have known that Towns Hospital had been founded on Towns' reputation of treating opium after reading *Reclaiming The Drinker* published in 1931. For reasons not known, but presumably related to the business of keeping Towns Hospital solvent in tough economic times, Towns wrote *Drug and Alcohol Sickness* the next year. Towns seemed always to compose his advertisements, and this 44 page "book" was just one more advertising brochure.

By now he had was 70 years old but was still robust and active, and for a man that believed work to be the primary human virtue, there was no hint of a retirement. He wrote this newest booklet using the same ideas of addiction to which he had consistently written before. Addicts suffered torture and mental anguish by involuntarily having to poison themselves. "Their cells are poisoned with locked-up toxins, from self-made poisons, due to faulty metabolism and deficient elimination."[1] Most addicts wish to be decent and normal, but the build-up and "retention of the putrification products of cell decay and food decomposition" kept them trapped in a living hell. However, according to Towns, the wells of sympathy had dried up for addicts and their prospects were just as dim as ever despite Towns' quarter of a century of efforts trying to help them.

By many these people are regarded as suffering from some form of insanity—afflicted quite as definitely from the standpoint of mental equilibrium as a paranoic[EEE], a paretic[FFF] or a homicidal maniac.[2]

Towns insisted as he had for years, that it was the collective failure of society to have maintained a "distorted and entirely unsympathetic view of the whole matter." He believed most drug addicts wished to "break the chains that [bound] them to their evil genii." While he conceded there were some hopeless degenerates that had no other future than a prison cell, they were rare exceptions.[3]

Towns had not moved one bit from his original belief that most drug addicts were victims of their physicians or druggists. The majority of addicts received little pleasure from their narcotics, he wrote. Whereas most of his views seemed unaltered, there were significant changes in what he decided not to write. There was no mention of how legislation that he advocated would fix this drug 'evil' once and for all. There was not any mention that narcotics had been illegal for more than a dozen years. He did not try to address where addicts had derived their favorite substances since narcotic prohibition, nor what addicts now had to pay to acquire their fix. Also missing was any mention of any trips to Washington D.C. where his ideas were heard by Congress as they were back in the 1910's.

In the second chapter of the book titled "Slaves of the Poppy," Towns exhibited growth of a kind: he had improved his knowledge of ancient mythology and history particularly focused on narcotic practices in early times. He used Homer's *Iliad and the Odyssey* as an example that

---

[EEE] - paranoic – a psychotic disorder characterized by delusions of persecution with or without grandeur, often strenuously defended with apparent logic and reason
[FFF] - paretic – a late manifestation of syphilis, characterized by progressive dementia and paralysis

opium had been used by the Greeks. Opium had been used by Helen, daughter of Zeus, to

cheer up warriors that believed Ulysses and other warriors had been killed. Towns then

asserted that Egyptians fed paregoric to babies, which proved misleading. The name paregoric

had not been formulated as a mixture until it was created by Jakob Le Mort in the early 18th

century.[4] Towns' references to ancient times might have reflected a desire to recover some of

his authority on the subject of drug addiction after the devastating April 30, 1932 JAMA book

review.

Towns continued to report what he considered to be the shortcomings of alternative

methods to the Towns Treatment. Other approaches only deprived the addict of his substance,

but left the "poisons" untouched, which could lead to relapse because the cause of craving was

not addressed. Simple deprivation was also believed to be an extreme torture. Such beliefs

explained why many addicts, desperate to be released from their bondage, were petrified at

the thought of being treated.

Suffering is intense. Restlessness, the morbid craving for morphine, crises of violent fury and

destructive mania—often leading to delirium and attempted suicide—may result.[5]

He admitted there were degenerates beyond help, those that would "indulge their

depraved appetite for any new form of sensuous indulgence." They were beyond hope, a

menace to society, and there was no sense in attempting to treat them. They were the ones,

the "obvious" ones, that most normal people visualized when the subject of narcotics arose, which distorted society's perception away from Towns' perceived reality that most drug addicts were innocent victims.[6]

In Chapter III entitled "Removing The Craving," he continued his relentless assertion that his critics and competitors failed to recognize that removing craving was mandatory for sustained recovery.

The cause is *not mental*. The effects of toxic drugs in producing definite pathological changes in organism, are not of the imagination. They are, on the contrary, as distinct and definite as is a broken leg, or a case of eczema. For they are brought about by a material agency—the accumulation in the system of small quantities of the drug to which one may be addicted—together with the saturation of the tissues by toxins developed by the inhibiting action of the drug.

This explains why the deprivation treatment, and every other treatment for those addictions, *which is not directed towards eliminating these inhibiting poisons and toxins from the system*, is so generally foredoomed to failure.[7]

Towns then recalled how his work in treating drug addicts began, but he seemed to do so through rose colored glasses. He omitted his first experiences recruiting addicted volunteers many of which were underworld characters. He began with his Oyster Bay encounter with then-Secretary of War William Howard Taft. When this story was originally reported by Peter Macfarlane in "The 'White Hope' of Drug Victims" in 1913, three men, "one a Chinaman, and two Americans," were treated in order to convince Secretary Taft of the validity of Towns' solution.[8] Here the number has grown to six.[9] By 1947 as reported in Towns' obituary, his legend increased: the number had grown to a dozen, and they were reported to be soldiers that were treated under the supervision of army physicians.[10] Clearly one must be cautious in reading Towns regarding dates or numbers.

Despite Dr. Alexander Lambert's published disillusionment with the effectiveness of any medical approach to treat alcoholism, and despite the opinions of his recently hired Dr. William D. Silkworth on the recovery rate at Towns Hospital in the early 1930's (which will be addressed in the next chapter), Towns made a bold claim.

As I look back over this work from its inception, one of the most interesting things to me, notwithstanding that treatment after treatment for drug sickness has been brought out, and although I have been in a position to study at first hand all these so-called treatments—for many of them have been demonstrated in my own hospital—today I can say with absolute assurance, that the treatment brought out and developed by me is the most effective treatment known to the medical world.[11]

He even went further with his claim that was about as close to a guarantee without actually being one.

It is perhaps because the Towns hospital is thus equipped that we can record practically no failure in this method, where the patient was eligible for such treatment.

In other words, we have *never had a negative result* in any case, free from physical disability, or from an incurable painful condition which enforced the continued use of an opiate—such as gall stones, cancer etc.[12]

He repeated the shortcomings of deprivation and how the addict naturally wished to avoid such places where *"such deprivation may mean death"* (italics in original).[13] Because the Towns' methodology allowed the poisons to be withdrawn in a relatively safe, painless manner, addicts voluntarily chose his solution and then stayed free of their addiction. Towns was positively convinced of his assertion.

For any many who would undertake of his own initiative the definite treatment of his own case, with all the suffering the deprivation treatment entails, can be thoroughly relied upon to refrain from ever again returning to a condition where a repetition of this experience would be necessary.[14]

Towns repetitively seemed to have great faith that the most patients, upon seeing the errors of their past that had led to their alcoholism and addiction, would respond rationally and intelligently given the chance. How grateful they would be to be free at last! The pragmatism of a job with its associated responsibilities provided Towns' basic "pre factum" regarding the recovery potential of a prospective patient. Most productive contributors would return to their roles once again to the betterment of everyone. It was the vagrant rich and vagrant poor that were without hope.

Chapter IV was titled "Codeine, Heroin, and Cocaine" and was quite similar to his past opinions on drugs. He reasserted that cocaine was the most harmful of habit forming substances, and then provided a rather colorful description of what he believed to be the experiences of a cocaine addict.

The exhalation, which is the first effect, may, and frequently does, take the form of wild frenzy, sometimes accompanied by the fantastic hallucinations and delusions that are associated with acute mania. This is followed by profound depression, and frequently a sensation as of worms or insects beneath the skin, and sometimes ocular and circulatory disturbances.

The cocaine habitué, who has been taking the drug for some time is usually pale, capricious as to appetite, and extremely emaciated. His urine is scanty. He may have palpitation and irregular heart action, color blindness or double vision, and may suffer from an eczema of the nose—especially the tip—together with the formation of ulcers on the nasal septum—or even perforations of the septum.[15]

He repeated the assertion that Towns Hospital also treated those prone to indulging in too much coffee or tea. In Chapter V, he explained how hypnotics could be treated as well. Additional substances claimed to be effectively dealt with included paraldehyde, chloral, Indian hemp, bromides, and a variety of sedatives used to enhance sleep. Implied in these claims was a need to expand his advertised solutions to help attract more clients.

Chapter VI had Towns return to a favorite topic of his: tobacco. The chapter was titled "Tobacco-Poisoned Nerves." He listed the hazards from smoking almost with a vengeance.

Any and all forms of smoking are liable to induce asthma and shortness of breath. Also disturbance in vision, ranging from diminution of vision to retro bulbar neuritis. Even blindness from toxic amblyopia may result from excessive indulgences in cigarettes.

Thousands of smokers suffer from headaches, vertigo, insomnia, unwillingness to exert themselves, "trigger temper" and mental irritability and trembling of muscles.[16]

Once more Towns did not bother to document what sources he used to make such observations. One can also be reminded that some writers in the future would mistake Towns for being a doctor.[17] Another source would call him a Ph.D.[18] With all his opinions regarding a medical solution for addiction, and as a founder of a hospital, one can understand why some thought him to be a graduate of a medical school.

He also had specific warnings for any women that decided to indulge in the tobacco habit.

Women who smoke to excess frequently suffer from menstrual irregularities and other disorders of the generative system . . . Also women, who are much less resistant to the effects of nicotine than are men, suffer from facial blemishes, sallow complexions, and a loss of tonicity in the skin tissue. This latter is due to the fact that their thyroid, the normal activity of which controls the elasticity of the skin, has been overworked in attempting to oxidize the tobacco toxins . . . If women could only realize that they are playing ostrich, in attempting to hide the facial depreciation caused by tobacco toxins by plastering cosmetics and creams on their skins, they would get rid of their obsession for tobacco, no matter at what cost.[19]

The final two chapters of this short but highly opinionated work were taken from his previous book almost entirely. Unlike his practice of the 1910's in which he may have used the same paragraphs as many as three times in five years in various publications, this time he used the same sentences, but shuffled the order. His previous book *Reclaiming The Drinker* had Chapter IX titled "Prevention of Alcoholic Insanity" and Chapter X titled the same as the book title, which was "Reclaiming the Drinker." In *Drug and Alcohol Sickness*, he reversed the order of these two chapters: Chapter VII was titled "Reclaiming the Drinker" and Chapter VIII was "Prevention of Alcoholic Insanity." Examination of the two books side by side shows sentence after sentence in common, with occasional words being intertwined to disguise the repetition or the order of the sentences being changed while the meaning remained identical. Thus, the book hardly passes as a work of new scholarship. Instead, it has more the nature of a repetitive advertisement. Neither of these works remained in print as of this writing.

Had this book been Towns' final career contribution, his name likely would have fallen into the large dustbin of history and this book would not have been written. Towns' career, however, was going to end in a quite unforeseen, productive manner. He has provided an example that, contrary to impatient and often self-defeating prognostications, never is it too late to try to start to do the right thing.

17) Dr. William D. Silkworth Hired by Towns 1929-1951

The slender thread that connected Charles Towns to Alcoholics Anonymous had begun a number of years before A.A. was founded. According to Dale Mitchel, in his book *Silkworth The Little Doctor Who Loved Drunks*, Doctor William Duncan Silkworth was hired as physician in charge of alcohol rehabilitation at Towns Hospital in the spring of 1929.[1] Mitchel wrote that Dr. Silkworth was promoted to "medical superintendent of Alcohol and Addiction" in 1932 and soon afterward to "general medical superintendent of the hospital."[2]

Prior to being hired at Towns, Dr. Silkworth had been interested in morphine and opium addiction for many years. He arrived at Bellevue Hospital in 1896 as a medical student and intern. At the age of 29 in 1902, Silkworth had opened the first of three private practices dealing with drug addiction, but all failed after just a few years.[3] In 1916 he had a brief period in which he "began to work full time developing a sanitarium for alcoholics and addicts near New York," but despite working almost to the point of exhaustion the venture soon failed.[4] He then became a practicing army physician treating soldiers in a hospital that specialized in the psychologically wounded. The job ended months after the world war concluded. During that period, Silkworth was recognized "as one of the few doctors who had patience and could work effectively with addicted soldiers."[5] By 1919, he was an associate physician at Broad Street Hospital, but soon afterward became a clinical assistant associated with the Columbia Presbyterian network, a relationship that lasted until 1929. During the 1920's there seemed to have been a somewhat bewildering association with multiple jobs. His main source of his income seems difficult to identify as he was listed as an associate physician by three different medical institutions.[6]

By 1925, Silkworth was working almost exclusively with alcoholics,[7] which suggests that he, too, may have had to avoid the potential criminal consequences of a doctor working with drug addicts that had evolved. Questions remain regarding why Silkworth seemed to need a job so badly by the time he went to work for Charles Towns. Silkworth's life savings were wiped out by the stock market crash,[8] but what were the circumstances that led him to be unemployed (or underemployed)? Nor is there an explanation why Towns felt that there was a vacancy at Towns Hospital that needed to be filled. As at least three doctors, and sometimes as many as nine, were claimed to be residents or consultants at Towns through advertising in previous years,[9] how many were on staff when Silkworth was hired? Additionally, how would one reconcile a $40 a week salary[10] with a title of medical director upon Silkworth starting work at Towns Hospital? The job title and reported salary do not seem to fit. A lower job title upon beginning his employment there seems plausible. Regardless, Silkworth did seem to be medically in charge, one way or the other, by 1932.

Author Dale Mitchel has also documented another past professional relationship that helped shape the doctor. Dr. Silkworth had previously known Dr. Alexander Lambert, the Towns' ally, and benefactor before Lambert had ever heard of Charles Towns.

While at Bellevue, Silkworth had the opportunity to study and be tutored by Dr. Alexander Lambert, a visiting physician and a man whose path he would again cross nearly thirty years later. Lambert was passionately interested in narcotic addiction, later becoming one of the most respected men in the field of treatment. He published his first of many articles while working with Silkworth at Bellevue. It was a time when in the development of medicine that saw new theoretical articles published almost daily.[11]

Author Dale Mitchel provided an interesting background to the often quoted Silkworth assertion that many an alcoholic has an allergy to alcohol: this concept came to Silkworth through Doctor Lambert.

Lambert references the *Quarterly Journal of Inebriety* in his early writings. From this, we can assume he was familiar with an 1876 article that introduced the theory of an allergy predisposing one to addiction. We can also assume this information had been shared with Silkworth. Both the concept of alcohol allergy and Silkworth's relationship with Dr. Lambert would become important footnotes in the history of Alcoholics Anonymous. Lambert had always presented a case for a physical connection to the predisposition of alcoholism.[12]

While Lambert would later distance himself from the use of belladonna that he had championed in the *Journal of the American Medical Association* in 1909, Lambert and Towns were not the only ones of that era that wrote about the potential for plant related treatments for addiction. Silkworth had written *Notes of the Jungle Plant* in 1908, which described a Malaysian plant that was "shown to belong to the order *Combretum sundiacum.*"[13] The plant was described in a similar way to Towns' belladonna treatment. While Silkworth did not go as far as Towns and Lambert and actually treat patients using this substance, he argued for the potential value of the approach.

The remedy, while not a panacea, seems to offer the best medium of reduction thus far given to the profession, and while my experiments have been confined solely to the practical demonstration of the plant, I am led to believe that there may be present in the remedy an active ingredient, anti-opium in its properties. The burnt opium in gradually decreasing doses certainly plays an important role in the treatment, but this alone, or in combination with any other form of medication, heretofore known, has been, on the whole, unsatisfactory.

Both physician and patient must work together in harmony, and the suffering incident to the discontinuance of a powerful drug must be mitigated as much as possible, if permanent results are to be obtained.[14]

Silkworth's concentration in the first decade of the 20th century was opium and morphine addiction in an era when "there was confidence that an addict was eminently curable."[15] Silkworth, just as Towns and Lambert, was a resident of New York City that long had "held the distinction of harboring the largest number of narcotic addicts in this country."[16] Silkworth, who eventually earned the title of "the little doctor that loved drunks" from those that learned to love him, might have earned the title of "the little doctor that loved addicts" if it was not for drug prohibition. The Harrison Act of 1914 and the resulting legal rulings probably drove Silkworth to concentrate on alcoholism—forces that drove Towns to do the same. Thus, Silkworth at the age of 56 found at Towns Hospital a way to continue what had been his lifetime career. He, just as so many other doctors, stopped publicly treating addicts openly because of the potential legal consequences.

Silkworth portrayed the environment at Towns Hospital a great deal differently than the way his boss Charles Towns did. Initially, Silkworth was reported to be quite depressed by the "miserable wreckage" that he found that came through the place.[17] He became convinced that he needed to make many changes.

> In the first years at Towns Hospital, Silkworth was disappointed with the results of the recovery of his patients. He wrote about his failures with compassion. Fatality rates were high across the nation when dealing with alcoholic withdrawal, and Towns Hospital was no different. Silkworth continued working with different therapies—including the use of various nutrients and vitamins—until he began to find a way to help the alcoholic reenter life without a compulsion to drink. He spoke frequently about the need for a reliance upon God and a firm foundation of spiritual strength in order to handle the obsession to drink.[18]

The actual recovery rate that Silkworth found at Towns Hospital was less than two percent.[19] Could there be any greater contradiction with Towns' written words? In *Drug and Alcohol Sickness,* made while Silkworth was medical director in 1932, Towns had claimed "we have *never had a negative result* in any case, free from physical disability . . ."[20] Some negative publicity about the hospital had spread in recent years as well.

> By 1930, many of the prior patients at Towns who had been reportedly "cured" were now speaking publicly about failure and relapse. . . Towns needed a new direction in treatment and validity and respect for their alcoholic detoxification program. William Duncan Silkworth could provide just that.[21]

Jobs in Silkworth's field of expertise probably were hard to come by during the Great Depression. Besides, Towns, who had his 70th birthday in 1932, may have turned over the day to day operations of the hospital to subordinates long before Silkworth arrived. Thus, the little doctor was probably free to do as he saw fit just as long as he behaved with proper restraint regarding his controversial boss. Towns Hospital gave Silkworth the opportunity to capitalize on his experiences, in a field of work he had learned to love while putting his mark on the practices of the hospital.

> Silkworth literally reinvented the treatment model at Towns Hospital. He worked personally and closely with every patient. . . . He grew to know the alcoholic and, like no other, gained great insight into the alcoholic mind. Silkworth found that the physical remedy only opened the mind to a spiritual level of recovery necessary for continuous sobriety.[22]

Contrast Silkworth working "personally and closely with every patient" with Towns' 1915 assertion that the physician should not be a friend of his patient prior to his hospitalization commencing or any time thereafter, not even after the patient had been released after being treated successfully.[23]

By the fall of 1933, William Griffith Wilson made his first visit to Towns Hospital.[24] He documented this visit in his autobiography *Bill W. My First 40 Years*.

> It was here that I met a little man who was destined for greatness in the annals of Alcoholics Anonymous, Dr. William Duncan Silkworth. As I came out of the fog that first time, I saw him sitting by the bedside. A great, warm current of kindness and understanding seemed to flow out

of him. I could deeply feel this at once, though he said barely a word . . . A shock of pure white hair gave him a kind of otherworldly look . . . At last I'd found someone who understood, and I understood myself. It raised the unbearable burden of shame and guilt.[25]

Wilson described what he remembered of his first hospitalization.

At Towns in those days, they gave one some sedative, an occasional shot of whiskey, which was taken down to nothing in about three days; meanwhile they plied you with castor oil and belladonna. How the world brightened up as my brain began to clear. Only now did I realize how badly I had been benumbed for month, yes, years. Poisoned body, poisoned mind, poisoned emotions. All these were on [the] mend at once. Dawn was coming, and I waited for the sunrise.[26]

The language of alcohol being poison, just as Towns had so often asserted, was quite present in Wilson's words. He then documented his first encounter with Charles Towns at the hospital, and here he wrote about him as "Charlie" for reasons that can only be surmised.

Graduated to my bathrobe, I ventured to the roof. There was a solarium up there, a pool table, and a lot of gymnastic apparatus. One forenoon I bumped into Charlie Towns, the proprietor. Charlie was one of those American success stories. He had been a poor Georgia farm boy and later, banging around the world, his travels had taken him to China, where he'd seen belladonna applied to opium addicts.[27]

Here we have strong evidence that Bill's memory was not infallible about this period, as Robert Thomsen had observed.[28] Wilson had dictated his recollections of those events two decades after they had taken place. According to Robert Thomsen, in *Bill W.*, Bill Wilson did not converse with Silkworth until Bill's second visit.[29] In addition, Towns did not just see belladonna being used in China as Bill relayed. Towns had taken the belladonna treatment to China with him after pioneering it in New York City before 1908. Wilson shared his memory how Charles Towns instructed him how to get sober.

Well, the subject of his lecture[GGG] was this: no booze, plenty of exercise with the dumbbells, and muscle up the old willpower. Of course, anybody could stop if they really wanted to, once the poison was taken out of them by the famous Towns-Lambert treatment.

I must say in fairness , though, that Charlie didn't talk too much about curing alcoholism. At one time their literature had used the word, but it had been dropped. Lots of the patients were repeaters, people who had no idea of stopping. These fellows just wanted to be put in shape to drink again.

All of this impedimenta covered Charlie's finer nature, which I was later to see, for he plays an important part in my narrative to come.[HHH] On this first meeting, though, he did jar me. The spectacle of his success and his vast will to live lustily[III] got me down.

[GGG] Bill Wilson's memory of being lectured by Charles Towns, 'lecture' being mentioned twice, might have contributed to the following paragraph having been written in Alcoholics Anonymous on pages 18 and 19 [italics added for emphasis]: "That the man who is making the approach has had the same difficulty, that he obviously knows what he is talking about, that his whole deportment shouts at the new prospect that he is a man with a real answer, that he has no attitude of Holier Than Thou, nothing whatever except the sincere desire to be helpful; that there are no fees to pay, no axes to grind, *no lectures to be endured*—these are the conditions we have found most effective. After such an approach many take up their beds and walk again."

No two people could have been set in greater contrast than he and Dr. Silkworth. Those long talks with that benign little man will be treasured among my dearest possessions unto the end of my days. We used to sit out in the sun in a corner hedged around with plants. During these talks, some of his own stories fell out.[30]

As the time frame of these treasured talks with Silkworth was not mentioned, one might guess that these are collective memories of Bill rather than just of his first visit to Towns Hospital. While, in years to follow, there would be writers that would refer to the belladonna treatment as quackery and Charles Towns as a quack, no such opinions are known to have been written by Bill Wilson. Bill, twenty years after his encounter with Towns and seven years after Towns' death, would rather have Towns remembered for his "finer nature," a characteristic Wilson seemed to practice with most of the people he met to his everlasting credit. Furthermore, when one reads "Belladonna and Its Alkaloids" in the August 1915 issue of *The American Journal of Clinical Medicine* by Finley Ellignwood, M.D. of Evanston, Illinois, a medical author and editor of the publication name *Ellingwood's Therapeutist*, Towns' use of belladonna was thought to have been state of the art by many qualified medical men.[31] The fact that Towns did not change with the times hardly should have earned him the derogatory title of a quack.

Wilson continued to outline how Silkworth was so different than Towns.

[HHH] *Bill W., My First 40 Years,* dictated in 1954, ends before Bill met Doctor Bob in Akron in May, 1935. No knowledge is claimed here to begin to answer why Bill's taped autobiography was not continued beyond that point. One can presume that Bill planned to write more about Charles Towns' contributions to the creation of the book *Alcoholics Anonymous,* but for reasons unexplained, that apparently never happened.

[III] Lustily - full of or characterized by healthy vigor. If any mention of tobacco took place during these conversations, Wilson ignored it.

I listened to this little man, entranced. God knows I had been surrounded by those who care and a few who still cared. But this one understood. And he cared, too, in a deep, special way. In his lifetime, the doctor was to talk to fifty thousand cases of alcoholism. But not one was a case; they were all human beings. He cared for them collectively and, more important, he cared for them severally. Each one was something very special in his book. I instantly perceived this. He had a way of making me feel that my recovery meant everything to him, it mattered so much. Not a great M.D., this man, but a very great human being.[32]

According to Bill, and unlike Towns, Silkworth did not lecture his patients. He never communicated to them "on the basis of lecturing or sermonizing." Because of these wonderful mannerisms, Wilson asserted that Silkworth "had more success with alcoholics, even before AA, than perhaps any individual in the world."[33] Wilson continued his praise for Silkworth saying that within "Silky's kit of tools" he found two substantial contributions to the principles that eventually were to comprise the fellowship of Alcoholics Anonymous. The first was Silkworth's "immense capacity to somehow engage the utter confidence of alcoholic sufferers," which included an "immense capacity for love" through his ability to "make an identification with us alcoholics." The second great contribution was that alcoholism was an illness, "an illness of mind and body, neatly packaged in those two words, the allergy plus the obsession."[34]

Bill Wilson left this first visit to Towns Hospital "a new man," but the new man did not stay new.[35] He could not recall when he became, as his wife Lois described him, "a drunken sot" again,[36] or how many months he had stayed sober.[37] Lois wrote, "There was nothing to do but get him back to Towns Hospital immediately."[38] This first relapse, which may have lasted until

July, 1934,[39] caused his marriage to "hit a new emotional low and his second visit to the hospital." Bill's next relapse took place after a shorter period of being sober than before.[40] He could not remember why he got drunk again. All he could recall is that his "hopelessness broadened and deepened" as he experienced drunk after drunk. He was often "taken drunk without knowing how or why."[41]

Of particular interest was his stated reason he did not want to go back to Towns Hospital. If the belladonna treatment was so horrific, if he had to go through fifty hours of literal hell through the quack medicine provided at Towns Hospital, he did not state that as the reason. Instead, he shamefully confessed he "couldn't take the doctor" again, meaning that he did not wish to face Doctor Silkworth.[42] But by September, 1934,[43] he was taken to Towns Hospital a third time in "terrific shape."[44] After three or four days, he was able to regain a "semblance of [his] faculties" before a "depression set in."[45]

Soon after Bill emerged from this third episode at Towns in late September, 1934[46] with the verdict that he could not "go on this way another year" if he were to live, and if he was to stay sober, he was going to have to be locked up somewhere where he could not get alcohol. This time he left the hospital "really terror stricken."[47] His sobriety lasted him until Armistice Day, 1934 when he downed a free scotch at a Staten Island bar senselessly though he said it was insane to do so.[48] This binge lasted about a month and included being visited by Ebby Thacher twice.[49] A very drunk Bill voluntarily arrived at Towns Hospital a fourth time on December 11, 1934.

Silkworth greeted him outside his office—Bill had to look away to avoid the hurt he knew would be in the old man's eyes—and then the good doctor placed an arm across his shoulder and said quietly, 'Well, now, boy, isn't it time you got upstairs and went to bed?'[50] [51]

Robert Thomsen relayed the very sorry condition to which Bill Wilson had sunk.

One afternoon, only a few weeks back, his bowels had turned to water and gushed down into his pants. And now, despite the sedation, all his thoughts and memories, even his strange disjointed dreams, were stained by his own terrible stench, his own unspeakable shame . . . Tomorrow or the following day he would have to leave, and at this thought a sudden chill would sweep over him, his whole body would be covered with a cold sweat. He could not go home. Out there were three choices. Only three. He could stop drinking. Or he would go insane. Or he would die.[52]

Years later, Wilson admitted receiving the belladonna treatment when *Alcoholics Anonymous* was published in 1939[53] in "Bill's Story" and in his autobiography in 1954.[54] Dale Mitchel documented the use of belladonna when he wrote "Wilson was treated with belladonna by Dr. Silkworth at Towns during this fourth visit. His treatment is documented in Towns Hospital case number 1152, in December 1934."[55] Because he mentioned belladonna specifically when he documented his first and fourth visits, as well as having described his fourth hospitalization in his autobiography to include belladonna as part of "the usual treatment," the available evidence suggests he received belladonna during each of his four visits. Not mentioned, not even hinted at by Wilson are any of the bizarre side effects as documented in the 1910's, including the "puke and purge" and "delirium, diarrhea and damnation" observations of others during the treatment. Had Wilson been treated with the belladonna four times in a year and a half, each time for fifty hours on the hour, with the outcome of greenish stools while being invaded constantly by nurses and doctors, may it be presumed that Wilson would have had far more to say about it? Even when, for example, Bill Wilson recounted his fourth visit to Towns in 1956, he said nothing about belladonna, but instead he said, "At first I was suspicious. I was afraid I was going to be evangelized."[56]

A much safer assumption would be, as Glenn F. Chestnut suggested in his article "Bill Wilson's Vision of the Light at Towns Hospital," that "they were not given very much belladonna"[57] under the direction of Doctor Silkworth relative to the 1910's when the Towns-Lambert treatment was considered state-of-the-art. Silkworth fully realized the shortcomings of belladonna in his observation of the miniscule recovery rate when he began work at Towns. Dr. Silkworth was not the only doctor that would be using at least some belladonna during the 1930's. Dr. Robert Holbrook Smith, AA's celebrated cofounder, used the "Towns [Hospital] treatment"[58] on a fellow named Eddie not that many weeks after the Akron doctor's sobriety date.[59] However, at no time was there any hint of a fifty hour, round-the-clock, bizarre show of puking and purging. Any belladonna dosages involved had to have been employed in relative moderation. Belladonna was also occasionally involved in other forms of medical treatments into the 1940's—one peculiar episode in Germany documented that.[60]

Bill's White Light Experience, which he sometimes referred to as his "hot flash," followed on or about December 14, and he left the hospital on December 18, 1934 never to drink again. In years to come, however, Bill's explanation of his visionary experience led some critics to assert that the event occurred because of the belladonna. In retrospect, after three decades of patients receiving the medicines provided by Towns; of the many side-effects experienced by thousands of patients; and of all the doctors that had been references for the hospital and its treatment, Bill Wilson emerged as the only known historic "hot flash." To attribute Bill's experience to belladonna becomes absurd! After all, if the solution could provide such a life-changing, positive, cataclysmic event, would not Charles Towns already have been advertising that virtue for decades? He, the one who could stretch the truth beyond the breaking point to promote his hospital, never advertised or reported anything by a patient that even remotely resembled a "hot flash," or the experience of a white light that was from a "God of the preachers."[61]

Bill Wilson had been alarmed[62] by this revelation immediately after it occurred. He thought he might have gone nuts. Upon Bill reporting the event to Dr. Silkworth, the physician provided positive and comforting feedback to Wilson. He said that he was familiar with a history of sudden experiences that forever change peoples' lives, even though the good doctor admitted that he did not understand what had happened to Wilson. "Anything is better than the way you were," Silkworth said.[63] Author Robert Thomsen recorded that Silkworth told Wilson that probably he had "undergone some tremendous psychic upheaval."[64] The doctor continued, "I'm a man of science, and don't pretend to understand these things at all, but I know they do happen and they sometimes cure alcoholics."[65] Here Silkworth provided essential reinforcement to Wilson at a most critical time, for which he continued to express his sincere gratitude for the rest of his life. Had Charles Towns rather than Dr. Silkworth been present when Bill asked if he were going insane, the atheist Towns[66] most likely would have lectured Bill

Wilson first. Second, Towns probably would have told Wilson that he was crazy!

18) The Job Offer at Towns Hospital – 1937?

Bill Wilson's revelation of light left him wanting to work with alcoholics immediately and intensely. After Bill was discharged from Towns Hospital on December 18, 1934, how many days or weeks passed before Bill returned to be with alcoholics? No answer was available at this writing. What is known is that Doctor Silkworth allowed a sober Bill Wilson to visit other patients at Towns Hospital until Bill was to leave for Akron, Ohio in May of 1935. Wilson left no doubt of how important these visits were when he wrote the following in "Bill's Story" of *Alcoholics Anonymous*.

> . . . I soon found out that when all other measures failed, work with another alcoholic would save the day. Many times I have gone to my old hospital in despair. On talking to a man there, I would be amazingly lifted up and set on my feet. It is a design for living that works in rough going.[1]

How did Silkworth know that Bill Wilson was staying sober in this period? Did Bill have to report to the good doctor first before contacting any patients? What might Bill have had to do if Dr. Silkworth was not there? When did Charles Towns first find out that Bill, a former patient, was wandering the halls of Towns Hospital? Was it before Bill left for Akron? Charles Towns had repeatedly written that he did not want to follow up with any of his patients as he had written just a few years before.

The alcoholic worth while must first be robbed of all his alcoholic crutches. He must not be left with some makeshift to lean on. Nor must he be restricted, kept track of, and followed up for some indefinite period of time . . . For there is nothing that bores the alcoholic so much as long conversations about drinking when he would give his soul for a drink.[2]

Was not Silkworth allowing Wilson to use Towns Hospital as an "alcoholic crutch?"

There is no recorded response from Charles Towns regarding any first encounter with Bill Wilson wandering the halls of Towns Hospital or working with a freshly arrived alcoholic patient. Wilson wrote in August of 1957 about his return there: "When I wanted to go to work with alcoholics, [Silkworth] led me to them right there in his hospital, risking his professional reputation."[3] The good doctor may have been risking quite a bit. What might have happened to Silkworth's reputation had Wilson showed up at the hospital drunk again? Could Towns have imagined that a patient of his hospital, who had been a three-time loser and was supposed to leave after being treated never to be heard from again, would be allowed to return and talk with Towns Hospital patients? How did Wilson continue visiting patients there when his efforts seemed to keep nobody else sober for any length of time?[4] No alcoholic seemed to benefit from these "six months of failure" to "dry up any drunks" by Wilson visiting the hospital except for Bill Wilson himself, who did stay sober.[5]

However, somehow Doctor Silkworth must have been listening, for he was the one that helped straighten Bill Wilson out.

Bill Wilson was preaching, said [Silkworth], and his preaching was driving his prospects away. He was talking too much . . . about his own spiritual experience. Why not talk instead about the illness of alcoholism? Why not tell his alcoholics about the illness that condemned them to go mad or die if they continued to drink? "Coming from another alcoholic, one alcoholic talking to another, maybe that will crack those tough egos deep down," Silkworth said. "Only then can you begin to try out your other medicine . . ."[6]

Did the atheist Charles Towns know that he had an ex-patient preaching to the patients at Towns Hospital in the first half of 1935? We do not know. Possibly Towns was away for some of the time, maybe on a winter vacation? The two men had met either during Wilson's first or second visit. Maybe Towns did not notice for a time that Wilson was a former patient and not a hired member of the staff?

According to Dale Mitchel, in his book *Silkworth*, the good doctor may not have been as far out on a limb letting Wilson wander around Towns as previously presumed. That was because the esteemed colleague of Towns and Silkworth, Doctor Alexander Lambert, made the recommendation to Silkworth to allow Wilson's participation at the hospital.

Silkworth's first mentor, Dr. Alexander Lambert, now in partnership with Charles Towns, convinced Silkworth to give Bill Wilson a chance as an official volunteer lay therapist at Towns Hospital; he would be a representative of AA.[JJJ] Silkworth had learned long ago, through the work of other lay therapists such as Baylor and Peabody, that doctors didn't have the only answer for alcoholism. He knew the benefits of one alcoholic helping another. Although hesitant at first, the staff at Towns Hospital began to develop a deep respect for this tall and handsome man named Bill Wilson who spent all his time trying to help other alcoholics.[7]

[J] As A.A. was not named until mid-1938, the use of the term here has to be an inadvertent mistake.

Bill Wilson went to Akron, Ohio in May of 1935, soon met Dr. Robert Holbrook Smith there, shared with the doctor how he had become sober, helped Dr. Bob regain his sobriety after one slip, and then stayed the summer at the Smith's house on 855 Ardmore Avenue. Wilson had shared his experiences, rather than preach or lecture, as Silkworth had recommended. These two former inebriates were able to help A.A. #3, Bill Dotson, get sober by the beginning of July. Bill was to return to New York in the fall of 1935, and return to visiting patients at Towns Hospital as well as at the Calvary Mission. He also continued to stay close to the Oxford Group and their American leader Sam Shoemaker until circumstances led to a separation in 1937.[8]

As early as the end of 1936, Towns was to recognize the potential of this former dipsomaniac becoming of a lay therapist at his hospital. Silkworth's role in changing Towns' mind was documented by Wilson when he wrote of the job offer in *Alcoholics Anonymous Comes of Age*. He wrote that Towns said,

> "Now I am not a religious man and you must know that I was mighty skeptical of this business when it first came in here. Silkworth really scared me by his co-operation with you. But that is all changed. I believe in you people. Your methods are going to work."[9]

For the first time in Towns' life, at the age of 72, Towns admitted that he had changed his mind! Towns had become, as William G. Borchert described in *The Lois Wilson Story, When Love Is Not Enough*, one of Wilson's greatest admirers and supporters . . ."[10] Did Silkworth do most of the convincing of Towns, or Wilson? Was it Dr. Alexander Lambert? If it was Wilson, December of 1936 for the job offer may be too early a date: only five men were listed as being sober in New York City by the end of that year. The fifth, Myron Williams, had a sobriety date of April, 1936. New York #6, William Ruddell, did not get sober until February, 1937. Could the job offer have been sometime in 1937, or later? A date in 1938 might even be a better guess.[11]

Bill Wilson talked about this job offer in a talk given in Atlanta, Georgia in 1951, and the number of sober men attributed to have been said by Charles Towns suggests the December, 1936 as being inaccurate—just too early.

And one day I was up at old Charlie Towns who owned a drunk tank where I'd originally dried out. Charlie called me in his office. He said, "Look Bill. I want to talk with you. Old Doc Silkworth[KKK] really has faith in this thing of yours. Now I do. You only got 40-50 members around here, but someday, my boy, we're going to fill Madison Square Garden with those drunks." I said, "Doc,[LLL] I used to think so, but I think you're a little imagined [sic]. "No," he said, "I really believe that." "Now," he said, "Look Bill. These other drunks are getting jobs. You're passing them up over their heads, they're going back to work, drunks may be pretty crazy but none of them are stupid, they can certainly earn money if they stay sober. And you two people, you and Lois, you're starving to death. And as to the Rockefellers, what have they done?[MMM] Now, look Bill, why don't you come in here and let me give you an office here and make it your headquarters. I think you can get on my staff as sort of a lay therapist. Call it anything you like. It

---

[KKK] "Old Doc Silkworth" was a highly unlikely statement by Towns, as Towns was eleven years older than Silkworth
[LLL] Bill Wilson called Towns a "Doc" here, suggesting he, too, thought that Towns was a doctor, which he, of course, was not.
[MMM] Wilson and Silkworth, among others, met with the Rockefeller Charitable Foundation in 1937. Towns' reference here may reflect a resentment that he was not included.

would be perfectly ethical. You know that I haven't tried to take any advantage of the fact that you got well in this place. We haven't tried to capitalize on the fact that Dr. Silkworth's idea of sickness was a vital contribution to your society. Why don't you come in here and I'll put you on a darn good drawing account. I'll do more. Years ago in 1929 in the days of strict stockbrokers, when they all had bankrolls this place used to make several thousands of dollars a month, Bill. Today were just about breaking even. Times are hard. A partner of mine pulled out and took some of the business with him.[NNN] If you come in and make a perfectly ethical hookup with me, I'll give you a third interest in this place."[12]

Bill did not mention what pay he had been offered in this 1951 talk (following Tradition Six, where "problems of money, property, and prestige divert us from our primary purpose"). Dale Mitchel documented the pay offer in his book *Silkworth*, where he also used a 1936 date as when the offer took place.

In 1936, Charles Towns offered Bill Wilson a full-time paying position at Towns Hospital, with obvious support from Dr. Silkworth. The offer included a salary of $700 a month (2015: $12,000 or $144,000 a year) and a percentage of any profits from the AA ward. This was more than four times the amount of money offered to Silkworth when he first accepted the job at Towns Hospital.[13]

William L. White and Ernest Kurtz called the Towns' offer to Bill Wilson one of the "Twelve Defining Moments in the History of Alcoholics Anonymous" in a paper by that name in

---

[NNN] There is the possibility that the former partner was Dr. Alexander Lambert, but that is not known.

2008.[14] The salary offer, and possible part ownership, had to have been hugely attractive to Wilson, who was broke and would be evicted eventually from the townhouse in Brooklyn in which his wife Lois had been born. There was plenty of precedent for Towns to offer Bill Wilson a job as a lay therapist by this time.

Towns' offer to Bill Wilson was preceded by a tradition of distinguished lay therapists in the alcoholism arena that included Courtney Baylor, Francis Chambers, and, most importantly, Richard Peabody whose book, *The Common Sense of Drinking*, was currently popular. Bill Wilson could have easily become part of this growing network[ooo] of lay therapists.[15]

Bill was quite flattered by the offer. He continued to explain what happened next during his 1951 talk in Atlanta.

I must confess that I was terribly tempted. But the temptation passed into a conviction that Charlie Towns was right. And as I went home, I fell prey to our familiar ill, I fell prey to a rationalization, a particularly good one because I got it right out of the Bible. I thought to myself, "Yes, Bill, the laborer is worthy of his hire." So I arrived home and Lois, after an all day standing at that department store, was home cooking supper for the drunks around the house none of which was getting well either. It was only the ones outside the house that got well. And I said, "Well, dear, we're gonna eat. Gonna make this tie up with Charlie Towns." Well, she didn't seem too enthusiastic, she did seem kind of nice. That night there was that meeting in the parlor, and the drunks came in throughout the neighborhood, someone told it was a very big

---

[ooo] Hard to understand the reference to 'this growing network' when Peabody had died under, at best, dubious circumstances in March, 1936

meeting with all of us there, and excitedly I told them of this new opportunity. And as I talked I saw their faces fall. And when I had finished there was a dead silence. And finally one of them spoke. And I now know that he spoke for the group conscience. He said, "Bill, we know that you and Lois are having a tough time. Maybe we can give you a lift." But he said, "Don't you know that if you tie this thing up to that particular hospital that every hospital in the country will laugh because Charlie Towns is selling God, the old atheist. Don't you know, Bill if you put yourself in that position you'll become a professional? Bill, you can't do this thing to us," said the group conscience. "No, you can't do this thing to us." So I listened to the group conscience for the first time, and I knew that it was right. And luckily, I had the grace to obey it. And at that moment, it flashed over to me, you have never been a teacher of this society, you have been its pupil.[16]

Years later, Bill Wilson documented the job offer in *The Twelve Steps and Twelve Traditions* when he wrote about how he obeyed what became known as "the group conscience."[17] This group guidance became Tradition Two[PPP] of the Twelve Traditions regarding how an A.A. meeting should be governed and how individual members should behave for the survival of the group. He wrote that he obeyed the will of the group and turned the job offer down. But in doing so, he also followed what had become Tradition Six[QQQ] by omitting any mention of the money and the potential personal benefits of a $700 dollar a month job offer while the Great Depression was still a reality. Here was a clear example of how a story written by Bill Wilson intentionally omitted significant information: he wanted to highlight principles regarding the necessity of a recovery group surviving together, without muddying the waters to

---

[PPP] Tradition Two – "For our group purpose there is but one ultimate authority—a loving God as He may express Himself in our group conscience. Our leaders are but trusted servants; they do not govern."
[QQQ] Tradition Six – "An A.A. group ought never endorse, finance, are lend the A.A. name to any related facility or outside enterprise, lest problems of money, property and prestige divert us from our primary purpose."

include his immense personal sacrifice or ego. Some say to make an important point, "that someone should put their money where their mouth is." Wilson did precisely that! Furthermore, he was humble enough to never write about the personal economic sacrifice that resulted, or complain of himself and his wife living temporarily as nomads until they were fortunate enough find a home a couple of years later.

White and Kurtz built on this remarkable decision when they wrote:

> By defining itself as a spiritual program, the fellowship declared that its most essential elements were not for sale. In retrospect, one can only speculate on what might have happened had Bill Wilson accepted the proffered patronage of Charles Towns and his hospital.[18]

What might have happened had Wilson taken the offer? Might Wilson, himself prone to mood swings and deep periods of depression, been able to stay sober despite his erratic emotions that plagued him for the rest of his life? A most well-known New York lay therapist, Richard Peabody, died in March of 1936, and many think he died drunk.[19] Might Wilson's life have ended like that? Would problems of "money, power, and prestige" have broken the fledgling fellowship apart? Would Charles Towns have been an unwitting protagonist that shattered this group of drunks from continuing to discover a spiritual solution to alcoholism? Who can say? But the significance of Bill Wilson turning down the Charles Towns' job offer grows in significance when one learns that, in 2015 money, Wilson turned down $144,000 a year and never complained a bit! He even admitted that the yet unnamed group conscience of the fellowship was his teacher, and he was but a pupil of it. Wilson not only learned money

could not buy happiness—money could not buy him sobriety either!

19) Towns' Contributions to Alcoholics Anonymous

At first glance, the chances that Towns made a significant contribution to Alcoholics Anonymous seem highly unlikely. His job offer to Wilson inadvertently might have destroyed the emerging fellowship before the group had attained any substantial momentum. His opinion in *Habits That Handicap* regarding drunks banding together to help each other had been entirely negative.

A man once told me: "I want to be helped, but not at the cost of compulsory association with others seeking help. I know that to be thrown into unavoidable contact with those worse than myself would hopelessly degrade me. I should not be willing to risk that, no matter how much good the treatment might do me" . . . At a time when nothing in the way of betterment can be expected of him unless he regains confidence in himself, such treatment does not strengthen, but cripples, a man's spirit.[1]

Despite his outspoken opinions of the futility of alcoholics trying to help each other, Towns ended his career with actions that repudiated much of those printed opinions written over the past quarter of a century. He even went so far as to help Wilson and his little band of recovering drunks by becoming their largest creditor. He provided financial backing for A.A. when times were tough. The April, 1939 publication of the book *Alcoholics Anonymous* seems very unlikely without his support.

Towns had become familiar with *The Common Sense of Drinking* by Richard Peabody, written in 1931, that was popular at the time.[2] Peabody had provided an example that a book could be written by a layman that outlined how recovered drunks could stay sober. Bill Wilson's partner at the time, Hank Parkhurst, had assembled a stock prospectus titled "Alcoholics Anonymous" in mid-1938 for a corporation to be formed called "The One Hundred Men Corporation," which boasted of the potential for great financial returns.[3] However, Towns never risked any of his money buying stock from the group that had never become incorporated.[4] Instead, he provided the little group of drunks an outright loan at apparently no interest—a very generous gesture. Bill Wilson remarked:

> Charlie believed in us mightily; so we had put the slug on Charlie for $2,500. Charlie didn't want any stocks; he wanted a promissory note on the book not yet written. So, we tapped Charlie for $2,500, which we routed around through the Alcoholic Foundation so it could be tax exempt; do you understand?[5]

In 1957, Wilson wrote in the *Grapevine* how Towns was a major financial backer of the book project.

> Dr. Silkworth had helped to convert Mr. Charles B. Towns, the hospital's owner, into a great AA enthusiast and had encouraged him to loan $2,500 to start preparation of the book *Alcoholics Anonymous*—a sum, by the way, which later amounted to over $4,000.[6]

Bill Wilson wrote Frank Amos, a non-alcoholic member of the Alcoholic Foundation (forerunner of the A.A. Board of Trustees), on January 4, 1939 about the status of the book project and the role that "Mr. Towns" had played.

You will remember that we made strenuous efforts last summer to secure private contributions by which to carry on our work, maintain an office and secretary, and afford me time to write. These efforts proved unexpectedly disappointing, and broadly speaking, we were then faced with the question of whether to let the matter drift, those of us particularly concerned returning to business; whether I should accept the offer of Harper Bros. which would enable me to write the book, but which would provide no means of taking care of its aftermath; or whether we should permit Mr. Charles Towns to contribute further, undertaking the publication of the book ourselves and financing this latter activity by stock subscription.

After consultation the last mentioned course was adopted. Mr. Towns has subsidized me at the rate of $200 per month plus $100 more per month for the secretary that has worked with me[7]. Stock was offered at the rate of $25 per share and a company that would become known as "The One Hundred Men Corporation." The proceeds of the stock issued to take care of our office expense, Hank Parkhurst, and the promotional requirements of the book.[8]

Nothing has been found so far that has provided convincing evidence on why Towns decided to provide such substantial financial support.[RRR] We know Towns listened to his employee Dr. Silkworth and his longtime ally Dr. Lambert regarding the positive influences of Wilson working with alcoholics. Changing one's mind is one thing. That does not account for atheist Towns risking a total of $4,000 (around $50,000 in 2015 money) on the publication of an author's first book: a book that outlined a recovery program that stressed the importance of

---

[RRR] Please see endnote 7 of this chapter for a listing of the Towns Hospital check register, which documents checks written at Charles Towns' directions to various members of the book project, most of them to Bill Wilson.

spirituality and turning one's will to a loving God while mentioning very little about hospitalization or treatment. Towns had turned 77 that year at a time in life when wisdom often dictates avoiding any risky investments. Why would Towns make a substantial loan for the creation of a book that refuted much of his life work, and on top of everything else, talked about God?

Some of Towns' motivations for the loan may have been revealed when he contacted the American Medical Association in hopes of them providing positive publicity for the as of yet unpublished book. The AMA had replied asking for information about A.A.. Towns turned to Wilson for help (italics added for emphasis) as documented in Wilson's January 4, 1939 letter.

Mr. Towns asked me to help him draft a reply, which stated, in effect, that there was no organization in the conventional sense of the word; that for the past four years[sss] the work has been financed by the alcoholics themselves; that recently the Alcoholic Foundation had been formed to administer matters of money and so forth; that the majority of trustees of that Foundation were disinterested and well known in New York City; that a few modest donations had been made to the Foundation; that the work would never be on a fee or professional basis; that outsiders could not deal with this group in financial matters touching the work without approval of the trustees; and finally, that Mr. Towns had advanced certain monies to promote publication of the book, but that Alcoholics Anonymous had not obligated themselves to him in any way (except for the return of his money); *that Mr. Towns hoped and expected his business*

[sss] Four years? Of course that cannot possibly be true. November 1937 is the date that is believed to be when the book or pamphlet project originated. Here we have 'salesman' Bill Wilson stretching the truth. The letter being quoted was dated January 4, 1939.

would increase on account of our group, because men in it had taken his treatment and

liked it, and would probably recommend that others do likewise if the occasion

warranted. Mr. Towns stated explicitly that that was his only relationship with us; and

that he saw no reason why it should ever be any different. He also added that the

Towns Treatment was in use in Akron,[TTT] with his consent, but at no profit to himself."[9]

So Towns probably loaned Wilson and the book project money because the decision

was good for the hospital. Was it? Just twenty-eight A.A. members are listed as getting sober in

New York between the beginning of 1938 and March of 1939,[10] and of those, we do not know

how many of them were Towns' patients. A rough estimate is that Towns Hospital required no

less than sixty patients a month to stay in business, maybe more.[11] There's no way to know at

this time how many patients were attracted to the hospital because of Towns' emerging

favorable support of A.A., or how many stayed sober and may not have become A.A.

members.[12] The number of actual members of A.A. getting sober during 1938 seems fewer than

what could sustain Towns Hospital for more than a few weeks. Before too long, Towns was to

feel quite nervous whether or not his loan would be repaid.[13] Wilson stated in his long letter of

January 4, 1939 that of the creditors of the project, Towns was to be paid off first, probably

because of the pressures Wilson was feeling from Towns.

Despite the generosity of Towns supporting the book project, however, the project and

its members remained just about dead broke. As the finished book was being published in

---

[TT] Here is additional indication that, according to Wilson, some version of the belladonna treatment was used in Akron.

Cornwall, New York in early April of 1939, Bill Wilson documented how they just got by with Towns' help in the paying of a hotel bill.

> By now our money supply was gone. The hotel bill was going to be twice as much as the cash we had . . . Henry [Parkhurst] had lately adopted the comforting theory that if God wanted something done we only had to keep running up bills which eventually He would pay. This was a heartening example of faith, but it did leave the practical question of who would be God's agent in the manner of the money. Our stockholders were already loaded for every share they could take; they had had it. Maybe good old Charlie Towns would be the man. So it fell my lot to go to New York and put the touch on him. Mr. Towns was not too favorably impressed when he heard where we stood, but he came through with the hotel bill and about a hundred dollars to spare.[14]

In this case, "God's agent" was, more than anyone else, Charles Towns. These loans were made to Works Publishing as an apparent business decision and not to Bill Wilson personally. Less than three weeks after the book was published in early April 1939, Wilson and his wife Lois were evicted from their home at 182 Clinton Street, Brooklyn in which Lois Wilson was born.[15] No record of Wilson asking Towns to lend him personal funds to pay his mortgage is known. Despite his financial insecurity, Wilson seemed to hold no animosity towards Towns, for in that same January 4, 1939 letter, Wilson had written:

> How can we be helpful to Mr. Towns within certain limits? For he certainly played fair with us.[16]

There are well-documented stories throughout A.A. history that initially almost nobody wanted the book despite Wilson's and Parkhurst's relatively amateurish publicity attempts. Towns' contact with the AMA did not have favorable results either. A rebuke of the new book was written in an October 14, 1939 the *Journal of the American Medical Association* review.

> The book under review is a curious combination of organizing propaganda and religious exhortation. It is in no sense a scientific book, although it is introduced by a letter from a physician who claims to know some of the anonymous contributors who have been "cured" of addiction to alcohol and have joined together in an organization, which would save other addicts by a kind of religious conversion . . . The one valid thing in the book is the recognition of the seriousness of addiction to alcohol. Other than this, the book has no scientific merit or interest.[17]

Sales of the book during the summer of 1939 were very discouraging. The first big break the book *Alcoholics Anonymous* was a direct result of Charles Towns, as Bill Wilson documented in 1957.

> One day in July, I went into New York City, where I visited Mr. Charles Towns. As in the case of Mr. Blackwell of Cornwall Press, we owed Charlie plenty of money. But both men had cheerfully gone along. As I stopped off the elevator onto the hospital roof garden, Charlie greeted me with a broad smile. He had been raising heaven and earth to get publicity for us and had succeeded. He had known Morris Markey, a well-known feature writer, for years. Intrigued with the story of A.A., Mr. Markey had approached Fulton Oursler, then editor of *Liberty Magazine*. That great

editor, writer, and friend-to-be had instantly seen the possibilities and had commissioned Morris

Markey to do a piece. "So," inquired Charlie, "when will you go to work with Morris?"

To our great delight, Morris soon hammered out an article which he titled "Alcoholics and God."

It was to appear in the September 30, 1939 issue of *Liberty*. This time we really hoped and

believed that we had turned the corner, and indeed we had.[18]

While waiting for the article to be published, Wilson and Parkhurst were flat broke until

they scraped by with an additional loan of $1,000 from another creditor named Mr. G.[19] The

magazine article resulted in eight hundred "urgent pleas for help" and several hundred books

were sold.[20] Charles Towns' persistent and repeated financial help had helped push Alcoholics

Anonymous into the light! If J. D. Rockefeller, Jr. and friends helped put A.A. on the map,[21]

Towns helped make the reason for the map necessary. No other individual provided the

amount of financial support that allowed the book to be written in the first place. No one else

provided the connections that led to the first substantial publicity, which resulted in hundreds

of book sales when they were so badly needed. Charles Towns, despite his abrasive personality

and history of stretching the truth, turned out to be the right man and the right time to push

Alcoholics Anonymous into its first substantial successes. At a minimum, Towns helped provide

a huge financial lift and publicity push to the society of recovered drunks born out of the early

days of "flying blind."

20) Epilogue

Creditor Charles Towns was repaid in full for the book project by Works Publishing in spring of 1940,[1] and after that event, nothing more has been found regarding the life of this

most unusual and controversial man until after his death on February 20, 1947 at the age of 85.[2] Colonel Ed Towns, the only son of Charles Towns, took over the administration of the hospital fully by 1944.[3] The obituary almost entirely concentrated on Towns' career in combatting narcotics, despite the fact that about three-fourths of his business by 1915 was in treating alcoholics, and the ratio went

Figure 36 - Charles Towns as he had appeared in *The American Magazine* in October, 1912

up after that. A mistaken mythology about Towns remained even after his death.

Towns had very strong allies in the belief that alcohol was a poison. Chapter XXI of Jelliffe's and White's *Diseases of the Nervous System* written in 1917 regarded alcohol in the following manner.

It is generally conceded that alcohol is a powerful poison and as such if taken in large quantities or over a long period of time produces serious damage to the individual , , , As a matter of fact the toxic properties of alcohol far outweigh any possible beneficent effects that it may have. In fact, it is questionable whether alcohol should be considered in any other sense than as a poison.[4]

The belladonna treatment may sound ridiculous by standards of today, and the temptation to refer to Towns as a quack has proved irresistible to some. However, the medical methodology of purging poisons did not originate with Towns. Doctor John Harvey Kellogg of Battle Creek, inventor of Granola, advocate of multiple daily enemas, and whose brother founded the Kellogg Company that invented Corn Flakes cereal to assist in morning regularity, was just one other example of how purging the colon was considered essential to good health around the time that Towns achieved notoriety.[5] Dr. Frank Carlisle published "The Drug Treatment of Morphism" in the February 8, 1917 issue of the *Boston Medical and Surgical Journal*. His treatment used scopolamine, one of the three active ingredients of belladonna,[6] instead of belladonna itself. He insisted that it was "of vital importance that the bowels should be made to act thoroughly each day. . . " (Carlisle's treatment is explained in the footnote as having many similarities to Towns').[7]

As mentioned previously, the highly esteemed Doctor Silkworth had advocated the potential properties of a Malaysian jungle plant in 1908 to have anti-opium properties, just as Towns had attributed to belladonna. While Silkworth was writing his first published paper on that subject, Towns was in China about to become an acclaimed anti-opium hero. Dr. David F. Musto again provided us a perspective on these times.

It will suffice to note that the Towns method had so many social and political pressures favoring it that refutation was difficult for a decade after its publication. It seemed to succeed because the alternatives - no effective medical cure for addiction, and the inaccuracy of some medical theories of the time - were unacceptable.[8]

Dr. Musto documented that atropine,[UUU] contained in belladonna, was an agent in the Towns Treatment that provided "a delirium confusion, a kind of twilight sleep which erased the memory of the withdrawal"[9] —a magic of sorts that helped the patient through the most unpleasant physical consequences from his addiction. As Ernest Kurtz eloquently outlined in *The Spirituality of Imperfection*, alcoholics and addicts quite often have been believers in a magic—such has been most often the bottom line of why, over time, they became so subservient to their substances.

[T]he "magic" of chemicals signifies the desperate (and doomed) attempt to fill a spiritual void with a material reality . . . Addiction has been described as the belief that whenever there is "something wrong with me," it can be "fixed" by something outside of me."[10]

[UUU] The August, 1915 *American Journal of Clinical Medicine,* p. 754-755, contained an article titled "Atropine as a Remedy for Irritant Gases." A gauze mask moistened with a solution of sodium bicarbonate or hypsulphate was recommended for gassed soldiers in the field. For exposed soldiers, oxygen by inhalation was the primary remedy. However, a Douglas V. Cow, of the pharmacologic laboratory of Cambridge University, recommended atropine to have great potential value when combined with oxygen. The experiments at this time involved only rabbits. This note is being included to emphasize the nature of legitimate experimentation with atropine for the times.

Thus, the Towns Treatment can be viewed as a pragmatic attempt for the times to provide a relatively quick fix for many patients that already were predisposed to believe in quick fixes! To refer to Towns as quack negates that, from a medical perspective, Towns was able to convince some of the most esteemed doctors in the United States of the effectiveness of his approach. These major references will be listed once more. Doctor Alexander Lambert, Towns' greatest ally, was to become President of the American Medical Association in 1919. Doctor Samuel Lambert, brother of Alexander and for a time dean of the College of Physicians and Surgeons at Columbia University, was listed as being associated with Towns Hospital. Doctor Smith Ely Jelliffe, M.D., Ph. D. was "Professor of Diseases of the Mind and Nervous System at the New York Post-Graduate Medical School and Hospital."[11] Doctor Richard C. Cabot of Massachusetts General Hospital was very highly respected as well.[12] To assert these esteemed men fell for a quack misses the mark! The claims of having all cravings removed in five days by being "unpoisoned" were convincing enough to the medical establishment because they had no better solution themselves.[13] Yes, the claims made by Towns in the years that followed became more out of step with reality as critics discovered that relapses were common and that the magic of the Towns Treatment was myth. However, provocative medical advertising, using the hindsight of today, permeated the medical journals in which Towns appeared (See the Appendix for just a few examples). Consequently, simply to call Towns a quack negates the fact that much of what passed for modern medicine during the decade of Towns' popularity, and afterward, looks primitive and naïve today. An open mind perusing medical journals of the 1910's will not take long to find all sorts of what appears to be ridiculous medical claims.[14] Towns' advertising materials and writings fit with the times.[vvv]

A dismissal of Towns as a quack also may discourage acknowledgment of his positive contributions. Towns refined a means of removing physical cravings for addictive substances in a relatively brief period that appeared to work—at least for a while. He was way ahead of his time in declaring that tobacco was hazardous to one's health. He was an advocate along with Doctor Kellogg for a healthy lifestyle almost a century before much of the popularity of physical fitness took hold in the United States. Wilson, who seemed to accent the positive virtues in most people and hoped to avoid causing conflict in his writing, omitted saying anything negative about Towns directly even when Wilson might have been personally offended by a Towns' opinion. Nothing has yet been revealed to have been written by Wilson that disputed Towns' very negative opinions regarding tobacco. Wilson, of course, had been an example one could continue smoking and quit alcohol, something that Towns repetitively had insisted was highly unlikely.[www]

Another positive contribution of Towns was his advocacy that an addicted employee should be treated medically rather than criminally. The Chapter "To Employers" of *Alcoholics Anonymous* resembled a long-standing Towns' belief: that an employee suffering from

[vvv] Advertised in *The Modern Hospital*, December, 1916 included Cook's Imperial Extra Dry Champagne: "is just stimulating enough to keep up the spirit of hopefulness in the patient, without any depressing after-effect." Anheuser-Busch's Malt-Nutrino beverage was "pronounced by the US. International Revenue Department as a A PURE MALT PRODUCT, and not an Alcoholic Beverage" despite containing 2% alcohol. Cascade Whiskey advertised three different types of whisky: "We wish to make clear to the medical superintendents and physicians the differences between the ordinary commercial brands of whisky and the Cased Whisky as we supply it for medicinal use."
[www] Did Wilson smoke cigarettes while trying to help alcoholics at Towns Hospital? For that matter, was smoking permitted at Towns Hospital by either the staff or the patients? Was Bill allowed to smoke his cigarettes at any time during any of his four visits there as a patient? (Wilson, who smoked through all his sobriety, died at the age of 75 of emphysema).

alcoholism could and should be retained, allowed to seek hospitalization, and returned to his productive role in society. Towns had written in 1912 that firing an addicted employee was a crime[15] and that Towns' methods of helping his patient were useless if the man could not return to his place of employment.[16] Towns surely would have lent his support for this chapter that is believed to have been written by Hank Parkhurst.[17] Towns' legacy does represent a forerunner to commonly accepted practices in many businesses today.

Towns' first book *Habits That Handicap* encapsulated most of his other works and the related brochures and advertising that preceded and followed. Towns' general claims for the belladonna treatment to be a solution for drugs, alcohol, tobacco, and a wide variety of other substances had nothing to do with the spiritual solution with which Alcoholics Anonymous was based, nor the singleness of purpose of dealing just with alcohol. Consequently, the early members of A.A. had to distance themselves from Towns just as they had to distance themselves from Frank Buchman of the Oxford Group after his 1936 controversial interview in *The World Telegram*, which included remarks about Hitler.[18] Controversy might have proven as hazardous to the emerging fellowship as professionalism. Wilson, while being honest about Towns' assistance to A.A., had to remain silent regarding Towns' eccentricities in Wilson's consistent desire to do everything possible to avoid turmoil and stick to the central issue: recovery from alcoholism.

The politics of Charles Towns included an unquestioned noble faith in the political efficacy of government. In the era in which *Habits That Handicap* was written, Towns most resembled a Wilsonian Democrat. Probably his idealism suffered severely from the United States repudiation of the League of Nations after World War I. Though Towns never specifically mentioned the League in any writings yet examined, Towns had repetitively asserted that narcotic addiction could be eliminated almost entirely if governments were the sole source and distributor of the substances. Implied through such advocacy was an unnamed international organization formed to oversee how governments worked together. The solution to narcotic addiction could be best achieved by government regulations and monitoring of how the drugs would be tracked through the requirement of doctors writing prescriptions and druggists distributing the drugs. Similar policies were to be enacted internationally. Towns considered such unanimity essential, which further implied that he believed citizens of vastly different cultures and governmental methods would share his perception of the crisis. Such was not to be the case.

A fair assumption would be that Towns, in his worst nightmare, could not have visualized the invention of amphetamines in the thirties, the discovery of LSD that followed, or the sheer variety and potency of new legal and illegal drugs that have evolved since. He never seemed to visualize that a moderate recreational usage of any drug could be a "high," or for that matter, considered fun, and that some people could successfully hide their addictions for decades. To him, drug prohibition was required because no individual was immune from becoming a threat to society. Any subordination of the will to any mood-altering substance was dangerous: a subtraction from the life of the "drug fiend" and everyone around him. The world would be a net gainer if narcotics, alcohol, and tobacco were eliminated and forgotten. His two books written in 1931 and 1932 may have been his way of trying to combat the opinions favoring the repeal of the 18th amendment and the legalization of alcohol consumption, which followed in 1933.

Towns was not immune to laws of unintended consequences. He advocated the medicalization of drug treatment and considered filling state prisons and county jails with drug addicts to reflect near barbaric practices that caused needless suffering. His advocacy of the Boylan Act for New York State and his support of the Federal Harrison Act passed by Congress in December, 1914 reflected his ideas for a national medical solution to drug addiction. He could not have foreseen that the Harrison Act would be used by the Treasury Department, through the Supreme Court, to criminalize drug addiction nationally in just five years. No comment regarding this unintended result was ever made by Towns—even when he published two books in the early 1930's. Had he realized his personal legal opinions would be bad for his business? Towns Hospital was very profitable until the late 1920's, so keeping his opinions to himself regarding Federal law seemed good for his finances, at least. The fears brought about by a world war and the actions of the Treasury Department had muted his voice: criminalization of narcotics was to be America's future.

However, Towns appeared rather naïve about politics altogether. He had clearly stated that since society had allowed alcohol to be legally sold, that society should be responsible for the inevitable negative consequences. Towns proposed "Alcohol Clearing Houses" should be built to provide universal solutions for all alcoholics resulting from society's mistaken permissiveness.[xxx] Municipalities or the state should be responsible for such facilities without complaint. That such hospitals might be in competition for the medical dollar with privately funded hospitals was not a concern of Towns. He seemed to consider himself above politics.

[xxx] As Towns had insisted that a fundamental part of his treatment required payment of a substantial fee upfront for which the patient would ultimately be responsible, he never seemed to address what Alcohol Clearing Houses would be expected to charge their patients.

Towns probably would have dismissed such criticism from doctors in private practice, or working for private hospitals, for their lack of vision and compassion.

His hospital survived him by eighteen years and continued despite the death of Dr. Silkworth in 1951. The reasons for the closing were outlined in a *New York Times* article dated June 6, 1965.

> The 50-bed institution at 293 Central Park West was a casualty of other detoxification methods, its inability to qualify for Blue Cross payments, and the rigors of a new Hospital Department code. It had pioneered in the "drying out" and "tapering off" process, always regarding alcoholism as a sickness. [19]

But, above all, Towns' lasting legacy began when he made a great decision to hire Dr. William Duncan Silkworth, and then support Silkworth's ideas in the years afterward when he saw they worked. Not only did Dr. Silkworth reinvent the treatment program at Towns Hospital, but also he was able to accomplish that feat while carefully avoiding public conflict with his very controversial superior. Silkworth happened to be the right man at the right time when a particularly obstinate drunk, Bill Wilson, made four visits to the hospital finally to get sober.[YYY] Silkworth provided needed support to Wilson immediately after his "hot flash" and during critical months of Wilson's early sobriety, but again, without Towns Hospital, Wilson may have never stayed sober. Wilson may have remained just one more nameless drunk, at some place such as Bellevue Hospital, who was doomed to jails, institutions, or death.

[YY] See endnote 43, of Chapter 17

Towns had enough of an open mind to loan Wilson and his group of drunks four thousand dollars for the book project despite his rejection of employment at Towns Hospital. Without those funds, which amounted to as much as half of the financing of the book Alcoholics Anonymous,[zzz] there might not have been a completed book project, or at minimum, it would have been substantially delayed at a time when Wilson and his wife were destitute. Towns also provided a much needed push that provided connections for the first published magazine article supporting the new book. He contributed mightily to the publicity necessary for Alcoholics Anonymous eventually to reach countless thousands baffled by their compulsive drinking without any hope for the future.

As this biography comes to a close, there is a realization of just how incomplete this work is. Very little regarding his personal life has been documented. Major life making decisions were mentioned without almost any understanding of why they took place. He worked in insurance in Georgia, for example, but where? What led him to move to New York? Where did he live and travel with his wife? Maybe many blanks can be filled in over time.

Charles Towns can be comprehended, however, as a man that had believed faith in oneself was essential—he wanted to reach each of his patient's sense of pride—precisely the opposite of a surrender or an admission of powerlessness practiced today in Twelve Step programs. While never publicly speaking of any shortcomings regarding his hospital, or expressing any regrets regarding his work near the end of his career, Towns' actions spoke for his own surrender to ideas he saw blossom in his very own hospital without him. Just as it became irrelevant whether or not Bill Wilson's "hot flash" was caused by belladonna, much of

---

[zzz] See endnote 7 of Chapter 19

Towns' written opinions became irrelevant, and forgivable as well, in light of what he finally did accomplish. His pride could have led him to dismiss this newly sober Wilson and his buddies with their desire to write a book. But that's not what happened. Charles Barnes Towns, when the future of the young fellowship of Alcoholics Anonymous was in the balance, made crucial contributions that helped the program to flourish. Anyone that has benefitted from the Twelve Steps, which A.A. has given to the world of recovery, owes a thank you to this almost forgotten atheist. Towns swallowed his pride by giving a boost to the spiritual program of Alcoholics Anonymous at a crucial time from which, indisputably, countless thousands have benefitted. As written in *Alcoholics Anonymous*, after all, "Drinkers like to help other drinkers."[20]

King Charles Barnes Towns saw a future recovery community that would fill Madison Square Garden: the A.A. Fellowship wanted no king to rule them. Accordingly, he humbly abdicated the rule of his castle, gave his blessings to the new movement Alcoholics Anonymous, and silently stepped into the shadows. If anybody remembered him at all, he was simply "Charlie."

21) Appendix

Figure 37 - A June, 1911 Ad in the Boston Medical and Surgical Journal showing the health properties of a pure malt product, which of course contained alcohol

Figure 38 - A June 29, 1911 ad in the Boston Medical and Surgical Journal, which recommended how doctors should prescribe "The Best Tonic" and not some cheap imitation.

Figure 39 - Ad in the June 1911 *Boston Medical and Surgical Journal* for Glyco-Thymoline of a medication to be placed in an infant's food or used with an enema

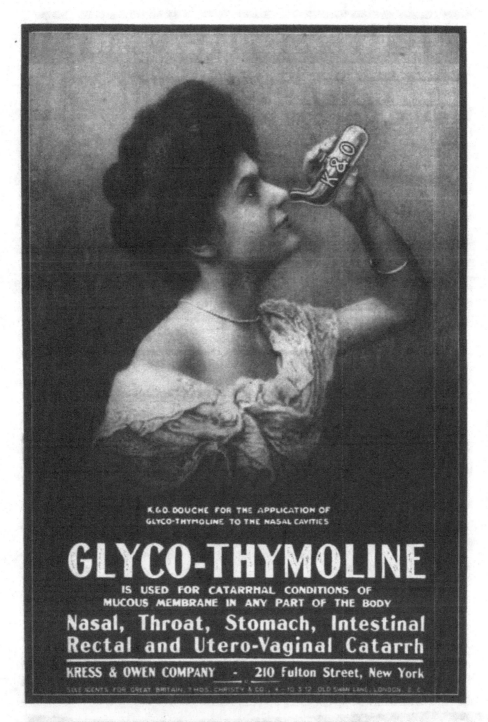

Figure 40 - A second ad for Glyco-Thymoline in the *Boston Medical and Surgical Journal*. Not only was the medication good for nursing babies, included here was a half dozen additional projected usages for the product. The ad also appeared many times in the1915 *Maryland Medical Journal*.

THE MODERN HOSPITAL—ADVERTISEMENTS

Liquid Petrolatum, Squibb

(Heavy, Californian)

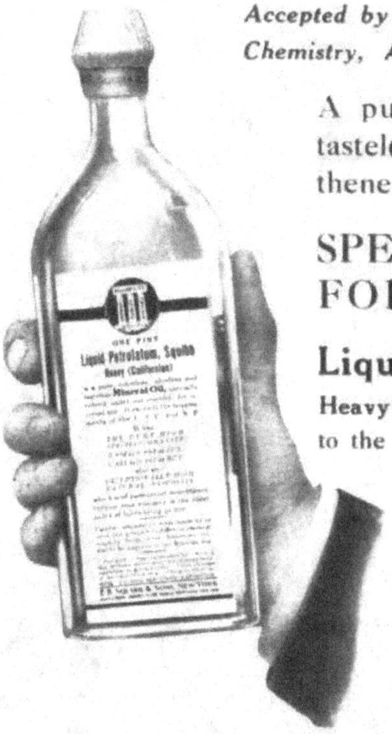

*Accepted by **the Council on Pharmacy and Chemistry, American Medical Association***

A pure, colorless, odorless, and tasteless mineral oil of the naphthene series of hydrocarbons.

SPECIALLY REFINED FOR INTERNAL USE

Liquid Petrolatum, Squibb, Heavy **(Californian), is recommended** to the **medical profession for preventing absorption of bacteria from the intestine and for restoring normal bowel functioning.**

It is the most viscous mineral oil on the market, which viscosity is true—i. e., natural—and is effective at the temperature of the inside of the intestine.

It may be administered in any quantities necessary. Its use does not form a habit.

As it is not absorbed, it is indicated to regulate the bowels during pregnancy and lactation.

Sold only in one-pint original bottles under the Squibb label and guarantee

Dr. Ferguson's concise handbook on Intestinal Stasis and Constipation will be sent free to any physician on request.

MEDICAL DEPARTMENT
E. R. SQUIBB & SONS, New York
Manufacturing Chemists to the Medical Profession since 1858

If you do not see in our advertising pages what you want, write us.

Figure 41 - A March, 1917 Ad appearing in *The Modern Hospital Magazine* for Liquid Petrolatum used to treat intestinal problems. The product may not have contained alcohol, but at the same time, the remarks that claim it not to be habit forming.

Figure 42 - An ad place in the April, 1917 issue of *The Modern Hospital* magazine by The J.L. Mott Iron Works featuring their work done at Towns Hospital with hydrotherapy

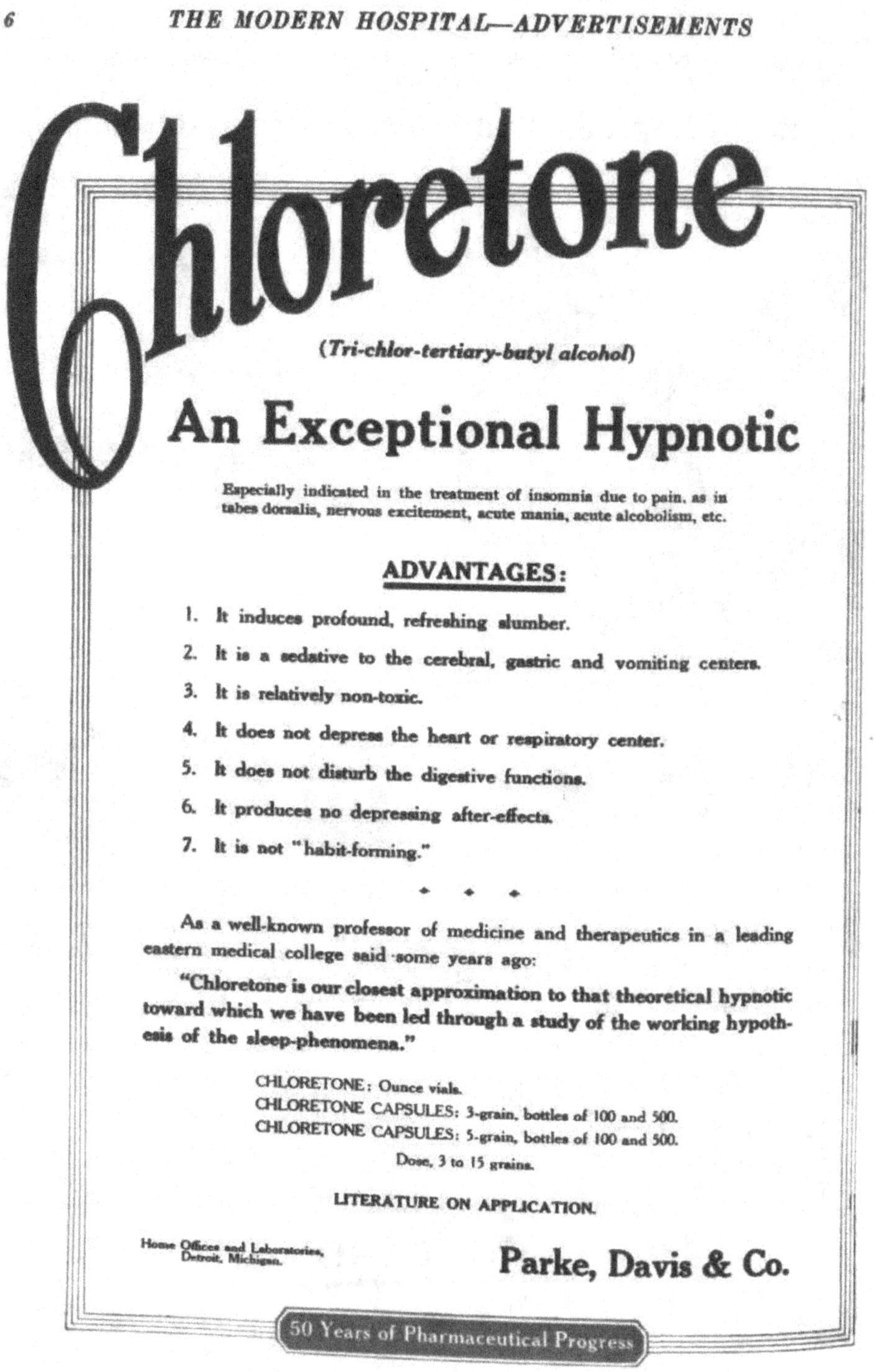

6 THE MODERN HOSPITAL—ADVERTISEMENTS

Chloretone

(*Tri-chlor-tertiary-butyl alcohol*)

An Exceptional Hypnotic

Especially indicated in the treatment of insomnia due to pain, as in tabes dorsalis, nervous excitement, acute mania, acute alcoholism, etc.

ADVANTAGES:

1. It induces profound, refreshing slumber.
2. It is a sedative to the cerebral, gastric and vomiting centers.
3. It is relatively non-toxic.
4. It does not depress the heart or respiratory center.
5. It does not disturb the digestive functions.
6. It produces no depressing after-effects.
7. It is not "habit-forming."

* * *

As a well-known professor of medicine and therapeutics in a leading eastern medical college said some years ago:

"Chloretone is our closest approximation to that theoretical hypnotic toward which we have been led through a study of the working hypothesis of the sleep-phenomena."

CHLORETONE: Ounce vials.
CHLORETONE CAPSULES: 3-grain, bottles of 100 and 500.
CHLORETONE CAPSULES: 5-grain, bottles of 100 and 500.
Dose, 3 to 15 grains.

LITERATURE ON APPLICATION.

Home Offices and Laboratories, Detroit, Michigan.

Parke, Davis & Co.

50 Years of Pharmaceutical Progress

Figure 43 - An ad for a hypnotic containing alcohol that appeared in the March, 1917 medical magazine *The Modern Hospital*

Figure 44 - a May, 1917 ad in *The Modern Hospital* featuring an extra dry champagne as being a health tonic

Figure 45 - A 1916 ad in *The Modern Hospital* featuring three kinds of whisky, which includes a "safe, medicinal whisky" that a doctor should consider safe to give to his patients

BOSTON MEDICAL AND SURGICAL JOURNAL [JANUARY 11, 1917]

Stanolind Liquid Paraffin

Stanolind
Trade Mark Reg U. S. Pat. Off.
Liquid Paraffin
(Medium Heavy)

Tasteless—Odorless—Colorless

During Pregnancy

STANOLIND Liquid Paraffin is an admirable laxative for use during pregnancy. It produces no irritation of the bowel, has not the slightest disturbing influence upon the uterus, and no effect upon the fetus.

The regular use of Stanolind Liquid Paraffin in the later months of pregnancy is an effective means of avoiding some of the serious dangers attending the parturient state because of sluggish bowel action.

Stanolind Liquid Paraffin counteracts to a definite extent an unfortunate dietetic effect on the intestine in this manner; the concentrated diet of our modern civilized life contains so little indigestible material that the residue is apt to form a pasty mass which tends to adhere to the intestinal wall. Stanolind Liquid Paraffin modifies this food residue, and thus tends to render the mass less adhesive.

Stanolind Liquid Paraffin is mechanical in action, lubricating in effect. Its *suavity* is one of the reasons why increase of dose is never needful after the proper amount is once ascertained.

A trial quantity with informative booklet will be sent on request.

Standard Oil Company
(*Indiana*)
72 West Adams Street
CHICAGO, U.S.A.   73

Figure 46 - *Boston Medical and Surgical Journal*, January, 1917. A March ad for this very same product promised relief from hemorrhoids

Figure 47 - *Boston Medical and Surgical Journal*, February, 1917. A rather unusual 'outstanding food' that promised favorable results for "infants, invalids, and the aged."

Figure 48 - *Boston Medical and Surgical Journal*, February, 1917. Top ad for The Fisk Hospital includes endorsement from a Towns' colleague Robert C. Cabot M.D.. Contains a physician advertising prices. Lower right shows an ad for the Towns Treatment

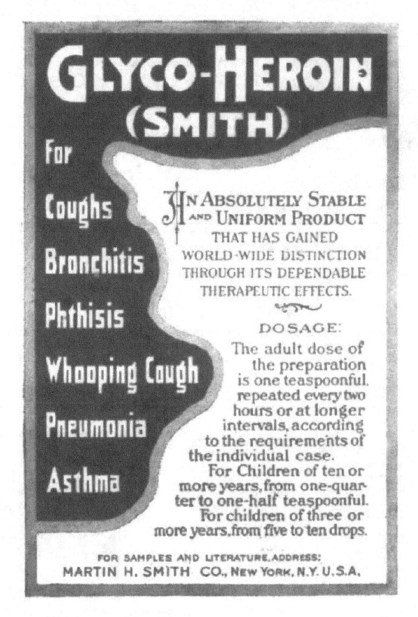

Figure 49 - December, 1914 ad in *The Medical Times*. This same ad appeared in the *Maryland Medical Journal* for January and February, 1915

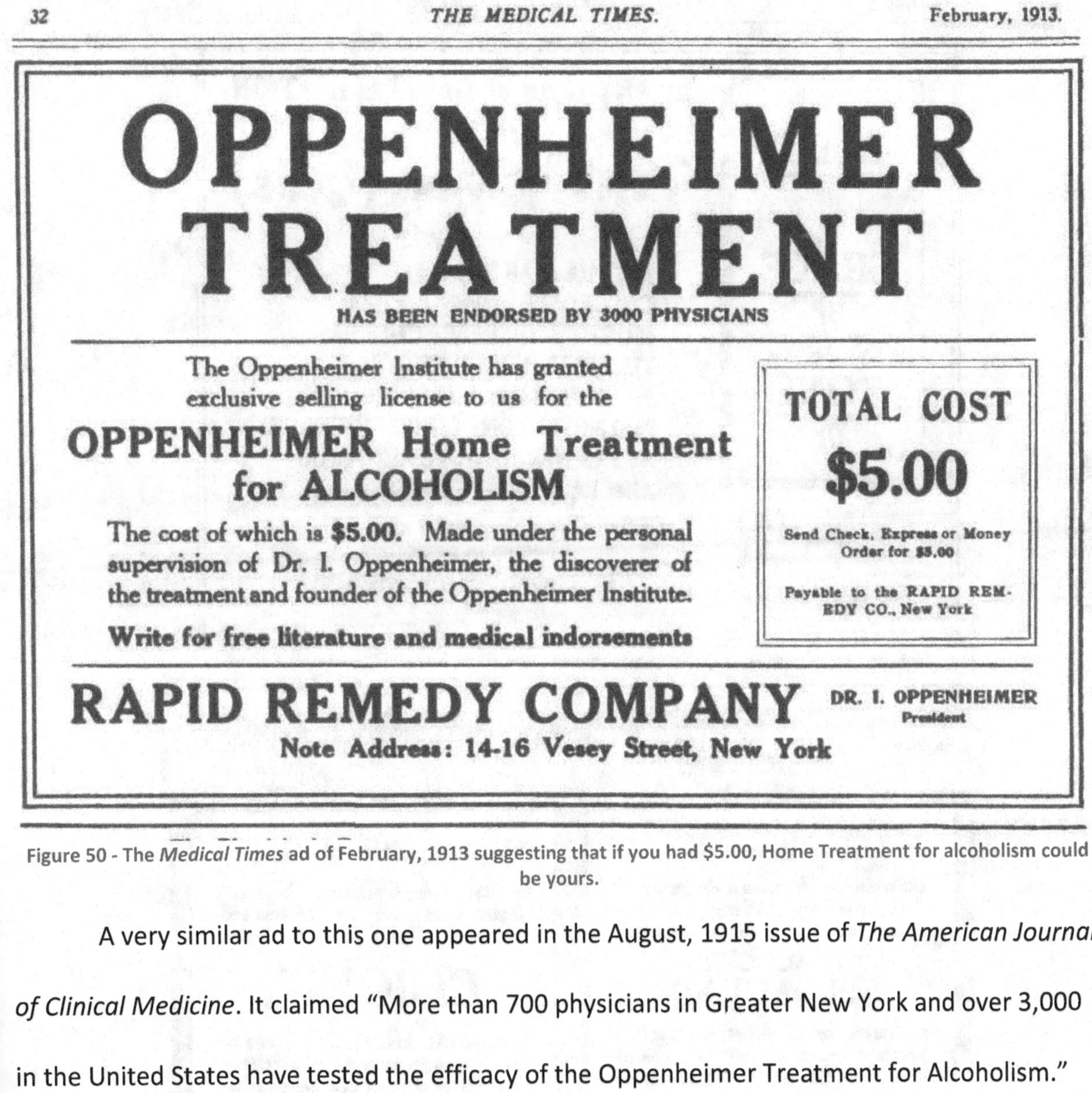

32 THE MEDICAL TIMES. February, 1913.

OPPENHEIMER TREATMENT

HAS BEEN ENDORSED BY 3000 PHYSICIANS

The Oppenheimer Institute has granted exclusive selling license to us for the

OPPENHEIMER Home Treatment for ALCOHOLISM

The cost of which is $5.00. Made under the personal supervision of Dr. I. Oppenheimer, the discoverer of the treatment and founder of the Oppenheimer Institute.

Write for free literature and medical indorsements

TOTAL COST

$5.00

Send Check, Express or Money Order for $5.00

Payable to the RAPID REMEDY CO., New York

RAPID REMEDY COMPANY

DR. I. OPPENHEIMER President

Note Address: 14-16 Vesey Street, New York

Figure 50 - The *Medical Times* ad of February, 1913 suggesting that if you had $5.00, Home Treatment for alcoholism could be yours.

A very similar ad to this one appeared in the August, 1915 issue of *The American Journal of Clinical Medicine*. It claimed "More than 700 physicians in Greater New York and over 3,000 in the United States have tested the efficacy of the Oppenheimer Treatment for Alcoholism."

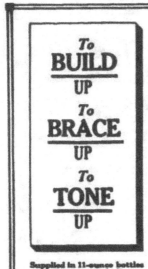
Figure 51 – The Pepto-Mangan ad found in the August, 1915 *Maryland Medical Journal* spoke volumes for the nature of patent medicines still available during these times. Patent medicines accounted for half of all drug sales as late as 1929 (See *The Origin of Compulsory Drug Prescriptions* by Peter Temin, 1978, p.2)

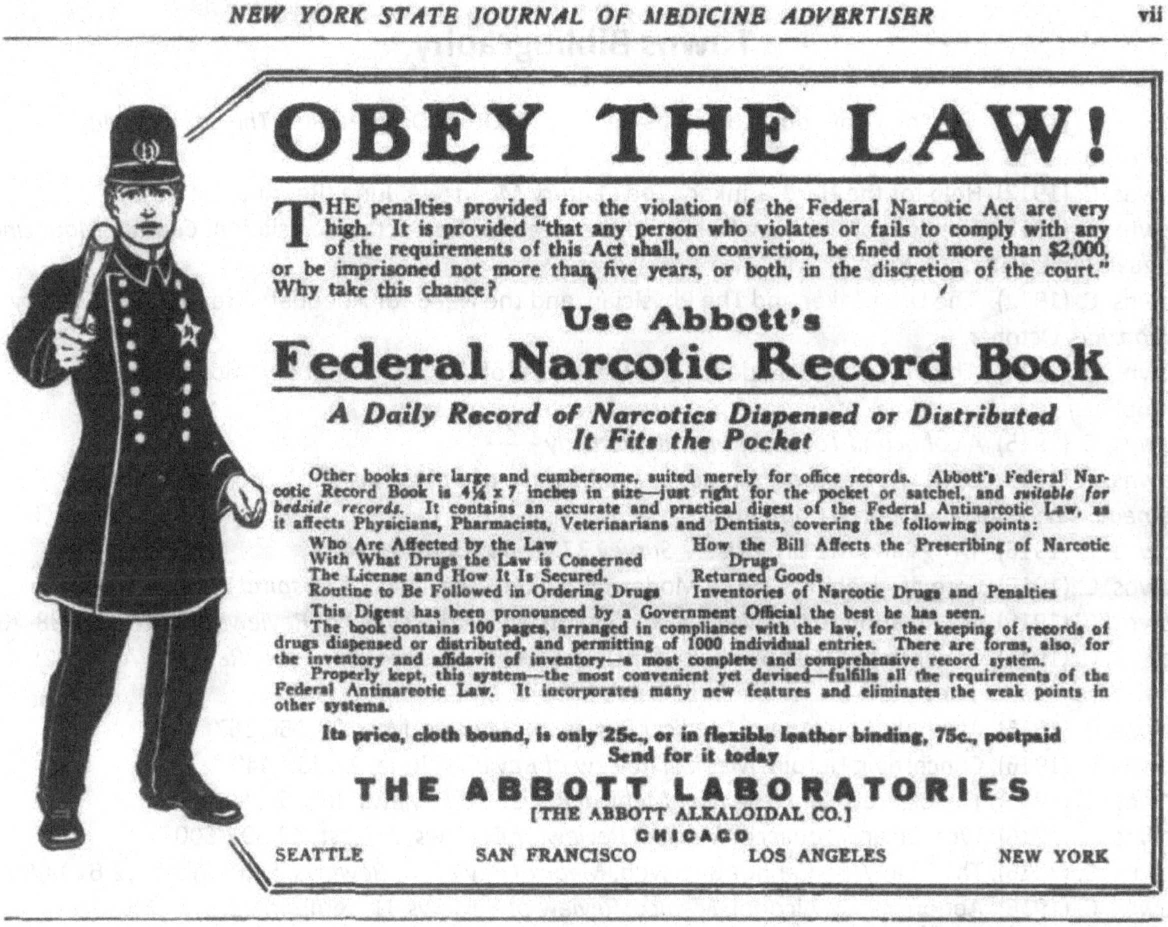

Figure 52 - This ad in the April, 1915 *New York State Journal of Medicine* was a result of the Harrison Ac

Towns Bibliography

Towns, C. (1912). The Injury of Tobacco and its Relation to Other Drug Habits. *The Century Magazine*, March, pp. 1-15.

Towns, C. (1912). Help for the Hard Drinker. *The Century Magazine*, June (Reprint) pp1-7).

Towns, C. (1912). The Peril of the Drug Habit and the Need for Restrictive Legislation. *Century Magazine*, August 84:580-587.

Towns, C. (1912). The Drug Taker and The Physician, and the Need for Adequate Treatment. *Century Magazine*, October,

Towns, C. (1914). The Physician's Guide for the Treatment of the Drug Habit and Alcoholism (8 page pamphlet).

Towns, C. (1915). *Alcohol and Tobacco, and the Remedy* ------

Towns, C. (1915, 1920). *Habits that Handicap: The Menace of Opium, Alcohol, Tobacco, and the Remedy.* NY: Funk & Wagnalls Company.

Towns, C. (1916). Drugs and the Drug User. *Survey* 37:47-49 (October 14).

Towns, C. (1916). Care of Alcoholics in the Modern Hospital. *The Modern Hospital* 7:(6):1-10 (Reprint).

Towns, C. (1916), My Relation to the Medical Profession, *Medical Review of Reviews*, March, 22:198-202

Towns, C. (1916), Government Responsibility for Drug Victims, *Medical Review of Reviews*, April, 22: 280-282

Towns, C. (1916), Alcoholic Reminders, *Medical Review of Reviews*, May, 22:366-367

Towns, C. (1916), Concerning Heroin, *Medical Review of Reviews*, June, 22:439-440

Towns, C. (1916), The Cigarette and the Boy, *Medical Review of Reviews*, July, 22:520-523

Towns, C. (1916), Women and Tobacco, *Medical Review of Reviews*, August, 22:599-600

Towns, C. (1916), The Man Who Cannot Be Saved, *Medical Review of Reviews*, September, 22:679-680

Towns, C. (1916), Aphorisms on Alcohol, *Medical Review of Reviews*, November, 22:832-835

Towns, C. (1916), The Future of Addict Legislation, *Medical Review of Reviews*, December, 22:905-911

Towns, C. (1916), Care of Alcoholics in the Modern Hospital, *The Modern Hospital*, 7(12):473-475

Towns, C. (1916). *Federal Responsibility in the Solution of the Habit-Forming Drug Problem.* NY: _____.

Towns, C. (1917). Successful Medical Treatment in Chronic Alcoholism. *The Modern Hospital,* 8 (1):6-10.

Towns, C. (1917). The Sociological Aspect of the Treatment of Alcoholism. *The Modern Hospital* 8 (2):103-106.

Towns, C. (1917). The Present and Future of Narcotive Pathology. *Medical Review of Reviews, N.Y.* 23:35-37. 113-119, 195-201.

Towns, C. (1917), Alcohol and the War, *Medical Review of Reviews*, June, 23:429-430

Towns, C. (1917), Alcoholism and Degeneration, *Medical Review of Reviews*, July, 23:507-510

Towns, C. (1917), The Necessity of Definite Medical Result, *Medical Review of Reviews*, 23:584-588, 640-642, 702-705

Towns, C. (1917), How to Eliminate the Alcoholic as an Insane Problem, *Medical Review of Reviews*, November, 23:761-765

Towns, C. (1917), Coffee Inebriety, *Medical Review of Reviews*, December, 23:825-828

Towns, C. (1917). *The Alcoholic Problem Considered in its Institutional, Medical, and Sociological Aspects* New York. (Published by the Author; Reprint of Modern Hospital Articles).

Towns, C. (1918), *The Work of Charles B. Towns Hospital and its Relation to the Medical Profession,* (Promotional Brochure Targeting Physicians), January, 16 pages

Towns, C. (1918), Psychology and Drugs, *Medical Review of Reviews*, January, 24:34-38

Towns, C. (1918), Alcohol and Antenatal Welfare, *Medical Review of Reviews*, February, 24:156-160

Towns, C. (1918), Inebriety and Drug Addiction, *Medical Review of Reviews*, April, 24:217-218

Towns, C. (NDa). The Habit That Destroys--How TO Destroy It   NY: Charles B. Towns Hospital (Promotional Article/Brochure).

Towns, C. (NDb). *Special Information for Physicians Concerning the Organization and Work of the Charles B. Towns Hospital 293 Central Park West, New York (Promotional Brochure).*

Towns, C. (1922). Hospital Treatment for Alcohol and Drug Addiction (Promotional Brochure Targeting Physicians, 27 pages).

Towns, C. (1928). *The Medical Treatment of Alcohol and Drug Addictions by Modern Hospital Methods.* New York City: Charles B. Towns Hospital (Promotional Brochure Targeting Physicians).

Towns, C. (1931). *Reclaiming the Drinker.* NY: Barnes & Company.

Towns, C. (1931). *The Menace of Opium* ---------

Towns, C. (1932). *Drug and Alcohol Sickness* NY: M.M. Barbour Co. In: Grob, G. (1981). *The Medical Profession and Drug Addiction.* NY: Arno Press Reprint.

General References and Suggested Readings

Books

Adams, Samuel Hopkins, *The Great American Fraud, The Patent Medicine Evil*, Project Gutenberg, December 1, 2013.

Al-Anon Family Group Headquarters, *Lois Remembers, Memoirs of the co-founder of Al-Anon and the wife of the co-founder of Alcoholics Anonymous,* 1600 Corporate Landing Parkway, Virginia Beach, VA 23454-5617, 1979.

Alcoholics Anonymous, *Alcoholics Anonymous*, Alcoholics Anonymous World Services, Inc., Fourth Edition, 2001.

Alcoholics Anonymous, *Alcoholics Anonymous Comes of Age*, 18th printing, Alcoholics Anonymous World Services, Inc, 1993.

Alcoholics Anonymous, *Pass It On: The Story of Bill Wilson and How the AA Message Reached the World*, New York; Alcoholics Anonymous World Services, Inc., 1984.

Alcoholics Anonymous, *DR BOB and the Good Oldtimers*, Alcoholics Anonymous World Services, Inc., 1980.

Alcoholics Anonymous, *Language of the Heart*, The AA Grapevine Inc., PO Box 1980, Grand Central Station, New York, New York, 10163-1980, 1988.

Alcoholics Anonymous, *Twelve Steps and Twelve Traditions,* Alcoholics Anonymous World Services, Inc., 1952, 1953.

B., Mel, *My Search For Bill W.,* Hazelden, Center City, Minnesota, 55012-0176, 2000.

Belenko, Steven R., *Drugs and Drug Policy in America*, Greenwood Press, 88 Post Road West, Westport, CT, 06881, 2000.

Bertram, Eva; Blachman, Morris; Sharpe, Kenneth; Andreas, Peter; *Drug War Politics, The Price of Denial*, University of California Press, Berkeley and Los Angeles, California, 1996.

Bewley-Taylor, David R., *The United States and International Drug Control 1909-1997*, Wellington House, 370 Lexington Ave., New York, NY, 10017-6550, 1999.

Blum, John Morton, *Woodrow Wilson and the Politics of Morality*, Little, Brown & Company, 1956

Borchert, William G., *The Lois Wilson Story, When Love Is Not Enough*, Hazelden, Center City, Minnesota 55012-0176

Cheever, Susan, My Name is Bill, Simon & Schuster, Rockefeller Center, 1230 Avenue of the Americas, New York, NY, 10020, 2004.

Courtright, David T., *Forces of Habit, Drugs and the Making of the Modern World*, Harvard University Press, Cambridge, MA and London England, 2002

Darrah, Mary C., *Sister Ignatia*, Loyola University Press, Chicago, Illinois, 60657, 1992.

Helmer, John, Drugs and Minority Oppression, The Seabury Press, 805 Second Ave., New York, NY, 10017, 1975.

Gahlinger, Paul, M.D., Ph.D., *Illegal Drugs*, published by Plume of the Penguin Group, 375 Hudson Street, New York, New York, 10014, January 2004

Glen R. Hanson, Peter J. Venturelli, Annette E. Fleckenstein, *Drugs and Society*, Eleventh Edition, Jone & Bartlett Learning, 5 Wall Street, Burlington, MA, 01803, 2012

Gordon, Ernest, *The Wrecking of the Eighteenth Amendment*, The Alcohol Information Press, Francestown, New Hampshire, 1943.

Fitzpatrick, Michael, *We Recovered Too, The Family Group's Beginnings in the Pioneers Own Words*, Hazelden, Center City, Minnesota, 55012, @2011

Jellinek, E. M., *The Disease Concept of Alcoholism*, College and University Press, New Haven, Conn, 1960.

Jelliffe, Smith Ely, White, William A.; *Diseases of the Nervous System, A Text Book of Neurology and Psychiatry*, Lea & Febinger, Philadelphia and New York, 1917.

King, Rufus, *The Drug Hang Up, America's Fifty-Year Folly*, Charles C. Thomas, Bannerstone House, 301-327 East Lawrence Avenue, Springfield, Illinois, 1972.

Kurtz, Ernie, *The Collected Ernie Kurtz*, iUniverse, Bloomington, IN 47403, 1999.

Kurtz, Ernest, *Not God*, Hazelden, Center City, Minnesota, 55012-0176, 1991, first published 1979 by Harper & Row Publishers, Inc., San Francisco.

Kurtz, Ernest and Ketcham, Katherine, *Spirituality of Imperfection*, Bantam trade paperback edition, January, 1994, originally published 1992.

Lobdell, Jared C., *This Strange Illness, Alcoholism and Bill W.*, Aldine De Gruyter, A division of Walter de Gruyter, Inc., 200 Saw Mill River Road, Hawthorne, New York, 10532, 2004.

Mitchell, Dale, *Silkworth The Little Doctor Who Loved Drunks*, Hazelden, Center City, Minnesota, 55012-0176, 2002.

Musto, David F., M.D., *The American Disease*, Origins of Narcotic Control, Oxford University Press, Inc., 200 Madison Avenue, New York, NY, 10016, 1973 & 1987.

Osler, William., M.D., *Modern Medicine*, Volume VII, Subtitle: "Diseases of the Nervous System," Lea & Fegler, Philadelphia and New York, 1910.

Pendergrast, Mark, *For God, Country and Coca-Cola, The Unauthorized History of the Great American Soft Drink and the Company that Makes It*, Collier Books, Macmillan Publishing Company, New York, NY, 10022, 1993.

Pittman, Bill, *AA The Way It Began*, Glen Abbey Books, PO Box 19762, Seattle, WA, 98109, 1988

Rock, Paul E., *Drugs and Politics*, Transaction, Inc., New Brunswick, NJ, 08903, 1977.

Schaler, Jeffrey A., Drugs, Prometheus Books, 59 John Glenn Drive, Amherst, NY, 14228-2197, 1998.

Temin, Peter, *The Origin of Compulsory Drug Prescriptions*, Working Paper, Department of Economics, Massachusetts Institute of Technology, 50 Memorial Drive, Cambridge, MA, 02139, 1978

Thomsen, Robert, *Bill W.*, Hazelden, Center City, Minnesota, 55012-0176, 1999; first published by Harper & Row, 1975.

Toland, John, *Adolph Hitler*, Volume II, Doubleday & Company, Garden City, New York, 1976.

White, William L, *Slaying The Dragon*, Chestnut Health Systems/Lighthouse Institute, Bloomington, Illinois, 61701, First and Second Editions, 1998 & 2014 (all quotes from 1st edition)

Wilson, Bill, *Bill W., My First 40 Years*, Hazelden, Center City, Minnesota, 55012-0176, 2000 by Stepping Stones Foundation.

Wing, Nell, *Grateful To Have Been There*, Hazelden, Center City, Minnesota, 55012-0176.

News Articles

Consumers Union, "The Harrison Narcotic Act (1914), Consumers Union Report on Licit and Illicit Drugs," by Edward Brechner & Editors, 1972.

New York Times, "Drug Habit Curable, Says Dr. Lambert," October 7, 1909

New York Times, "New Drug Law Hits Accidental Users," June 21, 1914.

New York Times, "Drug Smugglers Nullify New Laws," March 15, 1915.

New York Times, "Conquering The Habits That Handicap," August 8, 1915.

New York Times, "Federal Inquiry on Drugs Proposed," January 3, 1917

New York Times, "War is Increasing the Drug-Consuming Habit," April 29, 1917.

New York Times, "An Alcoholic's Savior, God, Belladonna or Both?", April 20, 2010, SCIENCE. section

Tapes and CDs

Bill Wilson, Atlanta, 1951, GSSA Archives, Macon, GA.

Jack Norris, Class A Trustee, Chairman of the Board of Trustees, Early Days in AA, Southeast Past Delegates meeting, Atlanta, GA 2/5/1972.

Web Sites

http://aaagnostica.org/2013/10/06/charles-b-towns/ Habits That Handicap, by Bob K.

Methoide.fcm.arizona.edu/infocenter/index.cfm?stid=164 The University of Arizona MethOIDE

http://azarius.net/smartshop/herbs/herbs-relax/lupulin/ azarious online smartshop.

http://barefootsworld.net/aacharles_towns.html "Charles B. Towns, Ph.D.".

http://www.cdc.gov/nchs/data/dvs/lead1900_98.pdf The Centers for Disease Control. publication "Deaths and Death Rates for Leading Causes of Death: Death Registration States, 1900-1998.

http://drvitelli.typepad.com/providentia/2012/12/seeling-the-belladonna-cure.html "Seeking he Belladonna Cure".

http://library.brown.edu/collections/kirk/casq/CASQ_v3n7_2008.pdf, CASQ, Culture Alcohol & Society Quarterly, Vol III, no 7, April, May, June 2008.

http://hindsfoot.org/lightbillw.pdf, Glenn F. Chesnut, "Bill Wilson's Vision of the Light at Towns Hospital".

http://www.druglibrary.org/schaffer/library/studies/cu/cu8.html Consumer Reports Magazine, "Consumers Union Report on Licit and Illicit Drugs," Edward M. Brechner and Editors of Consumer Reports Magazine, 1972.

http://www.encyclopedia.com/topic/Food_and_Drug_Act_of_1906.aspx Encyclopedia.com, Food and Drug Act of 1906

http://www.adherents.com/people/pk/John_Harvey_Kellogg.html "The Religious Affiliation of Dr. John Harvey Kellogg".

http:// http://www.morerevealed.com/library/coc/chapter2.htm "AA: Cult or Cure," Charles Bufe.

http://www.silkworth.net/gsowatch/aaws/ "Documents Concerning AAWS History, Who Wrote What in the Big Book"

http://silkworth.net/aahistorylovers/aa_history_lovers_messages.html "AA History Lovers".

http://silkworth.net/silkworth/silkworth_bio.html "The Roundtable of AA History, January 10, 1998, William Duncan Silkworth, MD (1873-1951).

http:// www.williamwhitepapers.com/pr/2008TwelveDefiningMomentsinAAHistory.pdf "Twelve Defining Moments in the History of Alcoholics Anonymous," William L. White, M.A. and Ernest Kurtz, Ph.D.

http://www2.potsdam.edu/alcohol/Controversies/1114796842.html#.VBENMXkg-Uk Alcohol Problems and Solutions, History of Alcohol and Drinking around the World, by David J. Hanson, Ph.D.

En.wikipedia.org – Wikipedia has been employed at occasional points for supplementary information, but never as a primary source regarding Charles Towns.

www.dailymail,co.uk/femail/article481822/Condemned-virgins-The-million-women-robbed-war.html The Daily Mail, Condemned to be virgins: "The two million women robbed by the war," September, 2007, Amanda Cable, a book review of *Singled Out, How Two Million Women Survived Without Men After The First World War* by Virginia Nicholson.

http://www.unodc.org/unodc/en/frontpage/the-1912-hague-international-opium-convention.html UNODC United Nations Office on Drugs and Crime

Http://www.history-magazine.com/bellevue.html, *Bellevue Hospital*, Edwin M. Knights Jr., M.D.,

Magazines - Journals

Boston Medical and Surgical Journal, Massachusetts Medical Society, New England Surgical Society, Vol. CLXIV, 1911, "The Towns-Lambert Treatment for Morphinism and Alcoholism", p. 676-677.

Boston Medical and Surgical Journal, Massachusetts Medical Society, New England Surgical Society, Vol ClXXVI, No. 6, February 8, 1917, "The Drug Treatment of Morphinism," Frank H. Carlisle, M.D., Norfolk, Mass, p. 209-210.

Colliers Magazine, Volume 52, November 29, 1913, "The White Hope of Drug Victims," Peter Clark MacFarlane, p. 16-17.

Consumers Union Report on Licit and Illicit Drugs, by Edward M Brecher and the Editors of Consumer Reports Magazine, 1972.

Journal of Studies on Alcohol, Blumberg, L. "The Ideology of a Therapeutic Social Movement: Alcoholics Anonymous,"1977, 38(11): 2126.

Literary Digest, "The War and the Dope Habit," June 9, 1917, p. 1776-1777.

Markings, Your Archives Interchange, "A.A. and Medicine Forge a Durable Relationship," Alcoholics Anonymous, Vol 25, No. 1, September-October 2005.

Maryland Medical Journal, The Medical Journal Company, Volume LVIII, December 1914-December, 1915.

Medical Review of Reviews, Volume XX, Jan-Dec 1914, Edited by Ira S. Wile, M.S., M.D.

Medical Review of Reviews, Volume XXI, Jan-Dec 1915, Edited by Ira S. Wile, M.S., M.D.

Medical Review of Reviews, Volume XXII, Jan-Dec 1916, Edited by Victor Robinson, Ph. C., M.D.

Medical Review of Reviews, Volume XXIII, Jan-Dec 1917, Edited by Victor Robinson, Ph. C., M.D.

Medical Review of Reviews, Volume XXIV, Jan-Dec 1918, Edited by Victor Robinson, Ph. C., M.D.

New York State Journal of Medicine, Volume XV, No. 4, April, 1915, "The Federal and State Laws in Relation to Habit-Forming Drugs," p. 129-131.

The American Journal of Clinical Medicine, "Belladonna and Its Alkaloids", Finley Ellingwood, M.D., Evanston, Illinois, August, 1915, p. 707-712.

The American Journal of Clinical Medicine, "Atropine as a Remedy for Irritant Gases," August, 1915. P. 754-755.

The American Journal of The Medical Sciences, Volume 154, December 6, 1917, Towns Hospital Ad.

The American Magazine, October, 1912, "Fighting The Deadly Habits, The Story of Charles B. Towns," Samuel Merwin, p. 708-717.

The British Medical Journal, "A Drastic Treatment for Alcoholism," p. 1249-1250, May 21, 1910

The Century Magazine, The Century Co., New York, New York, LXXXIII March 1912,766-772; LXXXIV June 292-298; August 580-587; October 853-859.

The Journal of the American Medical Association, Volume LIII, Number 13, September 25, 1909, "The Obliteration of the Craving For Narcotics," Alexander Lambert, M.D.

The Journal of the American Medical Association, Volume CXIII, Number 16, October, 14, 1939, "Alcoholics Anonymous" Book Review.

The Journal of the American Medical Association, Volume LX, Number 25, June 21, 1913, "The Treatment of Narcotic Addiction," Alexander Lambert, M.D.

The Journal of the American Medical Association, "Reclaiming The Drinker," Vol. XCVIII, Number 18, April 18, 1932, Book Review.

The Medical Critic and Guide, Volume Twenty One, January-December 1918, William J. Robinson, Ph.G., M.D., The Critic and Guide Company, 12 Mt. Morris Park West, New York.

The Medical Times, A Monthly Journal of Medicine, Surgery and the Collateral Sciences, Vol. XLI., No. 1, The Medical Times Company, 95 Nassua Street, New York.

The Medical Times, A Monthly Journal of Medicine, Surgery and the Collateral Sciences, Vol. XLII., January, 1914, The Medical Times Company, 95 Nassua Street, New York.

The Medical Times, A Monthly Journal of Medicine, Surgery and the Collateral Sciences, Vol. XLIII., January, 1915, The Medical Times Company, 95 Nassua Street, New York.

The Medical Times, A Monthly Journal of Medicine, Surgery and the Collateral Sciences, Vol. XLIX., January, 1921, The Medical Times Company, 95 Nassua Street, New York.

The Modern Hospital, Vol VII, July 1916-December 1916.

The Modern Hospital, Vol VIII, January 1917-June 1917.

The New Republic, "Drink and the Devil," January 15, 1916, p. 282-283.

Index

2

292 Central Park West, 241, 250
293 Central Park West, 38, 41, 243, 251, 261

A

AA The Way It Began, 8, 229, 230
Abolition of alcohol
    Would be a mistake, 285
Abolition of drugs and alcohol
    Reduce lunacy by 33%, 166
    Would reduce murder by 50%, 166
    Would reduce suicides by 60%, 166
Absinthe, 175, 226
    Destroying France, 227
Adams, Samuel Hopkins, 147
Addicts
    99% victims with intense longing to be free of habit, 140
    AMA's reference to A.A.'s 'kind of religious conversion', 327
    Ambulatory treatment criminalized in 1915, 161
    Became criminals in 1915, 161
    Believers in magic, 331
    By 1920 had become drug fiends, 237
    Cells of poisoned with locked up toxins, 287
    China with 160,000,000, 22
    Considered innocent victims, 19
    Cost of drugs always seems moderate, 76
    Could not be broken without medical aid, 23
    Deprivation
        Causes insanity, more often death, 139
    Differentiated from alcoholics, 174
    Doctors stopped treating, 299
    Easier to be one in prison than an alcoholic, 109
    Economically exploited, 74
    Fearful of the agony of deprivation, 91
    Indefinite maintenance of declared criminal, 246
    Innocent victims, 59
    Many petrified of treatment, 289
    Many physicians were addicts themselves, 90
    Monetary profit for treatment should not be involved, 82
    Most chose the Towns Treatment, 292
    Most were innocent victims, 290
    Most were victims, 61
    Most wished to break their chains, 288
    Must be treated or hell to pay, 70
    Must reduce risks of withdrawal, 70
    National policy required, 5
    No one with go to greater lengths, 69
    Not considered criminals, 5
    Not considered degenerates, 5
    Not stigmatized in 1906, 5
    Physicians
        15 percent of were, 91
    Physicians should have no personal contact with, 120
    Prescriptions had to be in decreasing dosages, 87
    Received little pleasure, 288
    Should be treated with compassion, 82
    Should not congregate with other addicts, 74
    Shrinks from publicity, 141
    Slaves, 172
    Some are hopeless, 128
    Sympathy rarely an effective treatment, 132
    Towns becoming an American crusader for, 29
    Towns claimed to cure 4,000 in China, 32
    Towns conveniently silent about consequences of drug prohibition, 288
    Towns more sympathetic with, 59
    Towns not interested in why one relapsed, 105
    Towns wanted to empty prisons of, 88
    Treated originally for condition long since disappeared, 260
    Victims entrapped in bondage, 171
    Victims of doctor or druggist, 151
Alcohol, 238
    Brandy
        Makes a man crazy, 274
    Called the worst of artificial stimulants by Towns, 102
    Compared to a clock hit by a brick, 173
    Curse to mankind, 177
    Deprivation of caused of wet brains and insanity, 50
    Drinkers on the high road to degeneration, 177
    Epidemic - most deadly, 273
    Formed in nature only as an excretion, 159
    Garbage of vegetation, 159
    Greater harm done by tobacco, 114
    Greater havoc than all the plagues, 48
    Greatest of humanity's curses, 48
    If used to excess, tobacco will be used to excess, 46
    Jellife and White
        Considered a poison, 330
    Liquor
        Makes a man brutal, dulls judgment, 273
    Prohibition of would benefit mankind, 166
    Towns
        King tottering into his grave, 160
        King was dying, 160
    Towns treatment adapted for, 43
    White Water of Death, 273
    Wine
        Makes a man crazy, 274
    World a net gainer if eliminated, 335
    World must find a solution for, 49
    World would gain if alcohol never again distilled, 48

Alcoholic delirium, 191
Alcoholic Foundation, 324
Alcoholics
    50% have syphilitic histories, 135
    Abused, 100
    All require treatment to be unpoisoned, 104
    Always looking for excuses, 133
    Believers in magic, 331
    Cannot avoid publicity, 141
    Deny, 140
    Detoxification by itself inadequate, 193
    Differentiated from addicts, 174
    Education the solution for, 193
    Friends to often sentimentalize or bully, 277
    Generous, magnanimous, quixotic, 50
    Gonorrhea plagues 90% of males, 136
    How to determine if worth treating, 56
    Many become addicts in prison, 109
    Many gradually hooked, 212
    Most were misunderstood, 53
    Older 1 to 2 oz. of whisky in treatment, 233
    Physical restraints barbaric, 192
    Prohibition didn't change ratio of in insane asylums,
        276
    Recovery should be in a hospital, not a jail, 107
    Sexual association not allowed, 136
    Should be expected to lie, 53
    Should be treated like invalids, 53
    Silkworth had more success with than any, 305
    So many smoked tobacco first, 114
    Society did not know what to do with them, 50
    Some are hopeless, 128
    Some become so through worry and grief, 49
    Some predisposed to alcoholism, 49
    Specialized hospital required to treat, 108
    Sterilization required if untreatable, 103
    Sympathy rarely an effective treatment, 132
    Their self-respect must be protected, 55
    Towns appears to be their best friend, 135
    Towns' basic strategy in treating, 100
    Towns becoming an American crusader for, 29
    Towns' recommendation for dealing with chronics, 134
    Towns the best friend of, 182
    Towns wishes not to know if yielded to madness, 138
    Treated no better than 100 years ago, 151, 277
    Wholly irresponsible, irrational, self-concerned, sub-
        human, 169
Alcoholics Anonymous, 6, 277, 311, 321, 338, 339
    28 members sober 1/38-3/39 in NY, 325
    A.A. # 3, Bill Dotson, 314
    Almost nobody wanted the book, 327
    AMA asking for information about, 324
    Belladonna, Page 7, 15, 307
    Bill Wilson co-founder, 3
    Bill Wilson emerging from fog first time, 301
    Board of Trustees, 322
    Creator of Twelve Steps, 339
    Crucial contributions by Towns, 339

Definitive History by Ernest Kurtz, xi
Drinkers like to help other drinkers, 339
Heavy smoker—Coffee Drinker, p. 135, 46
Lambert to Silkworth on allergy, 298
Much needed push, 338
Necessity to distance from Towns, 334
No obligation to Towns except the loan, 324
Possible delay from April, 1939 without Towns, 6
Possible sabotage by Towns, xii
Related to Towns' job offer to Wilson, 325
Saturday Evening Post, March 1941, 6
Silent about Towns' eccentricities, 334
Silkworth's contribution to A.A. principles, 305
Stock Prospectus, 322
Thread that ties Towns with A.A., 296
To Employers chapter, 333
Tobacco clouds at meetings, 46
Towns Helped when times were tough, 321
Towns loan of $4,000, 322
Towns provides first big break, 327
Towns push for the book, 328
Towns right man at right time, 328
Towns unlikely contributor, 321
Towns without spiritual similarities, 334
Tradition 2, 318
Tradition 6, 318
Wanted no king, 339
Alcoholics Anonymous Comes of Age
    Towns admitting he's not religious, 314
Alcoholism
    Could have been healed, 50
    Criminal actions resulting from, 276
    Disease
        Absolutely absurd to think it is, 194
        Partially true, 133
        Scientists have been misled, 133
        With a definite pathology, 278
    Lambert
        Best advised man in New York, 20
    Much of it could be eliminated, 143
    No case incurable until medical care attempted, 212
    No cure will exist ever according to Towns, 134
    Patient
        Seldom an angel, 172
    Patients wait until problem acute, 140
    Product of our imperfect social system, 102
    Towns
        No such thing as a cure, 194
        Realizes more required than just release from
            physical craving, 170
        Results from temptation more than sin, 188
        Results if one can't keep promises not to drink, 212
    Towns becoming a national authority on, 52
    Towns wished men would stay employed despite, 53
    Victims of this serious disease, 51
    Will eventually lead to insanity, 139
Alexander, Jack, 6
American Delegates to Shanghai

Announced victory of opium legislation in U.S., 31
American Journal of Clinical Medicine, 331
American lifestyle
    Reason for drug use, 71
American Medical Association, 89, 232, 272, 324
    8,500 doctors in 1900, 5
    Founded in 1847, 5
    Incorporated 1897, 5
    Standards for Medical schools in 1910, 5
American soldier
    No alcoholics treated worse, 197
Americans
    Demand medicine to stop a headache, 131
Amphetamines, 102, 141
Asthma
    Results from smoking tobacco, 294

B

Bacchus, 282
Barnum, P.T., 3
Barrymore, John, 251
Battle Creek, Michigan, 330
Bayer Aspirin, 154
Bayer Corporation, 154
Baylor, Courtney, 313
    Distinguished lay therapist, 317
Beer, 159, 273
    Brutishness results from drinking, 275
    Drinkers like its narcotic and stupefying effects, 276
    Hops
        Related to hashish, 274
    How a Babboon proved himself smarter than humans, 266
    Lupulin
        Active ingredient in hops, 274
    Makes a man slow-witted and abolishes judgment, 273
    Makes a man stupid, 274
    More noxious than wines or liquors, 273
    Some degenerate dogs drink it, 266
Belladonna, 191, 211, 229, 230, 231, 232, 280, 302, 308, 309, 330, 338
    No longer featured, 259
    Used in Germany in 1944, 308
    Wilson
        Called part of the usual treatment, 307
Belladonna delirium
    different from alcoholic delirium, 191
Belladonna poisoning, 233
Belladonna Treatment, xii, 15, 229, 303, 307, 330, 334
    As described by Alexander Lambert, 233
    Called quackery, 304
    Lambert distancing himself from, 298
    Maybe not so horrific after all, 306
    Similarities with Silkworth's Malaysian Plant, 298
    Used in Akron, 325
    Wilson likely received during all four visits, 307
Bellevue Hospital, 15, 20, 51, 72, 106, 152, 238, 297, 337

Silkworth arrived in 1896, 296
Silkworth tutored by Lambert at, 297
Bill W. My First 40 Years, 10, 301, 307
Black henbane, 231
Blue Cross, 337
Borchert, William G., 314
Boston, 35, 132, 135, 147, 239
Boston College, 79
Boston Medical and Surgical Journal, 35, 258, 330, 340, 341, 342, 343, 349, 350, 351
Bowers, Edwin F., 159
    Author of 'Aphorisms on Alcohol', 158
Boylan Act, 79, 82, 85, 87, 91, 125, 148, 185, 336
    Everyone knows that it is the work of Towns, 79
    Harrison Act was based on, 83
    Misdemeanor, $500 fine, one year sentence max, 82
    Musto description of, 79
    Towns praises the virtues of, 92
Boylan, John J.
    New York State Senator, 79, 148
Brent, Bishop Charles Henry
    Letter from China, 21
    US Chairman of China commission, 29
British Medical Journal, 232
Broad Street Hospital, 296
Bromides, 258, 293

C

Cabot, Richard C., M.D., 9, 147, 332
    Called Towns persuasive and dominating, 35
    Convinced of the efficacy of the Towns Treatment, 237
    No stranger to morphine, heroin & opium, 35
    Noted small amount of suffering in withdrawal, 35
    Praised Towns, 34
    Towns knows more than any doctor I have ever seen, 147
    Towns used name in 1922 brochure, 258
    Towns used to justify 80% recovery rate, 171
    Wondered if treatment worked without Towns, 35
    Wrote preface to *Habits That Handicap*, 124
California
    Cocaine required prescription in 1907, 161
Cambridge University, 331
Canada, 86, 176
    Belladonna native to, 230
    Ontario, 176
    Xanthoxylum native to, 231
Cannabis, 4, 274
Capone, Al, ix
Carlisle, Frank M.D., 330
Central Park, x, 38, 209, 235, 262, 263
Century Company, 147
Chambers, Francis
    Distinguished Lay therapist
        Follower of Richard Peabody, 317
Chestnut, Glenn F., 308

China, 2, 10, 18, 21, 22, 23, 24, 25, 27, 28, 33, 44, 186, 211, 226, 303, 330
   160,000,000 opium addicts, 52
   Bill Wilson's reference to, 302
   Bishop Brent letter to Roosevelt, 28
   Facing down the empress, 32
   International help with opium problem proposed, 29
   Opium problem, 29
   Opium smoking observations, 64
   Politics behind Towns' trip in 1908, 28
   Real reasons for Towns' trip, 240
   Tension between U.S. and, 28
   Towns' return from, 243
   US 2nd to China in opium consumption, 166
Chinese, 21, 28, 31, 90
   Being treated terribly in 1904 in U.S., 28
   Desire to exclude Chinese laborers in U.S., 28
   Embargo against the U.S., 28
   Roosevelt tries to ease embargo by, 29
   Treated cruelly in U.S., 28
Chinese government, 25
Chloral hydrate, 231, 293
   Classed as dangerous, 272
Cocaine, 4, 63, 83, 88, 129, 130, 131, 141, 171, 209, 224, 233, 237, 238, 252
   A proof of mixed sex relations, 95
   Addict
     No worse creature this side of hell, 172
   Alkaloid first isolated in 1855, 154
   Being sold ito children in Jersey City, 67
   Breaks down and degenerates tissue, 173
   Called a poison, 270
   Classed as dangerous, 272
   Compared to a clock hit by a brick, 173
   Eczema of the nose, 293
   Effects resemble alcohol, 228
   If alcoholic cannot get alcohol, he'll use, 225
   Leads to Murder, 129
   Makes user feel if he had no nose on his face, 129
   Most habit forming, 293
   No drug brings quicker deterioration, 130
   No patient worse this side of hell, 172
   Prohibition of would benefit mankind, 166
   Shortcut to prison or madhouse, 130
   Towns thought invented by Koller in 1884, 154
   Various early State laws, 161
Codeine, 45, 131, 293
Cohan, George M., ix
Colliers Magazine, 33, 72
Colorado
   Laws regulating cocaine in 1897, 161
Columbia Presbyterian network, 296
Columbia University, 332
Combretum sundiacum
   Malaysian Plant, 298
Copernicus, 278
Corn Flakes cereal, 330
Cornell University, 20, 147

Cornwall Press, 327
Cow, Douglas V., 331
Crack cocaine, 102, 141
Curse
   Addiction, 243
   Alcohol
     To mankind, 177
   Alcoholized parentage, 270
   Drug, 90, 163, 164, 247
   Drugs, alcohol and tobacco, 197
   Opium, 23, 31
   Upon parents for bringing up children irresponsibly, 217

D

Darwin, Charles, 159, 266
Deadly nightshade, 230
Delirium tremens, 192, 193, 219, 276, 277
Diminution of vision
   Results from smoking tobacco, 294
Dipsomania, 276
Dipsomaniac, 314
Diseases of the Nervous System, 256
   Negative opinions on alcohol, 329
Disturbance in vision
   Results from smoking tobacco, 294
Dotson, Bill
   A.A. #3, 314
Dreser, Heinrich, 153
Drug addict and alcoholic
   Third class treated at Towns Hospital, 255
Drug and Alcohol Sickness, 287, 295, 300
Drug Dealers
   Mininum penalty 20 years hard labor, 186
   Murderers, 186
Drug War Politics, 4, 5

E

Egyptians, 289
Eighteenth amendment repealed, 335
Ellingwood, Finley M.D., 304
Ellingwood's Therapeutist, 304
Elllis, Havelock, 146
Emerson, Ralph Waldo, 277
England, 187
Europe, 135, 210
   Belladonna native to, 230
Evil
   Alcohol, 158, 176, 177
   Alcoholic that is hopeless, 136
   Alcoholic that is very rich, or very poor, 137
   Drug, 124, 288
   Drug addiction, 65
   Drug and drink, 167
   Drug craving, 92

Drugs, 288
Habit forming drugs, 107, 210
   A united world problem, 210
Hashish, 225
Narcotics, 93, 94
Of the profit motive, 64
Opium, 28, 31
Opium smoking, 64
Sanatoriums that colonize, 123
Tobacco
   Leads to opium and alcohol, 114
War
   Out of evil good may come, 176

F

Fields, W. C., 251
Fleming, James W., M.D.
   Endorsement for four Towns brochures, 255
Flexner, Abraham, 147
France, 175, 176, 226, 227

G

Galileo, 278
Gambrinus, 275
Gangsters
   Many come from alcoholized parentage, 270
Gantry, Elmer, 3
Gehrig, Lou, ix
George III, 187
Georgia, 7, 10, 11, 25, 209, 262, 302, 338
   Atlanta, 315, 317
   Banned cocaine in 1902, 161
   Georgia born nerve, 27
   Georgia mad, 25
   LaGrange, 8
German
   Cruelty, 166
   Exporting drugs in toothpaste, 211
   Grand design for world conquest, 166
   Immorality, 166
   Poisoning U.S. School Children, 164
   Sabotaging wills of their enemies, 210
   Smuggling drugs into army training centers, 167
Germany, 154, 175
   Belladonna used in 1944, 308
   Munich, 271
Grapevine Magazine, 322
Great Britain, 175, 176, 226, 285
Gunmen
   Many come from alcoholized parentage, 270

H

Habits That Handicap, 89, 92, 110, 125, 146, 149, 150, 154, 157, 204, 214, 221, 276, 321, 334

called the most sober and important work, 147
Hague International Opium Convention of 1912, 224, 225, 226
Harrison Act, 78, 83, 85, 86, 87, 89, 92, 125, 184, 185
   2014 the 100th Anniversary of passage, 3
   25,000 doctors indicted, 247
   A tax act, 166
   Addicts driven to hospitals by legislation, 91
   Ambulatory treatment never stated as illegal, 161
   Court interpretation of, xi
   Criminalization of the addict, 158
   Dispensers of narcotics to be licensed, 84
   Fifty year impact of, 247
   Indefinite maintenance of addict illegal, 246
   Justifcation for, 165
   Life getting tough for addicts, 85
   Mutation into a criminal model, 88
   Not a prohibition bill at all, 83
   NY Boylan Act model for, 83
   Orderly marking of narcotics, 84
   Passage in December, 1914, xi
   Patent Medicine makers partially exempt, 84
   Silkworth probable impact on, 299
   Tax Act, 84
   Towns' advocacy of, 79
   Towns becomes silent about, 336
   Treasury Department Decision 2200, 87
   Treasury Department enforcement, 88
   Treasury Department interpretation of, 87
   Treasury Dept. actions favorable to Dr. Lambert, 89
Harrison, Francis Burton
   New York Congressman
      We are an opium consuming nation today, 83
Harvard University, 9, 34, 147
Hashish, 226, 274
   Among evil substances, 225
   Causes Mohammedan peoples to become dangerously violent, 275
   Contains same elements as in the lupulin glands of hops, 275
   Hops compared to, 275
   Hops in beer related to, 274
Headaches
   Results from smoking tobacco, 294
Helen, 289
Henbane, 231
Heroin, 4, 35, 63, 129, 131, 141, 209, 237, 252, 293
   Harrison Act restrictions described, 84
   History described by Towns, 153
   Named derived from the German word for strong, 153
   Towns' first patient, 154
Hill, Harold, 3
Holmes, Oliver Wendell, 146
Homer, 288
Hospital Treatment for Alcohol and Drug Addiction, 257, 264
Hubbard, Elbert, 154
Hudson River, 135

Hungarian
Never a drug user, 70
Huxley, Aldous, 141
Hyoscyamus, 191, 229, 231
Hypnotics, 100, 129, 242, 258, 293
Leads to moral degeneracy, 131
Second of Four Classes treated, 255
Should be regulated similarly to cocaine, 131
Towns condemns the use of, 130

I

Iliad and the Odyssey, 288
Illinois
Evanston, 304
Indian hemp, 293
Insomnia, 255, 260
Results from smoking tobacco, 294
Internal Revenue Service, 70, 83
Italians
Never a drug user, 70

J

Japan
Proposed to join opium conference, 29
Jelliffe, Smith Ely, M.D., 281, 329, 332
Co-author of *Diseases of the Nervous System*, 256
Endorsement for four Towns brochures, 255
Jesus, 278
Jewish Immigrants
The practical sagacity of their race is their surest safeguard, 70
Jews
Few become drug addicts, 70
Journal of the American Medical Association, 15, 33, 144, 147, 229, 258, 286, 289, 298
Review of *Alcoholics Anonymous*, 327

K

Keister, B. C., M.D.
Opium
Danger of degeneration into monkeydom, 166
Kelley, Howard A., M.D., 272
Kellogg Company, 330
Kellogg, John Harvey M.D., 330, 333
King, Rufus, 166
Kings County Hospital, 51, 72
Koller, Karl, 154
Kurtz, Ernest, xi
Alcoholics prone to be believers in magic, 331
Calls for amateurs, xii
Towns' job offer, 316, 319
William White Interview, xi

L

La Guardia, Fiorello H., ix
Lambert Treatment, 36
Lambert, Alexander M.D., 15, 93, 144, 147, 229, 232, 323
Administering the Towns Treatment, 229
Advocate of annual licensing of physicians, 81
Advocate of health insurance, 81
Advocate of standard fee schedule, 81
Allergy concept to Silkworth from him, 298
Became good friends with Towns, 20
Began to lose his enthusiasm, 238
Belladonna hallucinations described by, 232
Best advised man in NYC on drugs and alcoholism, 20
Called a 'comrade' of Towns, 81
Called founding father of American drug policy, 29
Complete disallusionment about treatment, 291
Convinced of the efficacy of the Towns Treatment, 237
Describes handling addicts and alcoholics, 232
Describes when treated patient will be comfortable, 234
Endorsed Towns & his treatment, 20
Endorsement for four Towns brochures, 255
Familiar with Quarterly Journal of Inebriety, 298
Gave treatment to 200, only 5% stayed off, 238
Informed Sec. William H. Taft about Towns & opium treatment, 21
Introduced Towns as straightforward - no faker, 20
Key player leading to narcotic prohibition, 29
Knew benefits of one drunk helping another, 313
No scientific solution to addiction until recently, 144
No stranger to morphine, heroin, & opium, 35
Passionately interested in narcotic addiction in 1896, 297
Personal physician to President Roosevelt, 21
Praises layman Charles Towns, 145
President of AMA in 1919, 332
Previous relationship with Dr. Silkworth, 297
Professor of clinical medicine at Cornell U., 20
Promoted Towns in NY Times, 32
Provided Towns valuable publicity, 33
Published the Towns formula for the world, 34
Recommended Wilson to visit patients at Towns, 313
Towns used name in 1922 brochure, 258
Towns used to justify 80% recovery rate, 171
Towns would not disclose secret formula, 20
Tutored Silkworth at Bellevue Hospital, 297
Wrote appendix to *Habits That Handicap*, 124
Lambert, Samuel M.D.
Endorsement for four Towns brochures, 255
Listed as associated with Towns Hospital, 332
Mistakenly credited in Pass It On, p. 101, 15
Le Mort, Jakob
Creator of paregoric, 289
League of Nations, 65
Leary, Timothy, 141
Libertinism, 265
Liberty Magazine, 6, 327

Looney Tune Cartoons, 273
LSD, 102, 141
Lusitania, 78
Luther, 278

M

Macfarlane, Peter Clark, 72
  Bishop Brent Letter, 21
  How Towns' first patients were treated, 17
  Praise for Towns, 33
  Taft patients reported by, 290
  The 'White Hope' of Drug Victims, 17
  Towns called 'humblest man from Georgia', 209
  Towns defiant in China, 26
  Towns' first patient, 12
  Towns in China, 25
  Towns just plain 'Georgia mad', 25
  Towns ordered to take down signs, 25
  Towns told to take down signs, 26
  Towns Treatment advocated, 36
  Towns' response to China challenge, 22
Malay Archipelago, 275
Marijuana, 4, 238, 274
Markey, Morris
  Author of 'Alcoholics and God' in *Liberty Magazine*, 327
Maryland Medical Journal, 42, 146, 352
Massachusetts General Hospital, 9, 34, 332
McCrae, Thomas, 147
Medical model of addiction and alcohol treatment, 6
Medical profession
  23% were victims of morphine habit, 166
Medical Review of Reviews, 11, 36, 79, 80, 144, 145, 146, 163, 178, 179, 184, 208, 217, 222, 224, 228, 270
  Towns
    Editor of the Department of Drug Addictions and Alcoholism, 158
Mental irritability
  Results from Smoking tobacco, 294
Merwin, Samuel, 9, 23, 72
  Alcohol
    Most insinuating and baffling enemies to the human character, 37
  Meeting with Towns, 22
  No author could portray Towns adequately, 10
  Suggests Towns goes to China, 22
  Towns praised by, 36
Mexico, 86
Mitchel, Dale, 296, 297, 298, 313
  Documented belladonna administered to Wilson, 307
  Has 1936 as date of Towns job offer to Wilson, 316
Modern Medicine, Its Theory and Practice, 147
Mohammedan peoples, 275
Monkeydom
  Worse than, 166
Morons
  Many come from alcoholized parentage, 270

Morphine, 4, 18, 35, 45, 63, 129, 131, 141, 154, 209, 228, 233, 237, 243, 252
  40 grains a day, 12
  Addiction to could become relic of the past, 88
  Addicts victims of their physicians, 174
  Ambulatory treatment criticized, 246
  Boylan Act impact on, 148
  Called a poison, 270
  Called dangerous, 272
  Cocaine addicts worse off, 173
  Doctors should not tell patient about, 61
  Dr. Cabot observes addicts at Towns, 35
  First addict of Towns had seen, 13
  Harrison Act restrictions described, 84
  Heroin roughly 3 times stronger, 153
  If not available, then alcohol, 225
  Leads to callous indifference to rights of others, 47
  Limit syringe access to, 59
  Most dosages of unnecessary, 60
  Patient
    Generally a good patient, 173
  Prohibition of would benefit mankind, 166
  Silkworth interested in, 296, 299
  Towns considered addicts of good patients, 172
  Towns describes sanitarium patients together, 75
  Treatment mandatory, 143
  U.S. Treasury criticism of indefinite treatment of, 246
  Will distort moral sense of best person on earth, 47
  Withdrawal suffering described, 289
Murder, 92, 129, 276
Musto, David F., M.D., 83
  Alexander brothers mistaken for each other at times, 15
  Belladonna Treatment described, 233
  Boylan Act described, 79
  Describing AMA in 1913, 5
  Disagreements with Towns described, 81
  Documented belladonna contained atropine, 331
  Explained why the Towns Treatment appeared to work, 239
  Explanation why Chinese so timid with Towns, 28
  Tennessee Narcotic Act of 1913, 161
  Towns mistaken for doctor, 37
  Towns would not change, 238
  Why the Towns Treatment seemed to work?, 330

N

Narcotics, 82
  Government Monopoly proposed by Towns to control, 65
  Called the worst of artificial stimulants by Towns, 102
  Contained in many patent medicines, 4
  Could be purchased by mail order, 4
  Could be purchased in grocery and general stores, 4
  Craving for obliterated in 5 days, 32
  Doctors becoming criminals by distributing, 162
  First U.S. Legislation regulating in 1909, 32

Greater harm being done by tobacco, 114

Law intended to control marketing of narcotics transformed into prohibition of, 86

Rigid government control of proposed by Towns, 65

Those dispensing substances should be licensed, 84

Towns advertising diminishes advertising for treatment of, 238

Towns believed addicts received little pleasure from, 288

Towns called 'The Solon of Narcotics', 148

Used in diarrhea and cough medicines, 131

World a net gainer if eliminated, 335

National Prohibition Enforcement Act

    Volstead Act, 78

Ness, Elliot, ix

Neurasthenia victim

    First class treated at Towns Hospital, 255

New York, 82, 90, 161, 185, 296, 336

    Boylan Act to set example for rest of country, 79

    Brooklyn, 317

    Legislature, 79

    Model for federal legislation, 82

New York City, ix, xii, 3, 11, 20, 22, 32, 35, 36, 38, 51, 72, 81, 135, 179, 211, 219, 235, 239, 262, 263, 303, 324, 325, 327, 353

    Addicts

        Estimated to be 300,000 in city, 167

    Six men sober by end of 1936, 315

    Towns arrived in 1901, 8

New York Post Graduate Medical School and Hospital, 332

New York State Journal of Medicine, 85, 116, 355

New York Times, 21, 32, 36, 80, 86, 165, 179, 337

Newton, Isaac, 278

Nicholas II, 159, 160, 175

Norman Kerr, M.D.

    All the alcohols are poisons, 226

Cigarettes the equivalent of, 46

Curse of, 31, 32, 44

Drinking excess coffee can lead to, 221

Evil, 28, 224

Harrison Act restrictions described, 84

If withdrawn, then alcohol, 69

Injecting becoming popular because of the syringe, 64

Law of 1909 limited to smoking opium, 31

Limited police powers to enforce, 31

Menace of, 148

Only 10% usage legitimate, 66

Opium law of 1909 to save face internationally, 31

Producing countries should make its prodction a monopoly, 66

Prohibition of would benefit mankind, 166

Silkworth interested in, 296, 299

Smoking compared to tobacco, 45

Smoking less viscious than morphine, 64

Smoking of, 64

Tobacco relation close to, 44

Towns claims of 4000 cures, 32

Towns exposes fake cures for, 24

Towns exposes phony cures, 25

Towns healing the world of the curse of, 32

Towns provides history of, 289

Towns solution for built Towns Hospital, 211

Towns Treatment world's only cure, 229

U.S. had no laws for in 1908, 30

Withdrawal symptoms described, 232

Oppenheimer Treatment for Alcoholism, 353

Osler, Sir William, 147

Oursler, Fulton

    Liberty Magazine Editor, 327

Oxford Group, 314

Oyster Bay, 290

O

Ohio

    Akron, 311, 314

        855 Ardmore Avenue, 314

        Towns claims Towns Treatment in use there, 325

Oinomania, 276

Opium, 2, 4, 22, 24, 29, 35, 43, 63, 64, 70, 73, 129, 131, 141, 173, 209, 226, 228, 233, 237, 252, 287, 299

    76 phony cures, 32

    A true inebriety, 226

    Addiction in Philippines, 21

    Alcohol mix dangerous, 70

    'As long as people can get opium, they will smuggle it.', 65

    Called a poison, 270

    Causes loss of responsibility, 62

    Ceases to stimulate, 45

    Charles B. Towns Anti-Opium Institute, 26

    China with 160,000,000 addicts, 22

    Chinese trying to eliminate, 23

P

Paraldehyde, 238, 293

Parkhurst, Hank, 322

    Amateurish publicity attempts, 327

    Flat broke, 328

Pass It On, 10, 15, 232

Patent medicines, 4, 5, 64, 66, 87, 148, 354

    Addictive themselves, 73

    Germans exporting drugs in, 211

    Partially exempt from Harrison Act, 84

    Until 1906, ingredients not required, 4

    Whistle blower Samuel Hopkins, 147

Patent-medicines, 63

Peabody, Richard, 313, 321

    Death of in March, 1936, 319

    Distinguished lay therapist, 317

Pearson, C. B., M.D., 228

Peiking, 25

Perversion, 265

Pharmacists, 5, 38, 58, 59, 80, 93, 335

Cannot be trusted to administer narcotics without oversight, 64
Could concoct their own brews, 131
Increasingly avoiding addicts, 209
Most addicts victims of, 288
Organized to resist change, 64
Source of addiction, 96
Too many making large profits, 63
Towns asks for their support, 163
Towns holds responsible for morphine addicts, 243
Philippine Commission
  Rejected terms of Towns' conditions, 21
Philippines, 2, 21, 22
Physician
  Addicts should quickly find themselves one, 82
  Comprised one-half of Towns Hospital patients, 71
  Creator of the drug problem in the United States, 68
  Had created the drug habit in the U.S., 71
  Increasingly avoiding addicts, 209
  Must become a sociologist, 167
  Must cut every excuse an alcoholic has for his habit, 133
  Must treat alcoholic without reservation, 134
  Narrow minded and wearing professional blinders, 167
  Primary source of addiction, 96
Pittman, Bill, 8, 229, 230
Pole
  Never a drug user, 70
Prohibition
  Alcohol
    Began January 16, 1920, 78
    Phenomena of recent times, 285
    Would diminish respect for law, 286
  Harrison Act
    Did not appear to be requiring, 83
  Narcotics
    Anti-vice crusaders appeared to have lost, 85
    Began in 1919, xi
    Clause in Harrison Act that was used to create, 85
    Evolved in 5 years, 78
    Hamilton Wright strong force for, 93
    Name of Towns all but forgotten, 3
    No Constitution Amendment required, 246
    Not Towns' original goal, 82
    Unlikely any 1914 legislator knew future of, 84
  U.S. Opium Law of 1909
    First step, 32
  Vodka
    Russia implemented in July 1914, 270
  World War I pushed into the background, 166
Prostitutes
  Many come from alcoholized parentage, 270
Prostitution, 165, 265
Psychologist, 127, 128, 132, 146
Pure Food and Drug Act of 1906, 4
Pythagoras, 278

Q

Quarterly Journal of Inebriety
  Contained theories of alcohol allergy in 1876, 298

R

Rape, 265
Rasputin, 159
Reclaiming The Drinker, 277, 284, 287, 295
Regulation
  Addiction
    Limit the problem of, 69
  Drugs
    The only answer, 67
  Hague Convention
    Realized all noxious substances required, 225
  Narcotics
    Considered essential, 68
  Opium
    The only solution, 65
    Would lessen sales of, 66
  Solution to narcotic addiction, 335
  Towns
    Caused doctors much paperwork, 94
    Could overrule personal desires, 96
    Goal was orderly oversight, 82
    Implied government would be void of corruption, 96
    Of upper world benefits under world, 96
  U.S. Treasury
    Punitive against perceived violators, 251
Retro bulbar neuritis
  Results from smoking tobacco, 294
Robinson, Victor
  Editor Medical Review of Reviews, 146
  Towns called a conspicuous figure in narcotics by, 147
Rockefeller Charitable Foundation, 315
Rockefeller, J. D., Jr, 328
Rockefellers, 315
Rockhill, William, 22
Roosevelt administration, 240
Roosevelt, Franklin Delano
  Actions to end alcohol prohibition in 1933, 265
Roosevelt, Theodore
  Desire to ease Chinese anger, 29
  President of the United States, 21
  Urges meetings of great powers about opium, 29
Root, Elihu, 30, 31
  Admonishes Wright, 30
  Secretary of State under Roosevelt, 30
Russell, Lillian, 251
Russia, 159, 160, 175, 226
  Prohibition of intoxicants, July, 1914, 270
Russian
  Never a drug user, 70

S

Sadism, 265
Sanatoria
    The less said about them the better, 145
Saturday Evening Post, 6
Seduction, 265
Shanghai, 25, 27, 29, 30, 31, 32, 74
Shoemaker, Reverend Sam, 314
Silkworth The Little Doctor Who Loved Drunks, 296, 313, 316
Silkworth, William D., M.D., 297, 316, 323, 337
    Advice to Bill Wilson, 312
    All 3 private practices failed, 296
    Allergy concept came through Dr. Lambert, 298
    Apparent confidence Wilson was sober, 311
    Argues for potential of Malaysian Plant treatment in 1908, 298
    Arrives at Bellevue as medical student in 1896, 296
    Associate physician with Broad Street Hospital, 296
    Believed an addict eminently curable, 299
    Bill Wilson
        Visit #1, 301
    Cared for drunks collectively and severally, 305
    Changed Towns' mind about Wilson, 314
    Claimed to be a man of science, 309
    Columbia Presbyterian network affiliate until 1929, 296
    Contributions to A.A. principles, 305
    Convinced of need to make big changes, 300
    Could provide a new direction for the hospital, 300
    Depressed by miserable recovery rate at Towns, 299
    Did not lecture, 305
    Different therapies at Towns Hospital, 300
    Doctors didn't have the only answer, 313
    Given opportunity to capitalize on experiences, 301
    Great Contribution
        Alcoholism was an illness, 305
        Gain utter confidence of alcoholic sufferers, 305
    Hired at $40 a week, 297
    Hired in 1929 for alcohol rehabilitation, 296
    In 1900's concentrated on opium and morphine, 299
    Lambert shared Quarterly Journal with, 298
    Life savings wiped out in Stock Market crash, 297
    Listened to Lambert to let Wilson visit patients, 313
    Might have been little doctor that loved addicts, 299
    More success with drunks than anybody, 305
    Need for a firm foundation of spiritual strength, 300
    Notes of the Jungle Plant, 298
    Opened first of 3 private practices in 1902, 296
    Physical remedy opened spiritual remedy, 301
    Practicing Army physician, 296
    Previous relationship with Dr. Alexander Lambert, 297
    Probably used belladonna moderately, 308
    Promoted to general medical superintendent, 296
    Promoted to medical superintendent in 1932, 296
    Provided helpful 'White light' Interpretation to Wilson, 309
    Providing essential reinforcement to Wilson, 309
    Recommendation to Wilson
        Talk about the illness, 313
    Reinvented treatment model at Towns, 301
    Risking his professional reputation, 312
    Says physician & patient must work together in 1908, 299
    Spoke of the need for a reliance on God, 300
    The little doctor that loved drunks, 299
    Towns Hospital Recovery rate at two percent, 300
    Towns opinions when Silkworth hired, 291
    Treating addicts hazardous to career, 299
    Wilson allowed to visit patients by, 311
    Wilson documents how Silkworth understood drunks, 304
    Wilson saying 'Old Doc Silkworth', 315
    Wilson says 'a great human being', 305
    Wilson says Silkworth different than Towns, 304
    Wilson sharing with Smith as recommended, 314
    Worked personally and closely with patients, 301
    Working with alcoholics only by 1925, 297
    Would have not met Wilson without Towns, 6
Simmons, Horace M., M.D., 157
Slavery, 144
Slaying The Dragon, 82, 85, 88
Smith, Robert Holbrook M.D.
    Belladonna use on Eddie, 308
    First meeting with Wilson, 314
    Wilson spends the summer of 1935 in Akron with, 314
Society
    Should be prepared to pay for consequences of alcohol, 50
    Should provide medical resources to recover, 151
Socrates, 278
Solanaceae family, 231
Somnifics, 258
South Africa, 275
South America
    Coca leaves chewed for many centuries, 154
Stacey, Frank R., M.D., 160
Star Trek, 123
Starling, Ernest H., 285
Stinking nightshade, 231
Strychnine, 231
    Used to combat patient's exhaustion, 234
Sulphonal, 258
Swift, George M., M.D.
    Endorsement for four Towns brochures, 255

T

Taft, William Howard
    Invited Towns to Washington, 21
    Secretary of Defense, Lambert told about Towns, 21
    Secretary of War, 1908, 21
    Wanted to send Towns to the Philippines, 21
Taft, William Howard
    Secretary of War, 290
Tennessee

Narcotic Act of 1913, 161
Tenney, Charles C.
    Member 1908 China Commission, 29
Thacher, Ebby, 306
The Action of Alcohol on Man, 285
The American Disease, 15, 28, 37, 79, 161, 233
The American Journal of Clinical Medicine, 304, 353
The American Magazine, 9, 72
The Century Magazine, 43, 52, 67, 90, 92, 93, 101, 110,
    130, 133, 134, 149, 187, 194, 279
The Cigarettist, 154
The Common Sense of Drinking, 317, 321
The Drug Hang Up, 166
The Lois Wilson Story, When Love Is Not Enough, 314
The Medical Sciences Ad, 206
The Medical Times, 40, 41, 42, 241, 242, 244, 245, 248,
    249, 250, 353
*The Medical Treatment of Alcohol and Drug Addictions by
    Modern Hospital Methods*, 264
The Modern Hospital, 38, 115, 116, 178, 179, 181, 188,
    189, 190, 193, 195, 199, 200, 201, 202, 203, 205, 208,
    344, 345, 346, 347, 348
    Asked to be more specific, 188
    Paying for two page ads, 204
    Reference to alcoholism not to be a disease, 278
    Towns amazing ad, 204
The Music Man, 3
The One Hundred Men Corporation, 322, 323
The Saturday Evening Post and the Tobacco Traffic, 157
The Spirituality of Imperfection
    By Ernest Kurtz, 331
The Towns-Lambert Treatment for Morphinism and
    Alcoholism
    by Dr. Richard. C. Cabot, 35
The Twelve Steps and Twelve Traditions, 318
Tien-Tsin, 25
Tobacco
    Cigarettes
        Gateway to alcohol and drugs, 44
        The Number one vice of humanity, 46
        Unsurpassed in corrupting young boys, 44
    Contributing to the degeneration of mankind, 114
    Filthy, smelly habit, 44
    Greater harm done by than alcohol or drugs, 114
    Leads to alcoholism and morphinism, 44
    World a net gainer if eliminated, 335
Tobacco addict.
    Fourth class treated at Towns Hospital, 255
Towns Hospital, 3, 18, 38, 72, 89, 114, 128, 146, 151, 164,
    170, 171, 181, 195, 204, 205, 209, 211, 235, 237, 238,
    241, 242, 244, 245, 246, 248, 249, 250, 251, 252, 259,
    262, 282, 283, 287, 291, 293, 297, 299, 304, 305, 306,
    307, 308, 311, 312, 313, 314, 316, 325, 332, 336, 337
    1922 brochure
        extended claims for Towns Hospital, 260
        Patients fell into four groups, 259
        physicians could be intimate with patients, 262
        rational after treatment, 261

    Three guiding principles, 263
    to attract doctors, 258
    50% of patients were physicians, 72
    A lucrative business, 34
    A most fascinating institution, 1
    Became just one more drunk tank, 6
    Closing, 337
    Complete confidentiality, 75
    Fatality rates high in alcohol withdrawal, 300
    Fee Fixed
        Gives Hospital the advantage, 120
    Fee up to $350, 72
    Four patients had died while being treated, 126
    Gave Silkworth an opportunity, 301
    Individual rooms, 75
    Letting a three time loser lose at, 312
    Move to 293 Central Park West in 1914, 38
    Not a single death in twelve years, 191
    One chance to recover only, 117
    Patients 'puked & purged, 232
    Physical restraints cruel and primitive, 192
    Physicians
        One half of those treated at Towns, 71
    Probable outcome of Harrison Act, 299
    Publicly speaking of failure and relapse, 300
    Recovery rate
        2% according to Silkworth, 300
        75 to 80%, 171
        75 to 90%, 236
        75%, 105
        80%, 167
        High claims led to criminalization, 247
        Shortcomings of, 308
        Towns could only guess, 243
    Silkworth disappointed with results, 300
    Silkworth hired for $40 a week, 297
    Silkworth hired in April, 1929, 296
    Silkworth promoted twice in 1932, 296
    Silkworth reinvented treatment model, 301
    Solarium Roof, 262
    Staff learned to respect Wilson, 313
    Towns hoped would go out of business, 143
    Treating alcoholics an afterthought, 211
    Treatment
        Pride essential to recovery, 75
    Used to make several thousand a month, 316
    Wilson allowed to visit patients there, 311
    Wilson did not want to face Silkworth, 306
    Wilson did not want to go back to, 306
    Wilson left a new man, 305
    Wilson offered third interest in, 316
    Wilson offered to work there for $700 a month, 316
    Wilson probably not given much belladonna, 308
    Wilson visiting patients at Towns, 312
Towns Treatment, 53, 145, 229, 289
    'When provided throughout the country', 106
    1922 brochure
        how blood stream relieved of impurities, 260

Addicts
    Should be given treatment prior to being forced to
        quit, 70
Administered without publicity in a few days, 55
Appearance of a revolutionary approach, 52
Atropine characteristics described, 331
Can prevent 25 to 35% from going to prison, 152
Cannot prevent repoisoning, 105
Claimed by Towns to be used in Akron, 325
Completely effective, 55
Diarrhea, delirium and damnation', 232
Discarded eventually, 6
Every physician already knows it, 55
Evidence accumulates it as being ineffective, 238
Free to every physician and to every hospital, 34
In the September, 1909 JAMA, 33
Ingredients available at any drug store, 55
Magic were myths, 332
No improvement thought possible, 34
Not a cure, 105
Obliterating the craving for narcotics, 37
Seemed neat and scientific in JAMA by Dr. Lambert in
    1909, 232
Seven days maximum, 106
Should be provided to prisoners before incarceration,
    142
Towns calls for proof of using tests not involving
    himself,, 124
Will obliterate terrible craving, 105
Towns, Charles Barnes, 329, 338
A practical student of cause and effect, 148
Above mercenary considerations, 1
Accused most churches dirty with tobacco, 113
Accused most colleges dirty with tobacco, 113
Addict
    Confirmed evader of responsibility, 72
    No Italians, Hungarians, Russians, Polish, 70
    No personal contact with physician essential, 120
    No torture compares with deprivation, 141
    Pride is his number one asset, 94
    Should never become acquainted, 75
    Wants others to take drugs, 72
Addiction
    How to get a definite mental change, 143
    Results from temptation more than sin, 188
    Source came from doctors and pharmacists, 96
Alcohol
    Alcohol considered a narcotic, 45
    Alcoholic must completely forever abstain, 56
    Caused body to retain poisons, 52
    Caused more death than any ten causes put
        together, 266
    Greater havoc than all the plagues, 48
    Greatest of humanity's curses, 48
    Loss to world incalculable, 53
    to be clean of, 3
    Waging relentless war against, 2
    Waging relentless warfare against, 2

White poison, 266
Alcohol effects appearing in great grandchildren, 223
Alcoholic must be restricted, tracked, followed, 312
Alcoholics
    40% of those in insane asylums, 101
    50% of Chronics have syphilitic histories, 135
    90% of chronic males victims of gonorrhea, 136
    All should be unpoisoned, 104
    Chronic cases should be force to work, 128
    Chronics only 25% recover, 135
    Colonization changes into convicts, 126
    Had been abused, 100
    Highly nervous, 49
    Hopeless should be unsexed, 136
    Most misunderstood, 53
    Must finish with promptly & conclusively, 138
    No one so hopeless has the vagrant rich, 127
    Predisposed, 49
    Self respecting pride is the main hope of, 57
    Should be expected to lie, 53
    Should be provided with alcohol if, 107
    Should be treated as invalids, 53
    Should not be treated as criminals, 53
    Warning issued to chronics, 137
Alcoholics Anonymous
    Provides outright loan, 322
Alcoholics Anonymous needed push, 338
Alcoholism
    Ailment of 1/3rd of the sick people in the world, 51
    Alcoholic the victim, 55
    Definite disease of alcoholism, 51
    Employee discharge a crime against society, 54
    Must give up tobacco to succeed, 46
    No cure for, 134
    Punishment has never yet cured a disease, 54
    Serious Disease, 51
Almost entirely forgotten in 2014, 6
Almost forgotten atheist, 339
American hero, 32
American Lifestyle pace, 71
An alcoholic must be robbed of all his crutches, 312
An undisputed king, 1
An unwitting protagonist, 319
Anything that acts like an opiate is an opiate, 38
Appeared to by like a philanthropist, 36
Atheist, 310
Became good friends with Alexander Lambert, 20
Became just one more sanitarium owner, 7
Begins writing monthly articles for the Medical Review
    of Reviews, 146
Believed prohibition a world-wide movement, 196
Belladonna
    Why was not a hot flash advertised, 309
benefactor to humanity, 2
Born on January 12, 1862 in LaGrange, Georgia, 8
Boylan Act the work of Towns, 148
Caffeine
    To be clean of, 3

Called a fraud, 81
Called a quack, 304
Called a quack by some today, 332
Called fool for giving up monetary profits, 34
Called Unselfish, 34
Chances of nature
    Right man in right place, 2
Change your mind and observe, 47
Changed his mind at age 72, 314
Charlie, 7, 10, 302, 339
    A.A. owed him plenty of money, 327
    Believed in A.A. mightily, 322
    Didn't want any stock, 322
    His finer nature covered, 303
    in A.A., not elsewhere, 302
    Lectured Bill Wilson, 10
    Loan routed through Alcoholic Foundation, 322
    loan to A.A. of $2,500, 322
    One of those success stories, 10
    owner of a drunk tank, 315
    Raising heaven and earth for A.A., 327
    Tells Wilson to work with Morris Markey, 328
    Towns the atheist selling God, 318
    Towns' job offer, 315
    Wilson asks Towns to pay hotel, 326
    Wilson first thought Towns was right, 317
Claimed in 1932 to never have had a negative result, 300
Claimed the Towns Treatment in Encyclopedias etc., 259
Claimed voters should decide about drugs for themselves, 168
Claims to have eliminated the hazard of alcoholic insanity, 191
Claims Towns Treatment used in Akron, 325
Cleanliness of mind
    Is godliness, 112
Cocaine
    No drug brings quicker deterioration, 130
    Proof of mixed sex relations, 95
    Shortcut to prison or madhouse, 130
    User feels he has no nose, 129
Coffee drinkers in excess thin almost to emaciation, 221
Colonization
    Only for hopeless mental cases, 75
Convinced a great many physicians of his approach, 332
Criminalized Narcotics unintentionally, 252
Delirium Tremens
    Never lost a single case, 100
Disease
    Alcoholism as disease only partially true, 133
Dismissed as quack, 4
Drug prohibition required, 335
Drugs
    Available in every prison, 142
    Can be exterminated in the U.S., 107
    Claims 15% of physicians to be addicts, 90

Claims more victims from opium than tuberculosis, 90
Cost to the addict moderate, 76
Destroys sense of responsibility, 74
Necessary above all else, 76
Only one way to be relieved of the curse of, 90
Real Cost to the world, 76
To be clean of, 3
Waging relentless war against, 2
Eighth Grade Education (a guess), 7
Emperor, 1
Employer
    Responsibilities of, 54
Encountered much prejudice because a layman, 34
Everyone in America with a personal interest, 2
Exercise
    Recommended as aftercare, 122
Fascinating man, 1
Federal legislation required, 96
Findings have made medical history, 161
Firing an addicted employee a crime, 334
First really intelligent crusade, 1
Found stock market exciting in NYC, 8
Genius, 2
Georgia
    Broke horses no other person could conquer, 8
    Farming became too easy, 8
    Life insurance followed railroading, 9
    studied arithmetic & grammar by self, 9
    takes to railroading, 9
Georgia mad at U.S. Minister, 25
Given boost into prominence by Wright and Lambert, 29
Had been highly critical of alcoholics helping each other, 321
Harrison Act
    Accused of practicing medicine without a license, 81
    Advocated government competition in medicine, 81
    Advocated unprecedented restriction of the private physician, 81
    Called the enemy of the average physician, 81
    Evoked hostility and resentment, 81
    Stimulated fear and enmity of the general practitioner, 81
Harrison Act shortcomings claimed, 86
Headache Medicines
    Alleges hundreds of deaths from, 131
Held in high esteem by Medical Profession, 2
His miraculous contribution to mankind, 6
Hospitals
    Did not know how to treat alcoholics, 100
Hypodermics
    Warning about availability of, 98
Inadvertently contributed to criminalize narcotics, 247
Key player leading to narcotic prohibition, 29
Knew of no writers that praised drugs, 141
Lasting Legacy, 337
Legislation

Potential benefits of to reduce drug addiction, 71

Will prevent many into the criminal class, 140

Mankind

Artificial stimulants irresistible, 102

Searches for exhilaration, 101

Medical solution stressed, 82

Merwin

the astonishing physical vitality, 10

'you can't beat Towns', 10

Mind changed by Silkworth about Wilson, 314

Mix in a grain of Towns, 1

Moralist not

A practical student, 114

Morphine and Tobacco create moral distortion, 47

Name all but forgotten, 3

Narcotics

Breaks down sense of moral responsibility, 44

Proposes worldwide government monopoly, 65

No one else had a better solution, 52

Nobody in the world knew quite so much, 1

Not a prohibition organization member, 188

Nurses

Addicted nurses more dangerous than doctors, 72

Cannot be trusted - too close to patient, 97

Probably more are addicted than doctors, 98

Should never be allowed unsupervised syringe use, 97

Offered Wilson $700 to work at Towns, 316

Opinions appearing socialist, 68

Opium

Addict different than alcoholic, 69

If withdrawn, alcohol used instead, 69

Originally scared by Wilson visiting patients, 314

Patent Medicines

Addictive themselves, 73

Patients

Better off dead than becoming drug addicts, 185

Compared to Broncos, 121

Never made a friend with one, 132

Rejects sympathy as being effective, 132

Reserved the right to refuse admission, 128

Personal experience rejected, 132

Persuasive and dominating, 1

Pharmacists

Addicted ones irresponsible, 72

Physicians

Accused as being addicts by, 5

Addicted ones a menace to society, 72

Addicted ones should be pitied rather than blamed, 94

Addiction could be eliminated once and for all, 93

Indicted as being ignorant of addiction, 90

Must account for every grain of narcotic, 93

Ones Critical of Towns Treatment called 'fakers' by, 125

Some called 'medical buzzards' by, 125

Strict impartiality required, 121

Pittman description of, 8

Please help put me out of business, 143

Praised by the Medical Review of Reviews, 144

Prisons

Predicted drugs would thrive there, 108

Treat before incarceration, 109

Private sanitariums methods should be ruled by law, 122

Prohibitionists

Towns an ally of, 96

Provided publicity through Liberty Magazine, 6

Providing 50% of funding for the book, 6

Providing A.A. first big sales opportunity, 327

Recovery

Essential the individual invest his own money in, 103

Recovery rate

%75 at Towns Hospital, 105

%80 at Towns Hospital, 167

20% at Bellevue Hospital, 106

75 to 90% at Towns, 236

75-80% at Towns, 171

Claims led to criminalization, 247

Most effective in the world, 291

Recovery Rate

Silkworth found %2, 300

Recreational drug usage inconcievable, 335

Reigned Supreme in 1910's, 5

Risking $4,000, 323

Sanatorium

Addicts should not congregate, 74

Colonization negative for patient, 75

Patient may become incurable there, 119

Small colony of drug users, 118

Strong criticism of, 114

Those that charge by week corrupt, 74

Three week max for giving patients drugs, 123

Saw world dazed and befuddled by substances, 38

Saying to Wilson that times are hard, 316

Saying Wilson's methods were going to work, 314

Should be taught in medical schools, 6

Silkworth contradicted Towns 1915 assertion, 301

Sincerity of Purpose, 2

Society

Should be willing to pay for consequences of alcohol, 108

Solon of Narcotics, 148

Some of the most opinionated writing of his career, 265

Spending all his spare time on legislative efforts, 148

Sterilization

For the hopeless, 103

Successful Treatment

Brief Treatment, 119

Syphillis compared to effect of alcohol on unborn infant, 223

Telling Wilson of Silkworth's vital contribution to Wilson's society, 316

The definite disease of alcoholism, 51

The Old Atheist, 318
Tobacco
  2nd to none in corrupting boys, 44
  Asserts tobacco blunts craving for alcohol, 46
  Corrupted morals of young boys, 110
  Damages a boy's work, 44
  If drunk, smokers don't care to smoke, 46
  Just like opium, 45
  Leads to callous indifference to rights of others, 47
  Narcotic Tobacco, 44, 45
  Relation to alcohol and opium very close, 44
  The only substance Towns ever used himself, 43
  To be clean of, 3
  Undoing of 75% of boys that go wrong, 111
  Waging relentless war against, 2
Towns approached State Senator John J. Boylan, 79
Towns Hospital
  Never a negative result, 292
Towns might have said Wilson was crazy, 310
Towns Treatment
  Failures come from the lack of a fixed fee, 117
  Should become medical school standard curriculum,
    51
Treatment
  As outpatient ridiculous, 73
  Must be administered by another, 74
  Reduction methods at home ridiculous, 74
Treatment hospitals
  Should be in every city, 108
Treatment no longer than seven days, 117
Treatment shortcoming in NY hospitals, 51
What bores the alcoholic most, 312
Wilson offered third interest in Towns by, 316
Woodrow Wilson advised, 179
World must listen to, 1
Would not reveal the secret formula, 20
Towns, Colonel Ed, 329
Towns, Jarrel Oliver
  Father of Charles Towns, 8
Towns, Mary L. Barbour
  Wife of Charles Towns, 8
Towns-Lambert Treatment, 15, 36, 124, 171, 175, 229,
  259, 308
  Lambert endorsed, named after him, 20
  Name used by Bill Wilson, 303
Toxic amblyopia
  Results from smoking tobacco, 294
Trigonal, 258
Tuberculosis, 90, 91, 271
Twelve Defining Moments in the History of Alcoholics
  Anonymous
  White and Kurtz, 316
Twelve Traditions of AA, 318

U

U.S. Commissioner of Internal Revenue, 161
U.S. Congress, 83, 184, 187, 210, 288, 336

Determined to exclude Chinese laborers, 28
Did not vote in narcotic prohibition, 86
Limited Police Powers, 31
U.S. Federal Government, 197
U.S. Federal Legislation, 3, 82, 84, 96, 187, 197, 210
U.S. House of Representatives
  Overrode Wilson's veto of the Volstead Act, 78
U.S. Minister to China
  Condemns Towns as trouble maker, 27
U.S. Opium Law of 1909, 32
U.S. Senate
  Overrode Wilson's veto of the Volstead Act, 78
U.S. State Department, 29
U.S. Supreme Court, 87, 158, 336
U.S. Treasury Department, 82, 85, 184, 246, 247, 251, 336
  Actions Supported by Dr. Lambert, 89
  Anything goes, 165
  Criminalization of narcotics in 5 years, 336
  Decision 2200, 126, 161, 246
    No Mention by Towns, 92
  Declared indefinite maintenance of addicts illegal, 246
  First seizures of illegal drugs in 1917, 166
  Harrison Act mutation, 88
  Impact on jails and prisons, 88
  Issues Decision 2200, May 11, 1915, 87
  Justification for Harrison Act rulings, 165
  Prosecutions filed by, xi
  Punitive measures of, 251
  Stand against ambulatory treatment, 246
  Took advantage of cure claims, 87
  Under a variety of prohibitionist pressure, 85
  Unexpected interpretation of Harrison Act, 86
U.S. v. Jin Fuey Moy, 158
Ulysses, 289
United Kingdom, 153
United States, 2, 29, 30, 32, 65, 78, 82, 86, 175, 184, 186,
  333, 353
  2nd to China in opium consumption, 166
  A different conception of the drug problem, 5
  Abandoned medical approach to treating addiction,
    239
  Belladonna native to, 230
  Brutality against Chinese, 28
  Citizen Towns had only known opium cure, 32
  Congress did nothing more than the Harrison Act for
    years, 161
  Dangers of tobacco ignored, 165
  Drug addiction a new issue to U.S. government, 20
  Had no opium laws in 1908, 30
  Harrison Act passed mainly for international
    obligations, 83
  Heroin introduced to by Bayer Corporation, 154
  limitations of first U.S. Opium law, 31
  Narcotic Prohibition in 5 years, 78
  No Federal drug laws, first in 1909, 4
  Repudiated League of Nations, 334
  Towns returning from China a hero, 32
  Wanted to show commitment to solve opium curse, 31

War increases narcotic fears, 45
World War I increased narcotic fears, 166
Xanthoxylum native to, 231
United States Alcohol Prohibition
Began January 16, 1920, 78
University College, London, 285

V

Venus, 282
Veronal, 258
Vertigo
Results from smoking tobacco, 294
Vodka, 160, 175, 226, 270
Volstead Act, 78, 246

W

Washington D.C., 21, 288
Welch, William H., M.D.
Ex-President of the AMA, 272
West Africa, 275
White, William A., M.D., 281, 329
White, William L., xi, 82, 85, 88, 235, 246
Towns' job offer, 316, 319
Wilson, Bill, 46, 215, 303, 311, 313, 321, 338, 339
Akron visit, May 1935, 314
Amateurish publicity attempts, 327
Being lectured by Towns, 303
Belladonna Treatment, 229
Belladonna Treatment – so called, 15
Calling Towns 'Doc', 315
Chances of meeting Silkworth without Towns remote, 6
Claimed Silkworth treated 50,000 alcoholics, 305
Could not remember why he got drunk again, 306
Explaining the Towns offer to Lois, 317
Flat broke, 328
Helps Towns draft reply to the AMA, 324
Hot flash, 309, 338
How did Silkworth know he was sober?, 311
Job offer made when?, xii
Lambert to Silkworth, let Wilson visit patients, 313
No alcoholic seemed to benefit from his visits, 312
No personal loan from Towns, 326
Offer to become lay therapist, 317
Offered $700 a month by Towns, 316
Omission of salary amount, 318
Partner Hank Parkhurst, 322
Pupil of this society, 318
Quit alcohol but not tobacco, 333
Recollection of *Liberty Magazine* origin, 327
Significance of declining job from Towns, 319
Silkworth's assistance to Wilson's 'White Light', 6

Silkworth's said Bill had been preaching, 312
Stretching the truth, 324
Taken drunk without knowing how or why, 306
Talks with Silkworth among his dearest possessions, 304
Three time loser, 312
Tobacco
Wilson never quit, 46
Towns
Didn't talk about curing alcoholism, 303
Towns' $2,500 loan, 322
Towns described, 10
Towns Hospital
1st visit, 301, 302
2nd visit, 306
3rd visit, 306
4th visit, 306
Towns Hospital four visits, 3, 337
Towns' job offer, 315, 316, 317
Towns paying hotel bill, 326
Towns should be remembered for his finer nature, 304
Towns staff gaining respect for, 313
Visiting patients at Towns, 311, 312
Visits Charles Towns one day in July, 1939, 327
White Light Experience, 3, 308, 311
Wilson offered third interest in Towns Hospital, 316
Wilson, Lois, 317
Not enthusiastic about job offer, 317
Wilson, Woodrow, 65, 187, 210
Crushed by defeat of U.S. refusal to join League, 78
Veto of Volstead Act, 78
Towns most likely a supporter of, 162
Urged by Towns to appoint committee, 179
World War I, 6, 78, 159, 160, 166, 175, 227
Towns
Has wrought incalculable good, 176
Wright, Charles Romley Adler, 153
Wright, Hamilton, M.D., 30, 31
Bypassed his own committee, 29
Called founding father of American drug policy, 29
Fell out of favor with Wilson administration, 93
Key player leading to narcotic prohibition, 29
Member 1908 China Commission, 29

X

Xanthoxylum, 191, 229, 231

Z

Zanthoxylum americanum, 231
Zeus, 289

Notes

Chapter 1 - Introduction

[1] *The American Disease, Origins of Narcotic Control*, David F. Musto, M.D., Oxford University Press, 200 Madison Ave., NY, NY, 10016, @1973, page 79

[2] *The American Magazine*, Samuel Merwin, "Fighting The Deadly Habits, The Story of Charles B. Towns," October, 1912, p. 717

[3] *Slaying The Dragon*, William L. White, Chestnut Health Systems, Lighthouse Institute, Bloomington, Illinois, 61701 @1998, p. 84 (All page numbers are from the 1998 edition).

[4] *The American Magazine*, Samuel Merwin, "Fighting The Deadly Habits," p. 708, 714

[5] "The "White Hope" of Drug Victims," *Collliers, The National Weekly*, Peter Clark MacFarlane, November 29, 1913, p 16

[6] *Boston Medical and Surgical Journal*, "The Towns-Lambert Treatment for Morphinism and Alcoholism," Massachusetts Medical Society, New England Surgical Society, Vol. CLXIV, May 11, 1911, Dr. Richard C. Cabot, M..D., p.676

[7] CASQ, Culture Alcohol & Society Quarterly, Vol III, no 7, April, May, June 2008, page 4.

[8] *The American Disease*, David F. Musto, page 82

[9] Bill Wilson talk, 1951, Atlanta, GA

[10] *Drug War Politics: The Price of Denial*; Bertram, Blackman, Sharpe & Andreas; U of Cal Press, Berkeley & LA, CA, p. 61

[11] http://www.encyclopedia.com/topic/Food_and_Drug_Act_of_1906.aspx Encyclopedia.com, Food and Drug act of 1906: "It would not stretch matters to say that the Pure Food and Drug Act of 1906 (P.L. 59-384, 34 Stat. 768), also known as the Wiley Act, stands as the most consequential regulatory statute in the history of the United States. The act not only gave unprecedented new regulatory powers to the federal government, it also empowered a bureau that evolved into today's Food and Drug Administration (FDA). The legacy of the 1906 act includes federal regulatory authority over one-quarter of gross domestic product, and includes market gatekeeping power over human and animal drugs, foods and preservatives, medical devices, biologics and vaccines. Other statutes (such as the Interstate Commerce Act of 1887, the Sherman and Clayton antitrust laws, and the Federal Trade Commission Act of 1914) have received more study, but the Pure Food and Drug Act has had the longest-lasting and most widespread economic, political, and institutional impact. . . . At the time, the Pure Food and Drug Act of 1906 was the most daunting intrusion by federal authorities into interstate commerce. Although other federal agencies could regulate prices and occupational safety, the USDA was now engaged in the regulation of the very manufacture and sale of products, in addition to advertising."

[12] Ibid., p. 62

[13] www.ama-assn.org/ama/pub/about-ama/our-history/ama-history-timeline.page?

[14] *The American Disease*, David Musto, p. 56

[15] *The American Disease*, David F. Musto, M.D., p 62: "The number of physician-addicts was high. Medicine was (and is) the leading profession in the rate of addiction, about 2 percent according to Wright's survey. The profession was commonly believed to be one of the causes of most of the other addicts in the nation, and evidence, nowhere contradicted before Congress, revealed that physicians were the principal offenders."

Chapter 2 – Beginnings 1862-1904

Col Ed. Towns, at the AA International in 1960: "My father was a Georgia boy whose schooling was very seriously curtailed through the efforts of a northern general named Sherman. And in fact not only did he never get any higher education. As a matter of fact, he was lucky to make it halfway through the first phase."

CASQ, Culture Alcohol & Society Quarterly, Vol III, no 7, April, May, June 2008, page 5

AA The Way It Began, Bill Pittman, Glenn Abbey Books, PO Box 19762, Seattle, WA, 98109, @1988, p. 84

"The "White Hope" of Drug Victims, *Collliers*, Peter Clark MacFarlane, p 16

[5] *Boston Medical and Surgical Journal*, May 11, 1911, Dr. Richard C. Cabot, M..D., p.676

[6] *The American Magazine*, Samuel Merwin, "Fighting The Deadly Habits," p. 714

[7] *Pass It On, The Story of Bill Wilson and How the A.A.Message Reached the World,* Alcoholics Anonymous World Services, Inc., New York, NY, p. 101

[8] *Bill W. My First 40 Years, An Autobiography by the Cofounder of Alcoholics Anonymous*, Bill Wilson, Hazelden, Center City, Minnesota, 55012-0176, (transcript of Bill Wilson recordings), p.. 106-107

[9] "The "White Hope" of Drug Victims," *Collliers*, Peter Clark MacFarlane, p 16

[10] "My Relation to the Medical Profession," *Medical Review of Reviews*, Charles B. Towns, p. 198

[11] The "White Hope" of Drug Victims," *Collliers*, Peter Clark MacFarlane,, p 16-17

[12] *Alcoholics Anonymous*, Alcoholics Anonymous World Services, Inc., p. 7

[13] My Relation to the Medical Profession," *Medical Review of Reviews*, Charles B. Towns, p. 198-199

[14] The "White Hope of Drug Victims," *Colliers*, Peter Clark MacFarlane, p. 16

[15] My Relation to the Medical Profession," *Medical Review of Reviews*, Charles B. Towns, p. 198-199

[16] *New York Times*, June 6, 1965. Colonel Ed Towns is quoted as having asserted "The hospital began in 1909 at 119 West 81st Street, and in 1914 moved to Central Park West."

[17] The "White Hope" of Drug Victims," *Collliers*, Peter Clark MacFarlane, p 17

Chapter 3 – Connections 1904-1908

[1] The "White Hope" of Drug Victims," *Collliers*, Peter Clark MacFarlane, p 17

[2] *Slaying The Dragon*, William L. White, p. 84

[3] *The American Disease*, David F. Musto, page 80

[4] Ibid., page 80

[5] Ibid., page 30

[6] The "White Hope" of Drug Victims," *Collliers*, Peter Clark MacFarlane, p 17

[7] Ibid., p 17

[8] Ibid., p 17

Chapter 4 – China 1908-1909

[1] *The American Magazine*, Samuel Merwin, "Fighting The Deadly Habits," p. 708-709

[2] The "White Hope" of Drug Victims," *Collliers*, Peter Clark MacFarlane, p 29

[3] Ibid., p 29

[4] Ibid., p 16

[5] Ibid., p 29

[6] *Forces of Habit, Drugs and the Making of the Modern World*, David T. Courtwright, Presidents and Fellows of Harvard College, 2002, p. 118: "[The head of British American Tobacco's] greatest success was in China, a country in which he [James Buchanan Duke] already had sizeable interests . . . Turning the pages he looked, not at the maps, but at the population figures. When he came to the legend 'Pop. 430,000,000,' he said, 'That is where we are going to sell cigarettes.'" P. 120: "Duke apparently hoped that BAT cigarettes would supplant opium smoking, which was under increasing attack by missionaries, nationalists, and other reformers in the early twentieth century . . . What is certain is that by 1916, a year when BAT's China cigarette sales were approaching—by some estimates they had already well exceeded—the 10 billion mark, this singularly addictive form of smoking had become popular with all classes and ages, including children."

[7] *The American Disease*, David F. Musto, page 30

[8] Ibid., p. 31

[9] Ibid., p. 31

[10] *Drugs and Minority Oppression*, John Helmer, The Seabury Press, 815 Second Ave., New York, NY, 10017, p. 38

[11] *The American Disease*, David F. Musto, p. 32. Note: Charles C. Tenney, secretary to the American Legation at Peking, should not be confused with Charles E. Terry, an early campaigner against drug addiction.

[12] *The American Disease*, David F. Musto, page 32-33

[13] Ibid, p. 34

[14] *The Medical Times*, "The Growing Menace of the Narcotic Drug Habit and the Efforts to Combat It," Honorable Edward Swann, Judge of the Court of General Sessions, New York, April 1914, p. 108: "At this conference it was resolved that no country should export opium to China; that remedies for the cure of the opium habit should be discovered, if possible; that all countries having concessions in China should see to it that all opium 'divans' were closed in their possessions, and that drastic measures should be taken against the use of morphine."

[15] The Drug-Taker and the Physician," Charles B. Towns, *The Century Magazine*, October, 1912, p. 856

[16] *New York Times*, October 7, 1909, "Drug Habit Curable, Says Dr. Lambert."

Chapter 5 – King Charles of New York City 1909-1919

[1] *The American Disease*, David F. Musto, page 82

[2] The "White Hope" of Drug Victims," Collliers, November 29-30, 1913, p 30

[3] *New York Times*, "Drying Out Hospital for Problem Drinkers Closes," June 6, 1965

[4] *Boston Medical and Surgical Journal*, May 11, 1911, Dr. Richard C. Cabot, M..D., p.676

[5] Ibid., p.676

[6] *The American Magazine*, Samuel Merwin, "Fighting The Deadly Habits," p. 716

[7] Medical Review of Reviews, Medical Bookland, Review of *Habits That Handicap*, p. 55

[8] "Conquering The Habits That Handicap," *New York Times*, August 8, 1915

[9] *The American Magazine*, Samuel Merwin, "Fighting The Deadly Habits," p. 708

[10] *The American Disease*, David F. Musto, p. 311

[11] *The American Magazine*, Samuel Merwin, "Fighting The Deadly Habits," p. 710

[12] *The Modern Hospital*, February, 1917, Charles B. Towns, Ad page 76.

Chapter 6 – *The Century Magazine* Articles 1912

[1] "The Injury of Tobacco, and Its Relation to other Drug Habits," Charles B. Towns, *The Century Magazine*, March, 1912, p. 766

[2] Ibid., p. 771

[3] Extraordinary statements that, more or less, were validated over time. *Forces of Habit, Drugs and the Making of the Modern World*, David T. Courtwright, Presidents and Fellows of Harvard College, 2002, p. 114: "The cigarette was to tobacco as the hypodermic syringe was to opiates; a revolutionary technology that permitted alkaloids to work more quickly and with stronger effect on the brain's reward system."

[4] "The Injury of Tobacco, and Its Relation to other Drug Habits," Charles B. Towns, *The Century Magazine*, March, 1912, p. 770

[5] Ibid. ,p. 770

[6] Ibid., p. 769

[7] Ibid., p. 768

[8] Ibid., p. 768

[9] *The Medical Times*, "The Growing Menace of the Narcotic Drug Habit and the Efforts to Combat It," Honorable Edward Swann, Judge of the Court of General Sessions, New York, April 1914, p. 108-109. Considered to be a representative sample.

[10] "The Injury of Tobacco, and Its Relation to other Drug Habits," Charles B. Towns, *The Century Magazine*, March, 1912, p. 771

[11] Ibid., p. 770

[12] Ibid., p. 771

[13] "Help For the Hard Drinker," Charles B. Towns, *The Century Magazine*, June, 1912, p. 292

[14] Ibid., p. 292

[15] Ibid., p. 292

[16] Ibid., p. 293

[17] In June 1914, the opinions of Charles Towns were solicited on the subject of how tobacco harmed young boys and how the substance led to "gambling, loose morals, drinking and everything else that is not worthwhile . . ." *The Medical Times*, "Smoking To the Boy Spells Worthlessness.", p. 171. By January 3, 1917, an article in the *New York Times* referred to Towns as 'an authority on anti-drug legislation."

[18] "Help For the Hard Drinker," Charles B. Towns, *The Century Magazine*, June, 1912, p. 294

[19] Ibid., p. 294

[20] Ibid., p. 294

[21] Ibid., p. 295

[22] Ibid., p. 295

[23] Ibid., p. 296

[24] Ibid., p. 297

[25] Ibid., p. 297-298

[26] Wikipedia, en.widipedia.org/wiki/Seven_Deadly_Sins

[27] *Slaying The Dragon*, William L. White, p. 85. "In 1914, fees at Towns Hospital ran from $200 to $350 for drug treatment ($75 in the Annex) and $75-150 for alcoholism treatment ($50 in the Annex)." However, over the years, there may have been additional latitude for reduction of these fees. In the book *Mrs. Marty Man* by Sally & David Brown, " . . . Towns required $100 up front . . ." on p. 115. When Bill Wilson entered the hospital drunk for the final time in December 1934, Wilson was sent upstairs to find a bed by Silkworth seemingly without any discussion of a fee for the broke Wilson that had spent his last pennies on beer. The Annex was located at 110 W. 82nd St., according to a July 1914 ad in *The Medical Times*. Just how long the Annex survived after the 1914 hospital move to 293 Central Park West is not yet known.

[28] *Slaying The Dragon*, William L. White, p. 85

[29] "The Peril of The Drug Habit," Charles B. Towns, *The Century Magazine*, August, 1912, p 580

[30] Ibid., p 581

[31] Ibid., p 582

[32] Ibid., p 582

[33] Ibid., p 581

[34] Ibid., p 581

[35] Ibid., p 582

[36] Ibid., p 582

[37] Ibid., p 582

[38] Ibid., p 582

[39] Ibid., p 583

[40] Ibid., p 583

[41] Ibid., p 583

[42] Ibid., p 584

[43] Ibid., p 584

[44] Ibid., p 584

[45] Ibid., p 584-585

[46] Ibid., p 585

[47] Ibid., p 585

[48] Ibid., p 587

[49] "The Drug-Taker and the Physician," Charles B. Towns, *The Century Magazine*, October, 1912, p. 853

[50] Ibid., p. 853

[51] Ibid., p. 854

[52] Ibid., p. 854

[53] Ibid., p. 854

[54] Ibid., p. 854

[55] Ibid., p. 854

[56] Ibid., p. 854

[57] Ibid., p. 857

[58] Ibid., p. 858
[59] Ibid., p. 859

Chapter 7 – The Harrison Act, December 1914

[1] The Wrecking of the Eighteenth Amendment, Ernest Gordon, @1943, The Alcohol Information Press, Francestown, New Hampshire, p. 286

[2] The American Disease, David F. Musto, p. 105

[3] The Sacred Heart Review, Boston College, Volume 57, Number 8, 3 February 1917, p. 6

[4] Medical Review of Reviews, Medical Bookland review of Habits That Handicap, January, 1916, p. 55

[5] The American Disease, David F. Musto, p. 102

[6] "New Drug Law Hits Accidental Users," New York Times, June 21, 1914

[7] Medical Review of Reviews, March, 1916, "My Relation to the Medical Profession," p. 198

[8] The American Disease, David F. Musto, p.102-103

[9] Medical Review of Reviews, December 1916, "The Future of Addict Legislation," p. 906

[10] The Medical Times, "An Analysis of the New York Anti-Narcotic Law," Judge Edward Swann of the Court of the General Sessions, New York, August 1914, p. 239-240

[11] Ibid., p. 239

[12] Slaying The Dragon, William L. White, p. 86

[13] Drug War Politics: The Price of Denial; Bertram, Blackman, Sharpe & Andreas; p. 67

[14] The American Disease, David F. Musto, p. 61

[15] Consumers Union Report on Licit and Illicit Drugs, by Edward M Brecher and the Editors of Consumer Reports Magazine, 1972

[16] Maryland Medical Journal, "The Harrison Anti-Narcotic Law," March, 1915, p. 76-77

[17] The Origin of Compulsory Drug Prescriptions, Peter Temin, Working Paper, Department of Economics, Massachusetts Institute of Technology, 50 Memorial Drive, Cambridge, MA, 02139, p. 1: "Before 1938, the only drugs for which prescriptions were needed were certain narcotics specified in the Harrison Anti-Narcotic Act on 1914."

[18] Drug War Politics: The Price of Denial; Bertram, Blackman, Sharpe & Andreas; p. 67

[19] Ibid., p. 68

[20] The New York State Journal of Medicine, Editorial: "The federal and State Laws in Relation to Habit-Forming Drugs," John Cowell MacEvitt, M.D. Editor, Vol. XV, April 15, 1915, No. 4., p. 129-131

[21] Slaying The Dragon, William L. White, p. 112

[22] Consumers Union Report on Licit and Illicit Drugs, by Edward M Brecher and the Editors of Consumer Reports Magazine, 1972

[23] Drugs and Drug Policy in America, Steven R. Belenko, p. 54,55, from "Drug Smugglers Nullify New Laws," New York Times, March 15, 1915

[24] Ibid., p. 55

[25] Slaying The Dragon, William L. White, p. 113: "In 1916, in the U.S. v. Jin Fuey Moy, the Supreme Court ruling in this case affirmed than an addict's possession of smuggled drugs was a violation of the Harrison Act. With this decision, the only way an addicted person could possess a drug was to obtain the drug through a physician. In 1919, in U.S. v. Doremus, the court ruled that the Act was constitutional in spite of the fact that it had been implemented for purposes other than revenue. In a critical decision announced the same day, The Supreme Court ruled in Webb v. United States that a physician prescribing morphine to an addict 'not in the course of professional treatment in the attempted cure of the habit,' but at a dosage 'sufficient to keep him comfortable,' was not within the meaning of the physicians' exemption of the Harrison Act, and was therefore illegal."

[26] Ibid., p. 113

[27] Illegal Drugs, Paul Gahlinger, M.D., Ph.D., published by Plume of the Penguin Group, January 2004, p. 60: "By 1930, 35 percent of all new convicts in the United States were being indicted under the Harrison Narcotic Act."

[28] Drugs and Minority Oppression, John Helmer, The Seabury Press, 815 Second Ave., New York, NY, 10017, @1975, p. 39

Chapter 8 – Habits That Handicap, August 1915

[1] *Drugs and Society*, Hanson, Venturelli, & Fleckenstein, 11th Edition, Jones & Bartlett Learning, 5 Wall Street, Burlington, MA, 01803, p. 254: "A number of physicians were addicted as well. One of the best-known morphine addicts was William Holsted, a founder of Johns Hopkins Medical School. Holsted was a very productive surgeon and innovator, although secretly an addict for most of his career. He became dependent on morphine as a substitute for his cocaine dependence (Brecher 1972)."

[2] *The Medical Times*, "The Abuse of Habit-Forming Drugs," July, 1913, p. 216: "The mortality statistics of the Census Bureau report that for the last ten years the annual average deaths indirectly due to poisons other than alcohol has reached the appalling figure of 5,000." Alcohol deaths are not specified.

[3] How could he have made such a claim without any supporting information whatsoever? The Centers for Disease Control publication "Deaths and Death Rates for leading Causes of Death: Death Registration States, 1900-1998 (www.cdc.gov/nchs/data/dvs/lead1900_98.pdf) lists 86,726 tuberculosis deaths in 1915, 100,789 deaths in 1917. According to *Drugs and Politics*, Edited by Paul E. Rock, @1977, by Transaction, Inc., New Brunswick, NJ: "Estimates vary, but almost certainly there were more than 100,000 addicts in the United States in 1914, many of whom were highly respected members of society." Death rates as listed in a 1920 table, created by the Metropolitan Life Insurance Company, does not mention alcoholism or drugs as a cause of death. Clearly the reference to tuberculosis is an unjustified sensationalism. However, such fearful claims were not just written by Towns: Rufus King's *The Drug Hang Up, America's Fifty-Year Folly*, Chapter 4, contains the following: "One 1916 estimate purported to establish that there were 200,000 highly dangerous drug fiends in the streets of New York City, not only lurking among marginal classes but ranging through the entire "upper world" as well . . . Estimates of the addict population in New York City alone jumped to 300,000 . . . On June 12, 1919, The Secretary of The Treasury reported that the United States was consuming ten to sixty times as much opium per capita as any other nation; that the number of opium users was somewhere between 200,000 and 4 million, and "probably more than" a million . . . " A 1923 study referenced by Rufus King reduced the nation's addict population to no more than 110,000.

[4] *Drugs and Drug Policy in America*, Steven R. Belenko, p. 43, from "Say Drug Habit Grips the Nation," *New York Times*, December 5, 1913: "Twenty three percent of the medical profession, the speaker continued, were now victims of the morphine habit."

[5] *Habits That Handicap*, Charles B. Towns, The Century Co., August, 1915, p. xii

[6] *Drugs and Society*, Hanson, Venturelli, & Fleckenstein, 11th Edition, Jones & Bartlett Learning, 5 Wall Street, Burlington, MA, 01803, p. 254 "By 1900, and estimated 1 million Americans were dependent on opiates (Abel 1980)."

[7] *Habits That Handicap*, Charles B. Towns, The Century Co., August, 1915, p. xiii

[8] Ibid., p. 48-49, 50

[9] Ibid., p. 50

[10] Ibid., p. 50

[11] Ibid., p. 57-58

[12] Ibid., p. 58

[13] Ibid., p. 61

[14] Ibid., p. 62

[15] Ibid., p. 72-73

[16] Ibid., p. 74

[17] Ibid., p. 74-75

[18] Ibid., p. 78-79

[19] Ibid., p. 84-85

[20] Ibid., p. 113-114

[21] Smith, Kline and French began selling amphetamine as an inhaler under the brand name Benzedrine as a decongestant in 1932. Methoide.fcm.arizona.edu/infocenter/index.cfm?stid=164

[22] Ibid., p. 115-116

[23] Ibid., p. 117

[24] *Ibid.,* p. 118-119

[25] *Habits That Handicap*, Charles B. Towns, p. 120 "[The recovery rate] varies enormously with the individual patients and one can only judge from one's experience. My personal experience is the 11 per cent of morphinists and 12 per cent of the alcoholics return for treatment. Doubling this percentage it still gives us 75 percent as remaining free from addiction. Of these a very high percentage are known to have stayed free."

[26] Habits That Handicap, Charles B. Towns, p. 121

[27] Habits That Handicap, Charles B. Towns, p. 122

[28] Ibid., p. 123-124

[29] Ibid., p. 124

[30] Ibid., p. 125

[31] A January 15, 1916 book review of *Habits that Handicap* in *The New York Times* began by discussing if the author of this book was a quack: " A QUACK, as everyone knows, is a person who pretends to skill, usually in medicine or surgery, and puffs his own wonderful remedy—making a loud and foolish noise. Mr. Towns claims he can stop the morphia habit. Is he a quack? Well, Dr. Alexander Lambert of New York and Dr. Richard C. Cabot of Boston have estimable names. They lend them to Mr. Towns. Dr. Lambert sent Mr. Towns to Dr. Cabot. Dr. Cabot regarded as "entirely impossible" the claims that Mr. Towns made. Experience converted him. He not only verified Mr. Towns' statements. He duplicated his methods and his cures. "I do not hesitate to say," Dr. Cabot writes, "that he knows more about the alleviation and cure of drug addictions than any doctor that I have ever seen."

[32] *Habits That Handicap*, Charles B. Towns,, p. 136-138

[33] Ibid., p. 138-139

[34] Towns was one of many contributors underneath the lead subject in the June 1914 *The Medical Times*, which was "Is Smoking Detrimental to Boys and Young Men?" (Vol. XLII., No. 6, p. 171-172). His article will be included here in full:

Smoking To The Boy Spells Worthlessness
Charles B. Towns
Superintendent of the Towns Hospital
New York

Tobacco has no greater foe that I. I view the subject from the standpoint of a man who was born and raised in the South, where every boy was expected to smoke, "Chaw" and "cuss" some as soon as his parents thought he was old enough to do so.

Very fortunate for boys who came along about my time, '62 there were no cigarettes. I was brought up on a farm, and my first smoking of tobacco was behind a barn—keeping out of sight of the elders. Had I been raised in this age in a big city, I unquestionably would have smoked cigarettes, for a time at least, until I was able of my own accord to learn that the use of tobacco is a bad business.

I voluntarily gave up tobacco twenty years ago, in disgust! I have never wanted to smoke since, and have always felt sorry for those who did.

There is nothing done at the present time to give the boys and young men of this age the right mental attitude about the use of this drug.

We must class the tobacco user as a whole among the most selfish of the animal kingdom. He thinks that his family should tolerate his smoking as often and as long as he pleases, that he should have a perfect right in private and public places, to use it irrespective of others feelings.

Tobacco, directly and indirectly, is the biggest possible factor in bringing about the boy's undoing. He must submit to his father's using it in his presence as he is growing up, and is told that he must not use it. We all know what this means sooner or later, and generally it is sooner.

The boy who begins smoking never does so in his parent's presence, nor with their consent. The boy beginning to use tobacco these days, begins with the worst form possible—cigarettes; as he must conceal his smoking it means he must begin to lie and this in the end will lead up to the boy's undoing.

The boy that will lie to his father about tobacco will lie about anything. He immediately cultivates that class of boys who are doing the same thing. We all know that with the fewest possible exceptions such boys are not looking for the clean things in life, nor discussing clean people and clean things. Not only is it the beginning of a systematic poisoning of the physical man, but it means a distortion of the moral man. In a short time you can begin to add gambling, loose morals, drinking and everything else that is not worth while, and which, sooner or later, spells "*worthlessness.*"

Materia medica tells us that nicotine, next to prussic acid, is the most powerful poison known to medicine. The only medical use that it can really be put to is to produce nausea; there are other drugs very much more desirable to meet such a condition.

Tobacco is harmful to every one who uses it, old or young. It cannot in any way contribute to anyone's physical or mental uplift. Some men are not so susceptible to the action of this drug as others; some are more economical in its user, and in the way in which they use it.

The reason that some men who have been using it for years apparently are in good health is that they are just a little harder to poison than the others. The use of tobacco in any form is a useless, stinking, dirty and injurious habit, and should be classed as the *world's worst form of drug habit*. It is more surely contributing to the degeneracy to the race than alcohol or opium! I believe that if we could eliminate the use of tobacco, we would lessen the excessive use of alcoholic stimulants 75%.

I hope some day to see nation-wide legislation which will compel the teaching to the young in public and private schools what tobacco, stimulants and drugs really are, and their action upon the human system. It should be made part of the school curriculum. If boys really knew what tobacco is, and what its effect would be on their health in the future, they would not want to use it.

Let us start out and give the boy an honest chance. Sooner or later the old tobacco-soaked individual will pass away. We must look to the new crop of youngsters for any real reform in this direction.

[35] *Habits That Handicap*, Charles B. Towns, p. 163
[36] Ibid., p. 165
[37] Ibid., p. 166-67
[38] Ibid., p. 169
[39] Ibid., p. 170
[40] Ibid., p. 170-171
[41] Ibid., p. 172
[42] Ibid., p. 174
[43] Ibid., p. 177
[44] Ibid., p. 177
[45] Ibid., p. 181
[46] Ibid., p. 177-178
[47] Ibid., p. 186
[48] Both Akron and New York early members of A.A. were hospitalized. Failure to submit to hospitalization indicated the alcoholic wasn't ready to get sober.
[49] *Habits That Handicap*, Charles B. Towns, p. 180-182
[50] Ibid., p. 182-183
[51] Ibid., p. 185
[52] Ibid., p. 190
[53] Ibid., p. 190
[54] Ibid., p. 192-193
[55] Ibid., p. 195
[56] Ibid., p. 195
[57] Ibid., p. 197
[58] Ibid., p. 198, 199
[59] Ibid., p. 198, 199
[60] Ibid., p. 198, 199
[61] Ibid., p. 201
[62] Ibid., p. 203
[63] *The New York Supplement, The Decisions of the Supreme and Lower Courts of Record of New York State,* Volume 165, June 11—July 30, 1917: Robertson vs. Charles B. Towns Hospital, p. 17: A patient was admitted on March 11,

[64] 1915. On March 14, the patient went mad, accused his roommate of trying to kill him, he then bolted out of the room, down the hall, to the lavatory. By the time a doctor could get to the patient, he had gone out a third floor lavatory window to his death. A jury had found the hospital liable for the patient's death, but two years later, a higher court reversed the decision and sent the case back to the lower court for a new trial.
Less than two years later, in January of 1917, he wrote "Successful Medical Treatment in Chronic Alcoholism" in *The Modern Hospital*, where he wrote "And so far as the hazard of death is concerned, it should be interesting for the reader to know that for the first twelve years of this work . . . we did not have a single death." How these two testimonies could have been reconciled by Towns, if he may have every tried to reconcile them, remains a mystery.

[65] *Habits That Handicap*, Charles B. Towns, p. 204

[66] Ibid., p. 207, 208

[67] Ibid., p. 209

[68] Ibid., p. 210

[69] Ibid., p. 211

[70] Ibid., p. 211

[71] *Ibid.*, p. 219-220

[72] "The Drug-Taker and the Physician," Charles B. Towns, *The Century Magazine*, October, 1912, p. 859

[73] *Habits That Handicap*, Charles B. Towns, p. 222

[74] *Ibid.*, p. 225-226

[75] *Ibid.*, p. 227

[76] *Ibid.*, p. 227-228

[77] *Ibid.*, p. 230-231

[78] *Ibid.*, p. 232

[79] Ibid., p. 233

[80] *Medical Review of Reviews*, "Stone Throwing in Modern Society," Lee Alexander Stone, M.D., Memphis Tennessee, November, 1915, p. 666" "Kelly estimates that venereal diseases cost America three billion dollars a year. Others claim that one out of every fifteen individuals met on the street or in society are syphilitics. Certainly it may be truthfully said that 90% of the male population of the United States have had gonorrhea. These two diseases are sapping at the very vitals of our civilization and are lowering the vitality of the individuals who, if they had never been infected, would have had their efficiency constantly at 100 percent.

Unless sanitarians and moralists get together and agree on some plan for handling prostitutes other than the one of persecution and prosecution of to-day, future races will have so degenerated in fifty years from the effects of venereal disease that nothing can be done for their regeneration."

[81] *Habits That Handicap*, Charles B. Towns., p. 234, 235

[82] Ibid., p. 237

[83] Ibid., p. 238-239

[84] Ibid., p. 236-237

[85] Ibid., p. 240

[86] Ibid., p. 243

[87] Ibid., p. 244

[88] Ibid., p. 245

[89] Ibid., p. 249

[90] Ibid., p. 246

[91] Ibid., p. 249, 250

[92] Ibid., p. 256-257

[93] Ibid., p. 262

Chapter 9 – *Medical Review of Reviews* December 1914 – July 1917

Medical Review of Reviews, "The Most Successful Treatment of Morphinism and Alcoholism Today," December, 1914, p. 618

[2] Ibid., p. 625

[3] Maryland Medical Journal, The Medical Journal Company, Volume LVIII, pages b-e in February, 1915, pages b-d in March, 1915.

[4] *Medical Review of Reviews*, January, 1916, Medical Bookland review of *Habits That Handicap*, p. 55

[5] Ibid., p. 55

[6] Ibid., p. 56-57

[7] Ibid., p. 58

[8] *Medical Review of Reviews*, March, 1916, "My Relation to the Medical Profession," page 200-201

[9] Ibid., p. 201

[10] Ibid., p. 202

[11] Ibiid., p. 202

[12] *Medical Review of Reviews*, April, 1916, "Government Responsibility for Drug Victims," p. 281

[13] *Medical Review of Reviews*, May, 1916, "Alcohol Reminders," p. 366

[14] Ibid., p. 366

[15] Ibid., p. 367

[16] *Medical Review of Reviews*, June 1916, "Concerning Heroin," p. 439

[17] The substance originated in the UK by C.R. Alder Wright. From Wikipedia:
Heroin /hɛroʊɪn/ (diacetylmorphine or morphine diacetate, also known as diamorphine (BAN, INN)) and commonly known by its street names of H, smack, horse, brown, black, tar, and others, is an opioid analgesic originally synthesized by C.R. Alder Wright in 1874 by adding two acetyl groups to the molecule morphine, which is found naturally in the opium poppy. It is the 3,6-diacetyl ester of morphine. Heroin itself is an inactive drug, but when inserted into the body, it converts into morphine. Illicit heroin is sometimes available in freebase form, dulling the sheen and consistency to a matte-white powder. Because of its lower boiling point, the freebase form of heroin is also smokable. It is prevalent in heroin coming from Afghanistan, which as of 2004 produced roughly 87% of the world supply in illicit raw opium. However, the production rate in Mexico has risen sixfold from 2007 to 2011, changing that percentage and placing Mexico as the second largest opium producer in the world. Wright's invention did not lead to any further developments, and diacetylmorphine became popular only after it was independently re-synthesized 23 years later by another chemist, Felix Hoffmann. Hoffmann, working at the Aktiengesellschaft Farbenfabriken (today the Bayer pharmaceutical company) in Elberfeld, Germany, was instructed by his supervisor Heinrich Dreser to acetylate morphine with the objective of producing codeine, a constituent of the opium poppy, pharmacologically similar to morphine but less potent and less addictive. Instead, the experiment produced an acetylated form of morphine one and a half to two times more potent than morphine itself. The head of Bayer's research department reputedly coined the drug's new name, "heroin," based on the German "heroisch," which means "heroic, strong.'

[18] *Medical Review of Reviews*, June 1916, "Concerning Heroin," p. 440

[19] From Wikipedia: Although the stimulant and hunger-suppressant properties of coca had been known for many centuries, the isolation of the cocaine alkaloid was not achieved until 1855. Various European scientists had attempted to isolate cocaine, but none had been successful for two reasons: the knowledge of chemistry required was insufficient at the time . . . The cocaine alkaloid was first isolated by the German chemist Friedrich Gaedcke in 1855. Gaedcke named the alkaloid "erythroxyline" . . . Niemann described every step he took to isolate cocaine in his dissertation titled *Über eine neue organische Base in den Cocablättern* (*On a New Organic Base in the Coca Leaves*), which was published in 1860—it earned him his Ph.D. and is now in the British Library. He wrote of the alkaloid's "colourless transparent prisms" and said that, "Its solutions have an alkaline reaction, a bitter taste, promote the flow of saliva and leave a peculiar numbness, followed by a sense of cold when applied to the tongue." Niemann named the alkaloid "cocaine" from "coca" (from Quechua "cuca") + suffix "ine" Because of its use as a local anesthetic, a suffix "-caine" was later extracted and used to form names of synthetic local anesthetics. In 1879, Vassili von Anrep, of the University of Würzburg, devised an experiment to demonstrate the analgesic properties of the newly discovered alkaloid . . . Karl Koller (a close associate of Sigmund Freud, who would write about cocaine later) experimented with cocaine for ophthalmic usage. In an infamous experiment in

1884, he experimented upon himself by applying a cocaine solution to his own eye and then pricking it with pins. His findings were presented to the Heidelberg Ophthalmological Society.

[20] *Medical Review of Reviews*, July 1916, "The Cigarette and the Boy," p. 523

[21] *Medical Review of Reviews*, August 1916, "Women and Tobacco," p. 599

[22] Ibid., p. 599-600

[23] *Medical Review of Reviews*, November 1916, "Aphorisms on Alcohol," p. 832

[24] Ibid., p. 832

[25] *Russia A History and An Interpretation*, Michael T. Florinsky, The MacMillan Company, 1947 & 1953, p. 1211: "The inspirer of the temperance crusade, according to Kokovtsov, was Rasputin. An inveterate drunkard, he could speak with authority on the ill effects of intemperance, and he sensed, of course, that the proposed policy would appeal to the tsar and the tsarina. Bar, a Rasputin appointee, inaugurated accordingly a perfunctory program of measures for the reduction of drunkenness, but he does not seem to have contemplated the abolition of the monopoly. With the mobilization of the Russian army in July 1914, liquor stores were temporarily closed, and in August the sale of intoxicants was prohibited, thus eliminating the chief source of state revenue." p. 1358-1359: [T]he decree of August 22, 1914 [extended] the duration of the war for the prohibition of the sale of liquor previously ordered for the period of mobilization. This venture into compulsory temperance would seem to have been a personal decision of the tsar, inspired, presumably, by Rasputin. . . . The abolition of the monopoly of spirits eliminated the largest single source of state revenue, an action believed to be unprecedented in the history of any country confronted with a grave emergency. The social effects of prohibition were similar to those in the United States under the Eighteenth Amendment. Prohibition was but loosely enforced, bootlegging flourished, peasants turned to various forms of home brew, and drunkenness was as prevalent as ever."

[26] *Medical Review of Reviews*, "The Responsibility of the Medical Profession in the Alcohol Question," Dr. Frank R. Starkey, Philadelphia, PA, October, 1915, p. 603: "The Russian Government long recognized that much of the suffering, poverty, indolence, inefficiency and crime of its citizens was due to alcohol, particularly in the form of vodka, and for many years it was the desire of the Czar to prohibit its use and abolish its manufacture, but because of the great hold it had upon his subjects, even with his unlimited power, he did not dare to so under ordinary conditions. This war, however, gave him his long desired opportunity and he arose to the occasion, giving to history one of the most far-reaching events of all time. The results already obtained have been so wonderful as to appear like magic. Notwithstanding the terrible struggle that his country is undergoing, the moral, physical and financial condition of his people are better today than ever before. Dogged brutality, idleness, poverty, desolation, crime and abject hopelessness are rapidly giving place to industry, efficiency, sense of family responsibility, prosperity and cheerfulness. Russia has risen to heights of individual morality and purpose never before dreamed of and which would have been an utter impossibility without this prohibitory mandate. . . . Shall we of the United States, who boast of our advanced civilization and far-seeing business acumen lag behind this formerly almost uncivilized country?"

[27] *Medical Review of Reviews*, November 1916, "Aphorisms on Alcohol , p. 834

[28] *Medical Review of Reviews*, December 1916, "The Future of Addict Legislation," p. 905

[29] Ibid., p. 907

[30] *The United States and International Drug Control, 1909-1997*, David R. Bewley-Taylor, Wellington House, 370 Lexington Ave., New York, NY, 10017-6550, @1999, p. 30

[31] *Medical Review of Reviews*, December 1916, "The Future of Addict Legislation," p. 908

[32] Ibid., p. 909

[33] Ibid., p. 910

[34] *The American Disease*, David F. Musto, p. 167, 175

[35] *Medical Review of Reviews*, January 1917, "The Present and Future of Narcotive Pathology," p. 35

[36] Ibid., p. 35

[37] *Drugs and Drug Policy in America*, Steven R. Belenko, p. 42-43, from "Say Drug Habit Grips the Nation," *New York Times*, December 5, 1913

[38] *The Drug War*, Rufus King, Chapter 4, www.druglibrary.org/special/king/dhu/dhu4.htm

Medical Review of Reviews, January 1917, "The Present and Future of Narcotive Pathology," p. 36,

"Eradication that is eighty per cent permanent is certainly entitled to be called 'scientific.'"

[40] *Medical Review of Reviews*, January 1917, "The Present and Future of Narcotive Pathology," p. 36, 37

[41] Ibid., p. 37

[42] Ibid., p. 37-38

[43] *Medical Review of Reviews*, February 1917, "The Present and Future of Narcotive Pathology," part 2, p. 113-114

[44] Ibid., p. 114

[45] Ibid., p. 116

[46] Ibid., p. 117

[47] Ibid., p. 117

[48] Ibid., p. 118

[49] *Medical Review of Reviews*, March 1917, "The Present and Future of Narcotive Pathology," part 3, p. 195

[50] Ibid., p. 196

[51] Ibid., p. 196

[52] Ibid., p. 196

[53] Ibid., p. 198

[54] Ibid., p. 198

[55] Ibid., p. 199

[56] Ibid., p. 200

[57] *Medical Review of Reviews*, June 1917, "Alcohol and the War," p. 430

[58] Ibid., p. 430

[59] *Medical Review of Reviews*, July 1917, "Alcohol and Degeneration," p. 508

Chapter 10 – The Peak, December 1916 – December 1917

[1] *The New York Times*, "Federal Inquiry on Drugs Proposed, Charles B. Towns Requests Appointment of Special Committee to Study Problem, Present Laws Conflicting, Findings of Investigators, He Thinks, Would Facilitate State Legislation," byline Washington, Jan 2., published January 3, 1917.

[2] *The Modern Hospital*, "Care of Alcoholics In The Modern Hospital," December, 1916, Charles B. Towns, p. 473

[3] Ibid., p. 473

[4] Ibid., p. 473

[5] Ibid., p. 473, 474

[6] Ibid., p. 475

[7] Ibid., p. 475

[8] The OCLC WorldCat listing (www.worldcat.org) for 'The Federal Responsibility in the Habit-Forming Drug Problem' listed three possible locations for this pamphlet as of January, 2015. Two locations were in New York City libraries, but both entries ended up pointing to the same pamphlet. This pamphlet literally was reported to have fallen apart when examined by a New York Public Library employee and not even a valid copy could be created. That left one complete copy at Ohio State University, which was copied and provided to me through the Gwinnett County Library, for which I am extremely grateful.

[9] *Federal Responsibility in the Drug Problem*, Charles B. Towns, p. 9

[10] Ibid., p. 9

[11] Ibid., p. 15-16

[12] Ibid., p. 16

[13] Ibid., p. 21

[14] Ibid., p. 22

[15] *The Modern Hospital*, "Successful Medical Treatment in Chronic Alcoholism," January, 1917, Charles B. Towns, p. 6

[16] Ibid., p. 7. However, in *Habits That Handicap*, p. 203, written two years before, he had written, "It is pleasant for me to add that during the whole fourteen years of my practice, although I have had thousands under treatment, many of them in exceedingly bad physical condition at the time the treatment was begun, with their drug

symptoms complicated by various and serious physical ailments and often accented by alcoholism, only four cases have died."

[17] Ibid., p. 7-8
[18] Ibid., p. 9
[19] Ibid., p. 9
[20] Ibid., p. 10
[21] Ibid., p. 10
[22] *The Modern Hospital*, "Sociological Aspect of the Treatment of Alcoholism," February, 1917, Charles B. Towns, p. 103
[23] Ibid., p. 103
[24] Ibid., p. 103
[25] Ibid., p. 104
[26] Ibid., p. 104-105
[27] Ibid., p. 105
[28] Ibid., p. 105
[29] Ibid., p. 106

Chapter 11 – The *Medical Review of Review* August 1917 – April 1918

[1] *Medical Review of Reviews*, August 1917, "The Necessity of Definite Medical Result," Charles B. Towns, p. 584
[2] Ibid., p. 584
[3] The "White Hope" of Drug Victims," Collliers, November 29-30, 1913, p 16
[4] "The War and the Dope Habit," *The Literary Digest* for June 9, 1917, p. 1776-1777
[5] *Drug War Politics*: The Price of Denial; Bertram, Blackman, Sharpe & Andreas; U of Cal Press, Berkeley & LA, CA @1996, p. 70
[6] http://www.druglibrary.org/special/king/dhu/dhu4.htm, The Drug Hang Up, America's Fifty-Year Folly, Chapter 4, Schaffer Library of Drug Policy
[7] *Medical Review of Reviews*, August 1917, "The Necessity of Definite Medical Result," Charles B. Towns, p. 585
[8] Ibid., p. 585
[9] Ibid., p. 586
[10] Ibid., p. 586
[11] *Habits That Handicap*, Charles B. Towns, p. 227
[12] *Medical Review of Reviews*, August 1917, "The Necessity of Definite Medical Result," Charles B. Towns, p. 587
[13] Ibid.,, p. 587
[14] Ibid.,, p. 587
[15] *Medical Review of Reviews*, September 1917, "The Necessity of Definite Medical Result," Part 2, Charles B. Towns, p. 640
[16] Ibid., p. 641
[17] *Medical Review of Reviews*, October 1917, "The Necessity of Definite Medical Result," Part 3, Charles B. Towns, p. 702
[18] Ibid., p. 702
[19] Ibid., p. 704
[20] Ibid., p. 704
[21] Ibid., p. 705
[2] *Medical Review of Reviews*, November 1917, "How to Eliminate the Alcoholic as an Insane Problem," Charles B. Towns, p. 764-765
[3] *Medical Review of Reviews*, December 1917, "Coffee Inebriety," Charles B. Towns, p. 825-827
[4] According to the U.S. Department of Veterans Affairs Fact Sheet, American Casualties suffered in World War I were: Battle Deaths: 53,402, Other Deaths in Service, 63,114, Wounded: 204,002. According to Wikipedia n.wikipedia.org/wiki/American_Expeditionary_Forces, "The first American troops . . . landed in Europe in June

1917 . . . but only in small scale . . . By the end of 1917, four divisions were employed in a large training area . . . At the beginning, during the Spring of 1918, the four battle-ready U.S. divisions were deployed . . ."

[25] www.dailymail,co.uk/femail/article481822/Condemned-virgins-The-million-women-robbed-war.html The Daily Mail, Condemned to be virgins: "The two million women robbed by the war," September, 2007, Amanda Cable, a book review of *Singled Out, How Two Million Women Survived Without Men After The First World War* by Virginia Nicholson

[26] *Medical Review of Reviews*, March 1918, "Alcohol and Antenatal Welfare," Charles B. Towns, p. 157

[27] Ibid., p. 157

[28] On 23 January 1912, the International Opium Convention was signed in the Hague by representatives from China, France, Germany, Italy, Japan, the Netherlands, Persia (Iran), Portugal, Russia, Siam (Thailand), the UK and the British oversees territories (including British India) . . . The International Opium convention consisted of six chapters and 25 articles. http://www.unodc.org/unodc/en/frontpage/the-1912-hague-international-opium-convention.html UNODC United Nations Office on Drugs and Crime

[29] *Medical Review of Reviews*, April 1918, "Inebriety and Drug Addiction," Charles B. Towns, p. 217

[30] http://www.unodc.org/unodc/en/frontpage/the-1912-hague-international-opium-convention.html UNODC United Nations Office on Drugs and Crime

[31] *Medical Review of Reviews*, April 1918, "Inebriety and Drug Addiction," Charles B. Towns, p. 217

[32] Ibid., p. 217

[33] Ibid., p. 218

[34] Ibid., p. 218

[35] Ibid., p. 218

[36] Ibid., p. 218

[37] *The Medical Times*, Vol. XLII, Vol. 6, New York, New York. Ads for the Pearson Home appeared throughout the 1914 year. Pearson authored an article in August, 1914 issue of the magazine titled "The Treatment of Morphinism."

Chapter 12 – The Towns Treatment

[1] *AA The Way It Began*, Bill Pittman, p. 164

[2] Wikipedia, en.wikipedia.org/wiki/Atropa_belladonna

[3] Wikipedia, en.wikipedia.org/wiki/Zanthoxylum_americanum

[4] Wikipedia, en.wikipedia.org/wiki/Hyoscyamus_niger

[5] *AA The Way It Began*, Bill Pittman, p. 167

[6] Ibid., p. 166

[7] *The American Disease*, David F. Musto, page 89

[8] *Pass It On*, Alcoholics Anonymous World Services, Inc., p. 101

[9] *The American Disease*, David F. Musto, page 82

[10] *The British Medical Journal*, May 21, 1910, "A Drastic Treatment for Alcoholism," p. 1249

[11] *The American Disease*, David F. Musto, page 82

[12] The "White Hope" of Drug Victims," Collliers, November 29-30, 1913, p 17

[13] *Medical Review of Reviews*, March 1917, "The Present and Future of Narcotive Pathology," part 3, p. 197

[14] *Slaying The Dragon*, William L. White, p. 85

[15] *AA The Way It Began*, Bill Pittman, p. 86

[16] *Medical Review of Reviews*, November 1917, "How to Eliminate the Alcoholic as an Insane Problem," Charles B. Towns, p. 764-765

Chapter 13 – The Fall from Grace

[1] *Reclaiming The Drinker*, Charles B. Towns, Preface

[2] *AA The Way It Began*, Bill Pittman, p. 86-87

[3] *The American Disease*, David F. Musto, page 88-89

[4] *The American Disease*, David F. Musto, page 89-90

[5] *The American Disease*, David F. Musto, page 102

[6] *Woodrow Wilson and the Politics of Morality*, John Morton Blum, Little, Brown & Company, @1956, p. 170

[7] *Reclaiming The Drinker*, Charles B. Towns, p.75-76

[8] *Slaying The Dragon*, William L. White, p. 113

[9] *Slaying The Dragon*, William L. White, p. 114

[10] Col Ed. Towns, talk given by, at the 1960 AA International, Long Beach, CA

[11] *The Lois Wilson Story, When Love Is Not Enough*, William G. Borchert, Hazelden, Center City, Minnesota 55012-0176, p. 209

Chapter 14 – *Four Brochures to Attract Physicians*

[1] *The Work of the Charles B. Towns Hospital and its Relation to the Medical Profession*, Charles B. Towns, January, 1918, p. 10-11

[2] Ibid., p. 5

[3] Ibid., p. 6

[4] Ibid., p. 6-7

[5] Ibid., p. 8

[6] Ibid., p. 9

[7] Ibid., p. 10

[8] Ibid., p. 13

[9] *The Special Work of the Charles B. Towns Hospital And Its Ethical Relations With The Medical Profession*, Charles Barnes Towns, Estimated @1919, p. 1

[10] *Bulletin of the American Academy of Medicine*, Volume IV, June 1899 to June 1900, The Chemical Publishing Company, Easton, PA, p. 597

[11] *Brooklyn Medical Journal*, Medical Society of the County of Kings, Brooklyn, NY, Volume XVIII, February, 1904, p. 58

[12] *The Special Work of the Charles B. Towns Hospital*, Charles B. Towns, p. 2

[13] Ibid., p. 2

[14] Ibid., p. 8

[15] Ibid., p. 9

[16] The significance of Towns advertising that there were no male nurses may be easily missed: *Bellevue Hospital*, Edwin M. Knights Jr., M.D., http://www.history-magazine.com/bellevue.html "[After the Civil War] Bellevue Hospital [had] a serious deficiency that limited its capacity to offer good medical care. Nothing could overcome the low level of nursing care. From its inception, Bellevue Hospital had depended upon people from the penitentiary to fill the jobs of nurses, attendants or helpers. Most of them worked without pay for the sake of board and lodging. It is unfair to paint them all with the same brush and accuse them of indifference or dishonesty, for some no doubt felt compassion for those unfortunate folk who were both ill and indigent, but the majority were uneducated and incompetent."

[17] *The Special Work of the Charles B. Towns Hospital*, Charles B. Towns, p. 13

[18] *Hospital Treatment for Alcohol and Drug Addiction*, Charles B. Towns, @1922, p. 3

[19] Ibid., p. 8

[20] Ibid., p. 4-6

[21] Ibid., p. 6

[2] Ibid., p. 6-7

[3] Ibid., p. 7

[4] Ibid., p. 16,17

[5] Ibid., p. 17

[6] Ibid., p. 11

[ ] Ibid., p. 17, 18

Ibid., p. 20, 21

Chapter 15 – *Reclaiming The Drinker* - 1931

[1] *The Wrecking of the Eighteenth Amendment*, Ernest Gordon, The Alcohol Information Press, Francestown, New Hampshire, @1943. FDR was the last President to be inaugurated on March 4. Before he was inaugurated, Congress passed the 21st amendment, repealing the 18th amendment, on February 20. By March 13, FDR advocated modification of the Volstead Act to allow the sale of beer, which was approved by Congress and went into effect on April 7. On March 31, Congress passed the Copeland-Celler Bill that removed the liquor limits that could be prescribed to a patient by a doctor. Full repeal of prohibition could not take place until the Utah Convention approved the 21st amendment on December 5, 1933.

[2] *Reclaiming The Drinker*, Charles B. Towns, M.M. Barbour Company, 521 Fifth Avenue, NY, NY, 1931, p.8

[3] Ibid., p.11

[4] Ibid., p.11

[5] From "History of Alcohol and Drinking around the World," David J. Hanson. Ph.D., http://www2.potsdam.edu/alcohol/Controversies/1114796842.html#.VBENMXkg-Uk
" While no one knows when beverage alcohol was first used, it was presumably the result of a fortuitous accident that occurred at least tens of thousands of years ago. However, the discovery of late Stone Age beer jugs has established the fact that intentionally fermented beverages existed at least as early as the Neolithic period (cir. 10,000 B.C.) (Patrick, 1952, pp. 12-13), and it has been suggested that beer may have preceded bread as a staple (Braidwood et al, 1953; Katz and Voigt, 1987); wine clearly appeared as a finished product in Egyptian pictographs around 4,000 B.C. (Lucia, 1963a, p. 216)."

[6] *Reclaiming The Drinker*, Charles B. Towns, p.13

[7] Ibid., p.13-14

[8] Ibid., p.17

[9] Ibid., p.23

[10] Ibid., p.25-26

[11] Ibid., p.26

[12] Ibid., p.28

[13] *Russia A History and An Interpretation*, Michael T. Florinsky, The MacMillan Company, 1947 & 1953, p. 1211

[14] *Reclaiming The Drinker*, Charles B. Towns p.29

[15] Ibid., p.32

[16] Ibid., p.38

[17] Ibid., p.39

[18] Ibid., p.40

[19] Ibid., p.40

[20] Ibid., p.42

[21] Ibid., p.42

[22] Ibid., p.43

[23] Ibid., p.45

[24] Ibid., p.46

[25] Ibid., p.50

[26] Ibid., p.51

[27] Ibid., p.51-52

[28] Ibid., p.52

[29] Ibid., p.52, 53

[30] Ibid., p.54

[31] Ibid., p.55

[32] Ibid., p.61

[33] Ibid., p.66

[34] Ibid., p.66

[35] Ibid., p.67

[36] Ralph Waldo Emerson, *Self-Reliance,* 1841, The Harvard Classics, Grolier Enterprises Corp., @1994, p.66

[37] *Reclaiming The Drinker*, Charles B. Towns, p.67

[38] *The Modern Hospital*, "Sociological Aspect of the Treatment of Alcoholism," February, 1917, Charles B. Towns, p. 103

[39] "Help For the Hard Drinker," Charles B. Towns, *The Century Magazine*, June, 1912, p. 293

[40] *Reclaiming The Drinker*, Charles B. Towns, p.69

[41] *Ibid.*, p.70

[42] *Reclaiming The Drinker*, Charles B. Towns, p.71-72. Authors note: Great care was attempted to find this quote in the text of *Diseases of the Nervous System,* but without success. Six editions of the work were published, the last in 1935. Towns supposedly referenced a 1929 edition, while the first edition dates from 1917. The fourth edition was searched that was published in 1923 without finding the attributed to the book by Towns.
Among some of the more notable quotes found in *Diseases of the Nervous System,* 1917, p. 847:
"It must be recalled that many psychoneurotics whose compulsive flights are alcoholic—and such are usually the flight from an unconscious homosexual conflict—are very superior types of people.
The life history of many an alcoholic shows him to be an inefficient individual. He is incapable of meeting reality efficiently every day . . . This is the inefficiency Adler believes Is dependent upon organ inferiority, or to use an older and more tried expression, it is constitutional. The reaction to such a feeling of inferiority drives the inefficient individual to find some way of escape from the horrid facts, the overburdening oppressions of reality. This he finds in alcohol which dulls his perception of reality and permits the world of phantasy to reign supreme. In this fool's paradise the alcoholic finds temporary surcease from the burdens he is but poorly equipped to bear."
P. 852-853: "Alcoholic Pseudoparanoia—In some patients with chronic alcoholism a fairly circumscribed delusional system may develop which characteristically takes the form of delusions of marital infidelity . . . Instead of realizing his own impotence, which is an inacceptable thought, he blames his wife for being untrue to him. These cases are essentially chronic and persist at least as long as the alcohol is indulged in, while even when it is removed they may be a long time clearing up and may perhaps go over into a chronic delusional state largely because of an unconscious homosexual fixation."

[43] *Reclaiming The Drinker*, Charles B. Towns, p.72

[44] *Medical Review of Reviews*, "The Responsibility of the Medical Profession in the Alcohol Question," Frank R. Starkey, M.D., Philadelphia, PA, October, 1915, p. 598, "Taking all the classes there are perhaps more men addicted to alcohol than women. Altho among the lower classes there are a great many women who use alcohol freely and among the idle well-to-do the number of females addicted to alcohol is much greater than is usually supposed, however, many are able to hide their indiscretion by resorting to patent medicines or the drinking of perfumes, which is extremely common among this class. The use of cocktails, etc., are almost constant accompaniments of many women's social affairs. At Bellevue Hospital the number of females under 32 admitted to alcohol wards exceeded males, between 33 and 35 more men than women were admitted, and at 58 or over there were again more women than men, in a series of eighteen thousand seven hundred sixty-eight cases.

[45] *Reclaiming The Drinker*, Charles B. Towns, p.72,73

[46] *Ibid.*, p.75-76

[47] *Ibid.*, p.77

[48] *Journal of the American Medical Association*, "Reclaiming The Drinker," Vol. XCVIII, Number 18, April 18, 1932, Book Review.

[49] *The Action of Alcohol on Man*, Ernest H. Starling, Longmans, Green and Co., 39 Paternoster Row, London, E.C. New York, Toronto, Bombay, Calcutta and Macras, @1923, title page

[50] *Ibid.*, Preface

Chapter 16 – *Drug and Alcohol Sickness* - 1932

Drug and Alcohol Sickness, Charles B. Towns, M.M. Barbour Company, 521 Fifth Avenue, NY, NY, 1932, p. 1
Ibid., p. 1-2
Ibid., p. 2

[4] The History of opium in medical practice, C. Allyn Pierson, http://callynpierson.wordpress.com/2011/09/02/history-of-opium-in-medical-practice/

[5] *Drug and Alcohol Sickness*, Charles B. Towns, p. 10

[6] *Drug and Alcohol Sickness*, Charles B. Towns, p. 11

[7] *Drug and Alcohol Sickness*, Charles B. Towns, p. 13

[8] The "White Hope" of Drug Victims," *Collliers*, November 29, 1913, p 17

[9] *Drug and Alcohol Sickness*, Charles B. Towns, p. 14

[10] The *New York Times* obituary for Charles B. Towns reported this story following Towns' death February 20, 1947: "Working always with physicians, he treated successfully many cases of drug addiction. In 1907, the late President William H Taft, then Secretary of War, sent twelve soldiers to Mr. Towns' hospital, where under clinical observation of Army physicians, they were successfully treated."

[11] *Drug and Alcohol Sickness*, Charles B. Towns, p. 15

[12] Ibid., p. 15-16

[13] Ibid., p. 16

[14] Ibid., p. 17

[15] Ibid., p. 18-19

[16] Ibid., p. 27

[17] Even Bill Wilson made that mistake in his 1951 talk in Atlanta when he referred to Towns as "Doc."

[18] http://barefootsworld.net/aacharles_towns.html "Charles B. Towns, Ph.D."

[19] *Drug and Alcohol Sickness*, Charles B. Towns, p. 28

Chapter 17 – Dr. William D. Silkworth Hired by Towns 1929-1951

[1] *Silkworth The Little Doctor Who Loved Drunks*, Dale Mitchel, Hazelden, Center City, Minnesota, p. 30. However, this date differs depending upon the source. *Pass It On*, p. 101, quotes Bill Wilson as having said, "'In desperation, he made connection with Towns Hospital. The pay was pitiful, something like $40 a week and board, I think.' But Bill said, Silkworth's arrival at Towns Hospital in 1930 was the turning point in the doctor's life". No additional support for the 1930 date is provided. Ernest Kurtz in *Not God* (repeated in the 1988 version *AA The Story*) has the date as 1924: "in 1924, after completing specialty training in neuropsychiatry, he became medical director of the Charles B. Towns Hospital in New York . . ." Bill Wilson in *Alcoholics Anonymous Comes of Age*, on page 13, does not provide a date, but does provide a job title of "Physician-In-Chief." The Round Table of AA History dated January 10, 1998 found in Silkworth.net has an additional date: "The respected Journal of Studies on Alcohol . . . reports Silkworth arrived at Towns in 1932. An article by Leonard Blumberg, (Professor of Sociology, Temple University, Philadelphia, Vol. 38.. No 11, 1977, "The Ideology of a Therapeutic Social Movement: Alcoholics Anonymous") says Dr. Silkworth worked at Towns from 1932 until his death in 1951. *Slaying The Dragon* uses 1930 as the date on page 141.

[2] *Silkworth*, Dale Mitchel, p. 37

[3] *Silkworth*, Dale Mitchel, p. 21. His first opened in 1902 and closed in 1906. "In early 1902, Silkworth opened his first of three private practices with dreams of someday owning a clinic." A second private practice existed from 1914-1916. The dates of the third private practice are not clear at this writing.

[4] *Silkworth*, Dale Mitchel, p. 26

[5] Ibid., p. 27

[6] Ibid., p. 29

[7] Ibid., p. 29

[8] *Pass It On*, Alcoholics Anonymous World Services, Inc., p. 101

[9] *The Modern Hospital*, June, 1917, Charles B. Towns, Ad page 76 (see Figure 25 for the number nine).

[10] *Silkworth,* Dale Mitchel, p. 54

[11] Ibid., p. 20

[12] Ibid., p. 20

[13] *Silkworth The Little Doctor Who Loved Drunks*, Dale Mitchel, Hazelden, Center City, Minnesota, p. 132, "Notes of the Jungle Plant (*Combretum Sundiacum*), February 24, 1908

[14] *Silkworth The Little Doctor Who Loved Drunks*, Dale Mitchel, Hazelden, Center City, Minnesota, p. 134, "Notes of the Jungle Plant (*Combretum Sundiacum*), February 24, 1908

[15] *The American Disease*, David F. Musto, page 78

[16] *The American Disease*, David F. Musto, page 79

[17] *Silkworth*, Dale Mitchel, p. 35

[18] Ibid., p. 34

[19] Ibid., p. 35-36

[20] *Drug and Alcohol Sickness*, Charles B. Towns, p. 15-16

[21] *Silkworth*, Dale Mitchel, p. 33

[22] Ibid., p. 33

[23] *Habits That Handicap*, Charles B. Towns, p. 180

[24] *Pass It On*, Alcoholics Anonymous World Services, Inc, p. 100

[25] *Bill W. My First 40 Years*, Bill Wilson, Hazelden, p. 104, 105

[26] Ibid., p. 106

[27] Ibid., p. 106

[28] *Bill W.*, Robert Thomsen, p. 175: "In fact, [Bill's] memories of this entire period, from 1933 until about the end of 1934, were totally disordered."

[29] Ibid., p. 174

[30] Ibid., p. 106-107

[31] "Belladonna and Its Alkaloids," *The American Journal of Clinical Medicine*, Finley Ellingwood, M.D., Evanston, Illinois, August, 1915, p. 707-712. "While I have used atropine very freely, the most of my observations, especially those upon children and, in fact, at the bedside, have been made with carefully prepared tincture of the plant-drug . . . belladonna is an excitant to the cerebrum, promoting active hyperemia . . . There is a characteristic syndrome present in congestive types of many diseases which rationally indicates the need for belladonna . . . Children very active and with big brains, who are disturbed nights by night-terrors or dreams or show other evidences of restlessness are relieved by belladonna . . . in diphtheritis, tonsillitis, croup, bronchitis, pneumonitis, pleuritic, and peritonitis, belladonna stimulates the capillary circulation in the engorged organs, thus quickly preventing the local effects of the acute congestion or inflammation . . . It is one of our best remedies for whooping cough . . . In the milder forms of insanity or other forms of mental disease, the Homeopathist prescribed belladonna where there was violent delirium . . . Some of our writers have claimed that belladonna is just as effective in preventing the development of diphtheria as it is in preventing scarlet-fever . . . Professor Whitford long advised belladonna for painful menstruation."

[32] *Bill W. My First 40 Years*, Bill Wilson, Hazelden, p. 109

[33] Ibid., p. 110, 111

[34] Ibid., p. 112, 113

[35] *Bill W. My First 40 Years*, Bill Wilson, Hazelden, p. 113. Message 3330 from Silkworth.net "AA History Lovers" has the second visit being in July of 1934, the third visit being in September 17, 1934. Afterward Bill stayed sober until Armistice Day, November 11, 1934, with the fourth visit on December 11, 1934.

[36] *Lois Remembers, Memoirs of the co-founder of Al-Anon and the wife of the co-founder of Alcoholics Anonymous*, Al-Anon Family Group Headquarters, Inc. 1600 Corporate Landing Parkway, Virginia Beach, VA, 23454-5617, p. 86

[37] *Pass It On*, Alcoholics Anonymous World Services, Inc. p. 106: "By the time the summer came . . . [soon afterwards] Bill wound up in Towns for the second time . . ."; *Bill W. My First 40 Years*, Bill Wilson, Hazelden, p. 114: " . . . I left Towns after the second trip with considerable renewal of hope."; *Bill W.*, Robert Thomsen, p. 176: 'In July he was put into Towns Hospital again, and again there was a memorable session with Silkworth."

[38] *Lois Remembers*, Al-Anon Family Groups, p. 86

[39] *Bill W.*, Robert Thomsen, p. 175: "Even years later, no matter how hard he tried, Bill could not remember the circumstances of his next drunk, or even when it started., whether it was a month or a couple of weeks after leaving Towns. He knew only that it was one of his worst and one that seemingly was impossible to stop. In fact, his memories of this entire period, from 1933 until about the end of 1934, were totally disordered. Yet strangely he remembered the shameful debilitating weakness, the black terror . . . " p. 176: "In July he was put into Towns Hospital again . . ."

[40] *Bill W., My First 40 Years*, Bill Wilson, Hazelden, p. 115

[41] Ibid., p. 115

[42] Ibid., p. 115

[43] This is the place of an ongoing dispute: whether or not Bill Wilson was at Towns three times, or four times, can be argued, and the confusion can come from the date of the third visit, which seems to make it the second. *Pass It On* (p. 108) and Bill W. in his autobiography both say this visit was in mid-summer of 1934. However, Bill W.'s biography clearly has "the second trip" to Towns, p. 114, followed by his "next relapse" and then going to Towns again at the bottom of p. 115. *Pass It On* has the second visit on p. 106 and the third on p. 108. Both of these books clearly have these two visits clearly differentiated from the December 11, 1934 last visit to Towns Hospital. Robert Thomsen stated "Four times in 1933-34, Bill was a patient at Towns Hospital . . ." on p. 174 of his *Bill W.* biography, but Thomsen only describes three visits himself. A July visit is described on p. 176. Lois Wilson describes Bill Wilson entering Towns Hospital in the vicinity of July, but leaving Towns in late September, 1934 on p. 87 of *Lois Remembers*. Clearly he was not there for two months, suggesting the July visit was the second and his third visit led to his departure in September. Message 3330 from Silkworth.net "AA History Lovers" has the second visit being in July of 1934, the third visit being in September 17, 1934. Afterward Bill stayed sober until Armistice Day, November 11, 1934, with the fourth visit on December 11, 1934. Ernest Kurtz wrote in *Not God* on p. 15: "Wilson was introduced to the Charles B. Towns Hospital, a drying out facility on Central Park West to which he was admitted four times in 1933-1934." Bill Pittman in AA The Way It Began wrote on p. 150: " . . . he was admitted to Charles B. Towns Hospital on four separate occasions in 1933 and 1934." *Language of the Heart*, p. 283: "As Jung had told Rowland that his case was hopeless and that medicine and psychiatry could do nothing more for him, so Silkworth told Lois on a fateful day in the summer of 1934 [visit #2], 'I am afraid that Bill Will have to be committed. There is nothing that I can do for him, or anything else that I know.' These were words of great humility from a professional. The scared me into sobriety for two months, although I soon resumed my drinking [leading up to visit #3]."

[44] *Bill W., My First 40 Years*, Bill Wilson, Hazelden., p. 115

[45] Ibid., p. 115

[46] *Lois Remembers*, Al-Anon Family Groups, p. 87

[47] Bill W., *My First 40 Years*, Bill Wilson, Hazelden, p. 117

[48] *Bill W.*, Robert Thomsen, p. 181

[49] Bill W., My First 40 Years, p. 132: "The area way bell at 182 Clinton Street rung, and there [Ebby] stood." That was Ebby's first after Bill's debauch that began on Armistice Day. The second visit of Ebby, p. 135: "One afternoon Ebby turned up with a friend, Shep Cornell."

[50] Ibid., p. 198

[51] Note that there was no mention of any fee being paid up front by the drunk Wilson, which Towns had once considered so essential to the recovery of an addict or alcoholic. The question of who paid how much for each of the four visits will not be addressed here. Who influenced Lois to originally get her husband to go to Towns is not addressed either. Names that appear related to one or both these subjects include Dr. Leonard Strong (Bill Wilson's brother-in-law), Dr. Clark Burnham (Lois' father), and Bill Wilson's mother Emily Strobel, formerly Emily Griffith Wilson.

[52] *Bill W.*, Robert Thomsen, p. 199, 200

[53] *Alcoholics Anonymous*, Alcoholics Anonymous World Services, p. 7

[54] *Bill W. My First 40 Years*, Bill Wilson, Hazelden, p. 140 "The usual treatment began. Barbiturates to temper me down, doses of belladonna, and a little sedative."

[55] Silkworth, Dale Mitchel, p. 48

[56] *We Recovered Too, The Family Group's Beginnings in the Pioneers Own Words*, Michael Fitzpatrick, Hazelden, Center City, Minnesota, 55012, 2nd Audio Track, Bill Wilson, June 1956. Note: As a former smoker myself, Bill Wilson's smoker's cough clearly audible in the recording.

[57] "Bill Wilson's Vision of the Light at Towns Hospital," Glenn F. Chesnut, http://www.hindsfoot.org/lightbillw.pdf

[58] The writing of Bill to Lois as quoted in *Dr. Bob and the Good Old Timers* on p. 78: "Bill told [Eddie] to wait [and not commit suicide] until they had a chance to talk. Then he and Bob 'tore over to Cleveland in the middle of the night, got him here and to the hospital and commenced to give him the Towns [Hospital] treatment. That, plus

more oxidizing has been magical,' Bill wrote Lois, 'and is creating a great stir at the City Hospital, where the doctors are all agog, being unable to do anything with these cases.' ("Oxidizing" was probably short for "Oxfordizing" . . .).

[59] *Dr Bob and the Good Oldtimers*, Alcoholics Anonymous World Services, Inc., New York, NY, @1980, p. 78.

[60] *Adolph Hitler*, John Toland, Volume 2, p. 933: "[On September 20, 1944, Doctor] Giesing checked the three X rays with Morell and was amazed that his colleague identified the cheekbones as the sinuses. There followed the daily examination of the patient in his bunker and Giesing noticed Hitler's face had an odd reddish tinge in the artificial light. Afterward Hitler was stricken with stomach pains and insisted on taking more than a half a dozen of the "little black pills" prescribed by Morell. Concerned by the continuing dosage, Giesing began to make caution inquiries. Linge showed him the pill container. Its label read: Antigas Pills, Dr. Koster, Berlin, Extract nux vomica 0.04; Extract belladonna 0.04.

Giesing was appalled. Hitler had been heavily dosing himself with two poisons—strychnine and atropine. Perhaps that explained his attacks, his growing debility; his irritability and aversion to light; his hoarse throat and strange reddish tinge of his skin . . . Morell advised Hitler to remain in bed all day but he insisted on getting up for his regular examination by Giesing. He, in turn, advised discontinuance of the cocaine treatment, [which was a ten percent cocaine solution to relieve the sinus] . . ."

[61] *Alcoholics Anonymous Comes of Age*, Alcoholics Anonymous Publishing, Inc., NY, NY, 1957, p. 63

[62] *Alcoholics Anonymous*, Alcoholics Anonymous World Services, p. 14

[63] Ibid., p. 14

[64] *Bill W.*, Robert Thomsen, p. 202

[65] *Bill W. My First 40 Years*, Bill Wilson , Hazelden, p. 148

[66] The assertion that Towns was an atheist was taken from a transcript of Bill Wilson's talk in Atlanta made in 1951. The following quote was related to the Towns job offer to Bill Wilson and the resulting group conscience when an unnamed person was attributed by Wilson to have said, "But he said, 'Don't you know that if you tie this thing up to that particular hospital that every hospital in the country will laugh because Charlie Towns is selling God, the old atheist.'"

Chapter 18 – The Job Offer at Towns Hospital – 1937?

[1] *Alcoholics Anonymous*,"Bill's Story," p. 15

[2] *Drug and Alcohol Sickness*, Charles B. Towns, M.M. Barbour Company, 521 Fifth Avenue, NY, NY, 1932, p. 33

[3] *Language of the Heart*, The AA Grapevine, Inc., PO Box 1980, Grand Central Station, NY, NY, @1988, p. 175

[4] *Bill W.*, Robert Thomsen, p. 210

[5] *Language of the Heart*, The AA Grapevine, Inc., PO Box 1980, Grand Central Station, NY, NY, @1988, p. 175. Bill Wilson's sobriety date is about December 14, 1934. He was in Akron, Ohio by May 11, 1935. That time described is five months, not six. Once again, numerical references or date references made by alcoholics should be heard or read with some skepticism.

[6] *Pass It On*, Alcoholics Anonymous World Services, Inc., p. 133

[7] Silkworth *The Little Doctor Who Loved Drunks*, Dale Mitchel, Hazelden, Center City, Minnesota, p. 53-54

[8] While the separation with the Oxford Group was permanent, the separation with Shoemaker was only temporary. As Bill Wilson said from the podium as he introduced Rev. Shoemaker at the A.A. International in St. Louis in 1955:" It is through Sam Shoemaker that most of A.A.'s spiritual principles have come. He has been the connecting link . . . His utter honesty, his tremendous forthrightness, struck me deep. I shall never forget it. I want to introduce Sam to you as one of the great channels, one of the prime sources of influence, that have gathered themselves together into what is now A.A." *Alcoholics Anonymous Comes of Age*, p. 261
Alcoholics Anonymous Comes of Age, Alcoholics Anonymous Publishing, Inc., p. 100.
Regarding the varying dates of the job offer, these are five sources and what date they used:
Alcoholics Anonymous Comes of Age, p. 99 ("In 1937")
Lois Remembers, p. 197 – When: December, 1936
Not God, p. 63-64, Mid 1937
Bill W. by Robert Thomsen – no date, "One afternoon" p. 232
Pass It On – no date, after September, 1936, "One day" p. 175

This list was found as part of message 3330 From Art Sheehan in AA History Lovers of Silkworth.net
An additional date is found in AA History Lovers, Message 2792, dated November 1, 2005, which uses the date of November 13, 1939.

[10] *The Lois Wilson Story, When Love Is Not Enough*, William G. Borchert, Hazelden, Center City, Minnesota 55012-0176, p. 145

[11] The evidence for a later date for the job offer provided here is entirely circumstantial. AA History Lovers (Silkworth.net) has a list of the first 100 sober in AA from John Barton (#8061) by date and location. Three men are listed as getting sober in New York City in 1935, thus by the end of 1935 there were four sober men who got sober there. Only one man is listed as getting sober in 1936 in New York, Myron Williams, in April. Six additional men got sober during 1937 on the east coast, making eleven in total. Twenty eight get sober in 1938. Charles Towns was reputed to have said, "Look here, Bill, I've got a hunch that the A.A. business of yours is someday going to fill Madison Square Garden . . . ," which appears on p. 64 of *Not God* by Ernest Kurtz, which Kurtz quotes from p. 100 of *Alcoholics Anonymous Comes of Age*. If only one man got sober in 1936 in New York City, how likely would it be that Charles Towns had said that sentence in 1936? Also, A.A. as a group name did not appear in 1936, but later, around mid 1938. Many more patients were present at Towns Hospital than are included in this list. Relapses are not included in the numbers included either. One can conclude that when AA history and dates are mentioned together, a skeptical approach may often be a valid one.

[12] Bill Wilson talk in Atlanta, GA, 1951, original tape in the GSSA Archives, Macon, GA. Again, note the reference to "40-50 members" while the AA History Lovers list has only five total in New York at the end of 1936. By the end of 1936, the AA History Lovers list has a total of 17 sober total, and 51 sober in all locations at the end of 1937. Was Charles Towns aware that most early sobrieties were in Akron and Cleveland and not New York?

[13] Silkworth *The Little Doctor Who Loved Drunks*, Dale Mitchel, Hazelden, Center City, Minnesota, p. 54

[14] *Twelve Defining Moments in the History of Alcoholics*

www.williamwhitepapers.com/pr/2008TwelveDefiningMomentsinAAHistory.pdf Published in revised form in:

White, W. & Kurtz. E. (2008). Twelve defining moments in the history of Alcoholics Anonymous. In Galanter, M. & Kaskutas, L., p. 7

[15] Ibid., p. 7

[16] Bill Wilson talk in Atlanta, GA, 1951, original tape in the GSSA Archives, Macon, GA.

[17] *Twelve Steps and Twelve Traditions*, Alcoholic Anonymous World Services, Inc., p. 138

[18] *Twelve Defining Moments in the History of Alcoholics*

www.williamwhitepapers.com/pr/2008**TwelveDefiningMoments**inAA**History**.pdf, p. 8

[19] *Slaying The Dragon*, William L. White, p. 101

Chapter 19 Towns' Contributions to Alcoholics Anonymous

[1] *Habits That Handicap*, Charles B. Towns, p. 100, 101

[2] *Slaying The Dragon*, William L. White, p. 131

[3] The sixteen page stock prospectus entitled 'The One Hundred Men Corporation," written in 1938, included a listing of the potential returns to the investor of a $25 investment based on how many books might be sold. Parkhurst wrote that if 10,000 books were sold, the investor would earn $10, if 25,000 were sold, $30, and so on. He also made the following claim: "Although it seems ridiculous, one estimate has been made of a half a million volumes within two years time" would be sold. Checks could be made out to "The Alcoholic Foundation" or "Henry G. Parkhurst, Inc." and could be mailed to Parkhurst's address in Newark, New Jersey. According to Hazelden's *The Book That Started It All* on pages 221 and 223, a half a million books were sold by 1964, or twenty eight years after Parkhurst's "ridiculous" estimate.

[4] *Alcoholics Anonymous Comes of Age*, Alcoholics Anonymous World Services , p. 187

[5] "How The Book Alcoholics Anonymous Came About," Bill W.'s speech at the Texas State AA Convention, June 12, 1954, p. 214, in *The Book That Started It All*, Hazelden, Center City, Minnesota, September, 2010

[6] *Language of the Heart*, The AA Grapevine, Inc., PO Box 1980, Grand Central Station, NY, NY, @1988, p. 176

[7] On April 3, 1957. T. G. Lewis answered Bill Wilson's request for a record of the checks written by Charles Towns from the Towns Hospital Check Register to help finance the book project. Those checks were listed as follows (reproduced from the facsimile letter as accurately as possible):

"W.G. Wilson

Date	Check No.	Amount	Remark on Check Stub:
March 1, 1938	6888	$50.00	Publicity by Mr. Towns
April 1	6856	500.00	Frank Amos
May 18	7085	500.00	Advance on book
August 25	7274	500.00	Alcoholics Anonymous
October 14	7369	200.00	W.G. Wilson
October 29	7392	100.00	H.G. Parkhurst
November 14	7438	200.00	W.G. Wilson
December 1	7471	50.00	Wilson by Mr. Towns
December 15	7510	200.00	Wilson by Mr. Towns
January 11, 1939	7555	300.00	W.G. Wilson
February 11	635	300.00	W.G. Wilson, Mr. Towns' personal check
March 31	659	200.00	W.G. Wilson, Mr. Towns' personal check
April 21	7777	300.00	Wilson by Mr. Towns
		3,400.00	
		794.66	For Printing A.A.
		$4,194.66	

These are the only checks that were marked on the stub, but there are quite a number charged to Mr. Towns that he received cash for.

Besides these, he paid for the articles to be published in the Medical Record and Modern Medicine, as well for the reprints for these. The Record was $60.00 per month and Modern Medicine $72.00 per month."

On page 15 of *Alcoholics Anonymous Comes of Age*, Bill wrote, ". . . Mr. Chapman did most of the work in raising the $8,000 which was needed to pay off the shareholders and Mr. Charles B. Towns in full . . ." Thus, the statement that Charles Towns funded one half of the expenditures of publishing the Big Book is justifiable.

[8] Bill Wilson to Frank Amos, January 4, 1939 – as read by Jack Norris, Class A Trustee, in Atlanta, February 5, 1972 at the Southeast Past Delegates Meeting. CD available at MountainRecordings.com

[9] Bill Wilson to Frank Amos, January 4, 1939 – as read by Jack Norris, Class A Trustee, in Atlanta, February 5, 1972 Later on in the same letter, Wilson introduced a discussion topic, which raises many an eyebrow today in how the book might have been popularized. Thought the name Rockefeller was not mentioned, the text suggests that Wilson had such a personality in mind:

"Suppose we could find, for example, a public spirited person or persons, who would agree to buy, say at half price, five or ten thousand books. These books might be distributed by the buyer to ministers, doctors, or hospitals of which there are six to seven thousand in the United States. Or, again, they might be placed in libraries. Perhaps, better still, in hotel rooms along with the Gideon Bible. This last might be the best bet of all for almost every man of us has passed hours of terror and depression in those lonely cubicles. Under these conditions the book would hit the man at his most receptive moment and it would be introduced accidentally except by another person. The approach in those places would be perfect."

[10] Silkworth.net/aahistorylovers/aa_history_lovers_messages.html, message 8061

[11] "Conquering The Habits That Handicap," *New York Times*, August 8, 1915: "In his own hospital in New York City he has fifty beds, and he receives and discharges an average of four patients each day." However, William White in *Slaying The Dragon*, p. 85 gave these numbers for 1915: "In that year, 693 men and 189 women, 573 of whom were addicted to alcohol, with the remaining patients addicted to other drugs, most of the narcotic family." Total of 882 patients gives roughly 75 a month. Assuming 75 would be profitable, 60 represents a rough guess at a break-even point. Also, reference the 1917 March *The Modern Hospital* ad (Figure 20) where over three thousand patients had been treated in the last three years.

[12] We can safely assume that by the time that *Alcoholics Anonymous* was published, the collective failure rate in Akron and New York had been quite high. In Robert Thomsen's *Bill W.* biography covering the meeting held with Wilson and Dr. Bob in Akron in the fall of 1937, they gathered to make a progress report: "There had been failures galore. Literally hundreds of drunks had been approached by their two groups and some had sobered up for a brief period, but then slipped away." P.239. By the time the book was published in April 1939, AA History Lovers lists about 100 sober drunks, but by then, the failures probably were hundreds higher than in the fall of 1937.

[13] *Alcoholics Anonymous Comes of Age*, Alcoholics Anonymous World Services ,p. 188

[14] *Alcoholics Anonymous Comes of Age*, Alcoholics Anonymous World Services , p. 171

[15] Silkworth.net/aagrowth/northern_nj_aahistory.html

[16] Bill Wilson to Frank Amos, January 4, 1939 – as read by Jack Norris, Class A Trustee, in Atlanta, February 5, 1972 at the Southeast Past Delegates Meeting. CD available at MountainRecordings.com

[17] *The Journal of the American Medical Association*, Volume CXIII, Number 16, October, 14, 1939, "Alcoholics Anonymous" Book Review

[18] *Alcoholics Anonymous Comes of Age*, Alcoholics Anonymous World Services , p. 176-177

[19] Ibid., p. 178

[20] Ibid., p. 178

[21] Ibid., p. 187

Chapter 20 - Epilogue

[1] *Alcoholics Anonymous Comes of Age*, Alcoholics Anonymous World Services , p. 188

[2] "Founder of Hospital Here for ted Victims is Dead"—Framed Control Bills, special to the *New York Times*. Bronxville, NY, February 20, 1947

Charles B. Towns, a pioneer in the treatment of drug addiction and founder and head of Charles B. Towns Hospital, 293 Central Park West, New York, died here today in the home of his son, Col. Ed Towns, 441 California Road, after a brief illness. His age was 85. Mr. Towns was an early exponent of legal control of the sale of narcotics. He framed the Boylan bill to regulate narcotics, which the State Legislature enacted in 1914. Two years later he acted he acted as consultant of the Congressional Ways and Means Committee in the framing of the Harrison Federal Narcotics Control Law.

A layman, Mr. Towns, shortly after the turn of the century, became interested in narcotics addiction. From another layman he received a formula for the medical treatment of narcotics which later won endorsement of leading physicians, including the late Dr. Alexander Lambert of this city, Professor of Clinical Medicine at Cornell University, and Dr. Richard Cabot of Boston.

Working always with physicians, he treated successfully many cases of drug addiction. In 1907, the late President William H. Taft, then Secretary of War, sent twelve soldiers to Mr. Towns' hospital, where under clinical observation of Army physicians, they were successfully treated. In 1908 Mr. Towns went to China and made a study of the use of opium there. He opened an maintained three hospitals in Tien-Tien, Peiking and Shanghai, where 4,000 patients were treated. The next year he attended the first International Opium Conference in Shanghai, where he demonstrated his treatment to the delegates. On his return further demonstrations of his treatment were held in clinics at Bellevue Hospital, under the direction of Dr. Lambert, and the latter published the details of the treatment in The Journal of the American Medical Association. The treatment was also used for alcoholic addiction.

During 1912 Mr. Towns contributed a series of articles to *The Century Magazine*, dealing with the effects of tobacco, alcohol, and morphine. His publications includes "Alcohol and Tobacco and the Remedy," "Habits That Handicap," "The Menace of Opium," "Reclaiming the Drinker," and "Drug and Alcohol Sickness." [End]
Note: Boylan Bill was in effect in mid-1914. Harrison Bill passed in December, 1914, and went into law April 1, 1915, not two years later.

[3] During Col. Ed Towns' address to the A.A. International in 1960 at Long Beach, CA, he said that he had been in administrative control of the hospital for sixteen years. The June 6th 1965 New York Times article on the closing of Towns Hospital includes Col Ed. Towns being in control for 21 years.

[4] *Diseases of the Nervous System*, Jelliffe and White, p. 844

[5] *The Religious Affiliation of Dr. John Harvey Kellogg, Influential Physician, Medical Science and Health Pioneer,* www.adherents.com/people/pk/John_Harvey_Kellogg.html. Dr, Kellogg was a devout Seventh-Day Adventist and a contemporary of Ellen G. White, co-founder of Seventh-day Adventism before being excommunicated from the church in 1906.

[6] "Scopolamine is one of three main active components of belladonna and stramonium tinctures and powders used medicinally along with atropine and hyoscyamine." http://en.mind-control.wikia.com/wiki/Scopolamine

[7] "The Drug Treatment of Morphinism," Frank H. Carlisle, M.D., Norfolk, Mass, *Boston Medical and Surgical Journal,* Vol CIXXVI, No. 6, February 8, 1917, p. 209-210, "Our routine is as follows: A mixture containing scopolamine hydrobromide and morphine hydrobromide is given hypodermically on the evening of the day of arrival, and repeated at intervals of six hours during the first twenty four. The early effects of scopolamine usually make their appearance during this period and are manifested by marked dryness of throat, with difficulty in swallowing, dilated pupils with blurred vision, and speech becomes difficult and rather jerky. The patient may now, or perhaps not until the following day, become mildly hallucinated (visual and auditory). In conversation his sentences are apt to be short, sharp and often incomplete, due no doubt to flight of ideas and hallucinatory control.

On the second day the intervals for injection are increased to eight, and on the third day, to twelve hours. In typical cases the depressant effect of the drug (scopolamine) presents itself at about this time, continuing as a rule to some degree through the third and fourth days. This stage is characterized by a sensation of great fatigue and drowsiness; the excitement is greatly reduced and the patient seeks his bed and should obtain sleep of from four to eight hours' duration.

On the fourth day there may be some nervousness and gastric disturbance, but usually no craving for morphia. At bedtime the final dose of the scopolamine-morphine mixture Is given, together with fifteen grains of trigonal. This is almost invariably followed by a comfortable night's sleep, lasting from six to eight hours.

Active purgation is obtained during the withdrawal period, through the liberal use of compound cathartic pills, cascara sagrada and salines. It is of vital importance that the bowels should be made to act thoroughly each day in order to rid the system of morphine and its byproducts, but the drastic catharsis recommended by some authorities does not in our experience appear necessary. . . .

Immediately after withdrawal of morphine, and for a period of several weeks, the individual is nervous, troubled with insomnia , and in a condition wherein he is torn between conflicting emotions; he is impulsive, lacks self-control, and if not restrained, may suddenly disappear. For these reasons, we insist upon a ward residence from one to two weeks . . .

Following a residence of from six to twelve weeks the individual may now leave the hospital with some assurance of success . . ."

[8] The *American Disease*, David F. Musto, p. 90

[9] The *American Disease*, David F. Musto, p. 89

[10] *The Spirituality of Imperfection*, Ernest Kurtz, p. 120

[11] *Diseases of the Nervous System*, Jelliffe and White, taken from the title page of the book

[12] *The American Disease*, David F. Musto, p.319, Chapter 4, Footnote #56: "Cabot was a consultant to a Brookline sanitarium, founded in November 1910, which used the Towns method. Dr. Cabot was as distinguished as Lambert and is credited with having inaugurated social work in American hospitals and pioneering psychiatric social work in American hospitals and pioneering psychiatric social work training. His contributions to social work, his medical services, and teaching of physicians were of the highest quality. His adoption of the Towns method can hardly be attributed to mercenary motives or ignorance."

[13] A medical approach to curing alcoholism was given to Rowland Hazard in 1928, and is listed here as an example of a cure provided by a licensed medical doctor of the times. From Stellar Fire: Carl Jung, a New England Family, and the Risks of Anecdote, Cora Finch, http://hindsfoot.org/jungstel.pdf, @2008, p. 28, "After returning to the United States, Rowland Hazard went into treatment with Dr. Edward S. Cowles in New York City. Dr. Cowles subscribed to an allergy theory of alcoholism. The allergy, he believed, irritated the membranes of the brain and spinal cord. His treatment included repeated lumbar punctures. Dr. Cowles believe that drawing off spinal fluid would decrease the pressure and protein content of the cerebrospinal fluid, and that this would eliminate the craving for alcohol. His methods were unorthodox and controversial, even by the standards of the time."

From *Diseases of the Nervous System*, Jelliffe and White, p. 851:

"Alcoholic Hallucinosis—This condition is also an expression of chronic alcoholism and may be preceded by attacks of delirium tremens. It is characterized by hallucinations, auditory predominating, in this respect strongly contrasted to delirium tremens, and delusions of a persecutory character which harmonize and are explanatory of the hallucinations. It is quite characteristic that the hallucinations and the delusions deal with sexual matters, the patient frequently being abused by 'the voice' for committing some sexual crime or is accused of sexual perversions . . . The condition is essentially an acute paranoid state and as such its explanation is the same as the explanation of paranoia. In other words, there is an unconscious fixation at the homosexual level, and this accounts for the very great frequency of the sexual character of the hallucinations and the references to sexual perversions.

[15] *Help For the Hard Drinker*, Charles B. Towns, p. 295

[16] *AA The Way It Began*, Bill Pittman, p. 163

[17] "Documents concerning AAWS history," www.silkworth.net/gsowatch/aaws "Who wrote what in the Big Book"

[18] The actual Frank Buchman quote in *The World Telegram*: "**I thank heaven for a man like Adolf Hitler**, who built **a front line of defence against the anti-Christ of Communism** . . . Of course I don't condone everything the Nazis do. Anti-semitism? Bad, naturally. I suppose Hitler sees a Karl Marx in every Jew. **But think what it would mean to the world if Hitler surrendered to the control of God.** Or Mussolini. Or any dictator. **Through such a man God could control a nation overnight and solve every** last, bewildering **problem . . . Human problems aren't economic. They're moral and they can't be solved by immoral measures**. They could be solved within a God-controlled democracy, or perhaps I should say a theocracy, and they could be solved through a God-controlled Fascist dictatorship." From "A God Guided Dictator, "*The Christian Century*, September 9, 1936. A detailed discussion, highly critical of how an A.A. Conference approved book *Pass It On* shortened and misused this quote, can be seen in *AA: Cult or Cure?*, by Charles Bufe, Chapter 2 as found in http://www.morerevealed.com/library/coc/chapter2.htm. The criticism centers around how Buchman was quoted in *Pass It On* in pages 170-171.The words in bold above appear in that A.A. book, and without the additional text of what was included in the Buchman interview found in *The World Telegram*. The omission of text provides another meaning. In any case, Wilson omitted any mention of Frank Buchman in his own writings, and here is but one example of the wisdom behind Wilson's desire to avoid controversy. On page 171 of *Pass It On*, there is the statement: "While most discussions of the incident, even by Buchman's critics, have vindicated him, the article brought the group into public controversy." Charles Bufe points out that no such vindication of the full quote of Buchman ever took place, since such a vindication would seem to validate "a God-controlled Fascist dictatorship."

On one other note regarding Mr. Bufe's title of his book *AA:Cult or Cure?*, Towns repeatedly ridiculed the concept that there was a cure for alcoholism. He was also described as an atheist. What are the chances of an atheist loaning a cult $50,000 in 2014 money? Thus, one may assume with some authority that atheist Towns would respond to Bufe's title with a response that A.A. was neither a cult nor cure.

[19] *New York Times*, "Drying Out Hospital for Problem Drinkers Closes," July 6, 1965

[20] *Alcoholics Anonymous*, Alcoholics Anonymous World Services , p. 112

Figure Cross Reference

Boston Medical and Surgical Journal, Volume CLXIV, May 11, 1911	Figure 28
	Figure 37
	Figure 38
	Figure 39
	Figure 40
Boston Medical and Surgical Journal, Volume CLXXVI, February 8, 1917	Figure 9
	Figure 46
	Figure 47
	Figure 48
Century Magazine, Vol. LXXXIII, March, 1912	Title 1 (page 43)

ntury Magazine, Vol. LXXXIV, June, 1912   Title 2 (page 48)
ntury Magazine, Vol. LXXXIV, August, 1912   Title 3 (page 58)
ntury Magazine, Vol. LXXXIV, October, 1912   Title 4 (page 68)
iers Magazine, Volume 52, November, 1913   Figure 1
ryland Medical Journal, Volume LVIII, August, 1915   Figure 51
dical Review of Reviews, Volume XX, December, 1916   Figure 13
                                                               Title 5 (page 149)
dical Review of Reviews, Volume XXIV, March, 1918   Figure 27
w York State Journal of Medicine, Volume 15, April, 1915   Figure 52
 American Journal of Medical Sciences, Volume 154, July 1917 Figure 26
 American Magazine, Volume LXXII, October, 1912   Figure 2
                                                               Figure 3
                                                               Figure 14
                                                               Figure 36
 Medical Times, Vol. XLI, February, 1913   Figure 50
 Medical Times, Vol. XLII, June, 1914   Figure 4
 Medical Times, Vol. XLII, July, 1914   Figure 5
 Medical Times, Vol. XLII, August, 1914   Figure 6
 Medical Times, Vol. XLII, October, 1914   Figure 7
 Medical Times, Vol. XLII,, December, 1914   Figure 8
                                                               Figure 49
 Medical Times, Vol. XLIX, January, 1921   Figure 29
 Medical Times, Vol. XLIX, February, 1921   Figure 30
 Medical Times, Vol. XLIX, March, 1921   Figure 31
 Medical Times, Vol. XLIX, April, 1921   Figure 32
 Medical Times, Vol. XLIX, May, 1921   Figure 33
 Medical Times, Vol. XLIX, June, 1921   Figure 34
 Medical Times, Vol. XLIX, July, 1921   Figure 35
 Modern Hospital, Vol. VII, December, 1916   Figure 11
                                                               Figure 12
                                                               Figure 15
                                                               Figure 45
 Modern Hospital, Vol. VIII, January, 1917   Figure 10
                                                               Figure 16
                                                               Figure 17
 Modern Hospital, Vol. VIII, February, 1917   Figure 18
 Modern Hospital, Vol . VIII, March, 1917   Figure 19
                                                               Figure 20
                                                               Figure 41
                                                               Figure 43
 Modern Hospital, Vol. VIII, April, 1917   Figure 21
                                                               Figure 22
                                                               Figure 42
 Modern Hospital, Vol. VIII, May, 1917   Figure 23
                                                               Figure 24
                                                               Figure 44
 Modern Hospital, Vol. VIII, June, 1917   Figure 25

Image Sources

Boston Medical and Surgical Journal, Volume ClXIV, No. 19, May 11, 1911, Boston Medical Library in the Francis A. Countway Library of Medicine

Boston Medical and Surgical Journal, 1917, Volume CLXXVI, No. 6, February 8, 1917, Harvard College Library from The Journal

Century Magazine, Vol. LXXXIII, March, 1912
http://www.unz.org/Pub/Century-1912mar-00766

Century Magazine, Vol. LXXXIV, June, 1912
http://www.unz.org/Pub/Century-1912jun-00292

Century Magazine, Vol. LXXXIV, August, 1912
http://www.unz.org/Pub/Century-1912aug-00580

Century Magazine, Vol. LXXXIV, October, 1912
http://www.unz.org/Pub/Century-1912oct-00853

Colliers Magazine, Volume 52, November, 1913, Library of the University of Illinois at Urbana-Champaign, Illinois

Maryland Medical Journal, Volume LVIII, August, 1915, University of Virginia Health Sciences Library

Medical Review of Reviews, Volume XXII, December, 1916, Boston Medical Library, 8 The Fenway

Medical Review of Reviews, Volume XXIV, March, 1918, Boston Medical Library, 8 The Fenway

New York State Journal of Medicine, Volume 15, April, 1915, Library of New York State Veterinary College, Ithaca, NY

The American Journal of Medical Sciences, Vol. 154, July-December 1917, Library of the University of Michigan

The American Magazine, Volume LXXIII, October, 1912, Library of the University of Michigan

The Medical Times, 1913, Volume XLI, Library of the University of Michigan, Homoeopathic Library

The Medical Times, 1914, Volume XLII, Library of the University of Michigan

The Medical Times, 1921, Volume XLIX, Library of the University of Michigan

The Modern Hospital, 1916 Volume VII, The University of Michigan Libraries

The Modern Hospital, 1917, Volume VIII, The University of Michigan Libraries